D0699999

Language Universals

Language Universals

Edited by
Morten H. Christiansen, Chris Collins,
and Shimon Edelman

OXFORD

UNIVERSITY PRESS

2009

OXFORD
UNIVERSITY PRESS

Oxford University Press, Inc., publishes works that further
Oxford University's objective of excellence
in research, scholarship, and education.

Oxford   New York
Auckland   Cape Town   Dar es Salaam   Hong Kong   Karachi
Kuala Lumpur   Madrid   Melbourne   Mexico City   Nairobi
New Delhi   Shanghai   Taipei   Toronto

With offices in
Argentina   Austria   Brazil   Chile   Czech Republic   France   Greece
Guatemala   Hungary   Italy   Japan   Poland   Portugal   Singapore
South Korea   Switzerland   Thailand   Turkey   Ukraine   Vietnam

Published by Oxford University Press, Inc.
198 Madison Avenue, New York, New York 10016

www.oup.com

Oxford is a registered trademark of Oxford University Press

Library of Congress Cataloging-in-Publication Data

Language universals / edited by Morten H. Christiansen,
Chris Collins, and Shimon Edelman.
p.   cm.
Includes bibliographical references and index.
ISBN 978-0-19-530543-2
1. Universals (Linguistics)   I. Christiansen, Morten H.
II. Collins, Chris   III. Edelman, Shimon.
P204.L358 2009
410.1'8—dc22
2008025741

9   8   7   6   5   4   3   2   1

Printed in the United States of America
on acid-free paper

PREFACE

The seeds for this book were sown when the three of us met for lunch at Banfi's Restaurant on the campus of Cornell University, Ithaca, New York, in October of 2003. We wanted to create a forum for discussing language that would transcend various seemingly unbridgeable theoretical differences. Taking a page from history, we decided to organize a symposium on language universals. In 1951, an informal meeting of linguists and psychologists at Cornell eventually led to the first Conference on Language Universals, convened at Dobbs Ferry, New York, in 1961. A vast volume of work across the cognitive and neural sciences over the decades since then has revealed much that is relevant to our understanding of the universals of human language. Clearly, the time was ripe to bring together scholars from different fields with a stake in language to present new insights into the nature of language universals. The resulting Cornell Symposium on Language Universals took place at the beginning of May 2004.

Because the Symposium was a great success, and because of the lack of recent interdisciplinary works describing the state of the art in research on language universals, we decided to put together this volume. Thus, most of the chapters in this volume stem from the Cornell Symposium on Language Universals; specifically, the chapters by Tom Bever, Andy Clark and Jennifer Misyak, Barbara Finlay, John Hawkins, Nobert Hornstein and Cedric Boeckx, James Hurford, Ralph-Axel Müller, Florencia Reali and Morten Christiansen, and Edward Stabler. Some of the Symposium participants were not able to contribute a chapter: Lila Gleitman, Paul Kiparsky, Christopher Manning, and Michael Tanenhaus. To fill some of the gaps in the volume, we were fortunate to be able to bring on board Emmon Bach and Wynn Chao, Joan Bybee, Steven Pinker and Ray Jackendoff, and Mark Steedman. Unfortunately, there is little in this volume on phonology and phonetics. It is in that area that there has been much recent productive debate on functionalist versus formal explanations of linguistic phenomena. This obvious gap in the coverage of the volume is due in part to the impossibility of covering all of linguistics in one book, and in part to the research interests of the editors.

Following the spirit of the Symposium, one of our goals in editing this book is to stimulate discussion between researchers who normally take very different perspectives on language and who don't often communicate with one another. For example, is it possible for a connectionist to have a productive dialogue with a generative syntactician? Can a functionalist be interested in the results of a mathematical linguist, and vice versa? Can a formal semanticist communicate with a psycholinguist? We have aimed to sidestep some of the usual debates and controversies, and to seek areas where discussion between the various disciplines and points of view is possible. In this way, we hope that this book will help set the agenda for future research. The study of language universals is a growing area of research across many disciplines. In bringing together in one place the positions of some of the most important people whose work has been central in shaping the research up to this point, we hope to uncover the central questions that need to be answered in the future.

There are many people who have contributed to this book in various important ways. In particular, we thank Rick Dale, Tejaswini Deoskar, Thomas Farmer, Bo Pedersen, and Aggrey Wasike for their help with the organization of the Cornell Symposium on Language Universals. We are also grateful to Catharine Carlin from Oxford University Press for her strong and continued backing of this project. Very special thanks go to our families, Anita Govindjee, Sunita Christiansen, Akuwa Collins, and Esti Edelman, for their patience and support during the editorial work. Last, but not least, our thanks go to the contributing authors for their willingness to make the revisions for which we asked, for gracefully accepting the inevitable delays in our editorial work, and, of course, for their well-written chapters.

We would also like to acknowledge the Cognitive Science Program at Cornell University for sponsoring the Cornell Symposium on Language Universals, as well as the additional support from the College of Arts and Sciences, and the Departments of Psychology and Linguistics at Cornell University. In addition, part of the editorial work was carried out while Morten was on sabbatical at the Santa Fe Institute, New Mexico, supported by a Charles A. Ryskamp Fellowship from the American Council of Learned Societies.

Morten H. Christiansen, Chris Collins,
and Shimon Edelman

CONTENTS

NOTES ON CONTRIBUTORS

EMMON BACH is Professor Emeritus of Linguistics at the University of Massachusetts, Amherst, and Professorial Research Associate at the School of Oriental and African Studies (University of London). He has taught also at Oxford University, Hampshire College, City University of New York, and the University of Texas, Austin, as well as at several Linguistics Institutes of the LSA. His primary research interests are syntax and semantics, and North American indigenous languages, especially Wakashan and other languages of the Pacific Northwest, and Western Abenaki. He lives in London.

THOMAS G. BEVER is Research Professor of Cognitive Science, Linguistics, Neuro-science, Psychology, and Language Reading and Culture at the University of Arizona. His research is at the intersection of those fields, motivated by a unifying question: what are the interactive formal and statistical sources of structural, behavioral, and neurological universals of language? He was founder of the first psycholin-guistics PhD program (at Columbia University), founder of The Center for the Sciences of Language at the University of Rochester, and cofounder of the journal *Cognition*.

CEDRIC BOECKX is Associate Professor in the Department of Linguistics at Harvard University, where he has been since 2003. He received his PhD in Linguistics from the University of Connecticut, Storrs, in 2001. He has held visiting positions at the Universities of Illinois and Maryland, and was an NWO fellow at Leiden University. His research interests are in theoretical syntax, comparative grammar, and archi-tectural questions of language, including its origins and its development in children and its neurobiological basis. He is the author of, among others, *Islands and Chains* (John Benjamins, 2003), *Linguistic Minimalism* (Oxford University Press, 2006),

Understanding Minimalist Syntax (Blackwell, 2008), and *Bare Syntax* (Oxford University Press, 2008). He has published numerous articles in journals such as *Linguistic Inquiry* and *Natural Language and Linguistic Theory*.

JOAN BYBEE (PhD, Linguistics, UCLA 1973) was on the faculty at the State University of New York at Buffalo from 1973 to 1989 and is now Distinguished Professor Emerita of the Department of Linguistics at the University of New Mexico. Bybee's research interests include theoretical issues in phonology and morphology, language universals, and linguistic change. Her books include *Morphology* (John Benjamins, 1985), *The Evolution of Grammar* (with Revere Perkins and William Pagliuca, University of Chicago Press, 1994), *Phonology and Language Use* (Cambridge University Press, 2001), and *Frequency of Use and the Organization of Language* (Oxford University Press, 2007). In 2004, she served as the President of the Linguistic Society of America.

WYNN CHAO received her PhD from the University of Massachusetts at Amherst, and teaches at the School of Oriental and African Studies, University of London. Her research is concerned with language universals and crosslinguistic variation, focusing on the constraints that linguistic structure imposes on the interpretation of elements in the nominal and verbal domains, and how these interact with ellipsis, quantification, and modification. Main areas of investigation include Romance and East Asian languages, especially Portuguese and Chinese, and patterns of language impairment in atypical populations.

MORTEN H. CHRISTIANSEN received his PhD in Cognitive Science from the University of Edinburgh in 1995. He is Associate Professor in the Department of Psychology and Co-Director of the Cognitive Science Program at Cornell University, as well as an External Professor at the Santa Fe Institute. His research focuses on the interaction of biological and environmental constraints in the processing, acquisition, and evolution of language, which he approaches using a variety of methodologies, including computational modeling, corpus analyses, psycholinguistic experimentation, neurophysiological recordings, and molecular genetics. He has edited volumes on *Connectionist Psycholinguistics* (with Nick Chater, Ablex, 2001) and *Language Evolution* (with Simon Kirby, Oxford University Press, 2003). He is currently working on a monograph, *Creating Language*: *Towards a Unified Framework for Language Processing, Acquisition, and Evolution* (with Nick Chater, Oxford University Press).

ANDY CLARK is Professor of Philosophy in the School of Philosophy, Psychology, and Language Sciences, at Edinburgh University in Scotland. He is the author of several books, including *Being There*: *Putting Brain, Body And World Together Again* (MIT

Press, 1997), *Natural-Born Cyborgs*: *Minds, Technologies and the Future of Human Intelligence* (Oxford University Press, 2003), and *Supersizing the Mind*: *Embodiment, Action, and Cognitive Extension* (Oxford University Press, 2008). His research interests include robotics and artificial life, the cognitive role of human-built structures, specialization and interactive dynamics in neural systems, and the interplay between language, thought, and action.

CHRIS COLLINS is Professor in the Department of Linguistics at New York University. He received a PhD in Linguistics from the Massachusetts Institute of Technology in 1993. His research interests are comparative syntax and the syntax of African languages. He approaches the issue of language universals through the in-depth study of various African languages, including Ewe, and most recently, N|uu, an endangered Khoisan language of South Africa.

SHIMON EDELMAN is Professor of Psychology at Cornell University, where he is also member in the graduate fields of Computer Science, Information Science, and Cognitive Science. His research interests include computational, behavioral, and neurobiological aspects of vision, as well as language acquisition and processing, and computational linguistics. His latest book is *Computing the Mind*: *How the Mind Really Works* (Oxford University Press, 2008).

BARBARA L. FINLAY received her PhD from the Department of Brain and Cognitive Science at MIT in 1976. She is presently the W. R. Kenan Jr. Professor of Psychology at Cornell University after a term of chair in that department, having held visiting appointments in Oxford, INSERM, University of Pará, Belém, Brazil, the University of Western Australia, and the Wissenschaftskolleg zu Berlin. Her principle research interests lie in "evo-devo," the study of the interrelationship of organization structure in development and evolution, as applied to the development of the mammalian visual system, and the evolution of cortex and cognitive function. She has also served as coeditor of *Behavioral and Brain Sciences* since 2002.

JOHN A. HAWKINS is Professor of English and Applied Linguistics at Cambridge University, and Professor of Linguistics at the University of California, Davis. He has held previous positions at the University of Essex (Colchester), the Max-Planck-Institute for Psycholinguistics in Nijmegen, and the University of Southern California in Los Angeles, and visiting appointments at institutions including UC Berkeley, UCLA, the Free University of Berlin, and the Max-Planck-Institute for Evolutionary Anthropology in Leipzig. He has broad and interdisciplinary interests in the language sciences and has published widely on language typology and universals, grammatical theory, psycholinguistics, and historical linguistics.

NORBERT HORNSTEIN is Professor of Linguistics at the University of Maryland, College Park.

JAMES R. HURFORD trained as an articulatory phonetician, and has written textbooks on semantics and grammar, and articles on phonetics, phonology, syntax, language acquisition, and pragmatics. His work is interdisciplinary, based in linguistics, but taking insights and data from anthropology, psychology, neuroscience, genetics, artificial intelligence, and philosophy. He attempts to reconcile the work of formal linguists studying words and sentences out of their communicative context, psycholinguists and neuroscientists studying the brain processes underlying language use, and anthropologists and sociolinguists who emphasize how language is embedded in social groups. His work emphasizes the interaction of evolution, learning, and communication. Early work focused on numeral systems, and this broadened to the topic of language evolution. He produced some of the earliest computer simulations of aspects of the evolution of language.

RAY JACKENDOFF is Seth Merrin Professor of Philosophy and Codirector of the Center for Cognitive Studies at Tufts University. He is past president of both the Linguistic Society of America and the Society for Philosophy and Psychology, and he was the 2003 recipient of the Jean Nicod Prize for Cognitive Philosophy. His most recent books are *Foundations of Language* (Oxford University Press, 2002), *Simpler Syntax* (with Peter Culicover, Oxford University Press, 2005), and *Language, Consciousness, Culture* (MIT Press, 2007).

JENNIFER B. MISYAK graduated from Williams College, where she received BA degrees in both Philosophy and Psychology, and was the college's first Cognitive Science concentrator. She also studied at Oxford University, where she was affiliated with Exeter College. Currently, she is pursuing doctoral work in the psychology department at Cornell University. Her research investigates individual differences in mechanisms for language and statistical learning, as well as cognitive development in infancy.

RALPH-AXEL MÜLLER received his PhD in Neurolinguistics from the University of Frankfurt/Main (Germany), and is now Professor of Psychology at San Diego State University and Associate Research Scientist at the University of California, San Diego. He was one of the first to apply positron emission tomography to the study of functional reorganization in children with early brain damage. His current research focuses on the brain bases of language development in typically developing children and language impairment in autism spectrum disorders, using functional magnetic resonance imaging and other MRI techniques.

STEVEN PINKER, a native of Montreal, received his BA from McGill University in 1976 and his PhD from Harvard in 1979. After teaching at MIT for 21 years, he returned to Harvard in 2003 as the Johnstone Professor of Psychology. Pinker has received numerous awards for his experimental research on cognition and language, his teaching, and his books, *The Language Instinct* (William Morrow, 1994), *How the Mind Works* (Norton, 1999), *The Blank Slate* (Viking, 2002), and *The Stuff of Thought* (Viking, 2007).

FLORENCIA REALI studied neurobiology as an undergraduate, obtaining a BS from Universidad de la Republica (UdelaR), Uruguay, in 2000. In 2002, she obtained an MS from UdelaR. She entered graduate studies at Cornell University, where she worked in Morten Christiansen's lab. Her work combined computational modeling and behavioral experiments to study various aspects of language evolution, acquisition, and processing. In 2007, she obtained her PhD in Psychology, after which she joined Tom Griffiths' lab at UC Berkeley as a postdoctoral fellow. There, she applies computational models of cognition to explore some questions about how we learn probabilistic properties of language.

EDWARD P. STABLER received his PhD from the Massachusetts Institute of Technology in 1981, and is now Professor of Linguistics at the University of California, Los Angeles, specializing in computational models of human language acquisition and use. His publications include *The Logical Approach to Syntax* (MIT Press, 1992) and *Bare Grammar: Lectures on Linguistic Invariants* (with Edward Keenan, CSLI, 2003). He is also a coauthor of the introductory textbook, *Linguistics* (edited by Victoria Fromkin, Blackwell, 2000).

MARK STEEDMAN is Professor of Cognitive Science in the School of Informatics at the University of Edinburgh, which he joined in 1998, after teaching for many years in Computer and Information Science at the University of Pennsylvania. He is Fellow of the British Academy, the Royal Society of Edinburgh, and the Association for the Advancement of Artificial Intelligence. His research interests cover issues in computational linguistics, artificial intelligence, computer science, and cognitive science, including syntax and semantics of natural language, parsing and comprehension of natural language discourse by humans and by machine, using Combinatory Categorial Grammar. Much of his current language research addresses issues in semantics, especially the meaning of intonation and prosody, as well as grounded semantically based language learning and wide-coverage parsing for robust semantic interpretation.

Language Universals

1

LANGUAGE UNIVERSALS: A COLLABORATIVE PROJECT FOR THE LANGUAGE SCIENCES

MORTEN H. CHRISTIANSEN, CHRIS COLLINS,
AND SHIMON EDELMAN[1]

Underlying the endless and fascinating idiosyncrasies of the world's languages there are uniformities of universal scope. Amid infinite diversity, all languages are, as it were, cut from the same pattern.

—Memorandum to the 1961 Dobbs Ferry Conference on Language Universals
(Greenberg, 1963/1966)

1.1. Language Universals: From Dobbs Ferry to the Present Time

Today, the idea that all languages are at least in part cut from the same pattern is perhaps not particularly controversial. In contrast, as is clear from the nature of the contributions to Greenberg (1963/1966), one of the main goals of the Dobbs Ferry Conference was to justify this thesis and articulate the uniformities that languages show. This is particularly clear in the appendix to Greenberg (1963/1966), "Memorandum Concerning Language Universals," which was distributed to the participants of the conference. In this memorandum, various notions of universals are introduced and compared, and it is suggested that language universals constitute "the most general laws of a science of linguistics."

Since the Dobbs Ferry Conference, the general perspective in the linguistic community on language universals has changed radically. The recent history of linguistics has been characterized by the intense search for these language universals, inspired in part by Greenberg's (1963/1966) seminal paper, and in part by the publication in 1957 of Chomsky's *Syntactic Structures*. These two publications have given rise to an explosion of work on language universals, ranging from work in formally oriented syntactic and semantic theories to the large number of typological studies inspired by Greenberg's 1963 paper. Although the origins of these two streams of thought are very different, the dividing line is becoming less clear. In an attempt to delineate possible parametric variation (and hence to isolate properties of universal grammar), generative work has become increasingly focused on a wide variety of typologically very different languages. The interpenetration and dialogue between these two streams of thought is one of the defining characteristics of the linguistics of the second half of the twentieth century and the beginning of the twenty-first century.

Therefore, at the present time, there is no need to justify the claim that language universals exist. All linguists (formally or functionally oriented) would recognize the search for the universal aspects of language as one of the most important areas of research in their field. As opposed to the state of affairs at the time of the 1961 Dobbs Ferry Conference, there are many well-articulated candidate universals that in some cases have been debated extensively. However, as evidenced by the broad spectrum of perspectives represented in this volume, opinions differ—sometimes strongly—over the exact nature of language universals, their origin, and how best to study them.

In putting together this volume, we wanted to construe the notion of language universal in the broadest sense possible, ranging from Hockett's (1960) design features (e.g., interchangeability, semanticity, arbitrariness, discreteness, displacement, openness, duality of patterning, etc.) to Greenberg's (1963/1966) implicational universals (e.g., "languages with dominant verb-subject-object (VSO) word order are always prepositional") to Chomsky's (1986) principles of Universal Grammar (UG) (e.g., recursion, structure dependence, subjacency, etc.). As this book shows, this list is far from complete. Thus, this volume also includes discussions of possible universals deriving from diachronic and historical processes (Bybee; Hurford; Reali & Christiansen, Chapters 2, 3, 14), performance constraints (Hawkins; Bever; Reali & Christiansen, Chapters 4, 6, 14), principles of "good design" (Hornstein & Boeckx, Chapter 5), neural components adapted for language through natural selection (Pinker & Jackendoff, Chapter 7), model-theoretic semantics (Bach & Chao, Chapter 8), the semantics of action planning (Steedman, Chapter 9), formal language theory (Stabler, Chapter 10), and biology (Müller; Clark & Misyak; Finlay, Chapters 11–13).

This book brings together contributions by language scholars from a variety of fields, seeking to forge new insights into the universals of language. The chapters take the form of original position papers by major figures in a variety of scientific fields with a stake in the study of language, including linguistics, psychology, computational linguistics, cognitive neuroscience, philosophy, and computer science. As such, the volume is intended to provide a snapshot of the current state of research and theoretical perspectives on language universals.

1.2. Varieties of Language Universals

The search for universals of language has been, and still remains, one of the central explanatory goals of the various disciplines involved in the study of language. By approaching the notion of language universals from an interdisciplinary perspective, we hope that the volume will allow the language sciences to make progress on the following questions: What are the possible sources of language universals? What are the most productive directions for future research into the problem of universals? And most importantly, how can communication be increased between linguistics and the other disciplines that participate in research on language universals?

In Chapter 2, Joan Bybee approaches linguistic universals from the viewpoint of the usage-based theory of language. She argues that from this perspective there are very few synchronic universals in the sense of features that can be found in all languages. The only synchronic universal that she reports having found in her work on morphology is that all languages have at least some minimal derivational morphology. More generally, Bybee argues that language change has to be taken into account in order to understand language universals. Factors relating to language use—such as frequency of usage—lead to grammaticalization, which tends to follow specific developmental paths. For example, she notes that discourse adverbs develop first from verb modifiers to clause modifiers, from a narrow scope to covering the whole clause, from concrete senses to more abstract ones, and from denoting specific content to indicating the speaker's attitude at the discourse level. Bybee suggests that language universals may be best viewed in terms of such unidirectional paths of linguistic change, driven by constraints arising from domain-general processes rather than ones that are specific to language.

James Hurford agrees that diachronic change is important to understanding language universals. In Chapter 3, he draws the reader's attention to two properties of languages that are, as he notes, not usually billed as universals: the ubiquitous irregularities and, what he considers to be the most striking universal of all, the tremendous expressivity of language. Hurford then proceeds to sketch an account of the former in terms of the latter. For that, he claims, it is necessary to widen the scope of the inquiry into universals from acquisition to production and to the diachronic or historical processes that link the two. By considering the life cycle of languages as well as their evolution and change, Hurford builds a case for diachronic explanation in the study of language universals, and illustrates its application to several of Greenberg's original examples. These ideas resonate in interesting and potentially productive ways both with classical and with new thinking about language. In noting that "language is like an ancient city, with buildings dating from different historical periods, but all still functioning," Hurford echoes Wittgenstein's (1953) remark in *Philosophical Investigations* (para. 18). At the same time, his hypothesis concerning the formative role of the "performance > competence > performance > competence" cycle in language change (cf. Christiansen & Chater, 2008) is likely to assume a key explanatory role in the study of language universals.

Whereas both Bybee and Hurford explore the possible diachronic causes of existing language universals (in Chapters 2 and 3, respectively), John Hawkins examines synchronic cross-linguistic patterns in grammars and language use. He proposes in Chapter 4 that "variation-defining" universals delimit the scope of possible variation across languages. Examples of such universals include the Greenbergian implicational universals and the parameters in the Government-Binding tradition. Hawkins argues that variation-defining universals are to be understood in terms of performance principles. For example, Hawkins explains the fact that verb-initial languages tend to be prepositional by showing that under certain assumptions a prepositional language where the verb precedes its object yields structures that are more efficiently parsed. Furthermore, he suggests that these same performance principles govern variation of structures within languages, dictating that following a verb, short prepositional phrases should precede long prepositional phrases.

In contrast to the performance-based universals discussed by Hawkins, the focus of Chapter 5 by Norbert Hornstein and Cedric Boeckx is on linguistic universals embodied in Universal Grammar (UG), a characterization of the innate properties of the language faculty. Approaching language universals from a minimalist perspective, they start out by contrasting I-universals (innate properties of UG) with E-universals (universals in the Greenbergian tradition). They point out that even if every language displayed some property P, it would not imply that P is an I-universal, whereas P would be considered an E-universal. Most of their chapter is devoted to considering UG and I-universals in light of recent minimalist syntactic theory. In particular, they make the point that I-universals will have to be rethought in light of Darwin's problem, or the logical problem of language evolution (see also Christiansen & Chater, 2008). Following Chomsky (2005), Hornstein and Boeckx raise the question of the relative importance of the following three factors in accounting for I-universals: (a) genetic endowment, (b) experience, and (c) language-independent principles. They conclude that the minimalist perspective suggests that I-universals—the key properties of UG—may not be genetically encoded but instead may derive from language-independent principles of good design.

Tom Bever adopts a minimalist approach to language, similar to Hornstein and Boeckx, but also seeks to incorporate elements from functional linguistics. Thus, in Chapter 6, he argues that linguistic universals need to be understood in terms of a model of language that incorporates both learned statistical patterns ("habits") and derivations ("rules"). In his Analysis by Synthesis model, sentences are initially given a basic semantic interpretation based on canonical statistical patterns of syntax, but sentences are also at the same time assigned a separate derivation, reflecting the syntactic relationship between constituents. This model leads Bever to differentiate between two types of language universals: (a) structural universals that relate to the minimalist core of the language faculty and manifest themselves in the existence of derivations, and (b) psychological universals that relate to how language is acquired and used (including performance-based constraints, such as those also discussed by Hawkins, Chapter 4). He also proposes a universal constraint on language that is necessary for his model to link statistical patterns with syntactic derivations. This constraint—the "canonical form constraint"—requires that all languages must have a set of statistically dominant structural patterns indicating the mapping between syntactic constructions and their meanings. Moreover, it should be possible to approximate the meaning of complex derivations in terms of such canonical patterns without recourse to a full derivational analysis. More generally, Bever sees his approach as complementary to the Minimalist program in that it seeks to determine what is minimally required to explain language acquisition and use.

In Chapter 7, Steven Pinker and Ray Jackendoff characterize language universals in terms of specific brain components that are available universally for the acquisition of language. Because each of these brain-related linguistic devices may not be utilized in every human language, linguistic patterns common to all languages do not necessarily follow from this approach. Pinker and Jackendoff suggest that evolution has endowed modern humans with a suite of adaptations that are specific to language (or for which language provided a strong selectional pressure). These adaptations for language include human specializations for both speech perception and production, as well as, more broadly, the duality of patterning (Hockett, 1960) evident in phonology as the combination of meaningless discrete sounds (phonemes) into meaningful units (morphemes). As examples of universal features of language that hold across all languages, Pinker and Jackendoff highlight the existence of words, construed as organized links between phonological, conceptual, and morpho-syntactic information, as well as the notion that all languages are designed to express conceptual structure. On the syntax side, they argue that the brain makes available a number of different syntactic devices that are reflected in human languages to a greater or lesser degree, including hierarchically organized phrase structure, word order, agreement between various constituents, and case marking. Thus, from the viewpoint of Pinker and Jackendoff, language universals arise primarily as a consequence of brain-related capacities that have evolved through natural selection and that are unique to humans and unique to language.

Although Pinker and Jackendoff note the importance of conceptual structure as a source of universal constraints on language, their chapter focuses primarily on linguistic devices outside of semantics. In contrast, Emmon Bach and Wynn

Chao, in Chapter 8, focus on semantic universals from the viewpoint of formal model-theoretic semantics. They start by outlining some general properties of semantic theory, including the notion of a "model structure" (the system of possible denotations), types of denotations, types of functions, and compositionality. On the basis of this general theory, the authors investigate the following questions: (a) Are the basic elements of the model structure universal? (b) Are the relations between syntactic categories and semantic interpretations universal? (c) Are there typological patternings related to either (a) or (b)? Whereas Bach and Chao hypothesize that the general model structure is the same for all languages, they outline research on a number of different "semantic typologies" where different semantic and syntactic properties seem to cluster together.

In Chapter 9, Mark Steedman takes a different approach to the notion of semantic universals. He opens his chapter by distinguishing those linguistic universals that are conditional and statistical (as in Greenberg's original list) from those that are absolute. The latter are further subdivided into substantive (e.g., the existence of nouns or of transitive verbs), functional (e.g., the existence of case, tense, etc.), and formal (e.g., the universal constraint noted by Ross (1967) that relates "gapping," or deletion of the verb under coordination, to base constituent order in the language). He then sets out to explain absolute universals in terms of the semantics of action planning—arguably, the driving force behind the emergence of language, construed as a means for communicating meaning as it is situated in the world. Steedman's formal approach to planning is based on a calculus of affordances (which, he notes, can be implemented in associative memory), such as those that are transparently encoded in the Navajo noun system, or in the Latin case system. The primitive operations in this calculus are function composition and type raising (the operation of turning an object of a given type into a function over those functions that apply to objects of that type). By resorting to the framework of Combinatory Categorial Grammar, Steedman reduces universals to functional application, composition, and type-raising rules. This allows him to develop a unified account for a wide range of formal universals, such as the fact that all natural languages are mildly context-sensitive, and the gapping direction in coordination.

Edward Stabler, too, adopts a formal approach to language universals but from the point of view of formal language theory and the theory of learnability, a point of view that was completely absent from the original 1961 meeting on language universals. In Chapter 10, he reports on research showing that it may be a universal structural property of human languages that they fall into a class of languages defined by mildly context-sensitive grammars. Stabler also investigates the issue of whether there are properties of language that are needed to guarantee that it is learnable. He suggests that languages are learnable if they have a finite Vapnik-Chervonenkis (VC) dimension (where VC dimension provides a combinatorial measure of complexity for a set of languages). Informally, a finite VC dimension requires that there be restrictions on the set of languages to be learned such that they do not differ from one another in arbitrary ways. These restrictions can be construed as universals that are required for language to be learnable (given formal language learnability theory). Stabler concludes by pointing out that formalizations of the semantic contribution (e.g., compositionality) to language learning might yield further insight into language universals.

In Chapter 11, Ralph-Axel Müller asks how the kind of language universals discussed in the previous chapters might be instantiated in human brains. He distinguishes between "shallow" and "deep" universals in cognition, the former being due to abstract computational properties, and the latter to properties of the neural architecture that supports the function in question, such as language. He proposes that shallow universals that are a matter of consensus in the linguistic community should be studied from a neurodevelopmental standpoint to seek their deep (i.e., biologically meaningful) counterparts. To examine the likelihood of there being deep universals that are specific to language, Müller conducts an extensive survey of genetic, anatomical, and imaging data, while advocating caution in their interpretation: both genes and input during development determine the function of the areas where language is traditionally assumed to reside. According to the explanatory synthesis he offers, the specific architecture of local brain areas (such as Broca's area) is not genetically predetermined but instead emerges as a result of its role and activity, given its particular location in functional networks. In conclusion, Müller suggests that a neurodevelopmental account of putative language universals is most likely to be based on organization and interaction of nonlinguistic "ingredient processes."

Using Müller's chapter as a point of departure, Andy Clark and Jennifer Misyak offer a critical perspective on the notion of innate universals. In Chapter 12, they describe their stance as "minimal nativism," according to which a brain area should be seen as embodying a kind of language universal if it is genetically predisposed toward fulfilling a certain sufficiently general linguistic function, for example by virtue of its strategic connectivity. On this view, Broca's area could still count as the brain locus of a linguistic universal, even if it supports other functions beside language. Having thus questioned one of the premises of Müller's argument, Clark and Misyak point out that its conclusion may still hold, if the "real story" of language involves languages adapting to humans (as hinted, e.g., by Hurford, Chapter 3—see also Christiansen & Chater, 2008).

Taking on a broad biological perspective, Barbara Finlay notes in Chapter 13 that the existence of universals in language would only be surprising if the rest of cognition, as well as the world at large, were unstructured. Given that the world is in some sense and to some extent predictable, universals should be sought in the structure of information it presents to the language system. A productive approach to the study of language universals could follow the lead of biology, where looking at the interplay of evolution and development is proving particularly effective.

The volume concludes with Chapter 14, in which Florencia Reali and Morten Christiansen note that natural languages share common features known as *linguistic universals* but that the nature and origin of these features remain controversial. Generative approaches propose that linguistic universals are defined by a set of innately specified linguistic constraints in UG. The UG hypothesis is primarily supported by Poverty of Stimulus (POS) arguments that posit that the structure of language cannot be learned from exposure to the linguistic environment. This chapter reviews recent computational and empirical research in statistical learning that raises serious questions about the basic assumptions of POS arguments. More generally, these results question the validity of UG as the basis for linguistic universals. As an alternative, Reali and Christiansen propose that linguistic universals should be viewed as functional features of language, emerging from constraints on statistical learning mechanisms themselves and from general functional and pragmatic properties of communicative interactions. The cognitive mechanisms underlying language acquisition and processing are proposed not to be qualitatively different from those underlying other aspects of cognition. Thus, this perspective calls for an interdisciplinary approach to the study of linguistic universals, where a full understanding of the language system would only be possible through the combined efforts of all subdisciplines in cognitive science.

1.3. The Importance of Interdisciplinary Research

It should be clear from the various chapters in this volume that language universals may derive from several different interacting sources: for example, a genetically specified UG, the interfaces between the language faculty (assuming UG) and other components of the brain, neural mechanisms and plasticity, processing constraints on language use, computational constraints on language learning and representation, factors related to the role of language as a medium of communication, and evolutionary dynamics of populations of language users. An intended contribution of this volume is to show that it is important to determine which of these various sources is at play and how the various sources interact. For example, some researchers may agree that some property, such as recursion, should be explained in terms of genetically specified neural structure, because it meets certain criteria for such an explanation, without necessarily agreeing that the structure is specifically "linguistic" (see Chapters 6, 7, 11, and 12 by Bever, Pinker & Jackendoff, Müller, and Clark & Misyak, respectively). Such a research strategy would force the linguist to state the property of recursion in a simple and clear form in order to enable the neuroscientist to isolate the mechanisms involved.

The full benefits of an interdisciplinary approach can only be reaped if we realize that such an approach opens entirely new avenues of research into universals. In the various disciplines concerned with language, the past half-century has seen, over and above regular progress, a few major conceptual revolutions (such as the ascendancy of cognitive psychology), and even the emergence of new fields (such as computational linguistics, formal semantics, and cognitive science). The new disciplines that together with linguistics form the contemporary field of brain/mind science offer both new twists on the issue of language universals and, more importantly, a glimpse of the possible place of universals in the grand scheme of things in cognition. Indeed, the quest for universals in linguistics is mirrored by very familiar-looking concerns in those other disciplines. Let us consider two examples, one structure related, and the other focusing on function.

Insofar as structure is concerned, a surprisingly fresh-sounding perspective on cognitive universals[2] is provided by a 1951 paper by Karl Lashley, *The problem of serial order in behavior*. Lashley writes:

> Temporal integration is not found exclusively in language; the coordination of leg movements in insects, the song of birds, the control of trotting and pacing in a gaited horse, the rat running the maze, the architect designing a house, and the carpenter sawing a board present a problem of sequences of action which cannot be explained in terms of successions of external stimuli.
>
> (1951, p. 113)

Although contemporary readers hardly need to be convinced that stimulus-response associations cannot explain cognition, it is worth pointing out that some of Lashley's examples, such as bird song or multijointed limb coordination, necessitate *hierarchically structured*, not merely properly sequenced, representations. Indeed, possible computational underpinnings of hierarchically structured representations are being intensely studied, for example, in vision, specifically in object and scene processing (e.g., Mozer, 1999). We note that although much more is known about vision and its neurocomputational basis than about language (not the least because of the ready availability there of animal models), the general characteristics of hierarchical visual representations are yet to be worked out, which suggests that intellectual cross-fertilization with linguistics could be especially effective here.

Turning from representations to the related issue of function, processes, and mechanisms, we observe that in vision, researchers have long been interested in identifying a core set of universal information-processing operations, or computational universals. The phenomena that need to be explained in vision range from so-called low-level perception (of color, texture, motion, surface shape, etc.), through mid-level perceptual organization and grouping, to high-level object and scene understanding. Echoing the minimalist hypothesis, suggesting that the complexity of language is mostly apparent (Chomsky, 2004), one may wonder whether the vast panoply of functions found in the arsenal of human vision can be reduced to a small set of computational primitives. In linguistics, the notion of a computational universal is exemplified by Merge and Move (Chomsky, 2004); it is not the place here to discuss candidates for similarly universal functional mechanisms in vision—suffice it to say that the possibility that such universals exist is being considered (e.g., Barlow, 1990; Edelman, 2008).

A possible methodological framework for facilitating comprehensive, cross-disciplinary studies of cognition had been proposed by Marr and Poggio (1977), who pointed out that cognition, as any other information-processing phenomenon, can only be fully understood if addressed simultaneously on a number of conceptual levels. These range from the most abstract computational level (what is the nature of the task, and what needs to be computed), through the algorithmic (what are the input and output representations, and how are the former to be mapped into the latter), to the implementational (what mechanisms can support the necessary computation, and what is their place in the brain).

Since its introduction, the Marr-Poggio approach has proven effective in various cognitive domains. Particularly instructive examples of the effectiveness of this approach can be found in the quest for computational universals, which are necessarily the farthest removed from behavioral and neurobiological data, and therefore the most difficult to substantiate. One such example is the interchangeability of space and time in cognitive representations—a possible computational universal identified by Pitts and McCulloch in a paper dealing with vision and audition, and titled, for reasons unrelated to the present book, *How we know universals* (1947). The idea that temporal quantities can be represented in the brain by spatial means has been supported by recent studies of auditory processing, which integrate behavioral and neurobiological data-gathering with computational analysis and modeling (reviewed in Shamma, 2001).

The recognition that universals will have different interacting sources suggests that a direction for future research will be the close collaboration of researchers from different disciplines with a stake in language, including linguistics, psychology, animal cognition, psycholinguistics, cognitive neuroscience, philosophy, computational linguistics, computer science as well as behavioral and molecular genetics. Given the ever increasing amount of research output in each of these disciplines, no single person can expect to cover all the bases. Thus, a complete understanding of the nature of language universals will by necessity require researchers to venture outside their home disciplines and invite collaborations with others.[3]

1.4. Toward an Integrated Understanding of Language Universals

In a multidisciplinary approach, it is not expected that there will be one answer to the question, "What are language universals?," nor have we tried to engineer one in this introduction. For this reason, we find that the study of language universals (perhaps along with the study of language acquisition and evolution) may provide one of the most fruitful areas of language research for cross-disciplinary collaborations. Unlike descriptive studies of particular languages, or cross-linguistic studies of particular syntactic or semantic phenomena, language universals often have a level of generality that make them well suited for collaboration between linguists and nonlinguists. We suggest that it is time to start a series of conferences on languages universals, which would take place every other year at a different university in the world. The conference could be modeled on the highly successful biennial language evolution conference that has been continuously growing in size and interdisciplinary breadth over the past 12 years. The proposed conference on language universals would force linguists to formulate their results in a way comprehensible to nonlinguistics, would induce nonlinguists to take an interest in working with linguistics, and would provide a forum where such collaborative efforts could be presented. We hope that this volume will provide part of the inspiration and impetus to establish such a conference series.

As another example of collaboration between linguists and nonlinguists, debate on language universals could take place in the context of co-taught courses at universities (which can be either at the graduate or undergraduate levels). Students and professors from different fields and very different theoretical backgrounds can benefit from such programmed interactions. Both undergraduates and graduates often find this kind of course rewarding, and college administrators normally look favorably upon this kind of interdisciplinary co-teaching.

Because of the wealth of findings and theories offered by the different disciplines, it is now more important than ever to actively seek an integrated understanding of the nature of human language universals, the cognitive and neural mechanisms behind them, and their manifestation among different languages. We see the book as a first step in this direction, providing contributions from scholars of language who work in a variety of fields, in an effort to stimulate insights from a variety of points of view.

Key Further Readings

To get some idea of the scope of the problem confronting any language researcher interested in language universals, one can take a quick look at the number of languages in the world, and their genetic affiliations and geographical distribution in the *Ethnologue* (Gordon, 2005; an online version available at: http://www. ethnologue.com/). This source provides a listing of all the languages found on earth. It does not give much structural information, but can serve as a useful starting point for anyone interested in typological patterns. For a searchable database of the structures of the world's languages, see *The World Atlas of Language Structures* (Haspelmath, Dryer, Gil, & Comrie, 2005), which is the latest development of the Greenbergian tradition of typological linguistics.

The point of departure for a historical perspective on language universals would be the report that was published following the first Conference on Language Universals, convened at Dobbs Ferry, New York, in 1961 (Greenberg, 1963/1966). Also of historical significance is Greenberg's short volume on language universals, which was recently published in a new edition (Greenberg, 1966/2005), and his article in *Science* (Greenberg, 1969) pointing to the study of language universals as a new frontier for research. Additionally, Hockett's (1960) paper in *Scientific American* on the universal features of human language as well as Chomsky's (1965) discussion of linguistic universals and UG provide insights into the early study of universal patterns of language.

As background literature for the present volume, Baker (2001) provides a nontechnical introduction to the generative grammar approach to language and the role of language universals in this framework. For an alternative approach to grammar and universals, as seen from the viewpoint of construction grammar, see Goldberg (2006). Culicover and Jackendoff (2005) seek to provide a bridge between generative and construction grammar approaches to syntax and linguistic universals.

More generally, the nature of language universals and their possible origins is a key question for current research on language evolution. Christiansen and Kirby (2003) contain a selection of papers on the evolution of language, providing insights into universals from many different theoretical and disciplinary perspectives.

Finally, each chapter in this volume contains a list of *Key Further Readings*, listing background literature relating to language universals as approached from a variety of viewpoints, including those of usage-based, evolutionary, typological, minimalist, psycholinguistic, semantic, and computational linguistics, as well as biology, neurobiology, and cognitive science.

Notes

1 The authors' names are in alphabetical order.

2 By "universal" in the expression "cognitive universals," we mean to refer to properties holding across humans and cognitive domains.

3 As a case in point, one of us—Chris Collins—has joined forces with Richard Kayne (NYU) and computer scientist Dennis Shasha (NYU) to develop an open database aiming to provide a comprehensive picture of syntactic, semantic, and morphological variation across human languages. In a similar vein, another of us, Morten Christiansen, has embarked on a major project to create a quantitative modeling framework for understanding universal patterns of language change, through interdisciplinary collaborations with typological linguist William Croft (UMN), phonetician Ian Maddieson (UC Berkeley), mathematical biologist Jon Wilkins (SFI), a physicist specializing in molecular phylogenetics, Tanmoy Bhattacharya (LANL), cultural anthropologist Daniel Hruschka (SFI), statistical physicist Eric Smith (SFI), theoretical evolutionary biologist Mark Pagel (Reading), and molecular anthropologist Mark Stoneking (MPI-EVA).

References

Baker, M. C. (2001). *The atoms of language*: *The mind's hidden rules of grammar*. New York: Basic Books.

Barlow, H. B. (1990). Conditions for versatile learning, Helmholtz's unconscious inference, and the task of perception. *Vision Research, 30*, 1561–1571.

Chomsky, N. (1957). *Syntactic structures*. The Hague: Mouton & Co.

Chomsky, N. (1965). *Aspects of the theory of syntax*. Cambridge, MA: MIT Press.

Chomsky, N. (1986). *Knowledge of language*. New York: Praeger.

Chomsky, N. (2004). Language and mind: Current thoughts on ancient problems. In L. Jenkins (Ed.), *Variation and universals in biolinguistics* (pp. 379–405). Amsterdam: Elsevier.

Chomsky, N. (2005). Three factors in language design. *Linguistic Inquiry, 36*, 1–22.

Christiansen, M. H., & Chater, N. (2008). Language as shaped by the brain. *Behavioral & Brain Sciences, 31*, 489–558.

Christiansen, M. H., & Kirby, S. (Eds.). (2003). *Language evolution*. Oxford: Oxford University Press.

Culicover, P. W., & Jackendoff, R. (2005). *Simpler syntax*. New York: Oxford University Press.

Edelman, S. (2008). *Computing the mind*: *how the mind really works*. New York: Oxford University Press.

Goldberg, A. E. (2006). *Constructions at work*: *The nature of generalization in language*. New York: Oxford University Press.

Gordon, R. G., Jr. (Ed.). (2005). *Ethnologue*: *Languages of the world* (15th ed.). Dallas, TX: SIL International.

Greenberg, J. H. (Ed.). (1966). *Universals of language* (2nd ed.). Cambridge, MA: MIT Press. (Originally published in 1963 as a report of the Dobbs Ferry Conference, NY, April 13–15, 1961).

Greenberg, J. H. (Ed.). (1969). Language universals: A research frontier. *Science, 166*, 473–478.

Greenberg, J. H. (2005). *Language universals—with special reference to feature hierarchies* (2nd ed.). Berlin: Mouton de Gruyter. (Original work published in 1966.)

Haspelmath, M., Dryer, M. S., Gil, D., & Comrie, B. (2005). *The world atlas of language structures*. Oxford: Oxford University Press.

Hockett, C. F. (1960). The origin of speech. *Scientific American, 203*, 88–111.

Lashley, K. S. (1951). The problem of serial order in behavior. In L. A. Jeffress (Ed.), *Cerebral mechanisms in behaviour* (pp. 112–146). New York: Wiley.

Marr, D., & Poggio, T. (1977). From understanding computation to understanding neural circuitry. *Neurosciences Research Program Bulletin, 15*, 470–488.

Mozer, M. C. (1999). A principle for unsupervised hierarchical decomposition of visual scenes. In M. S. Kearns, S. A. Solla, & D. Cohn (Eds.), *Advances in neural information processing systems 11* (pp. 52–58). Cambridge, MA: MIT Press.

Pitts, W., & McCulloch, W. S. (1947). On how we know universals: The perception of auditory and visual forms. *Bulletin of Mathematical Biophysics, 9*, 127–147.

Ross, J. R. (1967). *Constraints on variables in syntax*. Unpublished doctoral dissertation, Massachusetts Institute of Technology, Cambridge, MA.

Shamma, S. (2001). On the role of space and time in auditory processing. *Trends in Cognitive Sciences, 5*, 340–348.

Wittgenstein, L. (1953). *Philosophical investigations*. Oxford, UK: Blackwell.

2

LANGUAGE UNIVERSALS AND
USAGE-BASED THEORY

JOAN BYBEE

2.1. Universals in a Theory of Language

The treatment of similarities and differences among languages has always been central to theorizing about language. As Givón (2002) points out, linguistic science has gone through cycles in which the similarity and diversity of languages are alternately emphasized. American structuralism worked with certain structural properties that could be described given a certain procedure (e.g., phones, phonemes, morphs, morphemes, etc.) but avoided claims about more substantive categories and encouraged researchers not to impose a European model on the world's languages (Sapir, 1921; Whorf, 1945). Martin Joos (1957, p. 96) writes that in the American tradition "languages could differ from each other without limit and in unpredictable ways." At that stage in the history of linguistics, the diversity in the world's languages was emphasized. This is one area in which Chomsky (1965) definitely broke with his predecessors: he situated language universals squarely within a linguistic theory and established the tradition that a linguistic theory is required to say something about universals.

Chomsky's (1965) theory links language universals to child language acquisition by claiming that the universal aspects of language are genetically determined, that is, innate in the child. The basic idea follows from Jakobson's (1941 [1968]) observation of similarities in children's acquisition of phonology across languages and preferred patterns of phoneme distribution across languages. The crucial link between child language and universals would presumably be language change: change in the grammar takes place in first language acquisition, and thereby universals become manifest in the language. However, language change is much less studied in the generative framework, so that an understanding of how this occurs has not been fully worked out (but see Lightfoot, 1979, 1991; Roberts & Roussou, 2003).

17

In contrast, the theory I will discuss here, usage-based theory, sees a very different relationship between language universals, language change, and child language. As a much more empirically based theory, the fact that there are actually very few synchronic universals of language in the strong sense, that is, features that all languages have in common, means that there is much less emphasis put on universals of grammar as *static constraints*.

The formulation and explanation of language universals within a usage-based framework is based on the theories implicit or explicit in the work of Joseph Greenberg (1969, 1978), taken up and elaborated by Givón (1979 and elsewhere) and other functionalists, such as Li (1975, 1976), Thompson (1988, 1998), and Croft (2001, 2003), just to name a few. The underlying idea is that languages conventionalize frequently used structures so that use directly shapes structure. If language is used in similar ways in different cultures, similar grammars will arise.

Given that a number of factors are involved in this process, a variety of outcomes is possible. Because the factors are local to the communicative situation and the repetition of these factors in real-time events leads to the creation of grammatical patterns, this view of language makes it qualify as a complex system (Holland, 1998). Thus, complexity theory applies directly to this view of language in which grammar is emergent. Language universals (in the weak sense of statistical tendencies) are also emergent rather than given a priori.

2.2. Features of Usage-Based Theory

It will not be possible to give a full account of usage-based theory here; instead, I will only mention some specific features relevant to language universals (but see Barlow & Kemmer, 2000; Bybee, 2001, 2006a, for discussion). In terms of grammatical description, usage-based theory takes constructions, which are direct form-meaning pairings, to be the basic units of grammar (Goldberg, 2006). Construction grammar and usage-based theory emphasize the specifics of grammar, grammar on a level that is not likely to be universal. For instance, the following sentences exemplifying constructions have been studied in construction grammar (Fillmore, Kay, & O'Connor, 1988; Israel, 1996).

(1) What's a nice girl like you doing in a place like this?
(2) The inmates dug their way out of the prison.
(3) The more he digs, the dirtier he gets.

In these cases, the specific construction determines the meaning of the expression. Of course, more generalized constructions have also been studied. Goldberg (1995,

2006) has been especially interested in the ditransitive construction (*Mary gave Jim a book*), and Croft (2001) has studied a wide range of general constructions across languages.

Construction grammar in a usage-based framework would also take account of the fact that certain instances of constructions are also conventionalized. Thus (1) is not just an example of the "what is X doing Y" construction, but also a conventionalized instance of it. Using an exemplar model, constructions as well as particular instances of constructions can be registered in memory (Bybee, 2006a). New findings in child language research show that children learn constructions by first mastering specific instances (with particular lexical items, such as the ditransitive with *give*) before going on to generalize and use the constructions productively with other lexical items (Lieven, Pine, & Baldwin, 1997; Tomasello, 2003).

Croft (2001) argues explicitly against the universality of constructions, maintaining instead that each language defines its own constructions and the categories within them. "Constructions are language specific, and there is an extraordinary range of structural diversity of constructions encoding similar functions across languages" (p. 183). Croft surveys the types of voice (active, passive, and inverse) constructions across languages and concludes (as have others) that there are no static synchronic universals of the expression of voice. There are, however, similarities that can be discovered and Croft, following the Greenbergian theory of universals, attributes these similarities to the diachronic paths of development for voice constructions. As in other areas of grammar, diachronic work has revealed a limited number of paths of change for voice constructions. Because change is gradual, constructions change their properties only very gradually, with the result that across languages, constructions in the same functional domain will have both similarities and differences.

Usage-based theory also emphasizes the effects of frequency of use on cognitive representations. One major effect of token frequency is the strengthening or entrenchment of structures (Bybee, 1985, 2006a; Langacker, 1987). With repetition, sequences of elements become automatized and are processed as a single unit. Thus, patterns that are repeated for communicative reasons can become automated and conventionalized as part of grammar (Givón, 1979) (see section 2.6). Other effects of frequency of use will be discussed below.

2.3. Situating Universals in a Linguistic Theory

A fundamental question for any linguistic theory to address is the nature of the human genetic endowment that makes language possible. There are various ways to approach this question. Perhaps the most fundamental consideration is whether language similarities are to be attributed to domain-general or domain-specific processes and abilities. Domain-general abilities are those that are also used outside of language, in general cognition, and include categorization, use of symbols, use of inference, and so on. Domain-specific abilities would be those that are specific to language and not evidenced elsewhere. The ability to process speech auditorily may turn out to be quite specific to language and not a process used elsewhere. (See Chapter 7 for further discussion.)

Among the domain-specific abilities that have been proposed, one might distinguish between structural knowledge and processing abilities. The innate parameters of generative grammar would be structural knowledge—specific knowledge about how languages are structured. An example of a processing constraint that might be innate would be the parsing constraint discussed by Hawkins in Chapter 4). The structural knowledge would become manifest during the acquisition of language by children, but the processing constraint would affect choices of structures and thus influence grammar through usage.

Researchers have the right to make any sort of hypotheses they want; in effect, they can choose where they are going to look for universals. The most parsimonious of hypotheses would be that language is derived from general cognitive principles. Thus Lindblom, MacNeilage, and Studdert-Kennedy (1984, p. 187) urge us to "DERIVE LANGUAGE FROM NONLANGUAGE!" (emphasis in original). I agree that this should be the first line of attack, and we should hypothesize structures or abilities specific to language only when all other hypotheses fail.

A problem arises, however, in making the distinction between general cognitive tendencies and specifically linguistic ones. The main problem is that our conceptual framework for understanding our experience and the semantic packaging we use when talking about it are often difficult to distinguish. For instance, Jackendoff (2002) formulates a principle he calls Agent First, which expresses a strong tendency found in languages to put the agent of the verb in first position in the clause. He regards this principle as part of the Universal Grammar (UG) "tool kit." In contrast, Goldberg (2006) presents evidence that the salience of agents (actors) is a general cognitive bias; their salience would give rise to the tendency to mention them first. I do not know how to resolve this debate. Perhaps the best solution would be to give a rather strict definition for what would qualify as a linguistic universal and then search in general cognition for linguistic factors that manifest themselves only as tendencies. This leads to considerations of the next section.

2.4. How Universal Are Universals?

As mentioned above, serious work on crosslinguistic patterns turns up very few absolute universals. As someone who has been very interested in language universals and who has invested a great deal in empirical research trying to discover language universals, it is something of a disappointment to have to conclude that there are very few absolute synchronic universals of language. As reported in my book, *Morphology*, I surveyed the verbal morphology of 50 unrelated languages and found statistical patterns of great interest, but very few absolute universals, in the sense that one can say "all languages have x." One finding was that inflectional affixes on verbs appeared in a certain order with respect to the verb stem: aspect is the closest, then tense, and then mood; person-number affixes are farthest from the stem. There are exceptions to this ordering, making this only a tendency. The only absolute universal I found is that all languages have at least some derivational morphology.

A second study (Bybee, Perkins, & Pagliuca, 1994) was directed more at uncovering universal patterns of change, for these seemed to be the foundation for the synchronic tendencies discovered earlier. In this study we included both inflectional and periphrastic expressions associated with verbs in 76 languages. The type of synchronic universals that emerged was implicational: One can say, for instance, that if a language has any inflectional morphology at all, it will have a past or a perfective inflection. If it lacks inflection, it is likely, instead, to have a periphrastic marker, perfect or anterior (two names for the same thing). The diachronic paths of change uncovered were much more striking. This study focused on diachronic relations between lexical expressions and grammatical ones, and found a number of revealing similarities across unrelated languages indicating strong universals in the way new grammatical markers evolve. As Greenberg and Givón have noted, we here have facts of great potential for helping us understand the common basis upon which grammar evolves and a way of understanding the similarities among languages. (For further discussion, see sections 6.2 and 6.3, Chapter 6).

The paucity of true universals of synchronic language structure poses a great problem for the innateness theory. Crosslinguistic diversity leads to claims that these universals are very abstract and are disguised by other traits of languages. Newmeyer (2005) discusses the problems with trying to build typology and universals into a theory of grammar and concludes that processing constraints will account for many crosslinguistic patterns. Another approach is to propose a universal and innate "tool kit" that contains the possible grammatical devices that can be used (Jackendoff, 2002). A problem with this approach, as I see it, is that there is no account of how languages "pick and choose" from this tool kit the devices they use. This proposal needs a diachronic component before it can be evaluated. In the next section we consider how universal tendencies might emerge in specific languages.

2.5. How Do Universals Manifest Themselves?

As we have mentioned, in Chomskian theory universals emerge in child language acquisition. In two senses this approach has not been fully articulated. First, despite some similarities between preferred patterns in the languages of the world and in early child language, strict correspondences have been hard to locate, whether phonological, morphological, or syntactic. Indeed, trying to locate language universals empirically is not a major part of the generative research agenda. Instead, innate universals are taken as given, so any feature demonstrated to be present in a few languages can be considered universal. (See Newmeyer, 2005, for a discussion of the problems with this approach.)

Second, the actual link between child language and the properties of languages across the world has not been established. What is needed is an account of how children change language in such a way as to make the universals manifest. Although many writers assume that the child language acquisition process changes language (Halle, 1962; Kiparsky, 1968; Lightfoot, 1979; and many others both earlier and later; see Janda, 2001, for references), empirical evidence that this is actually the case is still lacking. Indeed, the few studies that compare language change with child language come up with as many differences as similarities. In phonology, Drachman (1978) and Vihman (1980) compare phonological alterations common in child language to sound changes found in the languages of the world and find great dissimilarities. For instance, whereas consonant harmony is common in child language (that is, a child tends to use the same consonant twice in a word, e.g., *dadi* for *doggie*), consonant harmony does not occur in the (adult) languages of the world. Rather, vowel harmony occurs in many languages, but not in child language. Hooper (1979) and Bybee and Slobin (1982) find both similarities and differences between the acquisition of morphology and morphological change. On the one hand, Hooper finds that children do learn basic or unmarked forms first and use them to make more complex forms, which mirrors some analogical changes. On the other hand, Bybee and Slobin report that some formations produced by young children are not continued by older children and adults. Slobin (1997) also argues that the semantic/pragmatic senses, such as epistemic meanings, produced by the grammaticization process are not available to young children. If child language acquisition were the vehicle for language change, one would expect a much closer correspondence between the formations caused by the two. In addition, sociolinguistic studies find that ongoing changes are most advanced in adolescents and preadolescents rather than in children in the midst of the acquisition process (Labov, 1982). (See Croft, 2000, for further discussion.)

Research in the usage-based framework finds that crosslinguistic tendencies are manifested as language is used, and can be identified in actual instances of language use and language change. Through repetition of the patterns that manifest these tendencies, conventionalized structures are created. Section 2.6 will be devoted to explaining what we know about how this occurs. But first, let us consider some of the correspondences between child language and language universals.

The implicational universals of Jakobson and Greenberg are of special interest here because they seem to show a correspondence between child language and universals. In Chapter 3, Hurford, based on Jakobson (1941 [1968]), poses the hypothesis, "Given a universal: 'If a language has X, it always has Y,' then X cannot be acquired unless Y has been acquired first" as a way of stating the relation between child language and universals. Hurford proposes that the development of language in children recapitulates the development of languages over time. He does not suggest that children mold language toward universals except in the very long run.

The first problem with moving directly from Jakobson's or Greenberg's implicational universals to child language is that there are many different types of relations stated as implications. For instance, the statement that if a language has nasal vowels it also has oral vowels ties together two phenomena that are related to one another: as we will see below, nasal vowels develop out of oral vowels. In contrast, the statement that if a language has person/number marked on the verb it will also have tense, aspect, or modality marked on the verb (Greenberg, 1963) relates categories of different types. One does not develop out of the other, but, rather, the two types of categories have different relations to the verb such that it is much more likely for tense, aspect, and modality to be marked on the verb than person/number. The statement that the presence of inflection in a language implies the presence of derivational morphemes also relates two phenomena that do not have a developmental relation to one another. There are only a very small number of cases in which it might be hypothesized that inflection became derivation and vice versa; in fact, derivation and inflection do not interact particularly in languages. Indeed, this statement is rather vacuous given that all languages have some derivational morphology. One could even say that if a language has nasal vowels, it has derivational morphology.

A second problem is that child language does not progress by the child learning all of one category before moving on to the next. Thus, it is difficult to know what exactly is meant by "acquisition" (see below). The third problem involves the relation between some of these implications and frequency. As Greenberg

(1966) has shown, unmarked categories (in phonology, morphology, and lexicon) are more frequent than marked ones in the languages in which they both occur. Thus, if children acquire unmarked categories earlier than marked ones, how do we know that it is not frequency in the input that determines the order of acquisition?

Let us consider some examples of implication universals to see what type of explanation they are amenable to. First, a phonological example: The following general statement about the distribution of oral and nasal vowels in the languages of the world seems to be true: The presence of nasal vowel phonemes in a language implies the existence of oral vowel phonemes. As predicted, it also appears to be true that children acquire some oral vowels before they acquire any nasal vowels, for instance, in French (Aicart-de Falco & Vion, 1987; Lalevée & Vilain, 2006). But when we consider how languages acquire nasal vowels, we see that it is in a completely different way than the way children acquire them. Nasal vowels develop from assimilation to a nasal consonant and subsequent loss of that consonant (Ferguson, 1963). Thus English words such as *camp*, *think*, and *went* have nasalized vowels owing to the presence of a following nasal consonant. Also, in English this nasal consonant is becoming shorter before a voiceless stop and may eventually disappear. When that happens, English will have phonemic nasal vowels. Because nasal vowels develop out of oral vowels, but only in certain contexts, in any language that has nasal vowels, they occur in fewer positions and thus less frequently than the oral ones (Ferguson, 1963). When children are acquiring vowels, they first use only oral vowels and substitute oral vowels for nasal ones. They do not develop the nasality only in the context of a nasal consonant. It is plausible that children learn oral vowels earlier because they are auditorily and articulatorily less complex, and they are also more frequent. So the relation between child language and language universals is actually quite indirect in this example.

Now consider the morphological tendency concerning tense, aspect, and mood versus person/number. To simplify the discussion, let us just consider aspect in relation to person/number agreement. In *Morphology: A Study of the Relation between Meaning and Form* (1985), I argued that aspectual meaning is more relevant to the meaning of the verb than person/number agreement because aspect modifies the perspective from which the situation described by the verb is viewed (Comrie, 1976). My argument is that because of the semantic affinity of aspect to the verb, markers of aspect that are grammaticalizing would be highly likely to fuse with the verb and form an affix (see the discussion in section 2.6). Personal pronouns can also reduce and fuse with the verb to form agreement inflections, but this is somewhat less likely because of the lower semantic relevance of person/number agreement to the inherent meaning of the verb. Thus, whereas aspectual markers can change a verb from meaning "to know" to mean "to find out" (e.g., the Spanish perfective forms of *saber*, "to know," mean "to find out"), or can change the role of the situation described by the verb from ongoing to bounded, person/number agreement just indicates whether the arguments are first, second, or third person, and singular or plural. These latter indicators leave the meaning of the verb intact.

Aspect seems to be acquired before person/number, but some important qualifications are necessary. Children do not acquire the aspectual system in its entirety before moving on to person/number agreement. They may start with some aspectual marking at early stages, but before the entire system is mastered, person/number agreement has already begun to develop. In addition, the first aspectual markings only occur on certain verbs; children do not at first use the same verb with two different aspects (Bloom, Lifter, & Hafitz, 1980; Tomasello, 1992), suggesting that their use is not fully productive until later. Still, let us say that children begin to use some aspectual marking before they use person/number marking (see Simoes & Stoel-Gammon, 1979, for Brazilian Portuguese). Why would this be? Probably for the same reason that aspectual markers fuse with verbs in diachronic change— aspect has a direct effect on the verb's meaning. Thus, at first children are not separating out the aspectual meaning from the verb meaning. *Fell* and *spilled* are punctual actions with results, whereas *playing* and *talking* are continuing activities. It is also important that in adult language use certain verbs also favor certain aspects as well (Stefanowitsch & Gries, 2003). Part of the motivation for the early pairing of certain verbs with certain aspects may be in the input. In any case, at least one of the same factors is involved in both child language and language change. Yet, we will see in section 2.6 that this does not necessarily mean that children are the main vehicle by which aspectual affixes develop.

Is the fact that languages readily develop aspectual markers on verbs and children readily acquire them an indication of an innate linguistic universal, or is it based on a more general universal of human cognition? Again, this question is very difficult to answer. It is possible that the innate linguistic abilities of children predispose them to look for a specific marker of aspect; it is also possible that the general cognitive makeup of human beings directs us to conceptualize events or situations in such a way that notions such as the completion or continuation of a situation are important to our thinking and interactions.

These examples show that the relations between stated universals of language, language change, and child language development are not simple relations and do not provide clear evidence for innate universals. We must always bear in mind that crosslinguistic generalizations such as the implicational laws just discussed are generalizations over many cases in different languages, but the more explanatory factors have to be sought by examining the nature of the relation and how these relations arise (Bybee, 1988). In the next section we will see how patterns of change that arise through language use can help us understand these generalizations across languages.

2.6. How Can Universals Derive from Usage?

2.6.1. *Conventionalization*

Languages are conventional, meaning that a community of speakers agrees upon the form-meaning correspondences of words and the patterns they occur in. The fact that *perro* in Spanish refers to approximately the same entities as *dog* in English is by convention. Similarly, the fact that the possessive phrase *Mary's dog* puts the possessor first and uses a clitic to mark possession, and Spanish *el perro de María* puts the possessor second and uses a preposition are conventions of the two languages. Even if these two ways of signaling possession are selected from a universal inventory or "tool kit," they still have to be conventionalized to enter a language and remain there.

Conventions can be established by fiat, as when someone names a baby or a pet or decides to call their new invention a *radio*. But none of this works unless other people also adopt the convention. In addition, a few rounds of repetition are necessary to lock the convention in place. Grammatical structures are also conventionalized, but they do not arise in the conscious manner in which naming takes place. They arise, instead, by the repetition of patterns or sequences of items that have proved useful within the context of conversational exchange.

The effects of repetition are interesting to consider. Haiman (1994, 1998) makes the point that repeated use leads to the development of linguistic patterns in a way that is parallel to the process of ritualization, which occurs with nonlinguistic patterns. Ritual gestures start out as functional, but as they are repeated and transmitted across generations, they undergo certain changes. For one thing, they become "emancipated" from their original function. Saluting as used in the military began in the Middle Ages when soldiers wore metal armor; when they greeted a fellow soldier, they lifted the faceplate to identify themselves as friendly. This originally functional act came to stand for a respectful greeting of a fellow soldier or officer; it became emancipated from its original function, and continues to be used even though metal armor is no longer worn. Because emancipation can also occur in the creation of grammatical structure, the direct functional motivation for these structures will not always still be operative synchronically.

Haiman also notes that repeated use leads to automation of the rituals and reduction in their form; again the salute is a good example. We will see below that in the process of grammaticalization, emancipation, automation, and reduction in form, all play an important role.

2.6.2. Grammaticalization Defined and Illustrated

The most pervasive process by which grammatical items and structures are created is the process of grammaticalization. Grammaticalization is usually defined as the process by which a lexical item or a sequence of items becomes a grammatical morpheme, changing its distribution and function in the process (Heine, Claudi, & Hünnemeyer, 1991; Heine & Reh, 1984; Hopper & Traugott, 1993; Lehmann, 1982 [1995]; Meillet, 1912). Thus English *going to* (with a finite form of *be*) becomes the intention/future marker, *gonna*. However, more recently it has been observed that it is important to add that grammaticalization of lexical items takes place within PARTICULAR CONSTRUCTIONS and, further, that grammaticalization creates new constructions (Bybee, 2003; Traugott, 2003). Thus, *going to* does not grammaticalize in the construction exemplified by *I'm going to the store* but only in the construction in which a verb follows *to*, as in *I'm going to help you*. The term is also used at times to include cases of change that do not involve specific morphemes, such as the creation of a grammatical word order pattern out of a commonly used discourse pattern.

Historical linguists have long been aware of grammaticalization as a way to create new grammatical morphemes, but it was research in the 1980s and 1990s that revealed the pervasiveness of grammaticalization. Crosslinguistic and historical documentation make it clear that grammaticalization is going on in all languages at all times and, further, that all aspects of grammar are affected. In addition, there is the further remarkable fact that across unrelated languages lexical items with very similar meanings enter into the process and give rise to grammatical morphemes with very similar meanings (Bybee et al., 1994; Bybee, 2006b). Consider these examples (and see Heine & Kuteva, 2002, for a wonderful catalog of such changes):

In many European languages, an indefinite article has developed out of the numeral "one": English *a/an*, German *ein*, French *un/une*, Spanish *un/una*, and Modern Greek *ena*. Although these are all Indo-European languages, in each case this development occurred after these languages had differentiated from one another and speakers were no longer in contact. Furthermore, the numeral "one" is used as an indefinite article in Moré, a Gur language of the Burkina Faso (Heine & Kuteva, 2002), in colloquial Hebrew (Semitic), and in the Dravidian languages Tamil and Kannada (Heine, 1997). Examples of demonstratives becoming definite articles are also common: English *that* became *the*; Latin *ille*, *illa* "that" became French definite articles *le*, *la* and Spanish *el*, *la*; in Vai (a Mande language of Liberia and Sierra Leone), the demonstrative *mɛ* "this" became a suffixed definite article (Heine & Kuteva, 2002).

The English future auxiliary *will* came from an Old English verb meaning "to want." Parallel to this, a verb meaning "want" became a future marker in Bulgarian,

Rumanian, and Serbo-Croatian, as well as in the Bantu languages of Africa—Mabiha, Omyene, and Swahili (Bybee & Pagliuca, 1987; Heine & Kuteva, 2002). Parallel to English *can* from "to know," Baluchi (Indo-Iranian), Danish (Germanic), Motu (Papua Austronesian), Mwera (Bantu), and Nung (Tibeto-Burman) use a verb meaning "know" for the expression of ability (Bybee et al., 1994). Tok Pisin, a creole language of New Guinea, uses *kæn* (from English *can*) for *ability*, and also *savi* from the Portuguese *save*, "he knows," for ability. Latin *potere* or *possum*, "to be able," gives French *pouvoir* and Spanish *poder*, both meaning "can" as auxiliaries and "power" as nouns. These words parallel English *may* (and past tense *might*), which earlier meant, "have the physical power to do something." Verbs or phrases indicating movement toward a goal (comparable to English *be going to*) frequently become future markers around the world not only in languages such as French and Spanish, but also in languages spoken in Africa, the Americas, Asia, and the Pacific (Bybee & Pagliuca, 1987; Bybee et al., 1994).

Of course, not all grammaticalization paths can be illustrated with English examples. There are also common developments that do not happen to occur in English. For instance, a completive or perfect marker meaning "have [just] done" develops from a verb meaning "finish" in Bantu languages, as well as in languages as diverse as Cocama and Tucano (both Andean-Equatorial), Koho (Mon-Khmer), Buli (Malayo-Polynesian), Tem and Engenni (both Niger-Congo), Lao (Kam-Tai), Haka and Lahu (Tibeto-Burman), Cantonese, and Tok Pisin (Bybee et al., 1994; Heine & Reh, 1984). In addition, the same development from the verb "finish" has been recorded for American Sign Language, showing that grammaticalization takes place in sign languages the same way as it does in spoken languages (Janzen, 1995).

For several of these developments I have cited the creole language, Tok Pisin, a variety of Melanesian Pidgin English, which is now the official language of Papua New Guinea. Pidgin languages are originally trade or plantation languages, which develop in situations where speakers of several different languages must interact though they share no common language. At first, pidgins have no grammatical constructions or categories, but as they are used in wider contexts and by more people more often, they begin to develop grammar. Once such languages come to be used by children as their first language, and thus are designated as creole languages, the development of grammar flowers even more. The fact that the grammars of pidgin and creole languages are very similar in form, even among pidgins that developed in geographically distant places by speakers of diverse languages, has been taken by Bickerton (1981) to be strong evidence for innate language universals. However, studies of the way in which grammar develops in such languages reveals that the process is the same as the grammaticalization process in more established languages

(Romaine, 1995; Sankoff, 1990). Tok Pisin in particular has had a long life as a second language before becoming the first language of a generation of children, and even while it was still a pidgin language has developed grammatical markers, such as *bai* for future from the English phrase *by and by*.

2.6.3. How Grammaticalization Occurs

The grammaticalization process occurs during language use. A number of factors come into play, and these factors have been discussed in the literature cited above. For present purposes, let us think of grammaticalization, as Haiman does (1994, 1998), as a process of ritualization. This allows us to think of it in domain-general terms. We have already noted that ritualization requires repetition. In fact, one of the changes that occurs in grammaticalization is an extreme increase in frequency of use of the grammaticalizing construction. Besides being one the factors that changes, frequency itself is an important catalyst in many of the other changes that occur.

Like other repeated instances of behavior, grammaticalizing sequences reduce phonetically. I have already mentioned *going to* reducing to *gonna*. We also have ongoing reduction in phrases such as *want to, have to, supposed to*. Looking back to the past, we find that English *-ed* is the reduction of *dyde*, "did"; Spanish first person singular future suffix *-é* is the reduced form of the Latin auxiliary *habeo*. Such reduction is due to the automatization of the phonetic gestures in these sequences; as these strings are repeated, they become more fluent with more overlap and reduction of gestures.

Automatization also leads to sequences of morphemes being processed as units (Boyland, 1996). The internal units of the grammaticalizing expression become less transparently analyzable and more independent of other instances of the same units. Thus *have* in *have to* becomes more distant from the *have* in another grammatical expression, the Perfect. The forms of *have* in the Perfect contract with the subject (*I've seen, he's taken*, etc.), but the forms of *have* in *have to* do not (**I've to go*). Of course, this is driven in part by the semantic changes that occur.

Semantic change occurs gradually and involves various types of change. On the one hand, components of meaning appear to be lost. Thus *gonna* no longer indicates movement in space; *will* no longer indicates "wanting to"; *can* no longer means "know" or "know how to," but only ability or possibility; *a/an* is still singular, but does not explicitly specify "one." This type of change has been called "bleaching." It comes about as these expressions increase the contexts in which they are used. Even though *can* still indicates the subject has the knowledge to tell truthfully in *I can tell you that she has gone with her uncle*, it does not indicate anything at all about knowledge in *walk as quietly as you can*.

However, not all semantic change involves loss of meaning (Traugott, 1989). In change by pragmatic inference, meanings that are frequently implied by the accompanying context are conventionalized as part of the meaning of the expression. Frequent contexts of use for *be going to*, such as *I am going to deliver this letter*, imply intention, and as a result intention to act has become an important part of the meaning of the *be going to* expression.

In this short sketch, I have identified several mechanisms of change, all of which are driven by increased usage: phonetic reduction, automatization, increasing autonomy, semantic bleaching, and pragmatic inference. These are the basic mechanisms of change that can act on any grammaticalizing material and render it part of the grammar. These same processes are at work in very common grammaticalizations, such as the *go* futures, and also in the rarer ones, such as futures from temporal adverbs (such as Tok Pisin *bai*). Although these processes explain similarities across languages, they also allow for and create differences: a future from *go* will have different semantic nuances than a future from *want*; a future that has recently grammaticalized will have a strong intention reading, whereas a future that has undergone more development may have no intention uses at all (Bybee et al., 1994). Thus, grammaticalization has great potential for explaining the similarities as well as the differences among languages.

2.6.4. *Grammatical Properties Arising from Language Use in Interaction*

Thompson and colleagues have explored a number of constructions as used in natural conversation with an eye toward explaining their crosslinguistic properties in terms of the interactions in which they occur. Let us consider as our example the crosslinguistic analysis of interrogation in Thompson (1998). Thompson explores interrogation and negation together as being somewhat comparable in that they have been analyzed as expressing clause-level operators, and all languages provide some means for asking questions and expressing negation. She finds that the crosslinguistic properties of questions, especially as compared to negatives, result from of the way they are used in conversation.

Crosslinguistically there are five strategies for marking interrogatives (Ultan, 1978):

a. Intonation changes from declarative utterances
b. Interrogative morphemes that occur at or very near the beginning of the utterance or at the end
c. Tag questions following a statement
d. Nonintonational phonological marking at the end of the utterance
e. Inversion of the verb with the first element in the utterance

Thompson (1998, p. 313) points out that all of these strategies "involve special marking either at the beginning or end of the clause/sentence/utterance, or involve prosodic patterns that characterize the entire clause/sentence/utterance." She goes on to consider the nature of the unit over which the interrogation strategy operates, noting that many descriptions use the term *utterance* because units smaller than a clause (such as a noun phrase) can be questioned. In the cases where better data is available, it is clear that the locus of operation for the interrogation marker is a prosodic unit such as the intonation unit. In contrast, sentence negation always involves a particle, affix, or special word that is positioned with respect to the predicate rather than a prosodic unit or utterance.

Thompson sees these special properties of the grammar of interrogation to be linked to the way questions occur in conversation. Questions seek information, and in natural conversation they typically occur as the first part of an adjacency pair (Schegloff, 1968; Schegloff & Sacks, 1973). The first part of a pair establishes the nature of what follows; if a question is posed, conversational conventions require that a new turn (from a different speaker) follow, and this turn should be relevant to the information sought by the question.

A major factor in turn, transition in conversation, is the prosodic structure of the utterance. Thus the grammatical marking of interrogation develops out of conversational pairings in which the prosodic unit is modified by strategies that elicit a response from the hearer. As mentioned above, these include modification of the prosodic or intonation unit itself, adding something to it at the beginning or end, or modifying the beginning or end. When such strategies are repeated, they become conventionalized and part of the grammar.

To continue the comparison with negation, negative clauses do not occur in conversation as parts of adjacency pairs with any frequency. Negative sentences can deny propositions internal to the conversation or completely external to it. They can offer new information, or they can remark on old information. Thus, their grammar does not reflect any turn-taking markers.

2.6.5. The Development of Discourse Markers

It appears likely that all grammatical structures arise from use in conversation, including the various structures discussed in section 2.6.2. Particularly clear examples are discourse markers. Discourse markers are not universal, but the way they develop is, according to Traugott and Dasher (2002). Discourse markers such as *indeed, in fact, actually,* and comparable markers in other languages start out with concrete semantic content and function as part of the propositional meaning of the clause. The original meanings of the three English adverbs mentioned just above are still clear to native speakers. *Indeed* came from Old English *in dede,* meaning "in action," as in the expression, "in word and in deed." As Traugott and Dasher explain, actions are observable, and the common inference is made that what is seen is true. Thus *in dede* came to be used to express "in actuality," as in this example from 1388:

(4)   ofte in storial mateer scripture rehersith the commune opynyoun of men, and affirmith not, that it was so *in dede*.
        "often where matters of history are concerned, scripture repeats men's common opinion, but does not affirm that it was so in actuality."
                                                               (c. 1388 Purvey, Wycliffe, p. 56)

As a further development, *in dede* takes on an epistemic function, meaning "in truth," as in the following example from 1452:

(5)   The men of þe town had suspecion to hem, þat her tydyngis were lyes (as it was in dede), risen.
        "The men of the town, being suspicious that their reports were lies (as was certainly true), rose"
                                                               (1452, Chronical Capgrave, p. 216)

In this example, *in dede* has scope over the whole clause "that their reports were lies" and comments on its truth, thereby making an epistemic evaluation.

From this epistemic function, *indeed* developed several discourse-related functions, by which it came to express the relations among clauses, as the speaker intends them. One of these was an adversative function, which contrasts the assertion with *indeed* with the previous assertion:

(6)   [teachers] sometime purposely suffering ["allowing"] the more noble children to vainquysshe, and, as it were, gyuying ["giving"] to them place and soueraintie, thoughe *in dede* the inferiour children haue more lernyng.
                                                               (1531, Elyot, p. 21)

Another such function, commonly used today, is additive:

(7)   any a one that is not well, comes farre and neere in hope to be made well: *indeed* I did heare that it had done much good, and that it hath a rare operation to expell or kill diuers maladies.
                                                               (1630 Taylor, Penniless Pilgrimage, p. 131C1)

The adversative and additive functions, then, have scope over entire clauses, and serve to express the relation between assertions.

Traugott and Dasher review the development of a number of such discourse adverbs in English and Japanese, and make the following generalization (see also Company Company, 2006, for comparable examples and analysis of Spanish discourse markers): The functional development is from verb modifier to clause modifier, from scope within the clause to scope over the whole clause, from relatively concrete senses to more abstract and nonreferential senses, and from contentful function to procedural function, which expresses the speaker's attitudes to the content of the discourse and the participants in it. These paths of development can be considered universals, because changes always follow the directions cited here and not the reverse. Note, however, that no synchronic universals of language result. These examples, along with the other examples of grammaticalization cited earlier, demonstrate that searching only for universals of synchronic structure is far too limiting.

What we learn from these examples is that when people use language, they are interested in much more than the content that the speaker has made explicit; as people converse, they are constantly making inferences about the speaker's attitude toward the truth of his/her statements, about the intentions of the speaker, and about relations the speaker is proposing among clauses. This online process of inferencing imbues words and constructions with meanings they may not have originally had, but note, meanings of certain restricted types. For this reason, Traugott and Dasher are able to state generalizations about the directions of change.

2.6.6. Processing Preferences

Another way that language use can give rise to certain kinds of structures is by the repetition of structures that are easier to process at the expense of structures that are more difficult to process. Hawkins (2004; Chapter 4) proposes the Performance-Grammar Correspondence Hypothesis: "Grammars have conventionalized syntactic structures in proportion to their degree of preference in performance, as evidenced by patterns of selection in corpora and by ease of processing in psycholinguistic experiments."

One of the processing preferences that Hawkins discusses is evident in the following two sentences:

(8)   The man waited for his son in the cold but not unpleasant wind.
(9)   The man waited in the cold but not unpleasant wind for his son.

In languages such as English, sentences with the longer phrase at the end (8) occur more often than those with the longer phrase internal to the clause (9). Hawkins argues that sentences of the type (8) are preferred because they allow all the constituents to be identified earlier than the type in (9), where the long phrase defers the second PP. So, this case constitutes another way in which actual language use feeds into grammar.

We might want to go even further than Hawkins in explaining how sentence structure arises. Hawkins assumes the existence of constituent structure as a universal, but does not comment on where it might come from. In Bybee (2002) I argue that constituent structure is also emergent from language use in that words that are commonly used together come to be processed together. As mentioned earlier, a well-known feature of neuromotor processing is that sequences of actions that are often used become processed as single units (Boyland, 1996). Words within constituents occur together more often than words across constituent boundaries; thus the constituents themselves can be conventionalized patterns based on language use. Because words within constituents are related semantically to one another, the starting point for this explanation is a strong tendency to put semantically related items together in an utterance. Then, with repetition and conventionalization, constituents will emerge.

2.7. Conclusion: Similarities and Differences

As noted earlier, the basic structure of the usage-based approach to universals is first articulated in Greenberg (1969). Greenberg identifies several "dynamic selective tendencies," or diachronic processes, that create language states. He says (1969, p. 186),

> Synchronic regularities are merely the consequences of such forces. It is not so much again that "exceptions" are explained historically, but that the true regularity is contained in the dynamic principles themselves.

This theory, then, aims to explain both the similarities and the differences among languages. Rather than having one source for similarities (universals) and one source for language-specific properties, all grammatical patterns are created by the same set of processes, whether the patterns are highly common or very rare. It is in this sense, then, that the universals underlying the structure of language are to be found in the processes that govern the way speakers choose structures online and the processes that are set in motion by repetition of the same patterns over and over again. Some of these processes are likely to be domain-general processes, as argued here. I propose (with many others) that we look first to domain-general processes before turning to language-specific processes. It should be borne in mind that the processes that create grammar in the languages of the world interact in complex ways; online processing, conversational interactions, repetition leading to conventionalization, and language acquisition will all play a role in our final understanding of the general and specific properties of human languages.

Key Further Readings

Croft (2003) is an introduction to the Greenbergian approach to typology and universals with an emphasis on morphosyntax. Some of the original works by

Greenberg are accessible and certainly worth reading. Greenberg (1963) contains the proposals for word order universals as well as a number of implicational universals of morphology. Greenberg (1966) demonstrates the importance of frequency of use in understanding the properties of marked and unmarked members of categories.

In phonology, Blevins (2004) presents her "evolutionary" approach to crosslinguistic distributional patterns, which she demonstrates to be based on diachronic universals. Bybee (2008) demonstrates that a structural tendency of languages (Structure Preservation), which results in only contrastive features being used in lexical alternations, can be explained by the convergence of several well-attested paths of diachronic change.

It is interesting also to read more about grammaticalization (also called grammaticization) in a crosslinguistic context. Bybee et al. (1994) is a study of the grammaticalization of tense, aspect, and modality in a sample of 76 unrelated languages. Heine and Kuteva (2002) compile from myriad sources across languages all the documented paths of change that create grammatical morphemes. This is a wonderful reference and work, and a fun book to browse in. John Haiman's 1994 article and 1998 book are both highly readable and extremely thought provoking; they examine the role of repetition in rituals and in language.

References

Aicart-de Falco, S., & Vion, M. (1987). La mise en place du système phonologique du francais chez les enfants entre 3 et 6 ans: Une étude de production. *Cahiers de psychologie cognitive*, 3, 247–266.

Barlow, M., & Kemmer, S. (Eds.). (2000). *Usage-based models of language*. Stanford: CSLI.

Bickerton, D. (1981). *Roots of language*. Ann Arbor: Karoma.

Blevins, J. (2004). *Evolutionary phonology: The emergence of sound patterns*. Cambridge: Cambridge University Press.

Bloom, L., Lifter, K., & Hafitz, J. (1980). The semantics of verbs and the development of verb inflections in child language. *Language*, 56, 386–412.

Boyland, J. T. (1996). *Morphosyntactic change in progress: A psycholinguistic approach*. Dissertation: University of California at Berkeley.

Bybee, J. L. (1985). *Morphology: A study of the relation between meaning and form*. Philadelphia: John Benjamins.

Bybee, J. L. (1988). The diachronic dimension in explanation. In J. A. Hawkins (Ed.), *Explaining language universals* (pp. 350–379). New York: Basil Blackwell.

Bybee, J. L. (2001). *Phonology and language use*. Cambridge: Cambridge University Press.

Bybee, J. L. (2002). Sequentiality as the basis of constituent structure. In T. Givón & B. F. Malle (Eds.), *The evolution of language out of pre-language* (pp. 109–132). Amsterdam: John Benjamins. Reprinted in Bybee (2007), pp. 313–335.

Bybee, J. L. (2003). Mechanisms of change in grammaticization: The role of frequency. In R. Janda & B. Joseph (Eds.), *Handbook of historical linguistics* (pp. 602–623). Oxford: Blackwell. Reprinted in Bybee (2007), pp. 336–357.

Bybee, J. L. (2006a). From usage to grammar: The mind's response to repetition. *Language, 82,* 529–551.

Bybee, J. L. (2006b). Language change and universals. In R. Mairal & J. Gil (Eds.), *Linguistic universals* (pp. 179–194). Cambridge: Cambridge University Press.

Bybee, J. L. (2007). *Frequency of use and the organization of language.* Oxford: Oxford University Press.

Bybee, J. L. (2008). Formal universals as emergent phenomena: The origins of structure preservation. In J. Good (Ed.), *Language universals and language change* (pp. 108–121). Oxford: Oxford University Press.

Bybee, J. L., & Pagliuca, W. (1987). The evolution of future meaning. In A. Giacalone Ramat, O. Carruba, & G. Bernini (Eds.), *Papers from the VIIth International Conference on Historical Linguistics* (pp. 109–122). Amsterdam: John Benjamins.

Bybee, J. L., Perkins, R., & Pagliuca, W. (1994). *The evolution of grammar: Tense, aspect, and modality in the languages of the world.* Chicago: University of Chicago Press.

Bybee, J. L., & Slobin, D. I. (1982). Why small children cannot change language on their own: Evidence from the English past tense. In A. Alqvist (Ed.), *Papers from the Fifth International Conference on Historical Linguistics* (pp. 29–37). Amsterdam: John Benjamins.

Chomsky, N. (1965). *Aspects of the theory of syntax.* Cambridge, MA: MIT Press.

Company Company, C. (2006). Subjectification of verbs into discourse markers: Semantic-pragmatic change only? In B. Cornillie & N. Delbecque (Eds.), *Topics in subjectification and modalization* (pp. 97–121). Amsterdam: John Benjamins.

Comrie, B. (1976). *Aspect.* Cambridge: Cambridge University Press.

Croft, W. (2000). *Explaining language change: An evolutionary approach.* Harlow, England: Longman Linguistics Library.

Croft, W. (2001). *Radical construction grammar: Syntactic theory in typological perspective.* Oxford: Oxford University Press.

Croft, W. (2003). *Typology and universals* (2nd ed.). Cambridge: Cambridge University Press.

Drachman, G. (1978). Child language and language change: A conjecture and some refutations. In J. Fisiak (Ed.), *Recent development in historical phonology* (pp. 123–144). The Hague: Mouton.

Ferguson, C. A. (1963). Assumptions about nasals: A sample study in phonological universals. In J. H. Greenberg (Ed.), *Universals of language* (pp. 53–60). Cambridge, MA: MIT Press.

Fillmore, C. J., Kay, P., & O'Connor, M. C. (1988). Regularity and idiomaticity in grammatical constructions. *Language, 64,* 501–538.

Givón, T. (1979). *On understanding grammar.* New York: Academic Press.

Givón, T. (2002). *Bio-linguistics: The Santa Barbara lectures.* Amsterdam: John Benjamins.

Goldberg, A. E. (1995). *Constructions: A construction grammar approach to argument structure.* Chicago: University of Chicago Press.

Goldberg, A. E. (2006). *Constructions at work: The nature of generalization in language*. Oxford: Oxford University Press.

Greenberg, J. H. (1963). Some universals of grammar with particular reference to the order of meaningful elements. In J. H. Greenberg (Ed.), *Universals of language* (pp. 73–113). Cambridge, MA: MIT Press.

Greenberg, J. H. (1966). *Language universals: With special reference to feature hierarchies*. The Hague: Mouton.

Greenberg, J. H. (1969). Some methods of dynamic comparison in linguistics. In J. Puhvel (Ed.), *Substance and structure of language* (pp. 147–203). Berkeley: University of California Press.

Greenberg, J. H. (1978). Diachrony, synchrony and language universals. In J. H. Greenberg, C. A. Ferguson, & E. Moravcsik (Eds.), *Universals of human language, Vol. 1: Method and theory* (pp. 61–92). Stanford: Stanford University Press.

Haiman, J. (1994). Ritualization and the development of language. In W. Pagliuca (Ed.), *Perspectives on grammaticalization* (pp. 3–28). Amsterdam: John Benjamins.

Haiman, J. (1998). *Talk is cheap*. Oxford: Oxford University Press.

Halle, M. (1962). Phonology in generative grammar. *Word, 18*, 54–72.

Hawkins, J. A. (2004). *Efficiency and complexity in grammars*. Oxford: Oxford University Press.

Heine, B. (1997). *Cognitive foundations of grammar*. New York: Oxford University Press.

Heine, B., Claudi, U., & Hünnemeyer, F. (1991). *Grammaticalization: A conceptual framework*. Chicago: University of Chicago Press.

Heine, B., & Kuteva, T. (2002). *World lexicon of grammaticalization*. Cambridge: Cambridge University Press.

Heine, B., & Reh, M. (1984). *Grammaticalization and reanalysis in African languages*. Hamburg: Helmut Buske Verlag.

Holland, J. H. (1998). *Emergence: From chaos to order*. New York: Basic Books.

Hooper, J. B. (1979). Child morphology and morphophonemic change. *Linguistics, 17*, 21–50.

Hopper, P., & Traugott, E. C. (1993). *Grammaticalization*. Cambridge: Cambridge University Press.

Israel, M. (1996). The way constructions grow. In A. E. Goldberg (Ed.), *Conceptual structure, discourse and language* (pp. 217–230). Stanford: CSLI Publications.

Jackendoff, R. (2002). *Foundations of language: Brain, meaning, grammar, evolution*. Oxford: Oxford University Press.

Jakobson, R. (1941 [1968]). *Child language, aphasia, and phonological universals*. The Hague: Mouton.

Janda, R. D. (2001). Beyond "pathways" and "unidirectionality": On the discontinuity of language transmission and the counterability of grammaticalization. In L. Campbell (Ed.), *Grammaticalization: A critical assessment*. Special issue of *Language Sciences, 23*(2–3), 265–340.

Janzen, T. (1995). The polygrammaticalization of FINISH in ASL. Masters' Thesis, University of Manitoba.

Joos, M. (1957). *Readings in linguistics I*. Chicago and London: University of Chicago Press.

Kiparsky, P. (1968). Linguistic universals and linguistic change. In E. Bach & R. Harms (Eds.), *Universals in linguistic theory* (pp. 171–202). New York: Holt, Rinehart and Winston.

Labov, W. (1982). Building on empirical foundations. In W. P. Lehmann & Y. Malkiel (Eds.), *Perspectives on historical linguistics* (pp. 17–92). Amsterdam: John Benjamins.

Lalevée, C., & Vilain, A. (2006). What does it take to make a first word? The development of speech motor control during the first year of life. In H. C. Yehia, D. Demolin, & R. Laboissiere (Eds.), *Proceedings of the 7th International Seminar on Speech Production* (pp. 83–90). Belo Horizonte, Brazil: Centro de Estudos da Fala, Acústica, Linguagem e Música.

Langacker, R. W. (1987). *Foundations of cognitive grammar, Volume 1: Theoretical prerequisites.* Stanford: Stanford University Press.

Lehmann, C. (1982 [1995]). *Thoughts on grammaticalization.* Munich: Lincom Europa.

Li, C. N. (Ed.). (1975). *Word order and word order change.* Austin: University of Texas Press.

Li, C. N. (Ed.). (1976). *Subject and topic.* New York: Academic Press.

Lieven, E. V., Pine, J. M., & Baldwin, G. (1997). Lexically based learning and early grammatical development. *Journal of Child Language, 24,* 187–219.

Lightfoot, D. (1979). *Principles of diachronic syntax.* Cambridge: Cambridge University Press.

Lightfoot, D. (1991). *How to set parameters: Arguments from language change.* Cambridge, MA: MIT Press.

Lindblom, B., MacNeilage, P., & Studdert-Kennedy, M. (1984). Self-organizing processes and the explanation of phonological universals. In B. Butterworth, B. Comrie, & Ö. Dahl (Eds.), *Explanations for language universals* (pp. 181–203). New York: Mouton.

Meillet, A. (1912). L'évolution des formes grammaticales. *Scientia* 12. Reprinted in A. Meillet, *Linguistique Historique et Linguistique Générale* (pp. 130–148). Paris: Edouard Champion, 1948.

Newmeyer, F. J. (2005). *Possible and probable languages.* Oxford: Oxford University Press.

Roberts, I., & Roussou, A. (2003). *Syntactic change: A Minimalist approach to grammaticalization.* Cambridge: Cambridge University Press.

Romaine, S. (1995). The grammaticalization of irrealis in Tok Pisin. In J. L. Bybee & S. Fleischman (Eds.), *Modality in grammar and discourse* (pp. 389–427). Amsterdam: John Benjamins.

Sankoff, G. (1990). The grammaticalization of tense and aspect in Tok Pisin and Sranan. *Language Variation and Change, 2,* 295–312.

Sapir, E. (1921). *Language: An introduction to the study of speech.* New York: Harcourt, Brace and World.

Schegloff, E. (1968). Sequencing in conversational openings. *American Anthropologist, 70*(6), 1075–1095.

Schegloff, E., & Sacks, H. (1973). Opening up closings. *Semiotica, 7,* 289–327.

Simões, M. C. P., & Stoel-Gammon, C. (1979). The acquisition of inflections in Portuguese: A study of the development of person markers on verbs. *Journal of Child Language, 6*(1), 53–67.

Slobin, D. I. (1997). The origins of grammaticizable notions: Beyond the individual mind. In D. I. Slobin (Ed.), *The crosslinguistic study of language acquisition, Vol. 5: Expanding the contexts* (pp. 1–39). Mahwah, NJ: Lawrence Erlbaum.

Stefanowitsch, A., & Gries, S. T. (2003). Collostructions: Investigating the interaction of words and constructions. *International Journal of Corpus Linguistics, 8*(2), 209–243.

Thompson, S. A. (1988). A discourse approach to the crosslinguistic category "adjective." In J. A. Hawkins (Ed.), *Explaining language universals* (pp. 167–185). Oxford: Basil Blackwell.

Thompson, S. A. (1998). A discourse explanation for the crosslinguistic differences in the grammar of interrogation and negation. In A. Siewierska & J. J. Song (Eds.), *Case, typology and grammar* (pp. 309–341). Amsterdam: John Benjamins.

Tomasello, M. (1992). *First verbs: A case study of early grammatical development.* Cambridge: Cambridge University Press.

Tomasello, M. (2003). *Constructing a language.* Cambridge, MA: Harvard University Press.

Traugott, E. C. (1989). On the rise of epistemic meanings in English: An example of subjectification in semantic change. *Language, 65,* 31–55.

Traugott, E. C. (2003). Constructions in grammaticalization. In R. Janda & B. Joseph (Eds.), *Handbook of historical linguistics* (pp. 624–647). Oxford: Blackwell.

Traugott, E. C., & Dasher, R. B. (2002). *Regularity in semantic change.* Cambridge: Cambridge University Press.

Ultan, R. (1978). Some general characteristics of interrogative systems. In J. H. Greenberg, C. A. Ferguson and E. Moravcsik (Ed.), *Universals of human language, Vol. 4: Syntax* (pp. 211–248). Stanford, CA: Stanford University Press.

Vihman, M. (1980). Sound change and child language. In E. C. Traugott, R. Labrum, & S. Shepherd (Eds.), *Papers from the Fourth International Conference on Historical Linguistics* (pp. 303–320). Amsterdam: John Benjamins.

Whorf, B. L. (1945). Grammatical categories. *Language, 21,* 1–11.

3

UNIVERSALS AND THE DIACHRONIC LIFE CYCLE OF LANGUAGES

James R. Hurford

3.1. Acquisition Is Only Half of the Story

A prevalent form of explanation for universals of language (expounded in many of Chomsky's works, e.g., Chomsky, 1965) links linguists' theoretical descriptions of languages with language acquisition. From my own perspective, this generative approach is only partially adequate, as the title of this section suggests. The next paragraph below sketches a typical way in which generative linguists steer a tactical course between what is significantly common to all languages (thus potentially hypothesized to be linked to some bias in language acquisition) and what is idiosyncratic to particular languages (implicitly because of some other, usually unspecified, processes).

Linguists are interested in the common framework on which all languages are built, that is, in universals of language; they also have to cope with the great diversity of languages. General scientific methodology dictates that the description of each language should be as elegant and economical as possible, consistent with the facts. This pushes the linguist to formulate general synchronic rules and principles as the "core grammar" of a language, with lists of idiosyncratic facts treated as peripheral. The lexicon, a store of arbitrary sound-meaning links, is the most obvious "peripheral" component. Somewhere between general principles applying to the core grammars of all languages and the idiosyncratic lexicon are the values of parameters fixed during language acquisition (Chomsky, 1981). Fixing a parameter amounts to making a generalization over, for example, head-dependent constituent order, or whether the language permits null subjects, or the precise barriers to syntactic movement rules. Languages vary along these parameters, and this variation, along with the arbitrary facts of the lexicon, contributes to the diversity of languages.

Language is not totally innate; what is learned, be it arbitrary lexical form-meaning mappings or the values of parameters, is what makes the diversity of languages. If language were totally innate, there would be linguistic universals only in the trivial sense that there would be a single truly universal language, the only one that humans could possibly speak. Two correspondences have emerged in linguistic theorizing over the past 50 years: associating universals with what is innate and diversity with what is learned. The associations are made more subtle by extending the scope of the term *universal* not only to what languages *must* be like (i.e., what is innate and must be part of an acquired grammar), but also to constraints on what languages *can* be like (i.e., what can be acquired).

Already implicit here, and acceptable as *part* of the theory of language, is the idea that universal facts about languages can be explained by innate constraints on language acquisition, either absolute as principles or less absolute as parameters. And the obviously correct definition of acquisition is that it requires some input. Not even the most ardent nativist would claim that a language grows in a child wholly without input. And, within the innate constraints, the language acquired is determined by the input. Children arrive at some compromise between their innate template for language and the data bombarding them. They make generalizations over the data where the data fit nicely with innate biases, and where they don't, if the data is salient or frequent enough, they just memorize idiosyncratic facts. Given this picture, and accepting the idea of some innate biases (of course all learning is biased—there is no such thing as unbiased learning), it is easy to see how some universal patterns emerge in languages, but it is much less easy to see where the diversity comes from. In short, what keeps languages so diverse among themselves, and what keeps each language so full of stuff that has to be learned? Why should there ever be, in the data to which the child is exposed, any salient or frequent examples that just require memorizing?

To highlight this question, consider the ubiquitous presence of irregularity in languages. In the everyday, nontechnical sense of *universal*, irregularities are universal in languages. Only artificial languages, like Esperanto, are mostly lacking in irregularities (though even the original Esperanto had a few irregularities). It seems a natural prediction that once Esperanto has been transmitted culturally in a sizeable population for a few centuries, it, too, will evolve more irregularities. Now, an irregularity, by definition, cannot be the outcome of an innate bias. The innate language acquisition device doesn't say, "When you acquire this verb, whatever you do, make sure it doesn't conform to any of the general rules in your language." We know that children overregularize irregular verbs, saying "comed" and "taked," until the data make them change their minds, and they learn the irregular forms. What keeps languages somewhat irregular? Why don't the undoubted innate biases of children toward regularity overcome the irregularities? Because the irregularities are too persistent and salient in the input data. But why? Innate dispositions cannot provide the answer.

Irregularities are doubtless bona fide parts of any language, as second-language learners know to their pain. One may take a dismissive attitude and pronounce that they are "not interesting" because they do not shed light on the nature of the innate language-learning bias, the faculty of language in the narrow sense, "FLN" (Hauser, Chomsky, & Fitch, 2002). True, they don't, except to show the limitations of the innate learning bias as an *explanans* for all the parts of any language. Defining the goal of linguistics as just the discovery of the innate learning biases is not the only choice. Many researchers come to the subject through exposure to individual languages, and with a curiosity about what forms them, warts and all. The project to explain what makes whole languages the way they are goes beyond even consideration of the faculty of language in the broad sense, "FLB" (Hauser et al., 2002), because "each actual 'language' will incorporate a periphery of borrowings, historical residues, inventions, and so on" (Chomsky, 1981, p. 8). Chomsky's discussion (1981, 1986) of the motivation for a study of the individual psychological aspects of language is useful, but he is dismissive of any wider consideration of such historical and social factors "which we can hardly expect to—and indeed would not want to—incorporate within a principled theory of UG" (1981, p. 8). I do not share his pessimism about saying something systematic about the social and historical factors affecting languages. Indeed, unless one has a clear picture of what the historical and social influences on the formation of languages may be, it will be hard to reliably isolate the remaining individual psychological contribution, Universal Grammar (UG).

Irregularities are preserved by being repeated often enough in each generation to force the learner to deviate from otherwise regular patterns. Irregularities are stored both privately inside the heads of speakers who have memorized them and publicly outside in the community where their frequent rehearsal ensures that they don't go away in the next generation. This highlights a fact obvious in itself, but oddly not built into much theorizing about the nature of language. Languages are socially transmitted. Children acquire grammars not by telepathic access to the grammars in their parents' heads but by exposure to utterances in context. Thus languages, like egg-chicken life forms, exist in two distinct life phases, which we can conveniently identify as competence and performance.

The distinction between competence and performance is indispensable to any account of the nature of language. Performance is the externally observable behaviour of speakers, mostly displaying the regularities of their language, but also inevitably including occasional disturbances, such as hesitations and false starts. Competence is whatever a speaker has in his/her head that determines the form-meaning pairs of the language the person speaks. Opponents of the competence/performance distinction should not assume that competence necessarily comes with all of the theoretical baggage accumulated by generative linguistics in the past decades. Some of this accumulation may be correct, but it is not itself part of the definition of competence. We may disagree about the details, some perhaps preferring a list of constructions, others a richly structured lexicon plus the Merge operation, and yet others a set of weighted connections between arrays of nodes encoding meanings and forms. But each speaker of a language has something in his/her head that constitutes the person's knowledge of that language. (And let's not get bogged down here in whether this is "knowing that" or "knowing how"— Ryle, 1949.) I have heard a linguist avoid the loaded word "competence" in favor of the circumlocution, "permanent memorial representations," but there is no distinction here, outside the politics of the subject. Competence exists as one phase in the life cycle of a language. Competence in a language is acquired by exposure to performance data. Give a child Cantonese performance data, and the child acquires Cantonese competence; Ashanti leads to Ashanti, Dutch to Dutch. Performance (plus the innate biases) causes competence. Equally clearly, competence shapes performance, as emphasized above. The life cycle of a language is [performance > competence > performance > competence > performance > competence] for as long as there are speakers. At the level of our discussion here, the alternative terms, I-language and E-language, are just as apt. E-language begets I-language, which begets E-language, and so on. The situation is complicated by many factors, including language contact, learning from one's peers as well as one's parents, and so on. But the two-phase nature of the life cycle of a language is well accepted by modern historical linguistics (Andersen, 1973; Kroch, 2000; Lightfoot, 1999).

The two-phase existence of languages has typically not been widely applied to explaining universals of language (but see Chapter 4 and references there). Much more common has been the stand-alone story, "Internalized competence grammars have the properties they have because children are innately disposed to acquire grammars with those properties." We need to augment this story with another: "Performance in a language has the properties it has because speakers are disposed to produce utterances with those properties." Obviously part of the relevant disposition is the speaker's competence in the language. But that is not all. The form of an utterance in context is chosen as a function of the proposition the speaker wishes to convey, the speaker's attitude to this proposition, and the speaker's assumptions about what the hearer already knows, to name the foremost factors. The morphosyntactic form having been chosen, further performance factors affect the phonetic form of the utterance, which might be subject to truncation, slurring, and so forth. Some of these factors are so common in human discourse that something systematic can be said about them. Performance is not all random noise, beyond the reach of systematic study. The style of study of how performance factors affect the shape of utterances is necessarily quite different from the typical logiclike formalizing style of syntactic theory. The study of performance involves, for example, (1) statistical issues of frequency, such as figure widely in sociolinguistics, for example, in the articles appearing in the journal *Language Variation and Change* and much work by William Labov and his collaborators (e.g., Labov, 2000), and (2) quantitative measurement along continuous dimensions, as in work relating phonetic performance to phonological competence (e.g., Ohala, 2005). The phenomenon of frequency brings us back to an explanation of the universality of irregularities in language.

The irregular forms in a language tend strongly to include the most frequent lexical items. This is certainly true of English verbs, for instance. An obvious model for explaining the universal frequency–irregularity correlation involves random performance modification of the pronunciation of words. Modified versions of the frequent words (e.g., *haved > had*) will be heard relatively frequently in discourse, giving the child learner a chance to acquire these forms by rote. Other less frequent forms may not always be exemplified in all their paradigm slots in the experience of the child, and the child, having heard no exemplar, will apply regular rules to produce the forms missing from its experience. This process has been computationally modeled by Hare and Elman (1995) and Kirby (2001).

Languages universally maintain at least a certain minimal level of complexity. Although no accepted measure of linguistic complexity exists, it is clear that languages differ in the complexity of their various subsystems. Some languages have complex case systems, others have none; some languages have complex noun class systems, others have none; some languages have complex tense/aspect morphology, others have none. It has been an article of faith among linguists that every language is roughly equally complex, overall. Edward Sapir expressed it thus: "We know of no people that is not possessed of a fully developed language. The lowliest South African Bushman speaks in the forms of a rich symbolic system that is in essence perfectly comparable to the speech of the cultivated Frenchman" (Sapir, 1921, p. 22). Interestingly, though, in the sentence immediately before his oft-quoted aphorism about Plato walking with the Macedonian swineherd, Sapir writes that "both simple and complex types of language of an indefinite number of varieties may be found spoken at any desired level of cultural advance" (Sapir, 1921, p. 219); so here at least he seemed to envisage the possibility of "both simple and complex types of language."

The doctrine that every language is equally complex may be too extreme. For example, David Gil claims that Riau Indonesian is in its basic grammatical organization simpler than linguists have typically been willing to admit of any language (Gil, 2001). And it looks as if the Amazonian language Piraha is overall simpler than many other familiar languages (Everett, 2005). But even Piraha maintains a high level of morphological complexity; it is clearly a human language, orders of magnitude more complex than anything a nonhuman could master. What keeps languages, universally, up to a minimal level of complexity?

Computational experiments in simulating the competence > performance > competence] cycle in the life of a language have shown that in order for a language not to collapse to an extreme simple state there needs to be some counterpressure to the generalizing and simplifying tendency built into acquisition. In one illustrative simulation (Teal & Taylor, 2000), computational agents learned finite state grammars from sets of strings presented to them, arriving at their preferred grammars on the basis of minimal description length (MDL). MDL-style acquisition values statistically salient generalizations, which hold over the input data. Once a generation of agents had acquired grammars in this way (from an initial hand seeded set of data), they in turn produced sentences consistent with their grammars for the benefit of the next generation of agent learners. And so it went on, for many generations. Note two things: this implements the [competence > performance > competence > performance] life cycle discussed above; and the simulated agents are only acquiring grammars defining sets of well-formed strings—no simulation of meaning is involved. The results show a steady downhill decrease in complexity of the grammars acquired by successive generations. This is typical of experiments in which the only activity of the learning agents is the construction of the simplest possible grammars accounting for the utterances observed. There is a hill-climbing effect whereby, over generations, languages, and their grammars become ever simpler, and in the limit would arrive at extreme simplicity, for instance, a one-sentence language. Language acquisition tends to reduce the entropy of the language generated by the acquired grammar relative to the entropy of the input corpus.

Pointing in exactly the same direction are computational simulations of the evolution of vowel systems, most prominently by de Boer (2001). The most common vowel system in languages is the five-vowel symmetrical {i, e, a, o, u} system. Other systems exist, but the common five-vowel system seems to be the one that strikes the optimal compromise between simplicity and the need to preserve distinctions. De Boer's model arrives at a distribution of vowel systems that is statistically very similar to the overall distribution of vowel systems in the world's languages. His system incorporates the cycle of learning and production discussed above, with one generation learning an internalized system from the products output by the previous generation. The model explicitly incorporates a mechanism occasionally injecting a new random vowel into the systems of his agents. If this mechanism were not present, the evolved systems would tend to collapse, over time, to a single vowel, due to the (realistic) presence of noise in the system, which allows vowels to wander through the vowel space, and the possibility of merger between originally distinct vowels when they get close to one another. Vowel merger is a simplification process in acquisition.

So why aren't languages maximally simple, comprising just one sentence, and having just one vowel? If diachronic simplification, of which the engine is generalizing induction by learners, were the only pressure acting on languages, we would expect them to collapse. Of course they don't, and we all know why. Languages are used to communicate a rich set of distinct meanings. Humans need all those different sentences to say the things they want to say. And we need a minimal number of vowels so that we can shorten sentence length, while still maintaining an acceptable level of semantic expressivity. All this is obvious. But it is nowhere built into theories of language universals based on properties of the language acquisition device. Emphasis on formal universals de-emphasizes semantic content. How do languages manage to stay so good for communication?

Innate learning biases can explain some universals of language. Learning is one process mediating the transitions between life phases in the history of a language. Learning extracts from input data, in the form of utterances in context, an internalized representation of the language system. But another process, *production*, uses the internalized system representation to give out utterances in context. Production starts with having something very specific that you want to express clearly in such a way that your specific meaning is likely to be understood by your hearer. Humans apparently have extremely rich conceptual/intentional systems, providing them with elaborate, subtly distinguished thoughts that they express in language. The most striking universal of language, often overlooked in the forest of technical detail, is the enormous communicative expressivity of languages. Learning, incorporating generalizations about the data observed, is a centripetal force in the history of languages, tending to reduce complexity. Production is the counterbalancing centrifugal force, tending to maintain and even increase complexity. Note the essential part played by production in the explanation of the universal frequency–irregularity correlation discussed earlier; in this case, speakers relax on considerations of distinctness and let economy of effort in production take precedence.

There is a general comprehension/production asymmetry observed both in acquisition (where production is typically behind comprehension) and adult processing (where people in general have wider comprehension abilities compared to what they actually produce). This may perhaps be a clue to the proportions of the influence that acquisition and production have on the maintenance and development of languages. But it is clear that without some effort to produce utterances clearly distinguished by their phonetic and grammatical structure, languages would not sustain the level of complexity that they do. In the effort to produce clearly differentiated utterances, some a priori biases must also operate, perhaps domain-specific to language, but perhaps dependent on factors not specific to language, such as natural ways of guiding the attention of others to a desired topic of conversation.

3.2. Languages Evolve Along Universal Paths

Consider Jakobson's famous *Kindersprache, Aphasie und allgemeine Lautgesetze* (Jakobson, 1941). All three elements in the original German title denote diachronic processes, the development of language in children, the loss of language in aphasics, and general sound laws. Sound laws, when Jakobson wrote, were universally understood as *historical*. Thus Grimm's Law is a sound law, describing a historical change in Germanic. But the linguistic intellectual climate of the second half of the twentieth century was dominated by synchrony when the quest for universals began to take center stage. And *allgemeine Lautgesetze*, accordingly, got fashionably rendered as *phonological universals* in the 1968 translation. The correspondence that Jakobson pointed out had a massively useful impact on the field, but the subtle mistranslation of *allgemeine Lautgesetze* as *phonological universals* steered explanation of universals away from a connection with diachronic language change. Jakobson's own discussion of sound laws in the book is for the most part stolidly synchronic, with Chapter 14, for example, being entitled (in the here faithful English translation) "Identical Laws of Solidarity in the Phonological Development of Child Language and in the Synchrony of the Languages of the World." A factor that probably deterred even Jakobson from making too much of the connection with the history of languages was the prevalent (and still prevalent) commitment to uniformitarianism, the idea that earlier stages of languages were just as complex as modern languages. It was acceptable to state that children start with a minimal consonant set, such as {m, p, t}, far smaller than found in any extant language, and that aphasic speech could degenerate to this minimum, but it was not so acceptable to speculate about "primitive" prior historical stages of languages. Nevertheless, in a few short passages, Jakobson does allow himself to speculate about "glottogony" (now sometimes called "glossogeny") and to refer to the "origin of language" once in a brief one-paragraph chapter. He articulates the "principle of language change" thus: "This principle is simple to the point of being trivial; one cannot erect the superstructure without having provided the foundation, nor can one remove the foundation without having removed the superstructure" (p. 93). Amen to that.

If one is seriously interested in the origins and evolution of the language faculty and of individual languages, it seems inescapable that languages had humble beginnings. Language, as Hockett (1978) put it, did not spring fully formed from Jove's brow. The [competence > performance > competence > performance] framework outlined in the previous section provides a dynamic essentially different from Darwinian natural selection. In biological evolution, there is no equivalent to the continuing zigzag between E-language and I-language; genotypes beget genotypes directly, and DNA is copied into more DNA. Thus, while still noting very general parallels between biological evolution and linguistic evolution (glottogony/glossogeny), as nineteenth-century theorists such as Schleicher (1873) did, we can envisage a framework for the evolution of languages in which Jakobson's parallel between child language and glottogony/glossogeny fits very naturally. Languages evolve along the paths they follow because they are learned by children following these same paths, and because children, having acquired a "foundation" on the basis of learning from exemplars of their parents, have the opportunity, when it comes to producing messages themselves, to invent some additional "superstructure" (to adopt Jakobson's terms). Not too much should be made of the term *invent* here. I use *invention* in the sense in which elements of Creole languages can be "invented" by the first generation of speakers on the basis of a pidgin. A spectacular case of such invention, in Nicaraguan Sign Language, has recently been extensively documented (Kegl, 2002; Kegl & Iwata, 1989; Kegl, Senghas, & Coppola, 1999; Senghas, 1995a, b, 2001, 2003). Beyond creolization, linguistic invention is spontaneous and very small in scale, like stretching the syntactic context of a verb beyond its previous limits, as children do, or starting to make a previously allophonic variation into a phonemic distinction, or using a word in a new metaphorical way. Inventions such as these are manifest in production. Some invention can also happily come under the heading "reanalysis" of the input data, whereas some invention genuinely stretches the boundaries of the language. Invention is a special, atypical form of acquisition, adding new structures to a language, assuming the inventive speaker learns from his/her own inventive performance by adding the new usage to the person's repertoire.

Individual languages evolve along lines very similar to the development of language in children. The accumulation of ontogeny over generations creates glossogeny. This idea is actually not so very different from the modern standard nativist explanation of language universals, which holds that languages have the properties they have because children are innately disposed to acquire languages with just such properties. The only difference is that the theory proposed here hypothesizes that languages may take a long stretch in their history to take on the forms indicated by innate dispositions. There can be, in a technical sense, immature subsystems of languages. Languages in their synchronic patterns exhibit "growth rings," layering of structure showing what stages they have evolved through. Universally, languages are subject to historical growth (and shrinkage). Not surprisingly, languages preserve signs of growth. Many of Greenberg's synchronically stated implicational universals can be interpreted in this way. And interpreting them in this way begins to show an explanation of why they should be true. (Of course, the quest for explanations is never ending; today's *explanans* is tomorrow's *explanandum*.) I will mention a few of Greenberg's original universals and discuss them in this light.

Greenberg's *Universal 34* states, "No language has a trial number unless it has a dual. No language has a dual unless it has a plural" (Greenberg, 1963). We can correlate this with a hypothesis about ontogeny: "No child can acquire a trial number unless it has already acquired a dual. No child can acquire a dual unless it has already acquired a plural." Next, here is a phonological universal: "If a language has VCC syllable rhymes, it has VC syllable rhymes; if it has VC syllable rhymes, it has V syllable rhymes," which generates the hypothesis, "A child can only acquire VCC syllable rhymes it if has already acquired VC syllable rhymes; it can only acquire VC syllable rhymes if it has already acquired V syllable rhymes." In general, we may advance the following hypothesis about a correlation between universals and ontogeny: "Given a universal, 'If a language has X, it always has Y,' then X cannot be acquired unless Y has been acquired first." All this is pretty much pure Jakobson.

Here is a case that needs a little more discussion: Greenberg's *Universal 29* states, "If a language has inflection, it always has derivation" (Greenberg, 1963). Translating this according to the formula proposed, we get, "A child cannot acquire inflection unless it has already acquired derivation." At first glance, this is false; children can acquire productive plural inflections and apply them to derived forms such as *statement* before they are able to productively derive a noun from a verb by suffixing—*ment*. In fact, however, no English speaker can productively derive a noun from a verb by suffixing—*ment*. Try it, as a thought experiment, with *arrive* or *kill* to give **arrivement* and **killment*—it doesn't work. So the sense in which a language "has" derivation is different from the sense in which a language has inflection. Inflection is a generally productive process, reflecting an internalized rule. Derivation is a sporadic historical process resulting from nonce invention by individuals, which just happen to "stick." Derived forms are learned by rote by children. After some education, people develop some metalinguistic awareness and can contemplate the hypothetical productive application of derivational processes, as I just did with **arrivement* and **killment*. It is obviously the case that no child can apply the plural inflection to a derived noun unless he or she has already acquired that derived singular form. In this limited sense, then, the correlation between universals and ontogeny holds in this case, too.

My argument in the previous paragraph does not relate, however, to the sense in which Greenberg intended his *Universal 29*. That argument involved processes of derivation and inflection as applied to the same stem (e.g., *statements*, *denationalizes*). But Greenberg was motivated by the following more general consideration: "There are probably no languages without either compounding, affixing, or both. In other words, there are probably no purely isolating languages. There are a considerable number of languages without inflections, perhaps none without compounding and derivation" (Greenberg, 1963). It can be clearly shown that much derivation is a historical process; I will give examples immediately below. Thus, this last statement of Greenberg gives credence to the claim that, in respect of their derivational morphology at least, all languages are the products of historical processes.

Structured derivational morphology can be clearly related to the idea of growth rings, layered traces of the historical development of a language. As an example, a search in the *Oxford English Dictionary* for the earliest recorded forms of the word *nation* and its derivatives shows the following pattern:

nation 1300
   national 1597
      nationally 1649, *nationality* 1691, *nationalist* 1715,
      nationalize 1800, *nationalism* 1836
            denationalize 1807, *nationalization* 1813, *nationalizer* 1883
                  denationalization 1814

The levels of indentation here show the degree of morphological complexity—the number of morphemes in each word. Clearly, words were derived and added to the language in historical sequence. The layers in the synchronic forms are like geological strata, reflecting phases of invention back in the past. Thousands more such examples can be found.

The idea of layers of structure reflecting previous stages of the language is not new. Hopper gives a good example:

> Within a broad functional domain, new layers are continually emerging. As this happens, the older layers are not necessarily discarded, but may remain to coexist with and interact with the newer layers.
>
> (Hopper, 1991, p. 22)

   a. *Periphrasis*: *We have used it* (newest layer)
   b. *Affixation*: *I admired it* (older layer)
   c. *Ablaut*: *They sang* (oldest layer) (ibid. 24)

Thus, in the oldest layer, it is not possible to isolate a single morpheme indicating past tense; it would be very implausible to claim that the stem of the word is the discontinuous shell, *s-ng*, and that the inserted *-a-* vowel is a "past tense morpheme." Much Proto-Indo-European verbal morphology was like this, and vestiges survive in the strong verbs of the Germanic languages. Affixation by a productive past tense morpheme—*ed*, as in *admired*, is historically older than the periphrastic construction seen in *have used*, where free-standing words are syntactically strung together. All three ways of expressing pastness (with a subtle semantic difference between the last two) are present in Modern English, but they date from different eras. In this way, a language is like an ancient city, with buildings dating from different historical periods, but all still functioning.

The general unidirectionality of grammaticalization suggested by writers such as Hopper and Traugott (1993) indicates an incremental growth in the complexity of languages, and it follows from Jakobson's "trivial" principle that the foundations must precede the superstructure (quoted above), that implicational universals have a diachronic explanation. This does not deny that language acquisition plays a role; rather it acknowledges the crucial role that acquisition plays in explaining linguistic universals, but stretches out its application over successive generations in the history of languages. This view of how languages get to be the way they are is also in complete conformity with what we know about how cultural institutions in general grow.

Wrapping up, this chapter has chosen to take the goal of linguistics to be an explanation of how whole languages get to be the way they are. Other scholars are free to choose a narrower goal, such as discerning the contribution made by innate individual psychological biases in determining the shape of languages. But more narrowly circumscribed goals also run the risk of blinkered vision, and one may too easily assume that the factor whose contribution one is investigating is the *only significant* factor involved, or that other possible factors are either trivial or too complex to study systematically. I have tried to show that we can gain some insight into the forces shaping languages by considering them as products of a historical spiral involving both acquisition and production, learning and speaking, and occasionally innovating, over many generations.

Key Further Readings

Bybcc (2006) provides an extended version of her Presidential Address given to the Linguistic Society of America in January 2005: "The impact of use on representation: grammar is usage and usage is grammar." The rhetoric in the title, suggesting a literal equivalence between grammar (for which I have accepted the term "competence") and usage (for which I have accepted the term "performance") is unfortunate. In the article itself, however, the rhetoric is modified to represent a view very similar to the two-phase cycle in the existence of languages that I have espoused in this essay. Joan Bybee has been a prominent exponent of this view.

Heine and Kuteva (2002) dare to go against the prevailing uniformitarianism and suggest that earlier forms of languages had much simpler inventories of grammatical categories than many modern languages, drawing on evidence from grammaticalization. Hopper and Traugott (1993) is a major source setting out the idea of incremental language growth leaving traces in the history of a language. Jakobson (1941) is a classic, readable book, setting the scene for the ideas set out here. Of my own work: Hurford (1991) sets out the basic idea of the life cycle of languages advocated in this chapter; Hurford (2002) surveys computational models implementing the idea of language evolution through a life cycle of learning and production.

References

Andersen, H. (1973). Abductive and deductive change. *Language, 49,* 765–793.

de Boer, B. (2001). *The origins of vowel systems.* Oxford: Oxford University Press.

Bybee, J. (2006). From usage to grammar: The mind's response to repetition. *Language, 82,* 711–733.

Chomsky, N. (1965). *Aspects of the theory of syntax.* Cambridge, MA: MIT Press.

Chomsky, N.(1981). *Lectures on government and binding.* Dordrecht, Holland: Foris Publications.

Chomsky, N. (1986). *Knowledge of language: Its nature, origin and use.* New York: Praeger.

Everett, D. (2005). Cultural constraints on grammar and cognition in Piraha: Another look at the design features of human language. *Current Anthropology, 46*(4), 621–646.

Gil, D. (2001). Creoles, complexity and Riau Indonesian. *Linguistic Typology, 5,* 325–371.

Greenberg, J. (1963). Some universals of grammar with particular reference to the order of meaningful elements. In J. H. Greenberg (Ed.), *Universals of language* (pp. 73–113). London: MIT Press.

Hare, M., & Elman, J. L. (1995). Learning and morphological change. *Cognition, 56*(1), 61–98.

Hauser, M., Chomsky, N., & Fitch, T. (2002). The faculty of language: What is it, who has it, and how did it evolve? *Science, 298,* 1569–1579.

Heine, B., & Kuteva, T. (2002). On the evolution of grammatical forms. In A. Wray (Ed.), *The transition to language* (pp. 376–397). Oxford: Oxford University Press.

Hockett, C. F. (1978). In search of Jove's brow. *American Speech, 53,* 243–313.

Hopper, P. J. (1991). On some principles of grammaticization. In E. C.Traugott & B. Heine (Eds.), *Approaches to grammaticalization* (Vol. 1, pp. 17–35). Amsterdam: John Benjamins.

Hopper, P. J., & Traugott, E. C. (1993). *Grammaticalization.* Cambridge: Cambridge University Press.

Hurford, J. R. (1991). Nativist and functional explanations in language acquisition. In I. Roca (Ed.), *Logical issues in language acquisition* (pp. 85–136). Holland: Foris Publications.

Hurford, J. R. (2002). Expression/induction models of language evolution: Dimensions and issues. In T. Briscoe (Ed.), *Linguistic evolution through language acquisition: Formal and computational models* (pp. 301–344). Cambridge: Cambridge University Press.

Jakobson, R. (1941). *Kindersprache, Aphasie und allgemeine Lautgesetze.* Uppsala: Almqvist & Wiksell. Translated as *Child language, aphasia and phonological universals* by A. R. Keiler, 1968. The Hague: Mouton.

Kegl, J. (2002). Language emergence in a language-ready brain: Acquisition issues. In C. Morgan & B. Woll (Eds.), *Language acquisition in signed languages* (pp. 207–254). Cambridge: Cambridge University Press.

Kegl, J., & Iwata, G. A. (1989). Lenguaje de Signos Nicaraguense: A pidgin sheds light on the "creole?" ASL. In R. Carlson, S. DeLancey, S. Gildea, D. Payne, & A. Saxena (Eds.), *Proceedings of the fourth meeting of the Pacific Linguistics Conference* (pp. 266–294). Eugene, OR: University of Oregon.

Kegl, J., Senghas, A., & Coppola, M. (1999). Creation through contact: Sign language emergence and sign language change in Nicaragua. In M. DeGraff (Ed.), *Language creation and language change* (pp. 179–237). Cambridge, MA: MIT Press.

Kirby, S. (2001). Spontaneous evolution of linguistic structure: An iterated learning model of the emergence of regularity and irregularity. *IEEE Transactions on Evolutionary Computation*, 5(2), 102–110.

Kroch, A. (2000). Syntactic change. In M. Baltin & C. Collins (Eds.), *Handbook of contemporary syntactic theory* (pp. 629–739). Malden, MA: Blackwell.

Labov, W. (2000). *Principles of linguistic change. Volume II: Social factors*. Oxford: Blackwell.

Lightfoot, D. (1999). *The development of language*. Oxford: Blackwell.

Ohala, J. (2005). Phonetic explanations for sound patterns: Implications for grammars of competence. In W. J. Hardcastle & J. M. Beck (Eds.), *A figure of speech. A Festschrift for John Laver* (pp. 23–38). London: Erlbaum.

Ryle, G. (1949). *The concept of mind*. London: Hutchinson.

Sapir, E. (1921). *Language: An introduction to the study of speech*. New York: Harcourt, Brace & World Inc.

Schleicher, A. (1873). *Die Darwinsche Theorie und die Sprachwissenschaft*. Weimar: H. Böhlau.

Senghas, A. (1995a). *Children's contribution to the birth of Nicaraguan sign language*. Ph.D. thesis, MIT.

Senghas, A. (1995b). The development of Nicaraguan Sign Language via the language acquisition process. In D. MacLaughlin & S. McEwen (Eds.), *Proceedings of the Boston conference on language development* (Vol. 19, pp. 534–552). Boston: Cascadilla Press.

Senghas, A. (2001). Children creating language: How Nicaraguan Sign Language acquired a spatial grammar. *Psychological Science*, 12(4), 323–328.

Senghas, A. (2003). Intergenerational influence and ontogenetic development in the emergence of spatial grammar in Nicaraguan Sign Language. *Cognitive Development*, 18, 511–531.

Teal, T. K., & Taylor, C. E. (2000). Effects of compression on language evolution. *Artificial Life*, 6(2), 129–143.

4

LANGUAGE UNIVERSALS AND THE PERFORMANCE-GRAMMAR CORRESPONDENCE HYPOTHESIS

JOHN A. HAWKINS

4.1. Introduction[1]

In this chapter I explore the kinds of variation-defining universals that Greenberg introduced in his seminal 1963 paper on word order. They took the form of implicational statements: if a language has some property (or set of properties) P, then it also has (or generally has) property Q. For example, if a language has subject-object-verb (SOV) order, as in Japanese, it generally has postpositional phrases ([the movies **to**] **went**), rather than prepositional phrases as in English (**went** [**to** the movies]). I will have much less to say about the other major type of universal, the absolute kind of the form "all languages (or no languages) have property P." These have been at the core of Universal Grammar (UG) within generative theories, and are subdivided into "substantive," "functional," and "formal universals" in Steedman (Chapter 9), who follows Chomsky (1995). When implicational universals were incorporated into generative grammar, in the Government-Binding theory of the 1980s (Chomsky, 1981), they became known as "parameters," and the innateness claimed for the absolute universals (Chomsky, 1965; Hoekstra & Kooij, 1988) was extended to the parameters (Fodor, 2001; Lightfoot, 1991). It was proposed that the child's linguistic environment "triggered" one innate parameter rather than another, based on the data of experience. (See Bever, Chapter 6, for a more recent formulation.)

The distinction between variation-defining and absolute universals has taken center stage recently with the publication of Newmeyer's (2005) book *Possible and Probable Languages: A Generative Perspective on Linguistic Typology*. Newmeyer argues (contrary to the position taken by Boeckx and Hornstein, in Chapter 5) that the major parameters proposed, the head ordering parameter, the pro-drop parameter, and so on, have systematic exceptions across languages, are probabilistic, and are not part of UG, which is concerned with defining possible versus impossible languages. Haspelmath (2006) gives a similar critique of parameters. In effect, these authors recognize what Greenberg (1963) first recognized: the majority of his implicational statements hold only "with more than chance frequency," and most of those he formulated as exceptionless have subsequently turned out to have exceptions (Dryer, 1992). Clearly, if these parameters are not correct descriptively, they are not innate either, and the kind of environmental trigger theory for language acquisition built around them fails, if the basic premise fails (the existence of innate parameters).

The question then arises: Where do we go from here in order to better understand crosslinguistic variation? A number of generative theorists are trying to improve the empirical adequacy of earlier predictions. Cinque (2005) is a laudable example, which combines Kayne's (1994) antisymmetry principle with painstaking typological work (but see Steedman [2006] for a critique and an alternative). Another research program, more in line with Newmeyer's (op cit) proposals, is the one I shall illustrate in this chapter. Together with many collaborators, I have been pursuing an empirical and interdisciplinary approach to language universals, comparing variation patterns *within* and *across* languages. That is, we have been examining variation both in usage (performance) and in grammars. This program makes extensive use of generative principles and of typologists' generalizations (Comrie, 1989; Croft, 2003), and integrates them with psycholinguistic models and findings.

There are two reasons why this has proved fruitful. First, a general correlation is emerging: the patterns of preference that one finds in performance in languages possessing several structures of a given type (different word orders, relative clauses, etc.) look increasingly like the patterns found in the fixed conventions of grammars in languages with fewer structures of the same type. Numerous examples will be given in what follows.

Second, if this correlation is even partly correct, it has far-reaching consequences for language universals and for the theory of grammar. It enables us to make predictions from performance data for grammatical conventions, and the grammatical patterns predicted are often unexpected from grammatical considerations alone. It helps us to understand not only why there are patterns across languages, but also why there are exceptions to these patterns and when they occur.

Greenberg (1966) was the first to draw attention to such correlating patterns in his discussion of markedness hierarchies like Singular > Plural > Dual > Trial/Paucal. Morphological inventories across grammars and declining allomorphy provided evidence for these universal hierarchies, while declining frequencies of use in languages with rich inventories suggested not only a correlation with performance but also a possibly causal role for it in the evolution of the grammatical regularities themselves (Greenberg, 1995, pp. 163–164). Givón (1979, pp. 26–31) meanwhile observed that performance preferences in one language, for definite subjects, for example, may correspond to an actual categorical requirement in another. In Hawkins (1990, 1994), I argued that the preferred word orders in languages with choices are those that are productively conventionalized as fixed orders in languages with less freedom. And in my 2004 book I examine many more grammatical areas in a systematic test of the following hypothesis:

(1)   *Performance-Grammar Correspondence Hypothesis* (PGCH)
        Grammars have conventionalized syntactic structures in proportion to their degree
        of preference in performance, as evidenced by patterns of selection in corpora and by
        ease of processing in psycholinguistic experiments.

There is a growing awareness of this basic correspondence in many branches of the language sciences. Haspelmath (1999) proposed a theory of diachrony in which usage preferences lead to changing grammatical conventions over time. Bybee and Hopper (2001) document the clear role of frequency in the emergence of grammatical structure. There have been intriguing computer simulations of language evolution, exemplified by Kirby (1999), in which processing preferences of the kind assumed for word order in Hawkins (1990, 1994) are incorporated in the simulation and lead to the emergence of the observed grammatical types after numerous iterations (corresponding to successive generations of language users). There have been developments in Optimality Theory, exemplified by Haspelmath (1999) and Aissen (1999), in which functional motivations of an ultimately processing nature are provided for many of the basic constraints. Stochastic Optimality Theory (Bresnan, Dingare, & Manning, 2001; Manning, 2003) incorporates the preferences of performance ("soft constraints") as well as grammatical conventions ("hard constraints"). Newmeyer (2005) advocates replacing generative parameters with principles derived from language processing, while Phillips (1996) and Kempson, Meyer-Viol, and Gabbay (2001) incorporate the online processing of language into the rules and representations of the grammar.

But despite this growing interest in performance-grammar correspondences, the precise extent to which grammars have been shaped by performance is a matter of intense debate. There are different opinions in the publications cited so far and in the chapters of this volume. In the present context, I shall accordingly focus on the empirical evidence for the PGCH in order to try and convince the next generation of researchers that there is a real generalization here and that it does need to be incorporated into theories of grammatical universals. In the next section (section 4.2), I briefly summarize a range of observed performance-grammar correspondences that support it. I then exemplify the testing of the PGCH in the area of word order (section 4.3), followed by a short discussion of relative clauses (section 4.4). Conclusions and further issues are summarized in section 4.5.

4.2. Examples of Proposed Performance-Grammar Correspondences

The Keenan and Comrie (1977) Accessibility Hierarchy (SU>DO>IO/OBL>GEN; cf. Comrie, 1989) has been much discussed in this context. Grammatical cut-off points in relativization across languages follow the hierarchy, and Keenan and Comrie argued for an explanation in terms of declining ease of processing down the lower positions of the hierarchy. As evidence, they pointed to usage data from languages with many relativizable positions, especially English. The hierarchy correlated both with declining corpus frequencies down the hierarchy and with evidence of increasing processing load and working memory demands under experimental conditions (Diessel & Tomasello, 2006; Hawkins, 1999; Keenan, 1975; Keenan & Hawkins, 1987; cf. section 4.4.1).

More generally, filler-gap dependency hierarchies for relativization and Wh-movement structures across grammars point to increasing complexity in the permitted gap environments. For example, grammatical cut-off points in increasingly complex clause-embedding positions for gaps correspond to declining processing ease in languages with numerous gap-containing environments (including subjacency-violating languages like Akan; Saah & Goodluck [1995]); cf. Hawkins (2004; Chapter 7) and section 4.4.2.

Reverse hierarchies across languages for gaps in simpler relativization domains and resumptive pronouns in more complex environments (Hawkins, 1999) match the performance distribution of gaps to pronouns within languages such as Hebrew and Cantonese in which both are grammatical (in some syntactic positions), gaps being preferred in the simpler, and pronouns in the more complex relatives (Ariel, 1999; Hawkins, 2004; Matthews & Yip, 2003); cf. section 4.4.1.

Parallel function effects (whereby the head of the relative matches the position relativized on) have been shown to facilitate relative clause processing and acquisition (Clancy, Lee, & Zoh, 1986; MacWhinney, 1982; Sheldon, 1974). They also extend relativization possibilities beyond normal constraints holding in languages such as Basque and Hebrew (Aldai, 2003; Cole, 1976; Hawkins, 2004, p. 190).

Declining acceptability of increasingly complex center embeddings, in languages in which these are grammatical, is matched by hierarchies of permitted center embeddings across grammars, with cut-offs down these hierarchies (Hawkins, 1994, pp. 315–321).

(Nominative) subject (S) before (accusative) object (O) ordering is massively preferred in the performance of languages in which both SO and OS are grammatical (Japanese, Korean, Finnish, German) and is also massively preferred as a basic order or as the only order across grammars (Gibson, 1998; Hawkins, 1994; Miyamoto, 2006; Primus, 1999; Tomlin, 1986).

Markedness hierarchies of case (Nom>Acc>Dat>Other), number (Sing>Plur> Dual>Trial), etc., correspond to performance frequency hierarchies in languages with rich morphological inventories (Croft, 2003; Greenberg, 1966; Hawkins, 2004, pp. 64–68).

Performance preferences for subjects that obey the Person Hierarchy (first > second > third) in English (whereby *the boy hit me* is preferably pas- sivized to *I was hit by the boy*) have been conventionalized into a grammati- cal/ungrammatical distinction in languages such as Lummi (Bresnan, Dingare, & Manning, 2001). Sentences corresponding to *the boy hit me* are ungrammatical in Lummi.

The distinction between zero agreement in local NP environments versus explicit agreement nonlocally in the grammar of Warlpiri matches the environments in which zero and explicit forms are preferred in performance in languages with choices (Hawkins, 2004, p. 160).

I believe these are the tip of a large iceberg of performance-motivated crosslin- guistic patterns. And if these correspondences are valid, then the classic picture of the performance-grammar relationship presented in Chomsky (1965) needs to be revised. For Chomsky, the competence grammar was an integral part of a perfor- mance model, but it was not shaped by performance in any way:

> Acceptability . . . belongs to the study of performance, . . . The unacceptable
> grammatical sentences often cannot be used, for reasons having to do . . . with
> memory limitations, intonational and stylistic factors, . . . and so on. . . . it would
> be quite impossible to characterize unacceptable sentences in grammatical
> terms . . . we cannot formulate particular rules of the grammar in such a way as to
> exclude them.
>
> (Chomsky, 1965, pp. 11–12)

Chomsky claimed (and still claims) that grammar was autonomous and UG was innate (see Newmeyer [1998] for a full summary and discussion of these points). The PGCH in (1) is built on the opposite assumption that grammatical rules *have* incorporated properties that reflect memory limitations and other forms of complex- ity and efficiency that we observe in performance. This alternative is supported by the correspondences above, and it makes predictions for occurring and nonoccurring grammars, and for frequent and less frequent ones. It accounts for many crosslin- guistic patterns that are not predicted by grammar-only theories and for exceptions to those that are predicted. In the next section, I illustrate the PGCH and this research method in greater detail.

4.3. Head Ordering and Adjacency in Syntax

I begin by examining some variation data from English and Japanese in which users have a choice between the adjacency or nonadjacency of certain categories to their heads. It turns out that there are systematic preferences in performance, mirror image ones interestingly between these languages, and an efficiency principle of Minimize Domains is proposed that describes these preferences. I then show that this same principle can be found in the fixed conventions of grammars in languages with fewer options. Specifically, this principle can give us an explanation, derived from language use and processing, for general patterns in grammars, for puzzling exceptions to these patterns, and for grammatically unpredicted data sets involving, for example, hierarchies.

The principle of Minimize Domains is defined at the outset (cf. Hawkins, 2004, p. 31):

(2)   *Minimize Domains* (MiD)

   The human processor prefers to minimize the connected sequences of linguistic forms and their conventionally associated syntactic and semantic properties in which relations of combination and/or dependency are processed. The degree of this preference is proportional to the number of relations whose domains can be minimized in competing sequences or structures, and to the extent of the minimization difference in each domain.

Combination: Two categories, A and B, are in a relation of combination iff they occur within the same syntactic mother phrase or maximal projection (phrasal combination), or if they occur within the same lexical co-occurrence frame (lexical combination).

Dependency: Two categories, A and B, are in a relation of dependency iff the parsing of B requires access to A for the assignment of syntactic or semantic properties to B with respect to which B is zero-specified, or ambiguously or polysemously specified.

4.3.1. *Syntactic MiD Effects in the Performance of Head-Initial Languages*

Words and phrases have to be assembled in comprehension and production into the kinds of groupings that are represented by tree structure diagrams. Recognizing how words and phrases combine together can typically be accomplished on the basis of less than all the words dominated by each phrase. Some orderings reduce the number of words needed to recognize a mother phrase M and its immediate constituent daughters (ICs), making phrasal combination faster. Compare (3a) and (3b):

(3)   a. The man vp[waited pp1[for his son] pp2[in the cold but not unpleasant wind]]

        1   2 3 4   5
        ----

       b. The man vp[waited pp2[in the cold but not unpleasant wind] pp1[for his son]]

        1   2 3 4 5 6   7   8   9

The three items, V, PP1, and PP2, can be recognized on the basis of five words in (3a) compared with nine in (3b), assuming that (head) categories such as P immediately project to mother nodes such as PP, enabling the parser to construct and recognize them online. For comparable benefits within a production model, cf. Hawkins (2004, p. 106).[2]

   Minimize Domains predicts that Phrasal Combination Domains (PCDs) should be as short as possible, and that the degree of this preference should be proportional to the minimization difference between competing orderings. This principle (a particular instance of Minimize Domains) is called Early Immediate Constituents (EIC):

(4)   *Phrasal Combination Domain* (PCD)
         The PCD for a mother node M and its I(mmediate) C(onstituent)s consists of the smallest string of terminal elements (plus all M-dominated nonterminals over the terminals) on the basis of which the processor can construct M and its ICs.
(5)   *Early Immediate Constituents* (EIC) [Hawkins, 1994, pp. 69–83]
         The human processor prefers linear orders that minimize PCDs (by maximizing their IC-to-word ratios) in proportion to the minimization difference between competing orders.

In concrete terms, EIC amounts to a preference for short before long phrases in head-initial structures like those of English—for example, short before long PPs in (3). These orders will have higher "IC-to-word ratios," that is, they will permit more ICs to be recognized on the basis of fewer words in the terminal string. The IC-to-word ratio for the VP in (3a) is 3/5 or 60% (5 words required for the recognition of 3 ICs). The comparable ratio for (3b) is 3/9 or 33% (9 words required for the same 3 ICs).

   Structures like (3) were selected from a corpus on the basis of a permutation test (Hawkins, 2000, 2001): the two PPs had to be permutable with truth-conditional equivalence (i.e., the speaker had a choice). Only 15% (58/394) of these English sequences had long before short. Among those with at least a one-word weight difference (excluding 71 with equal weight), 82% had short before long, and there was a gradual reduction in the long before short orders, the bigger the weight difference (PPs = shorter PP, PPL = longer PP):

(6) n = 323   PPL > PPs by 1 word   by 2–4   by 5–6   by 7+
[V PPs PPL]   60% (58)   86% (108)   94% (31)   99% (68)
[V PPL PPs]   40% (38)   14% (17)   6% (2)   1% (1)

Numerous other structures reveal the same weight preference in English (e.g., Heavy NP Shift); cf. Hawkins (1994, p. 183), Wasow (1997, 2002), and Stallings (1998).

A possible explanation for the distribution in (6) can be given in terms of reduced simultaneous processing demands in working memory. If, in (3a), the same phrase structure information can be derived from a 5-word viewing window rather than 9 words, then phrase structure processing can be accomplished sooner, and there will be fewer additional (phonological, morphological, syntactic, and semantic) decisions that need to be made simultaneously with this one, and less demands on working memory; (3a) is therefore more efficient. More generally, we can hypothesize that the processing of all syntactic and semantic relations prefers minimal domains, which is what MiD predicts (Hawkins, 2004).[3]

4.3.2. Minimal Domains for Lexical Combinations and Dependencies

A PCD is a domain for the processing of a syntactic relation of phrasal combination or sisterhood. Some of these sisters contract additional relations of a semantic and/or syntactic nature, of the kind grammatical models try to capture in terms of verb-complement (rather than verb-adjunct) relations, such as *count on your father* versus *play on the playground* (place adjunct). Complements are listed in the lexical entry for each head, and the processing of verb–complement relations should also prefer minimal domains, by MiD, (2).

(7)   *Lexical Domain* (LD)
         The LD for assignment of a lexically listed property P to a lexical item L consists of
         the smallest possible string of terminal elements (plus their associated syntactic and
         semantic properties) on the basis of which the processor can assign P to L.

One practical problem here is that the complement/adjunct distinction is a multi-factor one covering different types of combinatorial and dependency relations, obligatoriness versus optionality, etc., and is not always clear (cf. Schütze & Gibson,

1999). Hawkins (2000, 2001) proposes the following entailment tests as a way of defining PPs that are lexically listed:

(8)   Verb Entailment Test: Does [V, {PP1, PP2}] entail V alone or does V have a meaning dependent on either PP1 or PP2? Example: *The man waited for his son in the early morning* entails *the man waited*; *the man counted on his son in his old age* does not entail *the man counted.*

(9)   Pro-Verb Entailment Test: Can V be replaced by some general Pro-verb or does one of the PPs require that particular V for its interpretation? Example: *The boy played on the playground* entails *the boy did something on the playground*, but *the boy depended on his father* does not entail *the boy did something on his father.*

If V or P is dependent on the other by these tests, then the PP is lexically listed, that is, dependency is used as a sufficient condition for complementhood and lexical listing. The PPs classified as independent are (mostly) adjuncts or unclear cases.

When there was a dependency between V and just one of the PPs, then 73% (151/206) had the interdependent PP (Pd) adjacent to V, that is, their LDs were minimal. Recall that 82% had a short PP adjacent to V preceding a longer one in (2), that is, their PCDs were minimal. For PPs that were *both* shorter *and* lexically dependent, the adjacency rate to V was 96%, which was (statistically) significantly higher than for each factor alone.

We can conclude that the more syntactic and semantic relations whose domains are minimized in a given order, the greater is the preference for that order: multiple preferences result in a stronger adjacency effect when they reinforce each other, as predicted by MiD (2). MiD also predicts a stronger adjacency preference within each processing domain in proportion to the minimization difference between competing sequences. For PCDs, this difference is a function of the relative weights of the sisters; cf. (6). For LDs, it is a function of the absolute size of any independent PP (Pi) that could intervene between the verb and the interdependent PP (Pd) by the entailment tests, thereby delaying the processing of lexical co-occurrences.

(10) n = 206	Pi = 2–3 words	:4–5	:6–7	:8+
[V Pd Pi]	59% (54)	71% (39)	93% (26)	100% (32)
[V Pi Pd]	41% (37)	29% (16)	7% (2)	0% (0)

Multiple preferences have an additive adjacency effect when they work together, but they result in exceptions to each when they pull in different directions. Most of the 58 long-before-short sequences in (6) involve some form of lexical dependency between V and the longer PP (Hawkins, 2000). Conversely, V and Pd can be pulled apart by EIC in proportion to the weight difference between Pd and Pi (Hawkins, 2004, p. 116).

4.3.3. MiD Effects in Head-Final Languages

Long before short orders provide minimal PCDs in head-final languages in which constructing categories (V, P, Comp, case particles, etc.) are on the right. For example, if the direct object in Japanese is a complement clause headed by the complementizer *to*, as in (11), the distance between the complementizer and other constituents of the matrix clause, the subject *Mary ga* and the verb *it-ta*, will be very short in (11b), just as short as it is in the mirror image English translation *Mary said that* . . . . Hence the Phrasal Combination Domain for the matrix clause in (11b) is minimal. In (11a), by contrast, with the center-embedded complement clause, this PCD proceeds all the way from *Mary ga* to *it-ta*, and is much longer.

(11)   a. Mary ga   [[kinoo   John ga   kekkonsi-ta to]s it-ta]vp
             Mary NOM   yesterday John NOM married   that said
             Mary said that John got married yesterday.
         b. [kinoo John ga kekkonsi-ta to]s Mary ga [it-ta]vp

A preference for (11b) is accordingly predicted in proportion to the relative weight difference between subject and object phrases. By similar reasoning, a long-before-short preference is predicted for [{NPo, PPm} V] structures in Japanese, in alternations such as (12) (with *-o* standing for the accusative case particle, and PPm for a postpositional phrase with a head-final postposition):

(12)   a. (Tanaka ga)   [[Hanako kara]pp [sono hon o]np   katta]vp
             Tanaka NOM   Hanako from   that book ACC   bought,
             "Tanako bought that book from Hanako"
         b. (Tanaka ga) [[sono hon o]np [Hanako kara]pp katta]vp

Relevant corpus data were collected by Kaoru Horie and are reported in Hawkins (1994, p. 152). Letting ICs and ICL stand for shorter and longer ICs, respectively (i.e., with weight as the crucial distinction rather than phrasal type), these data are summarized in (13) (excluding the phrases with equal weights):

(13) n = 153	ICL>ICs by 1–2 words	by 3–4	by 5–8	by 9+
[ICs ICL V]	34% (30)	28% (8)	17% (4)	9% (1)
[ICL ICs V]	66% (59)	72% (21)	83% (20)	91% (10)

These data are the mirror image of those in (6): the longer IC is increasingly preferred to the left in the Japanese clause, whereas it is increasingly preferred to the right in English. This pattern has since been corroborated in experimental and further corpus data by Yamashita and Chang (2001), and it underscores an important principle for psycholinguistic models. The directionality of weight effects depends on the language type. Heavy phrases shift to the right in English-type (head-initial) structures, and to the left in Japanese-type (head-final) structures; cf. Hawkins (1994, 2004) for extensive illustration and discussion.

In (14), the data of (13) are presented for both phrasal type (NPo versus PP) and relative weight:

(14)

	NPo>PPm by			NPo=PPm	PPm>NPo by		
n = 244	5+	3–4	1–2		1–2	3–8	9+
[PPm NPo V]	21% (3)	50% (5)	62% (18)	66% (60)	80% (48)	84% (26)	100% (9)
[NPo PPm V]	79% (11)	50% (5)	38% (11)	34% (31)	20% (12)	16% (5)	0% (0)

Notice the preferred adjacency of a direct object NPo complement to V when weight differences are equal or small in (14). This interacting preference is plausibly a consequence of the fact that NPs are generally complements and in a lexical combination with V, whereas PPs are either adjuncts or complements, mostly the former; cf. section 4.3.2.

4.3.4. Greenberg's Word Order Correlations and Other Domain Minimizations

Grammatical conventions across languages reveal the same degrees of preference for minimal domains. The relative quantities of languages reflect the preferences, as do hierarchies of co-occurring word orders. An efficiency approach can also explain exceptions to the majority patterns and to grammatical principles such as consistent head ordering.

Let us return to the implicational universal with which I began this chapter (section 4.1). Greenberg (1963) examined alternative verb positions across languages and their correlations with prepositions and postpositions in phrases corresponding to (15):

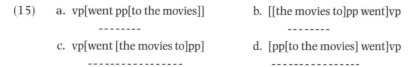

(15)   a. vp[went pp[to the movies]]   b. [[the movies to]pp went]vp
        --------   --------

        c. vp[went [the movies to]pp]   d. [pp[to the movies] went]vp
        -----------------   ----------------

(15a) is the English order, (15b) is the Japanese order, and these two sequences, with adjacent lexical heads (V and P), are massively preferred in language samples over the inconsistently ordered heads in (15c) and (15d). (16) summarizes the distribution in the database of Dryer's (1992) paper on the "Greenbergian correlations" (Hawkins, 2004, p. 124):

(16)   a. vp[V pp[P NP]] = 161 (41%)   b. [[NP P]pp V]vp = 204 (52%)
          c. vp[V [NP P]pp] = 18 (5%)   d. [pp[P NP] V]vp = 6 (2%)
          Preferred (16a) + (b) = 365/389 (94%)

The adjacency of V and P guarantees the smallest possible string of words, indicated by the underlinings in (15), for the recognition and construction of VP and of its two immediate constituents (ICs), namely, V and PP. Non-adjacent V and P in (15c) and (15d) require longer and less efficient strings for the parsing of phrase structure. That is, adjacency provides a minimal Phrasal Combination Domain for the construction of VP and its daughters, of the same kind we saw in the performance preferences of sections 4.3.1–4.3.3.

Consistent head ordering in grammars can be argued to derive from Minimize Domains (2), therefore. Conventions of ordering have emerged out of performance preferences, and one and the same principle can explain both the preferred conventions of grammar and the preferred structural selections in performance (in languages and structures in which speakers have a choice). MiD can also explain why there are two productive mirror-image types here, head-initial and head-final languages, exemplified by (15a) and (b), respectively: they are equally good strategies for phrase structure comprehension and production (Hawkins, 2004, pp. 123–126).

Purely grammatical approaches can also define a head ordering parameter (cf. Newmeyer, 2005, p. 43 and Haspelmath, 2006, for full references), and Svenonius (2000, p. 7) states that this parameter is "arguably not a function of processing." It is certainly possible that this is an autonomous principle of grammar with no basis in performance. But how do we argue for or against this?

A classic method of reasoning in generative grammar has always involved capturing significant generalizations and deriving the greatest number of observations from the smallest number of principles. An autonomous head ordering principle would fail to capture the generalization that both grammatical and performance data fall under Minimize Domains. The probabilistic and preferential nature of this generalization is also common to both. Moreover, many other ordering universals point to the same preference for small and efficient Phrasal Combination Domains, for example, in noun-phrase-internal orderings corresponding to (17) in English:

(17)   np[bright students s'[that Mary will teach]]
(17')   np[Adj N s'[C S]]   C = the category that constructs S': e.g., relative pronoun, complementizer, subordinating affix or particle, participial marking on V, etc. (Hawkins, 1994, pp. 387–393)

There are 12 logically possible orderings of Adj, N, and S' (ordered [C S] or [S C]). Just four of these have minimal PCDs for the NP (100% IC-to-word ratios), all of them with adjacent Adj, N, and C, namely, [N Adj [C S]] (Romance), [Adj N [C S]] (Germanic), [[S C] N Adj] (Basque), and [[S C] Adj N] (Tamil). These four account for the vast majority of languages, while a small minority of languages are distributed among the remaining eight in proportion to their IC-to-word ratios measured on-line (Hawkins, 1990, 1994, 2004). There appears to be no straightforward grammatical account for this distribution of occurring versus non-occurring and preferred versus less preferred grammars. The distribution does correlate with degrees of efficient processing in NP Phrasal Combination Domains, however.

4.3.5. Explaining Grammatical Exceptions and Unpredicted Patterns

Further support for the Minimize Domains explanation for head ordering comes from the grammars with exceptional head orderings. Dryer (1992) points out that there are systematic exceptions to Greenberg's correlations when the category that modifies a head is a single-word item, for example, an adjective modifying a noun (*yellow book*). Many otherwise head-initial languages have noninitial heads here (English is a case in point), and many otherwise head-final languages have noun before adjective (e.g., Basque). But when the non-head is a branching phrasal category (e.g., an adjective phrase as in English, *books yellow with age*), there are good correlations with the predominant head ordering. Why should this be?

When a head category like V has a phrasal sister, for example, PP in {V, PP}, then the distance from the higher head to the head of the sister will be very long when heads are inconsistently ordered and are separated by a branching phrase (e.g., vp[V [NP P]pp] in [15c]. An intervening phrasal NP between V and P makes the PCD for the mother VP long and inefficient compared with the consistently ordered counterpart (15a), vp[V pp[P NP]], in which just two words suffice to recognize the two ICs. But when heads are separated by a nonbranching single word, then the difference between, say, vp[V np[N Adj]] and vp[V [Adj N]np] is short, only one word. Hence, the MiD preference for noun initiality (and for noun finality in postpositional languages) is significantly less than it is for intervening branching phrases, and either less head ordering consistency or no consistency is predicted. When there is just a one word difference between competing domains in performance, cf. (6), both ordering options are generally productive, and so too in grammars.

MiD can also explain numerous patterns across grammars that do not follow readily from grammatical principles alone. Hierarchies of permitted center-embedded phrases are a case in point. For example, in the environment pp[P np[__ N]], we have the following center-embedding hierarchy (Hawkins, 1983):

(18)   Prepositional languages:

DemN	49%	NDem	51%
AdjN	32%	NAdj	68%
PosspN	12%	NPossp	88%
RelN	1%	NRel	99%

As the aggregate size and complexity of nominal modifiers increases (relative clauses exceeding possessive phrases, which in turn exceed single-word adjectives), the distance between P and N increases in the prenominal order and the efficiency of the PCD for PP declines compared with postnominal counterparts.[4] As efficiencies decline, the relative frequencies of prenominal orders in conventionalized grammatical rules declines also.

4.3.6. Minimal Domains for Complements and Heads in Grammars

Complements prefer adjacency over adjuncts in the basic orders of numerous phrases in English and other languages and are generated in a position adjacent to their heads in the grammars of Jackendoff (1977) and Pollard and Sag (1987). Tomlin's (1986) verb–object bonding discussion provides cross-linguistic support for this by pointing to languages in which it is impossible or dispreferred for adjuncts to intervene between a verbal head and its DO complement.

Why should complements prefer adjacency in grammars when there are basic ordering conventions? The reason, I suggest, is the same as the one I gave for the preferred orderings of complements (Pd) in performance in section 4.3.2. There are more combinatorial and/or dependency relations linking complements to their heads than linking adjuncts. Complements are listed in a lexical co-occurrence frame defined by, and activated by, a specific head (e.g., a verb); adjuncts are not so listed and occur in a wide variety of phrases with which they are semantically compatible (Pollard & Sag, 1994). The verb is regularly lexically dependent on its DO, not on an adjunct phrase: compare the different senses of "run" in *run the race/the water/the advertisement* (*in the afternoon*); cf. Keenan (1979). A direct object receives a theta-role from V, typically a subtype of Dowty's (1991) Proto-Patient; adjuncts don't get theta-roles. The DO is also syntactically required by a transitive V, whereas adjuncts are not syntactically required sisters. Processing these lexical co-occurrence relations favors minimal Lexical Domains (7).

4.4. Relative Clauses

Relative clauses have been well researched across grammars, and they are now receiving increasing attention in performance; so we can begin to compare the two sets of data in a further test of the PGCH (1). Relative clauses may exhibit a "gap" or a "resumptive pronoun" strategy (in Hebrew structures corresponding to *the students [that I teach (them)]*), or a structure with or without a relative pronoun (in English, cf. *the students [(whom) I teach]*). One of these strategies can be "fixed" or "conventionalized" in certain environments, whereas there can be optionality and variation in others. The issue is then whether the fixed conventions of grammars match the preferred variants of performance.

4.4.1. Gaps versus Pronouns

The selection from the variants in performance exhibits patterns: the retention of the relative pronoun in English is correlated (inter alia) with the degree of separation of the relative from its head; cf. Quirk (1957). The Hebrew gap has been shown to be favored with smaller distances between filler and gap (Ariel, 1999): that is, (19a) is significantly preferred over (19b) with a resumptive pronoun, while the pronoun becomes productive when "filler-gap domains" (Hawkins, 1999, 2004) would be larger, as in (20).

(19)   a. Shoshana hi ha-isha*i*   [she-nili ohevet 0*i*]   (Hebrew)
          Shoshana is the-woman   that-Nili loves
       b. Shoshana hi ha-isha*i*   [she-nili ohevet ota*i*]
                                   that-Nili loves her

(20)   Shoshana hi ha-isha*i*   [she-dani   siper   she-moshe rixel she-nili ohevet ota*i*]
         Shoshana is the-woman that-Danny said   that-Moshe gossiped that-Nili loves her

The distribution of the fixed variants across grammars also reveals patterns. In simple relative clauses in Cantonese, in which the subcategorizing verb would be adjacent to the head of the relative, a resumptive pronoun is ungrammatical (21b). In the more complex environment of (22) (with an intervening embedded VP), both gaps and resumptives occur (Matthews & Yip, 2003)[5]:

(21)   a. [Ng05 ceng2 0*i*] g02 di1 pang4jau5*i* (Cantonese)
             I   invite   those CL friend
             "friends that I invite"
         b. *[Ng05 ceng2*i* keoi5dei6*i*)] g02 di1   pang4jau5*i*
             I   invite   them   those CL   friend
(22)   [Ng05 ceng2 (keoi5dei6*i*) sik6-faan6] g02 di1 pang4jau5*i*
             I   invite (them)   eat-rice   those CL   friend
             "friends that I invite to have dinner"

More generally, the distribution of gaps to pronouns follows the Keenan and Comrie (1977) Accessibility Hierarchy (SU>DO>IO/OBL>GEN). This increasing preference for pronouns down the hierarchy provides a further piece of evidence for their claim that the AH correlates with declining ease of processing. Hawkins (1999, 2004) argued that there are indeed more complex domains for relative clause processing down the AH, measured in terms of syntactic node size and other correlated measures, and he argues further that resumptive pronouns minimize the lexical domains for argument processing, resulting in more efficient structures overall when relativization environments are complex.

In (19b) and (20), for example, the pronoun provides a local argument, *ota* (her), for lexical processing of *ohevet* (loves), whereas in (19a), lexical processing needs to access the more distant head *ha-isha* (woman) in order to assign a direct object to *loves*. The larger the distance between the subcategorizor and the relative clause head, the less minimal this Lexical Domain becomes, and the more efficient the copy pronoun becomes.

4.4.2. *Relative Clause Hierarchies*

A question that arises from the Accessibility Hierarchy is: What other grammatical hierarchies can be set up for relative clauses on the basis of cross-linguistic data, and do their ranked positions lend themselves to an account in terms of processing complexity? In Hawkins (1999, 2004), I proposed the following clause-embedding hierarchy for gaps:

(23)   infinitival (VP) complement>finite (S) complement > S within a complex NP

Relativization cuts off down this hierarchy in selected languages, much the way it does down the AH. Some languages exemplifying the cut-off points are summarized in (24):

(24)   Infinitival (VP) complement: Swedish, Japanese, English, French,
                                            German, Russian;
        Finite (S) complement: Swedish, Japanese, English, French;
        S within complex NP: Swedish, Japanese.

Standard German exhibits ungrammaticalities for relative clause gaps in finite complements; cf. (25). Corresponding gaps in infinitival complements such as (26) are grammatical (see Kvam, 1983, and Comrie, 1973, for similar data from Russian):

(25)   *Der Tierpark*i* [den*i* ich vermute s[dass alle Deutschen kennen 0*i*]] heisst ... (German)
        the zoo   which I suppose that all Germans   know   is-called
(26)   das Buch*i* [das*i* ich vp[0*i* zu finden] versucht hatte]/[das*i* ich versucht hatte [0*i* zu finden]]
        the book which I   to find tried   had / which I tried   had   to find
        "the book which I had tried to find"

English and French cut off at gaps within complex NP clauses, exemplified by (27) from English. This sentence contrasts with its Swedish counterpart, (28), in which the corresponding complex NP structure is completely grammatical (Allwood, 1982):

(27)   *I was looking for a bone*i* [which*i* I saw np[a dog s[that was gnawing on 0*i*]]]
(28)   ett ben*i* [som*i* jag ser np[en hund s[som gnager på 0*i*]]] (Swedish)
        a bone which I   see   a dog   which is-gnawing on

Corresponding to this last cut-off point, Saah and Goodluck (1995) have presented interesting experimental data from Akan (aka Twi), a language in which there is no grammatical subjacency condition outlawing gaps in complex NPs. Speakers nonetheless showed greater processing difficulty for gaps within a complex NP compared with an embedded finite clause; these processing data matched the grammatical cut-off data on the clause-embedding hierarchy (24).

4.5. Conclusions and Further Issues

The data of this chapter have shown that there are clear parallels between performance variation data and grammatical universals of the variation-defining kind. Hence, any proposed principles that apply to grammars only, such as innate parameters (Chomsky, 1981), are missing a significant generalization. One common principle evident in both is Minimize Domains (2). There is a correlation between the adjacency preferences of performance, in sections 4.3.1–4.3.3, and the adjacency conventions of grammars, sections 4.3.4–4.3.6. Further correlations between performance and grammatical variation were summarized in sections 4.2 and 4.4.

These correlations support the Performance-Grammar Correspondence Hypothesis in (1). The major predictions of the PGCH that are systematically tested in Hawkins (2004) are the following:

(29)   *Grammatical predictions of the PGCH* (Hawkins, 2004)
        (a) If a structure A is preferred over an A′ of the same structural type in performance, then A will be more productively grammaticalized, in proportion to its degree of preference; if A and A′ are more equally preferred, then A and A′ will both be productive in grammars.
        (b) If there is a preference ranking A>B>C>D among structures of a common type in performance, then there will be a corresponding hierarchy of grammatical conventions (with cutoff points and declining frequencies of languages).
        (c) If two preferences P and P′ are in (partial) opposition, then there will be variation in performance and grammars, with both P and P′ being realized, each in proportion to its degree of motivation in a given language structure.

We have seen in this chapter that such predictions are widely supported. Hence, principles of performance provide an explanation for variation-defining universals. Minimize Domains explains the Greenbergian correlations in (16) and other ordering patterns. It explains why there are two productive language types, head initial and head final: they are both equally efficient according to Minimize Domains (Hawkins, 1994, 2004). It explains puzzling exceptions to consistent head ordering involving single-word versus multi-word modifiers of heads (section 4.3.5). It also explains cross-linguistic patterns that are not predicted by grammatical principles alone, such as hierarchies of increasingly complex center embeddings in (18), and reverse hierarchies for some data versus others. For example, gap relatives cut off down the Keenan-Comrie Accessibility Hierarchy (if a gap occurs low on the hierarchy, it occurs all the way up), whereas resumptive pronouns follow an "if high, then low" pattern (section 4.4.1, and Hawkins, 1999).

Based on this evidence, I conclude, with Newmeyer (2005), that performance and processing must play a central role in any theory of grammatical variation and of variation-defining language universals. The PGCH gives good descriptive coverage. It also provides answers to explanatory questions that are rarely raised in the generative literature, such as the following: Why should there be a head ordering principle defining head-initial and head-final language types (Hawkins, 1990, 1994)? Why are there heads at all in phrase structure (Hawkins, 1993, 1994)? Why are some categories adjacent and others not (Hawkins, 2001, 2004)? Why is there a subjacency constraint, and why is it parameterized the way it is (Hawkins, 1999, 2004)?

They can be asked, and informative answers can be given, in the framework proposed here. The basic empirical issue involves conducting a simple test: Are there, or are there not, parallels between universal patterns across grammars, and patterns of preference and processing ease within languages? The data of this chapter suggest that there are, and the descriptive and explanatory benefits for which I have argued then follow.

Two further common principles of performance and grammar from Hawkins (2004) are summarized here without further comment:

(30)   *Minimize Forms* (MiF)
        The human processor prefers to minimize the formal complexity of each linguistic form F (its phoneme, morpheme, word, or phrasal units) and the number of forms with unique conventionalized property assignments, thereby assigning more properties to fewer forms. These minimizations apply in proportion to the ease with which a given property P can be assigned in processing to a given F.

(31)   *Maximize Online Processing* (MaOP)
        The human processor prefers to maximize the set of properties that are assignable to each item X as X is processed, thereby increasing O(nline) P(roperty) to U(ltimate) P(roperty) ratios. The maximization difference between competing orders and structures will be a function of the number of properties that are unassigned or misassigned to X in a structure/sequence S, compared with the number in an alternative.

Let me end this chapter with some general remarks on further issues. I distinguished in section 4.1 between variation-defining universals and absolute universals, and the data and discussion have been concerned with the former. I have argued that innate grammatical knowledge cannot be the ultimate explanation for them, but notice that it is still plausible to think in terms of Elman et al. (1996) "architectural innateness" as constraining the data of performance, which then evolve into conventions of grammar. The architectural innateness of the human language faculty enters into grammars indirectly in this way. Absolute universals can also be innately grounded as a result of processing constraints on grammars. When complexity and efficiency levels are comparable and tolerable, we get the variation between grammars that we have seen. But within and beyond certain thresholds, I would expect universals of the kind "all languages have X" and "no languages have X," respectively, as a result of processability interacting with the other determinants of grammars. The PGCH is no less relevant to absolute universals, therefore, with the extremes of simplicity/complexity and (in)efficiency being inferrable from actually occurring usage data. Systematic exploration of this idea is required in order see to what extent absolute universals can be explained through processing as well.

There can also be innate grammatical and representational knowledge of quite specific properties of the kind summarized in Pinker and Jackendoff's (Chapter 7) response to Hauser, Chomsky, and Fitch (2002). Much of phonetics, semantics, and cognition is presumably innately grounded, and there are numerous properties unique to human language as a result. See Newmeyer (2005) for the role of conceptual structure in shaping absolute universals, and also Bach and Chao (Chapter 8) for a discussion of semantically based universals.

The precise causes underlying the observed preferences in performance require more attention than I have given them here, and indeed much of psycholinguistics is currently grappling with this issue. To what extent do the preferences result from parsing and comprehension, and to what extent are they production-driven? See, for example, Wasow (2002) and Jaeger and Wasow (2005) for discussion of the different predictions made by production- versus comprehension-based theories for some of the data of this chapter. In addition, what is the role of frequency sensitivity and of prior learning in on-line processing? (e.g., Reali & Christiansen, 2007a, b).

A performance explanation for universals has consequences for learning and for learnability since it reduces the role of an innate grammar. UG is no longer available in the relevant areas (head ordering, subjacency, etc.) to make up for the claimed poverty of the stimulus and to solve the negative evidence problem (Bowerman, 1988). The result is increased learning from positive data, something that Tomasello (2003), connectionist modelers like MacDonald (1999), and also linguists like Culicover (1999) have been arguing for independently. These converging developments enable us to see the data of experience as less impoverished and more learnable than previously thought. The grammaticality facts of Culicover's book, for example, pose learnability problems that are just as severe as those for which Hoekstra and Kooij (1988) invoke an innate UG, yet Culicover's data involve language-particular subtleties of English that cannot possibly be innate (*the student is likely to pass the exam* versus *the student is probable to pass the exam*). See Hawkins (2004, pp. 272–276) for further discussion of these issues.

The explanation for cross-linguistic patterns that I have proposed also requires a theory of diachrony that can translate the preferences of performance into fixed conventions of grammars. Grammars can be seen as complex adaptive systems (Gell-Mann, 1992), with ease of processing driving the adaptation in response to prior changes. But we need to better understand the "adaptive mechanisms" (Kirby, 1999) by which grammatical conventions emerge out of performance variants. How do grammatical categories and the rule types of particular models end up encoding performance preferences? And what constraints and filters are there on this translation from performance to grammar? I outlined some major ways in which grammars respond to processing in Hawkins (1994, pp. 19–24) (by incorporating movement rules applying to some categories rather than others, defining certain orderings rather than others, constraining the applicability of rules in certain environments, etc.), and I would refer the reader to that discussion. How are these different rules then selected by successive generations of learners, and even by the same generation over time? I refer the reader here to Haspelmath (1999) and to Hurford (Chapter 3).

Key Further Readings

A non-technical introduction to the PGCH presented in this chapter is given in the first two chapters of Hawkins (2004). Chapters 5–8 of that book provide more detailed justification for the ideas presented here. An up-to-date introduction oriented to the concerns of typologists can be found in my chapter, "Processing efficiency and complexity in typological patterns," to appear in the *Oxford Handbook of Language Typology*, edited by Jae Jung Song. I give an introduction for psychologists, "Processing Typology and why psychologists need to know about it," in *New Ideas in Psychology* 25: 87–107 (2007). Greenberg's classic (1963) paper referenced below on the order of meaningful elements is essential reading for the study of variation-defining universals, and Newmeyer's (2005) book on possible and probable languages gives a good summary of both generative and typological approaches to these universals and a generative perspective that complements the typological and psycholinguistic perspective presented here. For introductions to typology, see Comrie (1989) and Croft (2003).

Notes

1 The following abbreviations are used in this chapter—Acc: accusative case; Adj: adjective; AH: Accessibility Hierarchy; C: category that constructs S'; CL: classifier; Comp: complementizer; Dat: dative case; Dem: demonstrative determiner; DO: direct object; EIC: Early Immediate Constituents; GEN: genitive; IC: immediate constituent; IO: indirect object;

L: lexical item; LD: lexical domain; MaOP: Maximize Online Processing; MiD: Minimize Domains; MiF: Minimize Forms; N: noun; Nom: Nominative case; NP: noun phrase; NPo: NP with accusative -*o* case particle; OBL: oblique phrase; OS: object before subject; P: preposition or postposition; PCD: phrasal combination domain; Pd: a PP interdependent with V; PGCH: Performance-Grammar Correspondence Hypothesis; Pi: a PP independent of V; Plur: plural; Possp: possessive phrase; PP: prepositional or postpositional phrase; PPL: longer PP; PPm: postpositional phrase; PPS: shorter PP; Rel: relative clause; S: sentence or clause; S': clause with one bar level; Sing: singular; SO: subject before object; SOV: subject-object-verb; SU: subject; UG: Universal Grammar; V: verb; VP: verb phrase.

2 Notice that sequences of [V PP PP] in English are compatible with different attachment options for the second PP. It could be attached to an NP within the first PP, to the VP, or to a higher S or IP. Low attachment to NP within the first PP will generally rule out the permutation option, and the predictions made here for relative ordering do not differ substantially between VP and S attachments (cf. Hawkins, 1994). There are multiple factors that can impact attachment preferences in on-line processing (plausibility, preceding context, frequency, etc.), as MacDonald, Pearlmutter, and Seidenberg (1994) have shown, and the calculation of domain sizes in (3) is made in effect from the speaker's perspective. The speaker knows that the second PP is permutable and is not to be attached within the first. Even from the hearer's perspective, however, notice that the second PP is not reached until the ninth word after the verb in (3b) compared with the the fifth word in (3a), and hence in all the structures in which high attachment is assumed on-line, (3b) will be a less minimal processing domain for phrase structure assignments than (3a).

3 Gibson's (1998) "locality" principle makes many similar predictions, and the wealth of experimental evidence that he summarizes there supports the MiD principle here.

4 In the parsing theory of Hawkins (1990, 1993, 1994), demonstrative determiners can construct NP just as N can, and this may explain the equal productivity of DemN and NDem in head-initial languages; both orders can construct NP at its outset.

5 The prediction I make for Cantonese performance is that the resumptive pronoun should be preferred in proportion to the complexity of phrases that intervene between the subcategorizer in the relative and the head of the relative. Cf. Hawkins (2004, p. 175) for the definition of a "filler-gap domain" that is assumed here (roughly the smallest domain linking the head to the position relativized on, either a gap or a subcategorizor).

References

Aissen, J. (1999). Markedness and subject choice in Optimality Theory. *Natural Language & Linguistic Theory*, *17*, 673–711.

Aldai, G. (2003). The prenominal [-Case] relativization strategy of Basque: Conventionalization, processing, and frame semantics, USC, UCLA: MS, Depts. of Linguistics.

Allwood, J. (1982). The complex NP constraint in Swedish. In E. Engdahl & E. Ejerhed (Eds.), *Readings on unbounded dependencies in Scandinavian languages*. Stockholm: Almqvist & Wiksell.

Ariel, M. (1999). Cognitive universals and linguistic conventions: The case of resumptive pronouns. *Studies in Language, 23*, 217–269.

Bowerman, M. (1988). The "No Negative Evidence" problem: How do children avoid constructing an overly general grammar? In J. A. Hawkins (Ed.), *Explaining language universals*. Oxford: Blackwell.

Bresnan, J., Dingare, S., & Manning, C. D. (2001). Soft constraints mirror hard constraints: Voice and person in english and lummi. In M. Butt & T. H. King (Eds.), *Proceedings of the LFG 01 conference*. Stanford: CSLI Publications.

Bybee, J., & Hopper, P. (Eds.). (2001). *Frequency and the emergence of linguistic structure*. Amsterdam: John Benjamins.

Chomsky, N. (1965). *Aspects of the theory of syntax*. Cambridge, MA: MIT Press.

Chomsky, N. (1981). *Lectures on government and binding*. Dordrecht: Foris.

Chomsky, N. (1995). *The minimalist program*. Cambridge, MA: MIT Press.

Cinque, G. (2005). Deriving Greenberg's universal 20 and its exceptions. *Linguistic Inquiry, 36*, 315–332.

Clancy, P. M., Lee, H., & Zoh, M. (1986). Processing strategies in the acquisition of relative clauses. *Cognition, 14*, 225–262.

Cole, P. (1976). An apparent asymmetry in the formation of relative clauses in modern Hebrew. In P. Cole (Ed.), *Studies in modern Hebrew syntax and semantics*. Amsterdam: North Holland.

Comrie, B. (1973). Clause structure and movement constraints in Russian. In C. Corum, T. C. Smith-Stark, & A. Weiser (Eds.), *You take the high road and I'll take the low node* (pp. 291–304). Chicago: Chicago Linguistic Society.

Comrie, B. (1989). *Language universals and linguistic typology* (2nd ed.). Chicago: University of Chicago Press.

Croft, W. (2003). *Typology and universals* (2nd ed.). Cambridge: Cambridge University Press.

Culicover, P. W. (1999). *Syntactic nuts: Hard cases, syntactic theory, and language acquisition*. Oxford: Oxford University Press.

Diessel, H., & Tomasello, M. (2006). A new look at the acquisition of relative clauses. *Language, 81*, 882–906.

Dowty, D. R. (1991). Thematic proto-roles and argument selection. *Language, 75*, 547–619.

Dryer, M. S. (1992). The Greenbergian word order correlations. *Language, 68*, 81–138.

Elman, J. L., Bates, E., Johnson, M., Karmiloff-Smith, A., Parisi, D., & Plunkett, K. (1996). *Rethinking innateness: A connectionist perspective on development*. Cambridge, MA.: MIT Press.

Fodor, J. D. (2001). Setting syntactic parameters. In M. Baltin & C. Collins (Eds.), *The handbook of contemporary syntactic theory* (pp. 730–738). Oxford: Blackwell.

Gell-Mann, M. (1992). Complexity and complex adaptive systems. In J. A. Hawkins & M. Gell-Mann (Eds.), *The evolution of human languages*. Redwood City, CA: Addison-Wesley.

Gibson, E. (1998). Linguistic complexity: Locality of syntactic dependencies. *Cognition, 68*, 1–76.

Givón, T. (1979). *On understanding grammar*. New York: Academic Press.

Greenberg, J. H. (1963). Some universals of grammar with particular reference to the order of meaningful elements. In J. H. Greenberg (Ed.), *Universals of language*. Cambridge, MA: MIT Press.

Greenberg, J. H. (1966). *Language universals, with special reference to feature hierarchies*. The Hague: Mouton.

Greenberg, J. H. (1995). The diachronic typological approach to language. In M. Shibatani & T. Bynon (Eds.), *Approaches to language typology*. Oxford: Clarendon Press.

Haspelmath, M. (1999). Optimality and diachronic adaptation. *Zeitschrift für Sprachwissenschaft, 18*, 180–205.

Haspelmath, M. (2006). Parametric versus functional explanations of syntactic universals. Leipzig: MS, Max Planck Institute for Evolutionary Anthropology.

Hauser, M., Chomsky, N., & Fitch, W. T. (2002). The faculty of language: What is it, who has it, and how did it evolve? *Science, 298*, 1569–1579.

Hawkins, J. A. (1983). *Word order universals*. New York: Academic Press.

Hawkins, J. A. (1990). A parsing theory of word order universals. *Linguistic Inquiry, 21*, 223–261.

Hawkins, J. A. (1993). Heads, parsing, and word order universals. In G. G. Corbett, N. M. Fraser, & S. McGlashan (Eds.), *Heads in grammatical theory*. Cambridge: Cambridge University Press, 231–265.

Hawkins, J. A. (1994). *A performance theory of order and constituency*. Cambridge: Cambridge University Press.

Hawkins, J. A. (1999). Processing complexity and filler-gap dependencies across grammars. *Language, 75*, 244–285.

Hawkins, J. A. (2000). The relative ordering of prepositional phrases in English: Going beyond manner-place-time. *Language Variation and Change, 11*, 231–266.

Hawkins, J. A. (2001). Why are categories adjacent? *Journal of Linguistics, 37*, 1–34.

Hawkins, J. A. (2004). *Efficiency and complexity in grammars*. Oxford: Oxford University Press.

Hoekstra, T., & Kooij, J. G. (1988). The innateness hypothesis. In J. A. Hawkins (Ed.), *Explaining language universals*. Oxford: Blackwell.

Jackendoff, R. (1977). *X-bar syntax: A study of phrase structure*. Cambridge, MA: MIT Press.

Jaeger, T. F., & Wasow, T. (2005). Production-complexity driven variation: Relativizer omission in non-subject-extracted relative clauses. Paper presented at the 18th Annual CUNY Sentence Processing Conference, Tuscon, Arizona.

Kayne, R. S. (1994). *The antisymmetry of syntax*. Cambridge, MA: MIT Press.

Keenan, E. L. (1975). Variation in universal grammar. In R. Fasold & R. Shuy (Eds.), *Analyzing variation in English* (pp. 136–148). Washington, DC: Georgetown University Press.

Keenan, E. L. (1979). On surface form and logical form. *Studies in the Linguistic Sciences, 8*, 163–203.

Keenan, E. L., & Comrie, B. (1977). Noun phrase accessibility and universal grammar. *Linguistic Inquiry, 8*, 63–99.

Keenan, E. L., & Hawkins, S. (1987). The psychological validity of the accessibility hierarchy. In E. L. Keenan, *Universal grammar: 15 essays*. London: Croom Helm.

Kempson, R., Meyer-Viol, W., & Gabbay, D. (2001). *Dynamic syntax*. Oxford: Blackwell.

Kirby, S. (1999). *Function, selection, and innateness: The emergence of language universals*. Oxford: Oxford University Press.

Kvam, S. (1983). *Linksverschachtelung im Deutschen und Norwegischen*. Tübingen: Max Niemeyer Verlag.

Lightfoot, D. W. (1991). *How to set parameters*. Cambridge, MA: MIT Press.

MacDonald, M. C., Pearlmutter, N. J., & Seidenberg, M. S. (1994). The lexical nature of syntactic ambiguity resolution. *Psychological Review, 101*(4), 676–703.

MacDonald, M. C. (1999). Distributional information in language comprehension, production, and acquisition: Three puzzles and a moral. In B. MacWhinney (Ed.), *The emergence of language*. Mahwah, NJ: Erlbaum.

MacWhinney, B. (1982). Basic syntactic processes. In S. Kuczaj (Ed.), *Language acquisition: Syntax and semantics*. Mahwah, NJ: Lawrence Erlbaum.

Manning, C. D. (2003). Probabilistic syntax. In R. Bod, J. Hay & S. Jannedy (Eds.), *Probability theory in linguistics*. Cambridge, MA: MIT Press, 289–341.

Matthews, S., & Yip, V. (2003). Relative clauses in early bilingual development: Transfer and universals. In A. G. Ramat (Ed.), *Typology and second language acquisition*. Berlin: De Gruyter.

Miyamoto, E. T. (2006). Understanding sentences in Japanese bit by bit. *Cognitive Studies: Bulletin of the Japanese Cognitive Science Society, 13*, 247–260.

Newmeyer, F. J. (1998). *Language form and language function*. Cambridge, MA: MIT Press.

Newmeyer, F. J. (2005). *Possible and probable languages: A generative perspective on linguistic typology*. Oxford: Oxford University Press.

Phillips, C. (1996). Order and structure. Ph.D. dissertation, MIT.

Pollard, C., & Sag, I. A. (1987). *Information-based syntax and semantics, Vol. 1: Fundamentals*, CSLI Lecture Notes No.13. Stanford: Stanford University.

Pollard, C., & Sag, I. A. (1994). *Head-driven phrase structure grammar*. Chicago: The University of Chicago Press.

Primus, B. (1999). *Cases and thematic roles: Ergative, accusative, and active*. Tübingen: Max Niemeyer Verlag.

Quirk, R. (1957). Relative clauses in educated spoken English. *English Studies, 38*, 97–109.

Reali, F., & Christiansen, M. H. (2007a). Processing of relative clauses is made easier by frequency of occurrence. *Journal of Memory and Language, 57*, 1–23.

Reali, F., & Christiansen, M. H. (2007b). Word chunk frequencies affect the processing of pronominal object-relatives. *The Quarterly Journal of Experimental Psychology, 60*, 161-170.

Saah, K. K., & Goodluck, H. (1995). Island effects in parsing and grammar: Evidence from akan. *Linguistic Review, 12*, 381–409.

Schütze, C. T., & Gibson, E. (1999). Argumenthood and English prepositional phrase attachment. *Journal of Memory and Language, 40*, 409–431.

Sheldon, A. (1974). On the role of parallel function in the acquisition of relative clauses in English. *Journal of Verbal Learning and Verbal Behavior, 13*, 272–281.

Stallings, L. M. (1998). Evaluating heaviness: Relative weight in the spoken production of heavy-NP shift. Ph.D. dissertation, University of Southern California.

Steedman, M. (2006) A Zipfian view of Greenberg 20. MS, University of Edinburgh.

Svenonius, P. (2000). Introduction. In P. Svenonius (Ed.), *The derivation of VO and OV*. Amsterdam: John Benjamins.

Tomasello, M. (2003). *Constructing a language*. Cambridge, MA: Harvard University Press.

Tomlin, R. S. (1986). *Basic word order: Functional principles*. London: Croom Helm.

Wasow, T. (1997). Remarks on grammatical weight. *Language Variation and Change, 9*, 81–105.

Wasow, T. (2002). *Postverbal behavior*. Stanford: CSLI Publications.

Yamashita, H., & Chang, F. (2001). "Long before short" preference in the production of a head-final language. *Cognition, 81*, B45–B55.

5

APPROACHING UNIVERSALS FROM BELOW: I-UNIVERSALS IN LIGHT OF A MINIMALIST PROGRAM FOR LINGUISTIC THEORY

Norbert Hornstein and Cedric Boeckx

5.1. Introduction

From the earliest days of generative grammar, the object of study has been the faculty of language (FL): those aspects of the mind/brain that underlie the fast, uniform, and seemingly effortless ability that humans have to acquire a natural language when placed in a linguistic environment, however rudimentary (sometimes radically so, as in the case of language creation/creolization; see Petitto, 2005). The supposition that such a capacity exists and is part of human nature (perhaps uniquely so)[1] rests on the trivial observation that humans are to language what birds are to flight and fish are to water; that is to say, barring pathology, any human child can acquire any human language and that this contrasts strikingly with the linguistic capacities developed by pets, plants, and artifacts when placed in similar environmental situations. For example, the authors have acquired (varieties of) French and English though they could just as well have acquired Swahili or Hindi or Polish or . . . if appropriately situated. We take the truth of this observation to be almost self-evident. Indeed, in our view, it takes heroic obtuseness, of a kind generally restricted to academics and intellectuals on the make, to be blind to these obvious facts. As we are not sufficiently bright to be so perverse, we will take it to be an irrefragable datum of the natural world. Given this, and given that *Universal Grammar* (UG) is simply one of the names for this distinctive capacity, it is impossible that linguistic universals can fail to exist. Of course, what the universals are is open to debate, even though their existence is, in our opinion, not rationally contestable. What, then, is the aim of linguistics? It is to describe and explain the fine structure of this capacity.

Following Chomsky, we can abstractly characterize the problem as follows. Call that part of the mind/brain specifically "concerned" with language the FL.

FL develops from an initial state S_I to a steady state S_S under the influence of linguistic experience (LE): $S_I \rightarrow_{LE} S_S$. A large part of the program of generative grammar has been to characterize the properties of S_I that make the mapping above possible given the information contained in LE. As S_I is assumed to be common across the species, and as any natural language can be characterized in terms of S_S, S_I must be quite abstract and general. We call S_I Universal Grammar. "Universal" is meant to distinguish S_I from the specific language particular properties coded in S_S (the grammar of a particular language); "Grammar" points to the other obvious fact: the natural language structures with which any given speaker is competent to embody, for all practical purposes, an infinite (unbounded) number of patterns. An infinite number of patterns cannot be stored as such.[2] They must be produced by a finite number of pattern generators (viz., rules). Rules, in the domain of language, we call "grammars," and so UG, which simply is the specification of the properties of S_I, includes a specification of recursive rule systems that S_I allows. To repeat, that UG exists *in some form* is a no-brainer given the obvious facts noted above (viz., that humans are "built" for language in ways different from house cats and desktops, that natural languages involve an unbounded number of patterns, that such patterns must be the product of rules of some sort, that any human child can learn any natural language). So is the conclusion that it involves, at least in part, a specification of the kinds of rules that characterize the allowable grammatical patterns. The challenging part of the enterprise rests not with these conclusions but in coming up with a detailed specification of the system; a characterization that is both general enough to cover the grammatical phenomena displayed in various natural languages, yet rich enough to support the mapping from S_I to S_S, given only the information in the linguistic experience of the child. This way of conceiving of the linguistic enterprise has been called biolinguistics, or *I-linguistics* (Chomsky, 1986), where *I* stands for internalist, intensional, individual, and, we would add (following a suggestion of Paul Pietroski), implementable (in wetware).

How are I-Universals and the UG structure of FL studied? The short answer is, any way one can. The longer answer involves identifying the research programs devised to advance this end. In Boeckx and Hornstein (2007), we offered a survey of what we take to be the major periods in the history of modern linguistics that have led to a considerable enrichment of our understanding of FL, hence of what counts as a linguistic universal. One particularly effective route into UG has been to consider the structure of FL against the backdrop of the "logical problem of language acquisition," aka "Plato's Problem." The problem amounts to this: The child ends up developing a linguistic system whose richness is much greater than what appears to be easily accessible from the input the child has access to, the primary linguistic data (PLD). This gap between the information in the input and the knowledge attained must be bridged somehow. Chomskyans propose that it is bridged by innate properties of our language faculty.[3] As a first approximation, these innate properties are what I-Universals are all about. It is those properties that direct language growth. By comparing the informational gap between what is attained and what the PLD makes available, it is possible to investigate the kind of structure that UG must have.

On this conception, I-Universals are likely to be (and have been found to be) quite abstract. They need not be observable. Thus, even were one to survey thousands of languages looking for commonalities, they could easily escape detection. In this they contrast with Greenbergian universals, which we would call E(xternalist)-Universals.[4] In fact, on this conception, the mere fact that every language displayed some property P does not imply that P is a universal in the I-sense. Put more paradoxically, the fact that P holds universally does not imply that P is a universal. Conversely, some property can be an I-Universal even if only manifested in a single natural language. The only thing that makes something an I-Universal on this view is that it is a property of our innate ability to grow a language. Universals so conceived are the laws of the faculty of language, and the aim of (bio-)linguistics is (at least) to uncover and refine these laws, laws that define the class of possible (I-)languages (not the probable ones).

In what follows we would like to discuss a second way of investigating the fine structure of FL that has emerged in the wake of the minimalist program (Chomsky, 1993, and subsequent work). Throughout, we will focus less on what syntactic universals one finds, and more on what properties the universals are expected to have. Specifically, we would like to show that although it has been standard practice in generative grammar to approach universals from "above" (assuming a richly specified UG, in order to address Plato's problem), the minimalist program outlines a project for approaching universals from "below," assuming a very minimal UG, in an attempt to address Darwin's problem, or the logical problem of language evolution.[5] As we shall see, this second approach becomes interesting to the degree that Plato's problem has been (at least partially) addressed. As we shall also see, Darwin's problem and Plato's problem share a common logic that makes pursuing answers to them in tandem rewarding.[6]

Here is the similarity in a nutshell: Given the richness and complexity of our human knowledge of language, the short time it takes for children to master their native languages, the uniformity displayed within and across languages during the acquisition process, and the poverty of the linguistic input to children, there doesn't seem to be any way out of positing some "head start" (in the guise of an innate component— Universal Grammar) in the language acquisition process. This head start not only allows linguists to make sense of the speed at which (first) languages are acquired, but also why the acquisition process takes the paths it takes (as opposed to the paths it could take). By minimizing the role of the environment, UG allows us to solve Plato's problem.

Similarly, in light of the extremely recent emergence of the language faculty, the most plausible approach is one that minimizes the role of the environment (read: the need for adaptation), by minimizing the structures that need to evolve, and by predefining the paths of adaptation, that is, by providing preadapted structures, ready to be recruited, or modified, or third factor design properties that emerge instantaneously, by the sheer force of physical laws.

5.2. Minimalism and Darwin's Problem

Over the last 50 years of research, generative grammarians have discovered many distinctive properties of natural language grammars (NLGs); for example, (a) NLGs are recursive; that is, their products (sentences and phrases) are unbounded in size and patterns produced and are made up of elements that can recur repeatedly; (b) NLGs generate phrases that display a very specific kind of hierarchical organization (viz., those described by X' theory); and (c) NLGs display nonlocal dependencies (as in Wh-movement, agreement with the inverted subject in existential constructions, or reflexive binding), which are subject to hierarchical (e.g., binding relations are subject to a c-command requirement) and locality restrictions (e.g., controllers are subject to the minimal distance requirements, and anaphors must be bound within local domains). These properties, among others, are reasonably construed as universal features of human grammars. A widely adopted (and to our minds very reasonable) hypothesis is that these characteristics follow from the basic organization of FL; that is, they derive from the principles of UG.

Given this, consider a second fact about FL: it is of recent evolutionary vintage. A common assumption is that language arose in humans in roughly the last 50,000–100,000 years (see Diamond, 1992). This is very rapid in evolutionary terms. It suggests the following picture: FL is the product of one evolutionary innovation (at the most two) that, when combined with the cognitive resources available before the changes that led to language, delivers FL. This picture, in turn, prompts the following research program: to describe the prelinguistic cognitive structures that yield UG's distinctive properties when combined with the one (or two) specifically linguistic features of FL.[7]

The approach, we would like to suggest, requires a specific conception of FL: It does *not* have a high degree of internal modularity. The reason for this is that modular theories of UG suppose that FL is intricately structured. It has many distinct components that interact in complex ways. On the assumption that complexity requires natural selection, and that natural selection requires time to work its magic (and lots of it: say, on the order of (at least) millions of years), the rapid rise of language in humans does not allow for this kind of complexity to develop.[8] This suggests that the highly modular structure of GB-style theories should be reconsidered (see Hornstein, 2001).

Fodor (1998) puts the logic nicely:

> If the mind is mostly a collection of innate modules, then pretty clearly it must have evolved gradually, under selection pressure. That's because . . . modules contain lots of specialized information about problem domains that they compute in. And it really would be a miracle if all those details got into brains via a relatively small, fortuitous alteration of the neurology. To put it the other way around, if adaptationism isn't true in psychology, it must be that what makes our minds so clever is something pretty general.

What holds for the modularity of the mind holds for the modularity of FL as well.[9] A highly modular FL has the sort of complexity that requires adaptation through natural selection to emerge. In addition, adaptation via natural selection takes lots of time. If there is not enough time for natural selection to operate (and 50,000–100,000 years is the blink of an evolutionary eye), then there cannot be adaptation, nor this kind of highly modular complexity. The conclusion, as Fodor notes, is that the system of interest, be it the mind or FL, must be simpler and more general than generally thought.

Lest we be misunderstood, let us make two points immediately.

First, this reasoning, even if sound (and it is important to appreciate how speculative it is, given how little we know about such evolutionary matters in the domain of language), does not call into question the idea that FL is a distinct specialized cognitive faculty. What is at issue is not whether FL is modular with respect to other brain faculties. Rather, what we are questioning is the internal modular organization of FL itself. The standard view inherited from GB is that FL itself is composed of many interacting grammatical subsystems with their own organizing principles. For example, the Binding Theory has its proprietary locality conditions (i.e., binding domains), its own licensing conditions (i.e., principles A, B, and C), and its own special domain of application (i.e., reflexives, pronouns, and R-expressions). So too for Control, Case Theory, Theta Theory, etc. It is this kind of modularity that is suspect as it requires FL to have developed a lot of complicated structure in a rather short period of time, both internal to FL itself and internal to each module of FL. If this is not possible because of time constraints, then rich internal modularity is not a property of FL.

Second, we are free to assume that the generalizations and "laws of grammar" that GB discovered are roughly empirically correct. In our opinion, one of the contributions of modern generative grammar to the study of language has been the discovery of the kinds of properties encapsulated in GB.[10] Reconsidering the internal modular structure of GB does not imply rejecting these generalizations.

Rather it adds to the linguistics research agenda one more goal: to show that these generalizations are the products of more primitive factors. The project would be to deduce these "laws" from more basic principles and primitives.[11]

A picture might be of service here to get the main point across.

(1)   Prelinguistic principles and operations → ?? → (roughly) GB laws.

This picture is intended to invoke the more famous one in (2).

(2)   Primary linguistic data (of L) → Uninersal Grammar (UG) → Grammar (of L)

The well-known picture in (2) abstractly represents Plato's problem, the logical problem of language acquisition. One studies UG by constructing systems of principles that can bridge the gap between particular bits of primary linguistic data (PLD) and language-particular grammars consistent with that PLD. Generativists discovered that the distance between the two is quite substantial (as the information provided by the PLD significantly underdetermines the properties of the final state of FL) and so requires considerable innate mental structure (including the principles of UG) to bridge the gap. GB is one well-articulated proposal for the structure of UG that meets this "poverty of stimulus" concern.

An important feature of the GB model is its intricate internal modularity as well as the linguistically dedicated aspects of its rules and principles. The modules in a GB system are specifically linguistic. By this we mean that their structures reflect the fine details of the linguistic domains that concern them rather than being reflections of more general cognitive mechanisms applied to the specific problems of language.[12] On this conception, FL is a linguistically dedicated system whose basic properties mirror the fine structures of problems peculiar to language: problems related to antecedence, binding, displacement, agreement, case, endocentricity, c-command, etc. These latter are specifically linguistic in that they have no obvious analogues in other cognitive domains. It is fair to say that GB is cognitively exceptional in that its principles and operations are cognitively *sui generis* and very specific to language.[13] In other words, GB endorses the view that FL is cognitively distinctive in that its internal structure displays few analogues with the principles and operations of other cognitive modules. In Chomsky's (2005) terminology, GB reflects the view that linguistic competence is replete with first factor kinds of ingredients and that third factor processes are relatively marginal to explaining how it operates.

The picture in (1) is modeled on that in (2). It proposes taking the reasoning deployed in (2) one step further. It relies on the belief that there is an analogy between learning and evolution. In both cases, development is partially a function of the environmental input. In both cases, it is also partially a function of the prior structure of the developing organism. In both cases, it appears that the prior "input" is insufficient to account for the state attained. In both cases, the "shaping" effects of the environment on the developmental processes require reasonable time during which the environment can "shape" the structures that develop.[14] The picture in (1) takes the evolution of the principles of UG as a function of the prelinguistic mental state of "humans" and something else ("??"). Given the evolutionarily rapid emergence of FL, we know that whatever "??" is, it must be pretty slight. We can investigate this process abstractly (let's call it the logical problem of language evolution, or *Darwin's problem*) by considering the following question: *What must be added to the inventory of prelinguistic cognitive operations and principles to deduce the principles of UG?* We know that whatever is added, though pretty meager, must be sufficient when combined with the resources of nonspecifically linguistic cognition to derive a system with the properties summarized by GB. In other words, what we want is an operation (or two) that, once added to more general cognitive resources, allows what we know about FL to fall out. On this conception, what is specifically linguistic about FL's operations and principles is exiguous. This is in strong contrast to the underlying ethos of GB, as noted above. The logic of Darwin's problem argues against the cognitive exceptionalism of FL. Its basic operations and principles must be largely recruited from those that were prelinguistically available and that regulate cognition (or computation) in general. FL evolved by packaging these into UG and adding one novel ingredient (or two). This is what the short time frame requires. What (1) assumes is that even a slight addition can be very potent, given the right background conditions. The trick is to find some reasonable background operations and principles, and a suitable "innovation."

Once again, the sense of the program is well expressed in Fodor (1998):

> It's common ground that the evolution of our behavior was mediated by the evolution of our brain. So what matters with regard to the question whether the mind is an adaptation is not how complex our behavior is, but how much you would have to change an ape's brain to produce the cognitive structure of the human mind. . . . Unlike our minds, our brains are, by any gross measure, very like those of apes. So, it looks as though small alterations of brain structure must have produced very large behavior discontinuities from the ancestral apes to us.

This applies to the emergence of our linguistic capacity as well, surely the most distinctive behavioral difference between us and our ape ancestors.

Note two more points: First, evolutionary explanations of behavior, as Fodor rightly insists, piggyback on changes in brain structure. This is why we would like our descriptions to be descriptions (even if abstract) of mechanisms and processes plausibly embodied in brains (see note 13). Second, as Fodor correctly observes, much of this talk is speculative, for very little (Fodor thinks "exactly nothing") is known of how behavior, linguistic or otherwise, supervenes on brain structure. In the domain of language, we know something about how linguistic competence relies on grammatical structure, and one aim of the minimalist program as we understand it is to investigate how properties of grammars might supervene on more primitive operations and principles that plausibly describe the computational circuitry and wiring that the brain embodies.

Many minimalist proposals can be understood as addressing how to flesh (1) out. Chomsky (2005) is the prime text for this. As he notes, there are three kinds of principles at work in any specific grammar: (i) the genetic endowment (specific to language), (ii) experience, and (iii) principles that are language or even organism independent. Moreover, the more that any of these can explain a property of grammar, the less explanatory work needs to be done by the others. What modern generative grammar has investigated is the gap between experience and attained linguistic competence. What minimalism is studying is the gap between the third factor noted above (nonspecifically linguistic principles and operations) and the first factor (what UG needs that is not already supplied by the third factor principles). The short evolutionary timescale, Chomsky (2005, p. 3) suggests, implicates a substantial role for principles of the third kind (as do Fodor's [1998] speculations noted above). The inchoate proposal in (1) is that this problem is fruitfully studied by taking the generalizations unearthed by GB (and its cognates; cf. note 10) as the targets of explanation (i.e., by treating GB as an effective theory).

Before moving on, we would like to emphasize one more point.[15] As conceived here, the minimalist program is clearly continuous with its GB predecessor in roughly the way that Darwin's problem rounds out Plato's. GB "solves" Plato's problem in the domain of language by postulating a rich, highly articulated, linguistically specific set of innate principles. If successful, it explains how it is that children are able to acquire their native languages despite the poverty of the linguistic input.[16] This kind of answer clearly presupposes that the sorts of mechanisms that GB proposes could have developed in humans. One source of skepticism regarding the generative enterprise is that the structures that UG requires if something like GB is correct could simply not have arisen by standard evolutionary means (e.g., by natural selection, given the short time period involved). But if it could not have arisen, then clearly human linguistic facility cannot be explained by invoking such mechanisms. Minimalism takes this concern to heart. It supposes that FL could arise in humans either by the shaping effects of experience (i.e., through natural selection) or as a by-product of something else, for example, the addition of new mechanisms to those already extant. For natural selection to operate, considerable amount of time is required. As it appears that FL emerged recently and rapidly as measured in evolutionary time, the first possibility seems to be ruled out. This leaves the "by-product" hypothesis. But a by-product of what? The short timescale suggests that the linguistic specificity of FL as envisaged by GB must be a mirage. FL must be the combination of operations and principles scavenged from cognition and computation in general *with possibly small adventitious additions*. In other words, despite appearances, FL is "almost" the application of general cognitive mechanisms to the problem of language. The *almost* signals the one or two innovations that the 50,000- to 100,000-year time frame permits. The minimalist hypothesis is that FL is what one gets after adding just a little bit, a new circuit or two, to general principles of cognition and computation. If this is "all" that is distinctive about FL, it explains how FL could have rapidly emerged in the species (at least in embryonic form) without the shaping effects of natural selection. The minimalist project is to flesh this picture out in more concrete terms.[17]

5.3. Two More Specific Minimalist Research Projects

To advance this theoretical goal, two kinds of projects are germane. The first adopts a reductive strategy, the goal being to reduce the internal modularity of UG by reducing apparently different phenomena to the same operations. This continues the earlier GB efforts of eliminating "constructions" as grammatical primitives by factoring them into their more primitive component parts (as Chomsky, 1993, advocated). Two examples will illustrate the intent.

An important example of reduction is Chomsky's (1977) proposal in *On Wh Movement*. Here, Chomsky proposes unifying the various kinds of constructions that display island effects by factoring out a common movement operation involved in each. In particular, Wh-movement, Topicalization, focus movement, tough constructions, comparative formation, and Relativization, all display island effects in virtue of involving Wh- (or later, A'-) movement subject to subjacency. What heretofore were treated as different kinds of constructions are henceforth analyzed as involving a common core operation (Wh/A'-movement) subject to a common condition (subjacency). The island effects the disparate constructions display are traced to their all having Wh/A'-movement as a key common component. In other words, sensitivity to island conditions is a property of a particular construction in virtue of having Wh/A'-movement as a subpart.

The reduction of island-sensitive constructions to those involving Wh/A'-movement as subpart does not (and was not taken to) imply that, for example, Topicalization and Relativization are *identical* constructions. Their distinctive features were and are obvious. However, despite their differences, because all these constructions use the same basic Wh/A'-movement operation, they will all be subject to the subjacency condition and so display island effects when this condition is violated. Thus, the island characteristics of these various constructions are explained by analyzing each as involving a common building block, the operation of Wh/A'-movement. Why do topicalization and relativization and question formation, etc., all obey island conditions? Because whatever their other differences, they all involve the operation of Wh/A'-movement and Wh/A'movement is subject to subjacency.[18]

A second example of this kind of reductive reasoning is pursued in Hornstein (1999, 2001) and Boeckx and Hornstein (2003, 2004, 2006). It attempts to reduce obligatory control and principle A to conditions on movement. More generally, the proposal is that all feature checking occurs under Merge, that Move involves an instance of Merge (viz., it is the complex of Copy and Merge), and that merging into multiple thematic positions via Move is possible. This has the effect of reducing oblig-atory control and principle A to the theory of movement (along with case theory, as first proposed in Chomsky, 1993) which, in turn, reduces the modularity of UG by reducing case, theta, and antecedence relations to those constructible via licit applications of Merge and Move. This can be construed as a version of the Chomsky (1977) program of reduction, but this time applied to the A-domain. Just as Topi-calization and Relativization involve the common operation of A'-movement (despite being different in many other ways), Control and Reflexivization (and Passive and Raising) involve the common feature of A-movement (despite being different in many other ways). What distinguishes Control from Raising (and Passive) on this concep-tion is not the primitive operations involved (they are identical in both cases), but the number of times A-movement (Internal-Merge) applies and the feature-checking positions through which elements are moved (e.g., Control and Reflexivization tran-sit through theta positions, unlike Raising and Passive). As in the case of Chomsky's (1977) thesis, this kind of reduction has explanatory virtues: Why are PRO and reflexives c-commanded by their antecedents? Because they are tails of chains formed by movement and the head of a chain always c-commands its tail. Why must reflexives and (obligatory controlled) PROs be locally licensed by their antecedents? Because they are residues of A-movement and thus only exist if something (viz., the antecedent) has moved from there in the way typical of A-movement (e.g., obeying minimality and least effort). Why does the controller typically obey Rosenbaum's (1970) Principle of Minimal Distance (PMD)? Because the control is an instance of movement, movement is subject to (relativized) minimality, and so the PMD is actually just an instance of this well-known constraint on movement.

Though reduction, if possible, is *always* methodologically favored because it enhances explanation, in the present context, it has one additional benefit. If achiev-able, it has the interesting consequence (interesting, given considerations mooted in section 5.2 above) of reducing the modularity characteristic of GB theories of UG. Binding, Control, Case checking, and theta role assignment result from the same basic operations subject to the same conditions. What differs are the features checked. Thus, though grammars check many different kinds of features, they do so using the same basic machinery, the operations Merge and Move, subject to mini-mality. Thus, for example, case features and theta features are checked by merging (via A-movement) near case and theta assigning heads, and Relativization, Topicalization, etc., by merging near Topic and Relative C^0 heads (via A′-movement). If this line of analysis is correct, then underlying the complexities of the many diverse linguistic relations sit two operations (viz., Merge and Move) and the conditions that they are subject to (e.g., minimality and something like subjacency).[19]

Given this line of thought, reduction has two alluring properties if successful: It increases explanatory power, and it simplifies the structure of FL. As the latter is a precondition for addressing the evolutionary question of how FL might have arisen in such a relatively short time, it contributes to the program schematized in (1) above. However, though reduction is a required first step, it is still only a first step. The next step is to factor out those features of FL that are irreducibly linguistic from those operations and principles recruited by FL from other cognitive domains. This constitutes a second minimalist project.

Consider an example from Hornstein (in press). Take the basic operation, Merge. It is normally taken to operate as follows: It takes two constituents as input, and combines them to form a novel constituent labeled by one of the inputs. Thus, a V can combine with a D to form an object labeled by the V: $\{V,D\}$.[20] Merge is subject to certain conditions. It is binary, it is subject to the Extension condition, and its product has only one label. One can reasonably ask whether this operation is "atomic," whether it is a primitive operation of FL or an instance of a more general cognitive operation, why it merges at most two constituents and not more, why it obeys the Extension condition, why only one constituent labels the output, why the merge involves labeling at all, what a constituent is, how it is different from Move, and so on.

All of these are reasonable questions, some of which have putative answers. For example, it is reasonable to suppose that an operation like Merge, one that "puts two elements together" (by joining them or concatenating them or comprehending them in a common set), is not an operation unique to FL. It is a general cognitive operation, which, when applied to linguistic objects, we dub "Merge." The Extension condition, which applies to all structure-building operations in grammar, is also plausibly a reflection of computational considerations that apply beyond the linguistic case. It has the property of preserving the structural properties of the inputs in the output. This is a "nice" property for a computational system to have because it avoids the revision (tampering with the properties) of previously computed information. Computations progressively add information. They never delete any. As grammars are computational systems (plausibly well-designed ones), we would expect them, if well designed, to have something like a montonic condition on structure building, like this one. Note that this reasoning explains why a computational operation like Merge obeys a condition like Extension. Extension is the linguistic expression of the *more general computational desideratum* of no tampering and as such is not specific to FL.

What of labeling? This is less obviously what we expect of computational operations. The labeling we see in FL leads to endocentric phrases (phrases that are headed
by a specific element). There is a lot of evidence to suggest that phrases in natural
languages are endocentric. Hence, it is empirically reasonable to build this into the
Merge operation that forms constituents by requiring that one of the inputs provide
a label. However, there is little evidence that this kind of endocentric hierarchical
structure is available outside FL. Nor is it obviously of computational benefit to have
endocentric labeling, for if it were we would expect to find it in other cognitive systems (which we don't). This suggests that endocentric labeling is a feature of Merge,
which is FL specific.[21]

We can keep on in this way until all the properties of Merge have been surveyed.
However, the point here is not to analyze Merge's various properties, but to illustrate
what it *could* mean to distinguish first factor from third factor features, those specific
to language and those part of the FL, though characteristic of biological and/or computational systems more generally. Recall, that in the best possible case, the truly
distinctive features of FL are small in number (one or two) and the rest of its properties are actually reflections of language-independent features of cognition and/or
computation. This is what we expect from a system that has only recently emerged.

Given (1), the project of finding the linguistically specific properties of FL is
bounded on the input side by the operations and principles available to FL/UG that
are not specific to language. It is bounded on the output side by the requirement
that the (small number of) linguistically specific primitives together with the previously available mechanisms derive the generalizations of GB. This project thus gains
teeth when considering the features of GB. If the project sketched in (1) is to be realized, then many apparently language-specific relations and operations will have to be
exposed as special instances of third factor features. This is no small task, given the
many grammatical notions (critical to the GB version of UG and many minimalist
accounts) that seem proprietary to language. Consider some examples.

In addition to Merge, which locally relates two expressions, Move is an operation that relates linguistic elements at a distance. A third operation is AGREE, which
can relate linguistic expressions without "displacement" (e.g., agreement in existential constructions in English). Then there is binding, which allows two nonadjacent
expressions to interact. Move, Bind, and AGREE relations are ubiquitous in language
but have no apparent analogues in other cognitive domains. In addition, there is
a plethora of relations like c-command, constituency, heads, maximal projections,
etc., that also seem unique to language. These notions critically exploit the specific
hierarchical structure characteristic of linguistic expressions and have no obvious
analogues in other domains. Are these all primitives of FL or are they the outward
manifestations in the domain of language of more general features of cognition?
The logic of Darwin's problem suggests the latter. The program is to show how this
could be so.

One way of approaching this task is via questions like the following. What is the relation between Merge, Move, and AGREE? There exist proposals that not all of these operations are primitive. Chomsky (2004) has proposed that Move is actually a species of Merge (Remerge). An earlier proposal of Chomsky's is that Move is the composite of two other operations, Copy and Merge. As for AGREE, in GB nonproximate agreement was an indication of covert Move. More contemporary accounts eliminate covert operations and substitute (long distance) AGREE. Are either Copy or (long distance) AGREE language specific? If not, then they are part of the background operations that were exploited to form FL. If so, they are first factor primitives whose emergence needs explanation. Here are other relevant questions: Why does movement target constituents? Why does it obey Structure Preservation? Why are anaphors generally c-commanded by their antecedents? Why do moved elements generally c-command their launch sites? Why are sentences hierarchically structured? And so on. GB has provided us with a rich description of what sorts of properties FL has. The minimalist program aims to understand why it has these properties and not others. We answer these questions by showing how these facts about grammatical processes could have rapidly emerged from the combination principles and operations not specific to language, and one or two innovations (preferably one) specific for language. Borrowing from Chomsky (1965), we can say that GB is (roughly) descriptively adequate in that it (more or less) correctly describes the laws of FL.[22] We can say that a minimalist hypothesis is explanatorily adequate if it explains how these laws could have emerged rapidly (i.e., by showing how a small addition specific to language combines with general cognitive principles to yield these laws).[23]

The two minimalist projects limned above clearly go hand in hand. Solving Darwin's problem will require reducing the internal modularity of FL by showing how the effects of a modular system arise from the interaction of a common set of operations and principles. This, then, sets up the second question regarding the source of these operations and principles. It is hoped that most are expressions of operations and principles characteristic of cognition and computation more generally. The minimalist bet is that these kinds of theoretical projects can be fruitfully pursued.

5.4. Minimalism and the Galilean Method

Chomsky (2007, p. 4) characterizes the shift in perspective brought on by minimalist concerns as follows:

> Throughout the modern history of generative grammar, the problem of determining the character of FL has been approached "from top down": How much must be attributed to UG to account for language acquisition? The M[inimalist] P[rogram] seeks to approach the problem "from bottom up": How little can be attributed to UG while still accounting for the variety of I-languages attained.

This view, he notes, prompts a particular style of investigation:

> [to] show that the [richly documented] complexity and variety [in language] are only apparent, and that the . . . kinds of rules can be reduced to a simpler form. A "perfect" [optimal] solution . . . would be to eliminate [those rules] entirely in favor of the irreducible operation that takes two objects already formed and attaches one to the other . . . , the operation we call *MERGE* [the simplest, smallest conceivable linguistic process].
>
> (Chomsky, 2001, p. 13)

This methodology, which is often characterized as "Galilean," has been extensively pursued in the domain of syntax in recent years (much more so than in other domains of grammar, perhaps for principled reasons of the kind explored by Bromberger & Halle, 1989). We would like to end this chapter by pointing to some of the more "Galilean" aspects of the enterprise as the minimalist style of research has been influenced by this more general methodological perspective.

Weinberg (1976) defines Galilean methodology thus:

> . . . we have all been making abstract mathematical models of the universe to which at least the physicists [read: scientists—CB/NH] give a higher degree of reality than they accord the ordinary world of sensation.

The Galilean program is guided by the ontological principle that "nature is perfect and simple, and creates nothing in vain," that nature "always complies with the easiest and simplest rules," and that "nature . . . does not that by many things, which may be done by few." (See, e.g., Galilei, 1962[1632], pp. 99, 397.)

In syntax, the task, then, to paraphrase Galileo, language always complies with the easiest and simplest rules, it employs only the least elaborate, the simplest, and easiest of means.

Although Galilean themes resonate with Chomsky's earliest writings (see Boeckx, 2006; Freidin & Vergnaud, 2001), such themes could not be systematically investigated before the 1990s because there was a more pressing goal: understanding how the child acquires the language of his or her environment, given the poverty of stimulus. It was only after the Principles-and-Parameters approach was found adequate in solving Plato's problem, in separating the universal from the language specific, and the principles from the parameters, that the shape of principles, the deeper *why* questions could begin to be asked.

It seems to us that the minimalist program and the logic of Darwin's problem fits well with a Galilean approach to the study of I-Universals.

5.5. Conclusion

This minimalist way of thinking has several interesting consequences. Here are two:

First, if correct, then some of the key principles of the language faculty may not be encoded in the genome. They may be what Chomsky (2005) calls third factor principles—principles of good design that transcend biology and open the door for nongenomic conception of nativism.

Second, if principles of good design are operative in FL, as the minimalist perspective suggests, then we shouldn't expect such principles to be subject to crosslinguistic variation. That is, minimalism leads to the claim that there can be no parameters within the statements of the general principles that shape natural language syntax, contrary to the vision of UG at the heart of Principles and Parameters theories, like GB (see Boeckx, 2008; Hornstein, in press). We believe that this conclusion is a natural consequence of the claim at the heart of the generative/biolinguistic enterprise that there is only language, Human, and that this organ/faculty emerged very recently in the species, too recently for multiple solutions to design specifications to have been explored.

In other words, whereas parameterized principles/universals made a lot of sense in the context of Plato's problem (GB-era), they make much less sense from the perspective of Darwin's problem.

To conclude, integrating the logic of Darwin's problem into the study of FL and I-Universals has already proven quite fecund in our view. It has raised new questions, suggested new analyses and grammatical mechanisms, and has led investigators to analyze the structure of UG and the source of I-Universals in new ways. Looking for answers to both Plato's problem and Darwin's problem in tandem has led to an approach to linguistic universals that may not only be internalist, intensional, and individual but also, perhaps for the first time, implementable in biological terms.

Key Further Readings

As in all previous stages of the generative enterprise, Chomsky's writings are required readings to understand the nature of minimalism. Chomsky's most recent essays have yet to be put together in book form (as were the early essays collected in Chomsky, 1995) and, as such, they remain to be streamlines, content-wise, but each one of them is indispensable. If we had to single one out, we would recommend Chomsky, 2004 (*Beyond explanatory adequacy*), to be read in conjunction with the less technical Chomsky, 2005 (*Three factors in language design*). In addition to Chomsky's works, readers can find overviews of linguistic minimalism ranging from the more philosophical (Boeckx, 2006; Uriagereka, 1998) to the more technical (Hornstein,

Nunes, & Grohmann, 2006; Lasnik, Uriagereka, & Boeckx, 2005), as well as a very useful anthology of minimalist studies in Boskovic and Lasnik (2007).

Notes

1   On the issue of uniqueness, see Hauser, Chomsky, and Fitch (2002), especially their notion of Faculty of Language in the Narrow Sense.

2   See Jackendoff (1994) for an excellent discussion concerning the open-ended diversity of linguistic patterns in natural languages.

3   This too is a rather trivial claim in its general form: *if* UG bridges the gap between PLD and S_S, then it cannot be features of the PLD that serve to bridge the gap. It must be some biologically given feature of humans that serves to bridge the gap. This is a truism. What may be contentious is whether some identified property outruns the reach of the PLD. In our opinion, the standard examples suffice to demonstrate that such "poverty of the stimulus" situations arise quite regularly and, hence, some "innate" features of humans are required to go from PLD to S_S. See Boeckx and Hornstein (2007) for further discussion.

4   This is consistent with the fact that comparative grammatical research, involving the comparison of properties of many languages, has yielded considerable insight into UG.

5   See Chomsky (2005, 2007).

6   On the parallelism between the two problems, see Boeckx (in press) and Hornstein (in press).

7   This clearly echoes the program outlined in Hauser et al., (2002).

8   The assumption that complexity requires natural selection is a standard assumption. For example, Cosmides and Tooby (1992), Dawkins (1996), Pinker (1997), and Pinker and Jackendoff (chapter 7). Dawkins's words serve to illustrate the general position:

> whenever in nature there is a sufficiently powerful illusion of good design for some purpose, natural selection is the only known mechanism that can account for it.
>
> (p. 202)

9   Fodor (2000) might not accept this inference, as he takes the program in linguistics to only be interested in knowledge, not mental mechanisms. We are inclined to think that Fodor is incorrect in his characterization of Chomsky's position. However, what is relevant here is that grammars are here construed as interested in the mechanics of linguistic mentation. The inventory of rules and principles describe real mechanisms of the mind/brain.

10   The generalizations characteristic of GB have analogues in other generative frameworks such as LFG, GPSG, Tag Grammars, Relational Grammar, etc. In fact, we consider it likely that these "frameworks" are notational variants of one another. See Stabler (chapter 10, this volume; 2007) for some discussion of the intertranslatability of many of these alternatives.

11   There is a term in the physical sciences for the status we propose for GB. The roughly correct theory whose properties are targets for explanation is called an "effective theory." Being an effective theory is already a mark of distinction, for to be one, a theory must have good empirical credentials. However, the term also implies that the structural properties of

an effective theory need further elucidation and which will come from being subsumed in a more general account. As such, treating GB (and its analogues; cf. note 10) as an effective theory is to at once praise its accomplishments and ask for more theoretical refinement.

12 Fodor (1998) characterizes a module as follows:

> A module is a more or less autonomous,
> special purpose, computational system. It's built to solve a very restricted
> set of problems, and the information it can use to solve them with is proprietary.

This is a good characterization of GB modules. They are autonomous (e.g., to compute case assignment, one can ignore theta roles, and similarly licensing binding relations can ignore case and theta properties) and special purpose (e.g., case versus theta versus binding). The problems each addresses are very restricted, and the concepts proprietary (e.g., binding, control).

13 As Embick and Poeppel (2005) observe, this is a serious problem for those aiming to find brain correlates for the primitives of FL (see also Müller, chapter 11). They dub this the granularity problem. They propose that one aim of linguistics and neuroscience should be to solve this problem by finding a level that can serve to relate the basic conceptions of each. Their concrete proposal is that an appropriate level of abstraction is the "circuit." Circuits are brain structures that compute simple operations. The aim is to find those primitive operations that are at once empirically grounded and that could be embodied in neural wetware. Given this, the goal for the minimalist will be to find a class of very basic primitive operations that plausibly underlie linguistic computations for consideration as candidates for possible neural circuits.

14 These analogies between learning and evolution have long been recognized. For an early discussion in the context of generative grammar, see Chomsky (1959). As Chomsky's review makes clear, the analogy between learning and evolution was recognized by Skinner and was a central motivation for his psychological conceptions.

15 This addition owes a lot to discussions with Paul Pietroski.

16 As the reader no doubt knows, this overstates the case. Principles and Parameters accounts like GB have not yet accounted for how children acquire language. The problem of how parameters are set, for example, is very difficult and as yet unresolved. For further discussion, see Boeckx (2008) and Hornstein (in press).

17 This way of stating matters does not settle what the mechanism of evolution is. It is compatible with this view that natural selection operated to "select" the one or two innovations that underlie FL. It is also compatible with the position that the distinctive features of FL were not selected for but simply arose (say, by random mutation, or as by-products of brain growth). This is not outlandish if what we are talking about is the emergence of one new circuit rather than a highly structured internally modular FL. Of course, once it "emerged," the enormous utility of FL would insure its preservation through natural selection.

18 It is worth observing that Chomsky (1977) also tries to reanalyze deletion rules like Comparative Deletion in terms of Wh/A'-movement. In effect, Chomsky argues that deletion rules that show island-like properties should be reduced to movement. This reduction serves

to explain *why* such rules obey island conditions, the latter being a property of this operation by eliminating a redundancy in the theory of UG (see Chomsky, 1977, p. 89).

19 If Move is actually an instance of Merge as proposed in Chomsky (2004), or the combination of Copy and Merge as proposed in (Chomsky, 1995), then we can reduce grammatical relations to various applications of Merge and feature checking.

20 Underlining identifies the expression that names the output. Labeling amounts to identifying one of the two merging elements. It is not an operation that need "write" the name of one of the two expressions as a label. For our purposes, it is equivalent to {X, {X,Y}} in current notation.

21 There is some evidence to suggest that endocentricity facilitates language learning. See de Marcken (1996).

22 The analogy to Chomsky (1965) is deliberate, but may be confusing unless the reader recalls that the locus of explanation has enlarged to include Darwin's problem so that an explanatorily adequate account cannot rest with simply providing an answer to Plato's problem.

23 We would be inclined to go further and incorporate Embick and Poeppel's proposal that an explanatorily adequate account provide a solution for the granularity problem as well.

References

Boeckx, C. (2006). *Linguistic minimalism: Origins, concepts, methods, and aims.* Oxford: Oxford University Press.

Boeckx, C. (2008). Approaching parameters from below. Ms., Harvard University. To appear in A.-M. di Sciullo & C. Boeckx (Eds.), *Biolinguistics: Language evolution and variation.* Oxford: Oxford University Press.

Boeckx, C. (in press). The nature of merge: Consequences for language, mind, and biology. In M. Piatelli-Palmarini, J. Uriagereka, & P. Salaburu (Eds.), *Of minds and language—The Basque country encounter with Noam Chomsky.* Oxford: Oxford University Press.

Boeckx, C., & Hornstein, N. (2003). Reply to "Control is not movement." *Linguistic Inquiry, 34,* 269–280.

Boeckx, C., & Hornstein, N. (2004). Movement under control. *Linguistic Inquiry, 35,* 431–452.

Boeckx, C., & Hornstein, N. (2006). Raising and control. *Syntax, 9,* 118–130.

Boeckx, C., & Hornstein, N. (2007). Les differents objectifs de la linguistique theorique [The varying aims of linguistic theory]. In J. Franck & J. Bricmont (Eds.), *Cahier Chomsky* (pp. 61–77). Paris: L'Herne.

Boskovic, Z., & Lasnik, H. (2007). *Minimalist syntax: The essential readings.* Oxford: Blackwell.

Bromberger, S., & Halle, M. (1989). Why phonology is different. *Linguistic Inquiry, 20,* 51–70.

Chomsky, N. (1959). Review of B. F. Skinner "Verbal behavior." *Language, 35,* 26–58.

Chomsky, N. (1965). *Aspects of the theory of syntax.* Cambridge, MA: MIT Press.

Chomsky, N. (1977). On Wh-movement. In P. W. Culicover, T. Wasow, & A. Akmajian (Eds.), *Formal syntax* (pp. 71–132). New York: Academic Press.

Chomsky, N. (1986). *Knowledge of language: Its nature, origin, and use*. New York: Praeger.

Chomsky, N. (1993). A minimalist program for linguistic theory. In K. Hale & S. J. Keyser (Eds.), *The view from Building 20: Essays in linguistics in honor of Sylvain Bromberger* (pp. 1–52). Cambridge, MA: MIT Press.

Chomsky, N. (1995). *The minimalist program*. Cambridge, MA: MIT Press.

Chomsky, N. (2001). Derivation by phase. In M. Kenstowicz (Ed.), *Ken Hale: A life in language* (pp. 1–52). Cambridge, MA: MIT Press.

Chomsky, N. (2004). Beyond explanatory adequacy. In A. Belletti (Ed.), *Structures and beyond: The cartography of syntactic structures* (pp. 104–131). Oxford: Oxford University Press.

Chomsky, N. (2005). Three factors in language design. *Linguistic Inquiry, 36*, 1–22.

Chomsky, N. (2007). Approaching UG from below. In U. Sauerland & M. Gaertner (Eds.), *Interfaces + Recursion = Language? Chomsky's minimalism and the view from syntax-semantics* (pp. 1–30). Mouton: de Gruyter.

Cosmides, L., & Tooby, J. (1992). Cognitive adaptations for social exchange. In J. Barkow, L. Cosmides, & J. Tooby (Eds.), *The adapted mind: Evolutionary psychology and the generation of culture*. Oxford: Oxford University Press.

Dawkins, R. (1996). *Climbing mount improbable*. Oxford: Oxford University Press.

Diamond, J. (1992). *The third chimpanzee*. New York: Harper.

Embick, D., & Poeppel, D. (2005). Mapping syntax using imaging: Prospects and problems for the study of neurolinguistic computation. In K. Brown (Ed.), *Encyclopedia of language and linguistics* (2nd ed.). Oxford: Elsevier.

Fodor, J. A. (1998). *In critical condition: Polemical essays on cognitive science and the philosophy of mind*. Cambridge, MA: MIT Press.

Fodor, J. A. (2000). *The mind doesn't work that way: The scope and limits of computational psychology*. Cambridge, MA: MIT Press.

Freidin, R., & Vergnaud, J.-R. (2001). Exquisite connections: Some remarks on the evolution of linguistic theory. *Lingua, 111*, 639–666.

Galilei, G. (1962[1632]). *Dialogue concerning the two chief world systems*. Berkeley: University of California Press.

Hauser, M. D., Chomsky, N., & Fitch, W. T. (2002). The faculty of language: What is it, who has it, and how did it evolve? *Science, 298*, 1569–1579.

Hornstein, N. (1999). Movement and control. *Linguistic Inquiry, 30*, 69–96.

Hornstein, N. (2001). *Move! A minimalist theory of construal*. Oxford: Blackwell.

Hornstein, N. (in press). *A theory of syntax*. Cambridge: Cambridge University Press.

Hornstein, N., Nunes, J., & Grohmann, K. K. (2006). *Understanding minimalism*. Cambridge: Cambridge University Press.

Jackendoff, R. (1994). *Patterns in the mind*. New York: Basic Books.

Lasnik, H., Uriagereka, J., & Boeckx, C. (2005). *A course in minimalist syntax*. Oxford: Blackwell.

de Marcken, C. (1996). *Unsupervised language acquisition*. Unpublished PhD thesis, MIT, Cambridge.

Petitto, L.-A. (2005). How the brain begets language. In J. McGilvray (Ed.), *The Cambridge companion to Chomsky* (pp. 84–101). Cambridge: Cambridge University Press.

Pinker, S. (1997). *How the mind works*. New York, NY: W. W. Norton & Company.

Rosenbaum, P. (1970). A principle governing deletion in English sentential complementation. In R. Jacobs & P. Rosenbaum (Eds.), *Readings in English transformational grammar* (pp. 20–29). Waltham, MA: Ginn.

Stabler, E. (2007). *Language structure, depth, and processing.* Paper presented at Mayfest 2007, College Park: University of Maryland.

Uriagereka, J. (1998). *Rhyme and reason.* Cambridge, MA: MIT Press.

Weinberg, S. (1976). The forces of nature. *Bulletin of the American Academy of Arts and Sciences,* *29*(4), 13–29.

6

MINIMALIST BEHAVIORISM: THE ROLE OF THE INDIVIDUAL IN EXPLAINING LANGUAGE UNIVERSALS

THOMAS G. BEVER

6.1. Background—The Evolution of Grammars

Since the late 1950s, it has been accepted that many universal properties of attested languages are due to behavioral constraints on language performance: these included the boundedness of sentence and word length, the limits on the number of words in the lexicon, restrictions on the amount of ambiguity in sentences, and so on. Excluding such performance-based universals isolates the computational processes involved in describing linguistic knowledge. The early phases of transformational syntax focused on a computational model of that knowledge. This model posited several enduring ideas about the computational basis for language:

(1)   a. Sentences involve derivations, from primitive/partial structures to surface forms.
        b. Syntactic operations are cyclic, that is, recursive, applying successively to their own output.

This set the role of behavioral theory and research within the Language Sciences. Initially, the question was about "the psychological reality of linguistic structures." That is, did the computational model involving transformations and derivations correctly describe what speakers deploy when they use language, not just descriptively, but in terms of the actual computational operations? This question dominated the first phase of modern psycholinguistics, led by George Miller and his students (Miller, 1962). Indeed it appeared initially that the transformational/derivational model was psychologically valid, sentences with more transformations are harder to process, sentences with shared underlying structures are perceived as related, and so on.

This initial success was overtaken by a rapid evolution of syntactic theory both with respect to its technical operations, and its related ontology. The major settled stages of generative syntactic theory between 1955–1970 and 1980–1990 were

(2)   a. Specific phrase structure generates underlying structures: many specific movement rules correspond to construction types (e.g., "passive, raising, question," etc.). Derivations are "guaranteed" to be correct by virtue of the application of the sets of rules.

       b. 1980–90: X-bar theoretic phrase structure is projected from lexical categories. Movement occurs where it can or is required by filtering constraints on derivations ("case theory," "binding principles." . . .). A set of parameters describe a small set of options how these filters and processes operate: each language has its own setting on each of these parameters).

At a technical level, derivations became less specific, less dependent on being triggered by specific structural indices, and more automatic; the corresponding ontological shift was from viewing syntax as describing the language that people know to describing the internal processes that result in language (for recent reviews of the development of generative syntax, see Boeckx, 2006; Chomsky, 2004; Freidin & Vergnaud, 2001; Hornstein & Boeckx, Chapter 5; Hornstein, Nunes, & Grohman, 2005; Lasnik, 2003; Martin & Uriagereka, 2000; Townsend & Bever, 2001, Chapter 3; Vergnaud, 1985).

The—perhaps ultimate—development in the trend to simplify syntactic theory is today's "minimalist program." This approach explicitly gives up the claim to be a particular theory of knowledge or processes of any kind. Rather, it is a framework for isolating the minimally required processes that could result in language. The approach takes as a boundary condition on possible languages the principle that language is an interface between humans' conceptual organization and motor systems. This idea was presaged in the early stages of generative grammar; for example, Miller and Chomsky (1963) noted that the existence of transformations and constraints on them that preserve recoverability of their source structures followed from the fact that language maps complex propositional structures onto a linear sequence. Today's minimalist program makes this feature of language the central constraint. The goal, then, is to discern the essential operations that meet that constraint as perfectly as possible (Chomsky, 1995, 2005; Lasnik, 2003).

This has started a renamed, if not totally new, kind of approach to the study of language universals, "biolinguistics." In this enterprise, the attempt is to show how a small number of minimally required processes can account for the essential computational operations in language. This is the focus of the "faculty of language." All other properties of attested languages are to be interpreted as functions of biological, psychological, or even social constraints (Hauser, Chomsky, & Fitch, 2002).

The main operation is cyclic "merge" of trees to form constituent hierarchies and derivations: if the head of a phrase is the same kind of constituent as the daughter of another phrase, the head can be merged with the daughter to form a more complex phrase. The process is cyclic in the sense that trees are constructed by iteration of the merge process from the most to least embedded phrase of a derivation. The process is recursive in the sense that it is possible for the daughter of one phrase to be the head of another. It is striking that these major computational features of the faculty of language now proposed within the minimalist program are essentially those in (1) above, except for X-bar theory, which is now itself rendered by cyclic merge. But the basic notion of cyclic operations has been the enduring properties of every variant of generative syntax for 50 years.

The simplification of grammatical processes has heightened the puzzle of language acquisition and its potential genetic basis. Traditional learning theory— essentially induction—cannot account for the discovery of most abstract features involved in sentence derivations. A new theory of learning is needed, and the default is "parameter setting"; that is, the child has a set of innate language-constraining parameters, and simply needs to pick up enough data from the environment to trigger one or another setting of each parameter (Fodor, 2001; Fodor & Sakas, 2004; Pinker, 1984; Yang, 2002).

How is the role of psychology in the explanation of linguistic universals changed by the developments within linguistic theory? In particular, has "biolinguistics" gone past "psycholinguistics," explaining everything of interest about language as a function of a few biological constraints and boundary conditions on the faculty of language, along with innate parameters that facilitate learning? If it has not yet done so, could it ever do so?

In what follows, I suggest that the answer to both questions is no. Formal approaches to explaining universals via abstracted biological constraints on the function of language, or by examining the data required to set parameters in an ideal learner, are limited to clarifying the boundary conditions on individuals learning and using language. Yet it is a collection of individuals that learn and use language, and we can profit by examining how they do this. The extent to which they do so by way of mechanisms not specific to language clarifies what we need to keep looking for as the essential universals of language.

6.2. Some Kinds of Psychological Constraints on Language Universals

We can distinguish three categories of language universals that may have explanations outside of the faculty of language:

(3)   a.   Constraints from language use;
            b.   Constraints from language acquisition;
            c.   Constraints from the neurological substrate.

6.2.1. Constraints from Language Use

Historically, many constraints on attested language universals have been based on models of sentence comprehension. An early classic instance of this was Chomsky and Miller's (1963) discussion of center embedding in English: they noted that one choice was to include a "recursion counter" as part of syntactic theory, limited to two in the case of center embeddings, but with no limit for right (or left) branching recursions. This would have increased the options available to grammars in many undesirable and unutilized ways. So the preferred alternative interpretation was that a center-embedded sentence is hard to understand because it requires extra processing memory to compute the output of an operation on an item that is itself incompletely computed by the same operation. Although I think this analysis is not entirely correct, it exemplifies several principles at work together in deciding if a universal, U_i, should be attributed to syntax or some other source.

(4)   a. U_i would require an otherwise unmotivated computational process, that is, the ability to count recursions.
            b. U_i can be explained as a special case of a process, motivated by some extralinguistic structure system.

General ideas on how comprehension works have been alleged to account for a number of syntactic universals and constraints. A simple example is heavy XP shifts, in which there is preference (sometimes a requirement) that a complex argument phrase be moved from its base (or semantically local) position to a position toward the end of a sentence.

(5)   a.   That Bill is in charge is likely → it is likely that Bill is in charge.
(5)   b.   For Bill to be in charge is likely—(it) is likely for Bill to be in charge → Bill is likely to be in charge.

In these cases, there is a clear preference (for some speakers, a requirement) that the complex phrase be placed at the end of the sentence. This exemplifies a simple principle, "save the hardest for the last" (Bever, 1970), on the assumption that phrase tree structures are assigned as part of comprehending a sentence. If a complex subtree appears first, it must be held in memory, while assigning a later simpler subtree, until the entire sentence tree structure is computed. But if the complex tree appears at the end of the sentence, its structure can be assigned as part of completing the entire sentence structure, and hence does not have to be held in memory. This constraint explains a number of cases of preferred, and sometimes required, constructions.

Hawkins, in Chapter 4 has argued that heavy phrase shifts actually vary according to the head/modifier order characteristic of each language: English is head initial, with a basic pattern of "head + modifier." But Japanese is a head final language with the opposite order; and Hawkins notes, Japanese constructions are often preferred with complex phrases prior to simpler ones. If true, this may show that the original "save the hardest for the last" principle is not based on the surface seriality of sentence input: rather, it is sensitive to the sequence of steps in phrase assignment, in which the head is first posited, and then modifiers are attached to it. Hawkins proposes a more general constraint on head–modifier distance to explain the facts. Which view is correct awaits further research. But both views share the concept that the order constraint follows from aspects of how sentences are processed in comprehension.

I will not spend further time here on such well-explored examples of how surface processes can constrain sentence constructions. Interested readers can consult Bever (1970), Bever and Langendoen (1971), and Bever, Carroll, and Hurtig (1976) for early examples of such ideas, and Hawkins (Chapter 4) for other instances. The basic moral is that sentence constructions that cannot be understood, or are hard to understand because of constraints on a serial comprehension process, will not be learned. In some cases, such as center-embedded sentences, this may block certain instances of otherwise grammatical sentences. In other cases, such constraints may be argued to limit the possibility of certain kinds of syntactic operations. This leads us to consider models of how sentence comprehension actually works.

6.2.2. The Integration of Associations and Rules in Sentence Comprehension

Current researchers on language comprehension generally start with one of two powerful and appealing ideas:

(6)   a. Meaning is extracted via associatively learned patterns;
(6)   b. Meaning is extracted from syntactic structures.

The associationist view dominated psycholinguistics (such as it was) for many years, until the cognitive revolution of the 1960s: it has been given new life in the form of computationally enriched connectionism (old fashioned associationism, plus various schemes for multilevel training, yielding a computationally tractable mediation SR theory—at least more tractable than the earlier ideas of Clark Hull, Charles Osgood, and colleagues). The idea is roughly that insofar as syntactic structures play a role in comprehension, they do so via the application of learned pattern templates. Problems with this view abound and are well understood. Major ones include the proper domain problem (what is the proper domain of an associative template?), proper organization of templates (how are overlapping and competitive templates organized?), and the recursive nature of syntactic structures (see the articles in Pinker & Mehler, 1988; also Steedman, Chapter 9). Nonetheless, although connectionist models are not adequate for the structure of language, they do capture an important property of behavior in ways more sophisticated than prior implementations of associationism—that is, that much of behavior depends on habits.

Realization of the importance of syntactic structures underlies many variants of syntax-first models of comprehension: on these models, syntax is assigned (somehow), and then meaning, context, knowledge, and other modalities of information are integrated with the assigned syntactic structure. These models characteristically give no initial causal role to statistical information, including eccentricities in the frequency of particular syntactic structures. Rather, syntax is first assigned based on structure building principles, and then statistical information and knowledge of all kinds can play a role in determining the final representation of meaning. The difficulty with these models is the persistent undeniable fact that statistical properties of sentences and meaning do appear to play some kind of immediate role in comprehension (see Townsend & Bever, 2001, Chapter 4).

The inadequacy of each kind of comprehension model alone reflects a duality in sentence processing: There are two well-known facts about language comprehension that require explanation by any adequate theory:

(7)   a. It is very fast: words in sentences are extra clear acoustically;
        b. Syntactic derivational histories are assigned as part of comprehension.

These two kinds of facts reflect a conundrum:

(8)   a. Sentences are horizontal, from "left" to "right";
        b. Derivations are "vertical" (i.e., if they were serial, 1964). They would sometimes span entire sequences, often "right" to "left," as in "raising" operations.

It is interesting and significant that each of these facts is explained by a corresponding view on processing: Associative templates are excellent at rapid pattern completion and apply immediately, going from signal to meaning. Syntactic structures as assigned build their derivations.

Townsend and Bever (2001) rehabilitated an analysis by synthesis model that embraces both kinds of information (Halle & Stevens, 1962). On this model, sentences are initially assigned a functional structure and meaning based on statistically dominant patterns; they are separately assigned a derivational history. In the ordinary run, the latter follows the former, perhaps by 100 milliseconds—that is, the model assigns correct syntax last, not first. This model has several features that are surprising in light of the goals of linguistics and presumptions about behavior:

- It is inelegant, simply gluing together the two kinds of processes;
- It involves understanding every sentence at least twice;
- It involves assigning a correct structure last;
- Initial meaning representations can be based on initially incorrect structures.

We adduced a full range of existing and new facts to support the model, indeed to support several of the surprising features. The reader is invited to consult the book for a full description. Here I focus on one case study, the comprehension of syntactic passives. Consider (9) to (12).

(9)   a.   Athens was attacked;
(9)   b.   Athens was ruined.

Classically, the passive form of verbs can be differentiated into "syntactic" versus "lexical" passives. The latter distribute in the same way as normal (stative) adjectives, motivating their categorization as lexically coded stative-like adjective forms.

(10)   a.   *Athens was quite attacked;
(10)   b.   *Athens looked attacked;
(10)   c.   Athens was being attacked;
(11)   a.   Athens was quite ruined;
(11)   b.   Athens looked ruined;
(11)   c.   *?Athens was being ruined.

The corresponding surface forms from a derivation in a theory that includes traces from movement looks schematically like the following:

(12)   a.   Athens was attacked [t-Athens];
(12)   b.   Athens was ruined.

Various studies have shown that there is some evidence that the trace is actually present in the mental representation of sentences with syntactic passives and not present in sentences with lexical passives. Typical studies show that shortly after the trace, the antecedent of the trace is more salient, for example, in a word probe paradigm. At the same time, the evidence suggests that the trace does not acquire its force in the representation immediately, but only after about a tenth of a second (Bever & Sanz, 1997; McElree & Bever, 1989).

These facts are given a handy explanation in the analysis by synthesis model. On that model, both kinds of "passives" are initially understood via a variant of the canonical sentence schema for English:

(13)   N V (N)⇒agent/experiencer action/predicate

That schema initially misassigns "attacked" as an adjective, part of a predicate phrase. That analysis, although syntactically incorrect, is sufficient to access a form of semantic information—modeled on the semantic interpretation schema for lexical passive adjectives. Thus, an initial comprehension of the sentence can be based on a syntactic misanalysis, which is eventually corrected by accessing the correct derivation. This sequence of processes also explains the fact that the evidence for the trace appears only after a short time has passed.

The psycholinguistic experimental literature of the last two decades is rife with controversy over how quickly and effectively statistically reliable information is assigned during comprehension. Much of this controversy has been presented under the rubric of proving or disproving that connectionist associative models can account for language behavior without recourse to linguistic derivational rules. Although not much light has come out of this controversy, it has documented that comprehenders are indeed sensitive to a wide range of statistically grounded information early in their comprehension. At the same time, experiments like the preceding also demonstrate that derivational structures are assigned as part of the comprehension process. Thus, the "inelegance" of the analysis by synthesis model in postulating two kinds of overlapping computational operations captures an evident fact that this is how people do it.

Aside from time-consuming and often inconclusive experimental investigations, this model explains a number of simple and well-known facts. Consider the following examples:

(14)   a. The horse raced past the barn fell.
(14)   b. More people have visited Paris than I have.

Our intuitions about each of these cases exemplifies a different aspect of the analysis by synthesis model. The first reflects the power of the canonical form strategy in English, which initially treats the first six words as a separate sentence (Bever, 1970). The entire sentence is often judged ungrammatical by native speakers until they see some parallel sentences of the same formal structure, or related to it:

(15)   a. The horse ridden past the barn fell.
(15)   b. The horse that was raced past the barn fell.
(15)   c. The horse racing past the barn fell.

The example is pernicious in part because of the canonical form constraint, and also because recovering from the misanalysis is itself complex: the correct analysis in fact includes the proposition that "the horse raced" (i.e., was caused to race). Thus, as the comprehender reworks the initial mis-parse, the correct analysis reinforces the incorrect surface analysis on which "the horse" is taken to be the subject of the embedded verb. This seduces the comprehender back into the mis-parse.

The second example (due to Mario Montalbetti), is the obverse of the first example. The comprehender thinks at first that the sentence is coherent and meaningful, and then realizes that in fact it does not have a correct syntactic analysis. The initial perceptual organization assigns it a schema based on a general comparative frame of two canonical sentence forms—"more X than Y," reinforced by the apparent parallel structure in X and Y (. . . have gone to Paris. . . . I have). On the analysis by synthesis model, this superficial initial analysis gains entry to the derivational parse system, which then ultimately blocks any coherent interpretation.

I do not expect to have convinced the reader of our model via such simplified examples alone: in our book, we organize a range of experimental and neurological facts in support of the general idea that an early stage of comprehension rests on frequent statistically valid patterns, followed by a more structurally complete assignment of a syntactic derivation.

An important consequence of the model for linguistics is that it requires certain universal features of actual languages in order to work. Most important is the otherwise surprising fact that actual languages have a characteristic set of statistically grounded structural patterns at each level of representation. It further requires that complex constructions with intricate derivations be functionally homonymous with simpler constructions in ways that allow the simpler constructional analysis to convey the more complex meaning at an initial prederivational stage of processing. In the next sections, I develop the implications of this for language learning and linguistic universals, and relate it to cognitive science in general.

6.2.3. Constraints Based on Acquisition

For centuries, the two ideas about comprehension mentioned above (1a,b, repeated below), have alternatively dominated the entire science of the mind:

(16)   a. Everything (real) is based on habits, prototypes, associations.
(16)   b. Everything (important) is based on rules, categories, computations.

The repeated scientific mistake has been to make either16a or 16b the only principle and to force it to account for everything. This has led to alternating prescriptive rejection of such superficially obvious facts as

(17)   a. Languages involve categorical operations;
(17)   b. Languages are learned.

That is, attempts by each school to account for everything mental have led to some correspondingly stark mottos:

(18)   a. Language cannot be learned by any "general" learning process;
(18)   b. Language cannot involve "ungrounded" symbolic computations.

Something has to be wrong here. Clearly, we need a theory that both explains what language is and how individual languages are learned by individual children. Any theory that requires language to be nonsymbolic is wrong: any theory that requires language to be "unlearned" is wrong. What we need to do is develop a learning theory that could work, and then see if it does work that way.

Today's theory, popular among structural linguists, is parameter setting—the child throws switches on universal language dimensions this way and that, based on impoverished evidence. A parameter setting model sets constraints on what such an acquisition theory must include: but it has almost the entire structure of attested and nonattested languages built in or autonomously constructable at the start (a tabula plena). Recent attempts to explore how parameter setting might work more fully still include prior knowledge of the set of grammars to try out (Yang, 2002), or even a scaffolding structure of proto-grammars designed to maximize efficient convergence on the correct grammar (Fodor & Sakas, 2004). Although the brute force of this model may overcome the "poverty of the stimulus," in itself it explains little about how the learning process unfolds in each individual, about interactions with emergent cognition, and about the role of individual motivations and introspections. At the very least, we need a theory of acquisition "performance" to understand the individual mechanics and dynamics of setting parameters.

The analysis by synthesis model we developed for comprehension can embrace parameter setting constraints, while also explaining other constraints on grammars in the framework of a general learning theory. We made some preliminary suggestions about this in our book, and I will expand on them a bit here. Basically, the idea is that the child alternates (logically, not always temporally) between developing statistically grounded syntactic/semantic patterns and providing structural derivations for sentences that fit those patterns. Indeed, the patterns that the child develops based on statistics of what he or she hears are just those patterns that adults rely on for comprehension; the derivations, which the child tries out to compute the patterns it has acquired, must converge on the same derivations as used by adults. There is a range of data suggesting that this model describes what individual children do during language acquisition. I just briefly sketch some salient facts here.

TABLE 6.1.   Percentage of Correct Acting Out Interpretations of
              Simple Sentences

Sentence	Age 2	Age 4
The dog bit the giraffe	90%	98%
It's the giraffe that the dog bit	87%	43%
The giraffe got bit by the dog	52%	27%
The dog ate the cookie	92%	96%
The cookie ate the dog	73%	45%
The cookie got eaten by the dog	55%	85%

First, perceptual and production strategies emerge from experience: young children compute initial stages of syntax based on initial structural assignments, independent of structural statistics or semantic probability, and then acquire statistical patterns.

There is considerable evidence that children under age 2 already have a basic grasp of the notion of agent, and in English have some sensitivity to word order (Golinkoff, 1975; Hirsh-Pasek & Golinkoff, 1993). We can show how this early capacity develops by systematically looking at the development of comprehension patterns in which they use puppets to act out short sentences. Two- and four-year-olds show a pattern of correctly acting out sentences (see Table 6.1, a recent replication of a study by me, Virginia Valian, & Jacques Mehler, first reported in Bever, 1970).

The early capacity of the 2-year-old suggests an available schema of the form NV = Agent (action). Most striking is the fact that the object cleft construction is correctly interpreted, although semantic constraints have a relatively small effect on the 2-year-old. This is consistent with the idea that the child has acquired a local categorical sequence syntactic strategy, but no general dependence on semantic information. The systematic performance at age four suggests that the child has now developed the more general sequence strategy, based on the canonical form of English mentioned above, on which the sequence initial noun is generally taken to be the agent; see (11) above.

(19)   #NV(N) = Agent, action (patient).

At the same time, the child now shows much more sensitivity to semantic constraints. In other words, the 4-year-old has acquired some statistical patterns for comprehension not yet available to the 2-year-old.

Another important fact is that children know about the difference between how they talk and how they should talk grammatically. There are numerous anecdotes reporting this awareness. For example, after one 3-year-old child (mine) was repeatedly teased by a (linguist) father (me) for using the incorrect weak past tense for go (i.e., "goed"), he finally said

(20)   Daddy, I talk that way, you don't.

This simple rejoinder shows that the child was aware of the distinction between the correct sentence form and his own dependence on forming the past tense with the regular ending. Awareness of this kind is consistent with the view here that the child develops statistical patterns as part of the overall acquisition process, which he or she can be aware of.

I also note that the model comports well with recent research showing that the infant is indeed a good extractor of certain kinds of patterns, and that Motherese actually has many statistically grounded properties that lead toward (but not all the way to) correct syntactic analyses. (e.g., Brent, 1996; Cartwright & Brent, 1997; Gerken, 1996; Golinkoff, Pence, Hirsh-Pasek, & Brand, 2005; Mintz, 2002, 2003, 2006; Redington & Chater, 1998). At the same time, there is now considerable research showing that infants are quite good at statistical inference from the presentation of serial strings with various kinds of structure (Gómez & Gerken, 1999; Marcus, Vijayan, Bandi Rao, & Vishton, 1999; Saffran, 2001, 2003; Saffran, Aslin, & Newport, 1996). Older children also show statistical sensitivity in developing grammatical and lexical ability (Bates & MacWhinney, 1987; Gillette, Gleitman, Gleitman, & Lederer, 1999; Moerk, 2000, Naigles & Hoff-Ginsberg, 1998; Yang, 2006).

The idea that the child acquires knowledge of syntax by way of compiling statistical generalizations and then analyzing them with its available syntactic capacities reflects a claim about how learning works in general that has been proposed in various forms for many years. For example, it is technically an expansion on the TOTE model proposed by Miller, Galanter, and Pribram (1960). An initial condition (statistically grounded pattern) triggers a Test meaning and an Operation (derivation), which triggers a new Test meaning, and then Exit. A different way of expressing this is in the classic work by Karmiloff-Smith and Inhelder (1973)—cognition advances in spurts, triggered by exposure to critical instances that violate an otherwise supported generalization.

The dual nature of the acquisition process is also related to classical theories of problem solving (e.g., Wertheimer, 1925, 1945). On such models, the initial stage of problem organization involves noting a conceptual conflict—if the answer is X, then Y is impossible, but if Y, then X is impossible. Characteristically, the solution involves accessing a different form of representation that expresses the relation between X and Y in more abstract terms. In language, this expresses itself, for example, as the superficial identity of passives and active constructions; the resolution of the problem is to find a derivational structure for the problem that shows how actives and passives are both differentiated and related derivationally. (In this sense, Piaget's attempts to explain language acquisition were well directed—albeit incomplete.) Hence, not only is language learning hereby interpreted in the context of a general learning device, it is also a special instance of a general problem solver. Language remains special because of its unique characteristics and role in human life; but it is no longer "special" because it is "unlearned."

The model also resolves some classical puzzles about acquisition. Notable is the problem of how children understand sentences before they have a grammatical analysis for them (Valian, 1999). The idea that the child maintains a list of grammatically unresolved sentences is unsatisfactory because any given list is heterogenous unless it is given some kind of prior ordering and structure. The analysis by synthesis model suggests that they rely on statistical patterns and occasional false analyses to generate an internal bank of meaning/form pairs that maintain the forms as puzzles for coherent derivational analysis.

The example-generating role of such internalized patterns cannot be overemphasized. To some extent, it mitigates the "poverty of the stimulus," the fact that the child receives sporadic, errorful, and limited input to work with. It allows the child to generate new exemplars of acquired patterns, thereby expanding its internal data bank of slightly different meaning/form pairs to be analyzed syntactically. This partially resolves, or at least clarifies the problem of how children access positive and negative feedback as guides to their emerging syntactic abilities, even if they treat each sentence initially as a unique item. On this view, the child can attempt derivation of a construction based on a subset of sentences of a given general pattern, and then "test" the derivational structure on other sentences of a similar pattern (Chouinard & Clark, 2003; Dale & Christiansen, 2004; Golinkoff et al., 2005; Lieven, 1994; Moerk, 2000; Morgan, Bonamo, & Travis, 1995; Saxton, 1997, 2000; Valian, 1999).

Other phenomena of acquisition fall out of this description. The most often ignored fact exemplified by the anecdote above (20) is that children are aware of the difference between how they understand/say certain meanings and how they should say them. How can this be? It is actually a different expression of the puzzle of how children can understand sentences for which they do not have a complete grammatical analysis: in this case, the child can show that he or she is explicitly aware of the distinction—making overt the fact that the child has an analysis available, although recognizing that it is not correct.

Note that there is no comfort here for empiricist associationists or any other model that attempts to show how computational structures are causally "grounded" or internalized from explicit patterns. The model assumes and requires that the child have the computational equipment to represent statistical patterns with some form of structure and to try out computational derivations that "explain" how one gets from the form to the meaning. However, the explicit role of statistical generalizations as a dynamic factor in the process of discovering structural rules may also lay the groundwork for a solution to an outstanding problem in parameter setting theory—what, in fact, are the appropriate and sufficient data to induce a child to set a syntactic parameter? (Fodor, 1998; Fodor & Sakas, 2004; Lightfoot, 1991; Pinker, 1984; Yang, 2002). A frequent discussion has involved the "subset principle," the idea that the parameters are set to a default, which can only be undone by exposure to a particular example that triggers the exceptional value of the parameter (Berwick, 1985; Pinker, 1984). This depends on languages being organized so that actual sentences exhibit the default values of a parameter, with the exceptional value being a "subset" of the default. The model of learning, which includes the development of statistical patterns, can explain this kind of apparent parameter setting without assuming that the default is specified in the infant's mind ahead of time. It is typically the case that the default value of the parameter also describes the more frequent kind of syntactic construction. Exposure to the more frequent constructions (sentences *with* apparent subjects) and the corresponding incorporation of a template lays the statistical groundwork for recognition of sentences with the default parameter setting (cf. Yang, 2002; see also Wonnacott, Newport, and Tanenhaus (2007)).

This way of thinking about how parameters are set during acquisition may reduce the requirement that all parameters are innately specified with a default value actually included. That in turn, leads to a dynamic interpretation of language learning, with the formation of patterns, and a subsequent (logically) assignment of structural analyses of the patterns, and of their exceptions. Again, the reader may come away with the false impression that this view is simply one in which statistical features and patterns explain what is learned (see Bates & MacWhinney, 1987, and their later writings). On our theory, this is only one quarter of the story; the other three quarters are as follows: (1) the (apparently automatic) mental isolation of the relevant dimensions of the parameters; (2) the emergence of structural processes, which provide integrated derivations for sentences exhibiting the learnable patterns; and (3) the availability of analysis by synthesis model, which integrates the statistical templates and derivational processes dynamically.

It is also useful to note that this structure resolves some of the limitations of each of the major approaches taken alone: access to statistical patterns mitigates the limitations of the poverty of the stimulus input, and access to parametric dimensions and derivational processes partially defines the domains over which statistical generalizations can be formed.

The analysis by synthesis model is, of course, only a model. Its major failing for many is that just as in its application to sentence comprehension, it is inelegant—a kluge that can embrace many other theories in a dynamic framework. I too would prefer a more elegant system. But behavioral facts do not allow that luxury, and no one, not even the most devoted evolutionists, has argued that all evolutionary developments move toward the most elegant and simple organizations. Most important for cognitive science in general is the fact that the model describes a special case of more general processes. This does not mean that language is not "special," drawing on numerous special capacities unique to it. But at least we see a way to recover the idea that language is learned in a dynamic manner, typical of all human learning, creativity, and aesthetic judgment.

6.2.3.1 Implications for Linguistic Universals—The Canonical Form Constraint

We now turn to the question of how acquisition processes might constrain languages to exhibit certain kinds of universal properties. There have been various approaches to the question of how acquisition constrains linguistic structures. Most ambitious have been attempts to show that formal learnability of derivational relations constrain those relations to be of certain types (e.g., Osherson & Weinstein, 1982; Wexler & Culicover, 1980). The enduring result of these investigations is a set of abstract constraints on possible kinds of derivational processes that guarantee recovery of inner from outer forms of sentences. Stabler (Chapter 10) and Steedman (Chapter 9) also note that the interrelation of semantic structures and learning syntax may account for certain universals. These investigations propose boundary conditions on the architecture of grammars. But they tell us little about the dynamics of actual acquisition processes. More recently Gleitman, Cassidy, Nappa, Papafragou, and Trueswell (2005) and Papafragou, Cassidy, and Gleitman (2007) have outlined how cognitive and informational constraints on conceptual learning interact with syntactic structures to shape lexical structures, and through them, certain aspects of syntactic structures.

The analysis by synthesis model of language acquisition requires that actual attested languages have a number of properties not explained by linearity constraints, nor by the usual array of computational linguistic universals or parameters. The most significant involve the existence of levels of representation and their interrelation. The model requires two features to start it off: it must have access to an initial syntactic vocabulary to characterize input sequences in some formal language; the input to the child must exhibit a standard, statistically dominant form—without this "canonical form constraint" (CFC), the language learning device cannot develop statistically valid generalizations. The CFC has at least two consequences for attested languages: mapping systems between levels of representation "conspire" to make sure there is a canonical form at each level of representation; mappings between forms of representation are unidirectional, from the more inner/abstract to the more superficial.

The notion of derivational conspiracies is not novel, be it in syntax or phonology (cf. Ross, 1972, 1973a). In the case of English, the vast majority of sentences and clauses have a canonical form in which there appears to be a subject preceding a verb:

(21)   a. The boy hit the ball.
(21)   b. The ball was hit by the boy.
(21)   c. It is the boy who hit the ball.
(21)   d. The boy was happy.
(21)   e. The boy seemed happy.
(21)   f. The boy was easy to see.
(21)   g. It was easy to see the boy.
(21)   h. Who saw the boy?
(21)   i. Who did the boy see?
(21)   j. Visiting relatives can be a nuisance.
(21)   k. The duck is ready to eat.

The coincidence of the surface forms reflects a constraint on derivations such that they almost all end up with similar phrase structures and surface case relations. This is despite the fact that the architecture of many grammatical theories—including all variants of generative grammar—would allow languages in which each underlying form is expressed in a uniquely distinct surface phrase organization and sequence. On our interpretation, such computationally possible languages will not be learned because they make it hard for the language learning child to develop an early statistically based pattern that it can internalize and manipulate for further stages of acquisition.

There are numerous levels of representation mediating between the propositional form of sentences and the linear string: syllabic, morphological, declension/conjugational, phrase, sentence. Attested languages have a canonical form at each level—canonical syllable, morphology, declension, conjugation, phrase (right versus left branching), sentence syntax. The canonical form can constrain the computational relations between levels to ensure its maintenance (conspiracies).

If there is a canonical form at each level, then for effability, it must embrace more than one derivational relation to input levels—this means that the derivation from one level to another will generally not be completely discoverable via operationalist principles based on surface forms. Rather, some form of problem solving via hypothesis generation and testing is required. This explains an otherwise puzzling fact about languages—why is each level distinct from the others, and not subject to operational discovery procedures? Languages with transparent subset relations between levels could have the same expressive power as existing ones: in that case, each level of representation would offer direct evidence of its relation to the derivationally prior level. If every derivation had such a distinct surface form, it would fulfill the role of syntax as mapping each hierarchical propositional structure onto a linear sequence. But then there would not be a surface canonical form and, hence, the language would not be learnable.

Accordingly, on this view, actually attested languages have mapping relations between levels that are unidirectional because they are many-to-one from inner to outer forms. Put in the terms of the modern "biolinguistic metaphor," syntax defines operationally opaque derivations to relate meaning to sound. The existence of derivations is a structural universal of the language faculty in the narrow sense— but the opacity of the derivations, and hence their directionality, is a universal of the language faculty in the broad sense—a function of what makes languages learnable by a general learning process (Hauser, Chomsky, & Fitch, 2002).

6.2.3.2 Special Implication for EPP—A Nonsyntactic Principle after all?

The preceding discussion offers an explanation for why sentence forms tend to converge on a common superficial form. This may offer an explanation for one of the more problematic syntactic constraints, which is still an anomaly within the minimalist framework. This is the so-called extended projection principle (EPP). This principle was first proposed to account for the appearance of subject-like phrases in sentences, so-called expletives—basically a principle that all sentences have to have (surface) subjects. For example, consider the following sentences:

(22)   a. John seemed foolish.
(22)   b. Foolish is what John seemed (to be).
(22)   c. What John seemed (to be) was foolish.

Each of these has a constituent in the subject position, but with a different semantic role. This suggests that the subject position must always have an overt phrase. In some cases, the subject position is filled with a word that has no semantic role in the sentence ("it"), further demonstrating the force of the EPP.

(22)   d. It seemed that John was foolish.

The EPP has been initially proposed as a fixed syntactic universal, part of the set of syntactic constraints that all languages must respect. Although more or less correct for English, the EPP has been further studied and a number of troubling facts have emerged (e.g., see discussions in Epstein & Seely, 2002; Lasnik, 2001; Richards, 2003; and papers in Svenonius, 2002):

- It may not be universal (e.g., Irish, as analyzed by McCloskey, 1996, 2001).
- It can have a variety of expressions in different languages (e.g., in a standard relation to focus as opposed to subject, in intonation patterns, etc.).
- It generally corresponds to the statistically dominant form in each language.
- It has not found a formal derivation within syntactic theories or the minimalist program—that is, it simply must be stipulated as a "syntactic" constraint on derivations.

The conclusion generally appears that the EPP may be a "configurational" constraint on derivations—it requires that sentences all conform to some basic surface pattern. Epstein and Seely (2002, p. 82) note the problem this poses for the minimalist program:

> If (as many argue) EPP is in fact "configurational," then it seems to us to undermine the entire Minimalist theory of movement based on feature interpretability at the interfaces. More generally, "configurational" requirements represent a retreat to the stipulation of molecular tree properties. . . . It amounts to the reincorporation of . . . principles of GB . . . that gave rise to the quest for Minimalist explanation. . . .

In other words, EPP is a structural constraint that has to be stipulated in the minimalist framework, and is one that at the same time violates some of that framework's basic structural principles and simplicity.

We can now treat the EPP as a U_i in the manner discussed above. There are two potential explanations of EPP phenomena. Either it is indeed a syntactic constraint, part of universal syntax in the narrow faculty of language, or it is a constraint on learnable languages, basically an expression of the canonical form constraint; sentences have to "sound" like they are sentences of the language to afford the child a statistical entree into acquiring the language.

How can we decide between these two explanations? We can apply the same logic as Miller and Chomsky applied to restrictions on center embedding: First, the EPP adds a stipulated constraint to grammars, which would otherwise be formally simpler. Second, the EPP appears to be a heterogenous constraint, with different kinds of expressions in different languages, not always strictly syntactic. Third, the canonical form constraint is independently attested and motivated: it explains statistical properties of language, stages of acquisition, and significant facts about adult language processing. Thus, we can conclude that the phenomena that motivated the EPP are actually expressions of the canonical form constraint (CFC). That is, languages could violate the EPP like phenomena so far as structural potential is concerned, but in so doing would violate the CFC and therefore not be learnable.

Syntacticians may object that this line of reasoning can appear to be circular. That is, many specific syntactic processes in individual languages appear to be explained by the EPP, governing not just the acceptability of sentences, but indeed their grammaticality. For example, in the examples at the beginning of this chapter on heavy phrase shift, it is clear that some phonological phrase must appear in surface subject position to maintain grammaticality of the sentences with displaced phrasal complements. Thus, the EPP constraint does not merely exert "stylistic" preferences on sentence constructions, it (can appear to) dictates syntactic requirements on derivations involving movement or other constraints.

What is at issue is the source of the constraint that results in processes that appear to conform to the EPP. On the view presented here, the child learns sentence constructions that conform to the canonical form constraint and tends not to learn constructions that do not. But on our interpretation, the notion of "learn" can be glossed as "discovers derivations for, using his or her available repertoire of structural devices. . . ." This allows for the discovery by the child of a wide range of structural derivational processes that maintain the CFC. Thus, we can accept that for individual languages there are specific derivational processes that conform descriptively to the EPP. But we argue that the EPP itself is merely a descriptive generalization, which reflects acquisition constraints as its true cause.

Note that the canonical form constraint can be different in different languages. For example, in inflected languages, the canonical form may involve particular suffixes, and not constituent order. Slobin and Bever (1982) found that the early canonical form that children arrive at in Serbo-Croation or Turkish conform to canonical properties in those languages. In Serbo-Croation, this involves a mixture of order and inflectional properties; in Turkish, with largely free constituent order, the canonical form appears to be two arguments and a verb, in which one of the arguments has a clear object suffix.

6.2.4. Constraints from Neurological Substrates

Consider now a speculative case study of computational constraints on the faculty of language based on neurological considerations. Although it has some logical force and a small amount of supporting data, my main purpose is to flesh out the range of ways we can consider where universals of language may come from. The claims are strong and require much more empirical demonstration than there is space for here.

One of the enduring properties of syntactic operations has been an upward moving cycle. That is, in every generative model, operations iterate from the most to the least embedded part of a sentence. This has often appeared as a constraint on movement "upward," from a more to a less embedded constituent. Attempts to define top-down computation (Phillips, 1995, 1996, 2003; Phillips & Wagers, in press;

Richards, 2001, 2002) characteristically involve "look-ahead" templates, or feature codings, which simulate "upward" constraints, and involve computational demands that increase geometrically with string length.

The priority of upward movement has recently found an explanation (Chomsky, 2004, 2005). Merge, as a successive operation that forms trees, has two possible expressions at each iteration: "Internal" merge results in new membership of X and prior Y within the same constituent, and "external" merge results in an X outside of a prior X and Y, in effect, a "copy" of the now more embedded X. Because the latter is by definition higher in the emerging hierarchy, upward "movement" is rendered if movement is interpreted as "copying by a higher constituent and deletion of the lower identical one." Thus, "movement" is now represented as copying, with default constraints on expressing only the least embedded copy of a constituent. That is, upward "movement" is a natural result of recursion, which itself has been proposed as the essential computational operation critical to language evolution (Hauser, Chomsky, & Fitch, 2002).

One possible route for this evolution is that the capacity for recursive merge appeared as a single (set of) mutations, which immediately led to more powerful minds. But another possibility is that recursive merge was "exapted" from other modalities with a long prior evolutionary background. An obvious candidate is from vision, because the brain areas devoted to language in humans are largely homologous to areas evolved for vision in our close biological relatives. The question that arises then is, what are the computational devices—if any—that might have evolved to solve visual problems, which could later transfer as the neurological basis for recursion in language?

Consider first some basic facts about motion perception. If a 0 moves from the left below to the right under temporal constraints consistent with motion (say, a fifth of a second), what we see is a dot in motion arriving at the right side:

0 . . . . >0

The motion may appear continuous. This is the basis for the well-known "phi phenomenon," in which motion is deduced from discrete presentations at a distance from each other (Breitmeyer, 1984; Kolers, 1972; Rock, 1983; Wertheimer, 1912). The organization of motion from one point to another is not only deductive, but later positions can "absorb" earlier ones. For example, in well-known cases of "metacontrast," the initial representation can become invisible as a separate entity (Ramachandran & Gregory, 1991; Shepard & Judd, 1976). In such cases of metacontrast, we perceive the final location of the 0 and the sensation that it moved to get there, but the representation of the original 0 is itself subsumed under the final representation: the simplest computational representation of this classic phenomenon in fact involves a form of merge, in which the final representation is organized as a function of its precursor(s).

This analysis, along with the assumption that only the highest representation in the structure is perceived, can explain the fact that the sequence of prior representations can be seen as an object in motion, arriving at the final point. Each of the "snapshots" that the eye captures is subsumed by the next, resulting in recursive iteration of the entire motion sequence.

This process of the perception of integrated motion is a potential computational foundation for the exaptation of recursive merge into language functions. Of course, we cannot test this directly, but we can consider some empirical predictions of our computational-recursive interpretation of simple motion. In particular, the metaphor of "movement" as "recursive copying" from less to more embedded structures suggests the hypothesis that real visual movement is easier to perceive from more to less embedded parts of a visual scene.

We have run a series of investigations of this (Bever, Lachter, & Weidenbacher, in preparation), showing that indeed movement is easier to perceive from an embedded part of a scene than into the embedded part. One way we test this is by studying the effectiveness of perceived motion between a small square and a larger square that contains the smaller square (there are various appropriate controls for attention and other factors). The results confirm the general hypothesis.

Suppose we take this to support the idea that "upward" movement is computationally prefigured in the visual system such that it provided the computational basis for exaptation into linguistic computations. In no way does this explain away the faculty of language as the result of "general" cognitive or visual processes. Rather, it would be an example of appropriation of structures and processes evolved for one purpose by another function. This is not an unusual idea in evolutionary theory.

But we owe ourselves an argument as to why "upward" movement took on priority in the visual system in general—many computational processes other than hierarchical merge might have been adaptive for motion perception. A full discussion of this involves consideration of the visual perception of biological movement. There is emerging evidence for special visual mechanisms that recognize biological motion as a function of hierarchically structured input, which requires upward integration of subvectors of motion into an overall vector (Pomplun, Liu, Trujillo, Simine, & Tsotsos, 2002; Tsotsos et al., 2005). This could be the basis for a generalization of hierarchical processing. A simpler and more classically Darwinian argument is that the perception of objects that appear from behind other objects is more salient and more important in survival of any species than perception of objects that move behind another object. Things jumping out at you are more likely to be efficiently nutritious or effectively dangerous than things jumping away and hiding.

Of course, our results and speculation are only part of a much larger empirical and theoretical story that we must support before we can come to the strong conclusion that upward movement (or its correspondent, downward control) in language structures is the result of corresponding constraints developed for vision. I mention it here as an example of the kind of investigation that can be pursued as part of delimiting and understanding the boundary conditions on syntactic operations and their evolution.

6.3. Conclusion

Language may have design features that are responsive to its role as an interface between thought and behavior. It may also rest on specific genetically structured filters or computational capacities, which may explain other universal properties. But it is also learned and performed by individual children, with individual motives and learning principles, all of which may be more general than language itself. I have explored a few of such cases in outline form, not to convince you that we know the answers, but to outline the potential range of constraints on universals that extend well beyond the idealized function of language itself.

In a sense, this represents a return to a classic notion of the "ideal speaker/hearer/learner" (cf. Chomsky, 1965). Today's minimalist syntax is a framework for the exploration of language as the optimal solution for the interface between thought and speech—the idea in part is to define the minimal assumptions about the universal faculty of language just sufficient to account for its structure. The goal is to explain language as it is, not humans' knowledge of it. The ideas raised in this chapter can be taken as examples of the complementary study—what is minimally required to account for the idealized knowledge and use of language.

Key Further Readings

The topics touched on in this chapter include among others, the history of syntax, current minimalism, current theories of language behavior, theories of language acquisition, the extended projection principle, as well as general theories of learning and vision. That is a lot of territory to cover in any limited set of readings. The reader is invited to select from the bibliography those that intrigue him or her. The main technical theme, however, is the integration of statistical and structural kinds of knowledge in behavior and learning. I have attempted to sketch a theory of learning, which is more general than just for language, but which has implications for language learning and structure. The main goal is to capture the two enduring generalizations about behavior, that it depends on habits, and that it depends on symbolic computations.

Background readings for the chapter include the following: On the history of transformational grammar, Hornstein and Boeckx (Chapter 5), Lasnik and Depiante (2000); on the history of grammar in relation to psychological models, Townsend and Bever (2001); on the EPP, Svenonius (2002), McGinnis and Richards (in press); on connectionist treatments of language in relation to grammar, Pinker and Mehler (1988); on acquisition models that combine conceptual and linguistic information, Gleitman et al. (2005); on current ideas about the evolution of language, Hauser et al. (2000), Pinker and Jackendoff (Chapter 7), Piatelli-Palmarini and Uriagereka (2004); for general discussion of universals in relation to syntactic theory, Piattelli-Palmarini, Uriagereka, and Salaburu (in press).

Acknowledgments

This chapter has benefited from discussions with at least the following persons: Andrew Carnie, Noam Chomsky, Heidi Harley, David Medeiros, Steven Ott, and Massimo Piatelli-Palmarini.

References

Bates E., & MacWhinney, B. (1987). Competition, variation, and language learning. In B. MacWhinney (Ed.), *Mechanisms of language acquisition* (pp.157–193). Hillsdale, NJ: Erlbaum.

Berwick, R. (1985). The acquisition of syntactic knowledge. Cambridge, MA: MIT Press.

Bever, T.G. (1970). The cognitive basis for linguistic structures. In J. Hayes (Ed.), *Cognition and the development of language* (pp. 279–362). New York: Wiley.

Bever, T.G., Carroll, J. M., & Hurtig, R. (1976). Analogy or ungrammatical sequences that are utterable and comprehensible are the origins of new grammars in language acquisition and linguistic evolution. In T. G. Bever, J. J. Katz, & D. T. Langendoen (Eds.), *An integrated theory of linguistic ability* (pp. 149–182). New York: T.Y. Crowell Press.

Bever, T., Lachter, J., & Weidenbacher, H. (in preparation). Asymmetries in motion perception.

Bever, T. G., & Langendoen, T. (1971). A dynamic model of the evolution of language. *Linguistic Inquiry, 2,* 433–463.

Bever, T. G., & Sanz, M. (1997). Empty categories access their antecedents during comprehension. *Linguistic Inquiry, 28,* 68–91.

Boeckx, C. (2006). *Linguistic minimalism: Origins, concepts, methods, and aim.* New York: Oxford University Press.

Breitmeyer, B. G. (1984). *Visual masking.* New York: Oxford University Press.

Brent, M. R. (1996). *Computational approaches to language acquisition.* Cambridge, MA: MIT Press.

Cartwright, T. A., & Brent, M. R. (1997). Syntactic categorization in early language acquisition: Formalizing the role of distributional analysis. *Cognition, 63*, 121–170.

Chomsky, N. (1965). *Aspects of the Theory of Syntax*. Cambridge, MA: MIT Press.

Chomsky, N. (1995). *The minimalist program*. Cambridge, MA: MIT Press.

Chomsky, N. (2004). Beyond explanatory adequacy. In Belletti, A. (Ed.), *Structures and beyond—The cartography of syntactic structures* (Vol. 3, pp. 104–131). Oxford, UK: Oxford University Press.

Chomsky, N. (2005). Three factors in the design of language. *Linguistic Inquiry, 36*, 1–22.

Chomsky, N., & Miller, G. (1963). Introduction to the formal analysis of natural languages. In D. Luce, R. Bush, & E. Galanter (Eds.), *Handbook of mathematical psychology* (pp. 269–321). New York: Wiley.

Chouinard, M. M., & Clark, E. V. (2003). Adult reformulations of child errors as negative evidence. *Journal of Child Language, 30*, 637–669.

Dale, R., & Christiansen, M. H. (2004). Active and passive statistical learning: Exploring the role of feedback in artificial grammar learning and language. In *Proceedings of the 26th Annual Conference of the Cognitive Science Society* (pp. 262–267). Mahwah, NJ: Lawrence Erlbaum.

Epstein, S., & Seely, D. (2002). *Derivation and explanation in the minimalist program*. Malden, MA: Blackwell Publishing.

Fodor, J. (1998). Unambiguous triggers. *Linguistic Inquiry, 29*, 1–36.

Fodor, J. D. (2001). Setting syntactic parameters. In M. Baltin & C. Collins (Eds.), *The handbook of contemporary syntactic theory* (pp. 730–738). Oxford, UK: Blackwell Publishers.

Fodor, J. D., & Sakas, W. G. (2004). Evaluating models of parameter setting. In A. Brugos, L. Micciulla, & C. E. Smith (Eds.), *BUCLD 28: Proceedings of the 28th Annual Boston University Conference on Language Development* (pp. 1–27). Somerville, MA: Cascadilla Press.

Freidin, R., & Vergnaud, J. R. (2001). Exquisite connections: Some remarks on the evolution of linguistic theory. *Lingua, 111*, 639–666.

Gerken, L. A. (1996). Phonological and distributional cues to syntax acquisition. In J. Morgan & K. Demuth (Eds.), *Signal to syntax: Bootstrapping from speech to grammar in early acquisition* (pp. 411–426). Mahwah, NJ: Erlbaum.

Gillette, J., Gleitman, L., Gleitman, H., & Lederer, A. (1999). Human simulation of vocabulary learning. *Cognition, 73*, 35–176.

Gleitman, L., Cassidy, K., Nappa, R., Papafragou, A., & Trueswell, J. (2005). Hard words. *Language Learning and Development, 1*, 23–64.

Golinkoff, R. M. (1975). Semantic development in infants: The concepts of agent and recipient. *Merrill-Palmer Quarterly, 21*, 181–193.

Golinkoff, R., Pence, K., Hirsh-Pasek, K., & Brand, R. (2005). When actions can't speak for themselves: Infant-directed speech and action may influence verb learning. In T. Trabasso, J. Sabatini, D. W. Massaro, & R. C. Calfee (Eds.), *From orthography to pedagogy: Essays in honor of Richard L. Venezky* (pp. 63–79). Mahwah, NJ: Erlbaum.

Gómez, R. L., & Gerken, L. A. (1999). Artificial grammar learning in one-year-olds: Leads to specific and abstract knowledge. *Cognition, 70*, 109–135.

Halle, M., & Stevens, K. N. (1962). Speech recognition: A model and a program for research. RLE Reports: Reprinted in J. A. Fodor & J. J. Katz (Eds.), *The structure of language: Readings in the philosophy of language*. Englewood Cliffs, NJ: Prentice-Hall.

Hauser, M., Chomsky, N., & Fitch, W. T. (2002). The faculty of language: What is it, who has it, and how did it evolve? *Science, 298,* 1569–1579.

Hirsh-Pasek, K., & Golinkoff, R. M. (1993). Skeletal supports for grammatical learning: What the infant brings to the language learning task. In C. K. Rovee-Collier & L. P. Lipsitt (Eds.), *Advances in infancy research* (Vol. 8, pp. 299–338). Norwood, NJ: Ablex.

Hornstein, N., Nunes, J., & Grohman, K. (2005). *Understanding minimalism.* Cambridge, UK. Cambridge University Press.

Karmiloff-Smith, A., & Inhelder, B. (1973). If you want to get ahead, get a theory. *Cognition, 3,* 195–212.

Kolers, P. A. (1972). Aspects of motion perception. *Memory & Cognition, 30,* 678–686.

Lasnik, H. (2001). A note on the EPP. *Linguistic Inquiry, 32,* 356–362.

Lasnik, H. (2003). *Minimalist investigations in linguistic theory.* New York: Routledge.

Lasnik, H., & Depiante, M. (2000). *Syntactic structures revisited.* Cambridge, MA: MIT press.

Lieven, E. (1994). Crosslinguistic and crosscultural aspects of language addressed to children. In C. Galloway & C. J. Richards (Eds.), *Input and interaction in language acquisition* (pp. 56–74). New York: Cambridge University Press.

Lightfoot, D. (1991). *How to set parameters.* Cambridge, MA: MIT Press.

Marcus, G. F., Vijayan, S., Bandi Rao, S., & Vishton, P. M. (1999). Rule-learning in seven-month-old infants. *Science, 283,* 77–80.

Martin, R., & Uriagereka, J. (2000). Some possible foundations of the minimalist program. In R. Martin, D. Michaels, & J. Uriagereka (Eds.), *Step by step: Essays in honor of Howard Lasnik* (pp. 1–24). Cambridge, MA: MIT Press.

McCloskey, J. (1996). Subjects and subject positions in Irish. In R. Borsley & I. Roberts (Eds.), *The syntax of the Celtic languages* (pp. 241–283). Cambridge, UK: Cambridge University Press.

McCloskey, J. (2001). The distribution of subject properties in Irish. In W. Davies & S. Dubinsky (Eds.), *Objects and other subjects* (pp. 157–192). Dordrecht: Kluwer Academic Publishers.

McElree, B., & Bever, T. G. (1989). The psychological reality of linguistically defined gaps. *Journal of Psycholinguistic Research, 18,* 21–35.

McGinnis, M., & Richards, N. (Eds.). (in press). *Proceedings of the EPP/Phase workshop.* Cambridge, MA: MIT Working Papers in Linguistics.

Miller, G. (1962). Some psychological studies of grammar. *American Psychologist, 17,* 748–762.

Miller, G., & Chomsky, N. (1963). Finitary models of language users. In R. D. Luce, R. Bush, & E. Galanter (Eds.), *Handbook of mathematical psychology* (Vol. II, pp. 419–492). New York: Wiley.

Miller, G., Galanter, E., & Pribram, K. (1960). *Plans and the structure of behavior.* New York: Holt.

Mintz, T. H. (2002). Category induction from distributional cues in an artificial language. grammatical categories in speech to young children. *Cognitive Science, 26,* 393–424.

Mintz, T. H. (2003). Frequent frames as a cue for grammatical categories in child directed speech. *Cognition, 90,* 91–117.

Mintz, T. H. (2006). Finding the verbs: Distributional cues to categories available to young learners. In K. Hirsh-Pasek & R. M. Golinkoff (Eds.), *Action meets word: How children learn verbs* (pp. 31–63). New York: Oxford University Press.

Moerk, E. (2000). *The guided acquisition of first-language skills.* Westport, CT: Ablex.

Morgan, J. L., Bonamo, K. M., & Travis, L. L. (1995). Negative evidence on negative evidence. *Developmental Psychology, 31,* 180–197.

Naigles, L. R., & Hoff-Ginsberg, E. (1998). Why are some verbs learned before other verbs? Effects of input frequency and structure on children's early verb use. *Journal of Child Language, 25,* 95–120.

Osherson, D., & Weinstein, S. (1982). Criteria of language learning. *Information and Control, 52,* 123–138.

Papafragou, A., Cassidy, K., & Gleitman, L. (2007). When we think about *thinking:* The acquisition of belief verbs. *Cognition, 105,* 125–165.

Pinker, S. (1984). *Language learnability and language development.* Cambridge, MA: Harvard University Press.

Pinker, S., & Mehler, J. (1988). *Connections and symbols.* Cambridge, MA: MIT Press.

Phillips, C. (1995). Right association in parsing and grammar. In C. Schütze, J. Ganger, & K. Broihier (Eds.), *Papers on language processing and acquisition* (pp. 37–93). *MIT Working Papers in Linguistics* 26.

Phillips, C. (1996). *Order and structure.* Unpublished doctoral dissertation, Massachusetts Institute of Technology, Cambridge.

Phillips, C. (2003). Linear order and constituency. *Linguistic Inquiry, 34*(1), 37–90.

Phillips, C., & Wagers, M. (in press). Relating structure and time in linguistics and psycholinguistics. In G. Gaskell (Ed.), *Oxford handbook of psycholinguistics.* Oxford, UK: Oxford University Press.

Piatelli-Palmarini, M., & Uriagereka, J. (2004). The immune syntax: The evolution of the language virus. In L. Jenkins (Ed.), *Variation and universals in biolinguistics* (pp. 341–377). Oxford: Elsevier.

Piattelli-Palmarini, M., Uriagereka, J., & Salaburu, P. (Eds.). (in press). *Of minds and language: The Basque country encounter with Noam Chomsky.* New York: Oxford University Press.

Pomplun, M., Liu, Y., Trujillo, J., Simine, E., & Tsotsos, J. (2002). A neurally-inspired model for detecting and localizing simple motion patterns in image sequences. Workshop on Dynamic Perception, Bochum, Germany.

Ramachandran, V. S., & Gregory, R. L. (1991). Perceptual filling in of artificially induced scotomas in human vision. *Nature, 350,* 699–702.

Redington, M., & Chater, N. (1998). Connectionist and statistical approaches to language acquisition: A distributional perspective. *Language and Cognitive Processes, 13,* 129–191.

Richards, N. (2001). *Movement in language.* Oxford, UK: Oxford University Press.

Richards, N. (2002). Lowering and cyclicity: Attraction by X from Spec XP. In M. Hirotani (Ed.), *Proceedings of NELS, 32.* Amherst, MA: GLSA.

Richards, N. (2003). Why there is an EPP. *Gengo Kenkyu, 123,* 221–256.

Rock, I. (1983). *The logic of perception.* Cambridge, MA: MIT Press.

Ross, J. (1972). The category squish: Endstation Hauptwort. In P. Perntau, et al. (Eds.), *Chicago Linguistic Society, 8,* 316–328.

Ross, J. (1973a). A fake NP squish. In C. Bailey & R. Shuy (Eds.), *New ways of analyzing variation in English* (pp. 96–140). Washington, DC: Georgetown University Press.

Ross, J. (1973b). Nouniness. In O. Fujimura (Ed.), *Three dimensions of linguistic theory* (pp. 137–257). Tokyo: TEC Corporation.

Saffran, J. R. (2001). Words in a sea of sounds: The output of infant statistical learning. *Cognition, 81*(2), 149–169.

Saffran, J. R. (2003). Statistical language learning: Mechanisms and constraints. *Current Directions in Psychological Science, 12,* 110–114.

Saffran, J. R., Aslin, R. N., & Newport, E. L. (1996). Statistical learning by 8-month-old infants. *Science, 274,* 1926–1928.

Saxton, M. (1997). The contrast theory of negative input. *Journal of Child Language, 24,* 139–161.

Saxton, M. (2000). Negative evidence and negative feedback: Immediate effects on the grammaticality of child speech. *First Language, 20,* 221–252.

Shepard, R. N., & Judd, S. A. (1976). Perceptual illusion of rotation of three-dimensional objects. *Science, 191,* 952-954.

Slobin, D. I., & Bever, T.G. (1982). Children use canonical sentence schemas: A crosslinguistic study of word order and inflections. *Cognition, 12,* 229–265.

Svenonius, P. (2002). *Subjects, expletives, and the EPP.* New York: Oxford University Press.

Townsend, D., & Bever, T. G. (2001). *Sentence comprehension.* Cambridge, MA: MIT Press.

Tsotsos, J., Liu, Y., Trujillo, J., Pomplun, M., Simine, E., & Kunhao, Z. (2005). Attending to visual motion. *Computer vision and image understanding, 100,* 3–40.

Valian, V. (1999). Input and language acquisition. In W. C. R. T. K. Bhatia (Ed.), *Handbook of child language acquisition* (pp. 497–530). New York: Academic Press.

Vergnaud, J. R. (1985). Dépendance et niveaux de représentation en syntaxe. *Lingvisticae Investigationes Supplementa, 13,* 351–371.

Wertheimer, M. (1912) Experimentelle Studien über das Sehen von Bewegung. *Zeitschrift für Psychologie, 61,* 161–265.

Wertheimer, M. (1925). *Drei Abhandlungen zur Gestalttheorie.* Erlangen: Verlag der Philosophischen Akademie.

Wertheimer, M. (1945). *Productive thinking.* New York: Harper.

Wexler, K., & Culicover, P. (1980). *Formal principles of language acquisition.* Cambridge, MA: MIT Press.

Wonnacott, E., Newport, E., & Tanenhaus, M. (2007). Acquiring and processing verb argument structure: Distributional learning in a miniature language. *Cognitive Psychology, 17,* 662–707.

Yang, C. (2002). *Knowledge and learning in natural language.* New York: Oxford University Press.

Yang, C. (2006). *The infinite gift.* New York: Scribner.

7

THE COMPONENTS OF LANGUAGE: WHAT'S SPECIFIC TO LANGUAGE, AND WHAT'S SPECIFIC TO HUMANS[1]

STEVEN PINKER AND RAY JACKENDOFF

7.1. The Issue of What Is Special to Language

In the context of contemporary mentalist study of language, one way of couching the question of language universals is in terms of language acquisition: What components are universally available in the brains of language learners that make possible the relatively rapid acquisition of language? The present chapter addresses this question—the character of the human language capacity. We should be clear, however, that the answer to this question may not yield characteristics common to all human languages—a more traditional interpretation of "language universals"— in that some components of the universal brain capacity may not be universally deployed.

Here we are more concerned with the question of what kind of biological system language is, and how it relates to other systems in our own species and others. This question embraces a number of more specific ones. The first is which aspects of the faculty are learned from environmental input and which aspects arise from the design of the brain (including the ability to learn the learned parts)—the language capacity in our sense. To take a clear example, the fact that a canine pet is called *dog* in English but *chien* in French is learned, but the fact that words can be learned at all hinges on the predisposition of children to interpret the noises made by others as meaningful signals.

A second question is what parts of a person's language ability (learned or built-in) are specific to language and what parts belong to more general abilities. Words, for example, are specifically a part of language, but the use of the lungs and the vocal cords, although necessary for spoken language, are not limited to language. The answers to this question will often not be dichotomous. The vocal tract, for example, is clearly not exclusively used for language, yet in the course of human evolution it may have been tuned to subserve language at the expense of other functions, such as breathing and swallowing.

A third question is which aspects of the language capacity are uniquely human, and which are shared with other groups of animals, either homologously, by inheritance from a common ancestor, or analogously, by adaptation to a common function. This dimension cuts across the others. The system of sound distinctions found in human languages is both specific to language and uniquely human (partly because of the unique anatomy of the human vocal tract). The sensitive period for learning language may be specific to certain aspects of language, but it has analogues in developmental phenomena throughout the animal kingdom, most notably bird song. The capacity for forming concepts is necessary for language, as it provides the system of meaning that language expresses, but it is not specific to language: it is also used in reasoning about the world. And because other primates engage in such reasoning, it is not uniquely human (though parts of it may be). As with the first two questions, answers will seldom be dichotomous. There will often be mixtures of shared and unique attributes, reflecting the evolutionary process in which an ancestral primate design was retained, modified, augmented, or lost in the human lineage. Answers to this question have clear implications for the evolution of language. If the language faculty has many features that are specific to language itself, it suggests that the faculty was a target of natural selection. If, on the other hand, it represents a minor extension of capacities that existed in the ancestral primate lineage, it could be the result of a chance mutation that became fixed in the species through drift or other nonadaptive evolutionary mechanisms (Pinker & Bloom, 1990).

One hypothesis about what is special about language is proposed by Hauser, Chomsky, and Fitch (2002) (henceforth HCF). They differentiate (as we do) between aspects of language that are special to language (narrow language faculty) and the faculty of language in its entirety, including parts that are shared with other psychological abilities (broad language faculty). They propose that "the narrow language faculty comprises only the core computational mechanisms of recursion as they appear in narrow syntax and the mappings to the interfaces" (i.e., the interfaces with mechanisms of speech perception, speech production, conceptual knowledge, and intentions). They further suggest that "most, if not all, of the broad language faculty is based on mechanisms shared with nonhuman animals" and that the narrow language faculty—the computational mechanism of recursion—is recently evolved and unique to our species" (p. 1573). They go on to speculate that recursion may not even have evolved for language itself but for other cognitive abilities such as navigation, number, or social relationships. In other words, HCF propose that recursion is the only thing that distinguishes language (a) from other human capacities and (b) from the capacities of animals. These factors are independent. The narrow faculty of language might include more than recursion, falsifying (a). Or it might consist only of recursion, although parts of the broad faculty might be uniquely human as well, falsifying (b).

As HCF note (p. 1572), the two of us have both advanced a position rather different from theirs, namely that the language faculty, like other biological systems showing signs of complex adaptive design (Dawkins, 1986; Williams, 1966), is a system of coadapted traits that evolved by natural selection (Jackendoff, 1992, 1994, 2002; Pinker, 1994b, 2003; Pinker & Bloom, 1990). Specifically, the language faculty evolved in the human lineage for the communication of complex propositions. HCF contrast this idea with their recursion-only hypothesis, which "has the interesting effect of nullifying the argument from design, and thus rendering the status of the narrow language faculty as an adaptation open to question" (p. 1573).

In this chapter we contrast our view with HCF's. We will show that there is considerably more of language that is special, though still a plausible product of the processes of evolution. We will assess the key bodies of evidence, coming to a different reading from HCF's. We organize our discussion by distinguishing the conceptual, sensorimotor, and specifically linguistic aspects of the broad language faculty in turn.

7.2. Conceptual Structure

Let us begin with the messages that language expresses: mental representations in the form of conceptual structure (what HCF call the "conceptual-intentional system"). The primate literature, incisively analyzed in HCF, gives us good reason to believe that primates possess some of the foundations of the human conceptual system, such as the major subsystems dealing with spatial, causal, and social reasoning. If chimpanzees could talk, they would have things to talk about that we would recognize. For instance, Cheney and Seyfarth (1990, 2006) develop detailed arguments that vervet monkeys and baboons make use of combinatorial concepts such as *x is kin of y*, *x is dominant to y*, and *x is an ally of y* in understanding the relationships among others with whom they interact. These can be seen as precursors of the far more elaborate human versions of these concepts.

Some aspects of the human conceptual system, such as Theory of Mind (intuitive psychology) and parts of intuitive physics, are absent in monkeys and questionable or at best rudimentary in chimpanzees (HCF; Povinelli, 2000; Tomasello, Carpenter, Call, Behne, & Moll, 2005). They are special to humans, though not special to language. We add that many other conceptual systems, though not yet systematically studied in nonhuman primates, are conspicuous in human verbal interactions, but are hard to discern in any aspect of primates' naturalistic behavior.

They include essences (a major component of intuitive biology and chemistry), ownership,[2] multipart tools, fatherhood, romantic love, and most moral and deontic concepts. We suspect that these abilities, like Theory of Mind, are absent or discernable only in rudimentary form in other primates. These too would be uniquely human aspects of the broad language faculty, serving also as part of a system for nonlinguistic reasoning about the world.

In addition, there are domains of human concepts that are probably unlearnable without language (Jackendoff, 1996). For example, the notion of a *week* depends on counting time periods that cannot all be perceived at once; we doubt that such a concept could be developed or learned without the mediation of language. More striking is the possibility that numbers themselves (beyond those that can be subitized) are parasitic on language—that they depend on learning the sequence of number words, the syntax of number phrases, or both (Bloom, 1994a; Wiese, 2004). Vast domains of human understanding, including the supernatural and sacred, the specifics of folk and formal science, human-specific kinship systems (such as the distinction between cross-cousins and parallel cousins), and formal social roles (such as "justice of the peace" and "treasurer"), can be acquired only with the help of language.[3] The overall picture is that there is a substrate of combinatorial conceptual structure in chimps, overlain by some uniquely human but not necessarily language-based subsystems, in turn overlain by subsystems that depend on the preexistence of linguistic expression. Thus, it is impossible to say that conceptual structure as a whole is uniquely human, or uniquely linguistic, or neither; the system is the result of a mixture of evolutionary old and new factors.

7.3. Speech Perception

Turning to the sensorimotor end of language, a longstanding proposal about the narrow language faculty is Alvin Liberman's hypothesis that "Speech is Special" (SiS): speech recognition is a mode of perception distinct from our inherited primate auditory analyzers, in being adapted to recover the articulatory intentions of a human speaker (Liberman, 1985, 1991; Liberman, Cooper, Shankweiler, & Studdert-Kennedy, 1967; Liberman & Mattingly, 1989).

One of the first kinds of evidence adduced for SiS, dating to the 1950s, was the existence of categorical phoneme perception, in which pairs of phonemes differing in, say, voicing (e.g., *p* and *b*) are discriminated more accurately than pairs of stimuli separated by the same physical difference (in this case, in voice-onset time) but falling into the same phonemic category (both voiced, or both unvoiced). This particular bit of evidence for human uniqueness was deflated in the 1970s by findings that chinchillas make similar discriminations (Kuhl & Miller, 1975). HCF cite this as evidence against SiS, together with three other findings: that certain animals can make auditory distinctions based on formant frequency, that tamarin monkeys can learn to discriminate the gross rhythms of different languages, and that monkeys can perceive formants in their own species' vocalizations. These phenomena suggest that at least some aspects of the ability to perceive speech were present long before the advent of language. Of course, some version of this conclusion is unavoidable: human ancestors began with a primate auditory system, adapted to perform complex analyses of the auditory world, and it is inconceivable that a system for speech perception in humans could have begun de novo.

How much of the human capacity for phonetic perception is present in other species? Most experiments testing the perception of human speech by nonhuman animals have them discriminate pairs of speech sounds, often after extensive operant conditioning (supervised learning). It is not surprising that some animals can do so, or even that their perceptual boundaries resemble those of humans, because auditory analyzers suited for nonspeech distinctions might suffice to discriminate among speech sounds—even if the analyzers humans use are different (Trout, 2001, 2003b). For example, a mammalian circuit that uses onset asynchrony to distinguish two overlapping auditory events from one event with a complex timbre might be sufficient to discriminate voiced from unvoiced consonants (Bregman & Pinker, 1978). But humans do not just make one-bit discriminations between pairs of phonemes. Rather, they can process a continuous, information-rich stream of speech. In doing so, they rapidly distinguish individual words from tens of thousands of distracters despite the absence of acoustic cues for phoneme and word boundaries, while compensating in real time for the distortions introduced by coarticulation and by variations in the age, sex, accent, identity, and emotional state of the speaker. And all of this is accomplished by children as a product of unsupervised learning. A monkey's ability to be trained to discriminate pairs of phonemes provides little evidence that its auditory system would be up to the task accomplished by humans. It would be extraordinarily difficult at present to conduct experiments that fairly compared a primate's ability to a human's, fully testing the null hypothesis.

Moreover, there is considerable evidence which suggests that speech is indeed special (Anderson, 2004; Liberman, 1985, 1991; Remez, 1989, 1994; Trout, 2001, 2003b). First, speech and sound are phenomenologically different: under certain conditions, a given sound can be perceived simultaneously as part of a syllable and as a nonspeech-like chirp (Liberman & Mattingly, 1989), or a stretch of sound can be heard to flip qualitatively between speech and nonspeech (Remez, Pardo, Piorkowski, & Rubin, 2001).

Second, in humans the perception of speech dissociates in a number of ways from the perception of auditory events (the latter presumably using the analyzers we share with other primates). Neuroimaging and brain-damage studies suggest that partly distinct sets of brain areas subserve speech and nonspeech sounds (Hickok & Poeppel, 2000; Poeppel, 2001; Trout, 2001; Vouloumanos, Kiehl, Werker, & Liddle, 2001). A clear example is pure word deafness, in which a patient loses the ability to analyze speech while recognizing other environmental sounds (Hickok & Poeppel, 2000; Poeppel, 2001). Cases of amusia and auditory agnosia, in which patients can understand speech yet fail to appreciate music or recognize environmental sounds (Peretz, Gagnon, & Bouchard, 1998; Poeppel, 2001), show that speech and nonspeech perception in fact doubly dissociate.

Third, many of the complex hallmarks of speech perception appear early in infancy (Eimas & Miller, 1992; Miller & Eimas, 1983). Recent studies suggest that young infants, including neonates, prefer speech sounds to nonspeech sounds with similar spectral and temporal properties. These include sounds that would have been indistinguishable in the womb, hence the preference cannot be explained by learning in utero (Vouloumanos & Werker, 2004a, 2004b).

Fourth, comparisons among primates turn up significant differences between their abilities to perceive speech and our abilities. For example, monkeys fail to categorize consonants according to place of articulation using formant transitions alone (Sinnott & Williamson, 1999). They discriminate /ra/ from /la/ at a different boundary from the one salient to humans (Sinnott & Brown, 1997). They fail to segregate the initial consonant from the vowel when compensating for syllable length in discriminating phonemes (Sinnott, Brown, & Borneman, 1998). They fail to trade off the duration of the silent gap with the formant transition in perceiving stop consonants within consonant clusters (Sinnott & Saporita, 2000). They fail to show the asymmetrical "magnet effect" that characterizes infants' discrimination of speech sounds varying in acoustic similarity to prototype vowels (Kuhl, 1991). And their subjective similarity space among vowels (measured by discrimination reaction times analyzed by multidimensional scaling) is very different from that of humans (Sinnott, Brown, Malik, & Kressley, 1997). Chimpanzees, too, have a subjective similarity space for vowels that differs from humans' and, like macaques, have difficulty discriminating vowel pairs differing in advancement or frontness (Kojima & Kiritani, 1989). Quail (Trout, 2003a)[4] and budgerigars (Dooling & Brown, 1990) that have been trained to discriminate human speech sounds also show patterns of discrimination and generalization that differ from those of humans. A recent review of research on speech perception in humans, chinchillas, budgerigars, and quail showed that the phoneme boundaries for humans and animals differed in more than a third of the studies (Sinnott, 1998). These findings must be qualified by the fact that (a) some of them may be matters of quantitative auditory tuning rather than qualitative differences in the auditory system, and (b) that human speech perception necessarily reflects the effects of extensive experience listening to a specific language. Nonetheless, if findings of similarities between humans and animals trained on human speech contrasts are taken as evidence that primate audition is a sufficient basis for human speech perception, findings of differences following such training must be taken as weakening such a conclusion. We conclude that SiS stands, and phonetic perception should be taken as part of the narrow language faculty.

7.4. Speech Production

On the articulatory side of speech, HCF cite two arguments against evolutionary adaptation in the human lineage. One is the discovery that the descended human larynx (which allows a large space of discriminable vowels, while compromising other functions) can be found in certain other mammalian species, where it may have evolved to exaggerate perceived size. HCF note that although a descended larynx "undoubtedly plays an important role in speech production in modern humans, it need not have first evolved for this function," but may be an example of "preadaptation" (in which a trait originally was selected for some function other than the one it currently serves). But this suggestion, even if correct, does not speak to the issue of whether the human vocal tract (and not just recursion) was evolutionarily shaped to subserve human language. Modifications of function are ubiquitous in natural selection (e.g., primate hands, bear paws, and bat wings are adaptations that evolved by natural selection from the fins of fish), so the fact that a trait was initially shaped by selection for one function does not imply that it was not subsequently shaped by selection for another function. Thus, even if the larynx originally descended to exaggerate size, that says nothing about whether its current anatomical position was subsequently maintained, extended, or altered by selection pressures to enhance speech.

Moreover, the argument that the larynx's position was adapted for size exaggeration is weak. The human larynx is permanently descended in women, children, and infants past the age of 3 months (Lieberman, 1984), all of whom speak or are learning to speak and none of whom, in comparison with adult males engaged in intrasexual competition, had much evolutionary incentive to exaggerate size if doing so would incur costs in other functions. Compare this with a related trait that is clearly adapted to size exaggeration in intrasexual competition, namely, lowered vocal fundamental frequency. This trait, as expected, is specifically found in males of reproductive age. Moreover, even with its descended larynx, the human supralaryngeal vocal tract is no longer than what would be expected for a primate of our size, because the human oral cavity has shortened in evolution: humans, unlike chimpanzees, don't have snouts (Lieberman, 2003). Finally, the descended larynx is only part of a suite of vocal-tract modifications in human evolution, including changes in the shape of the tongue and jaw, that expand the space of discriminable speech sounds despite compromises in other organic functions, such as breathing, chewing, and swallowing (Lieberman, 1984, 2003), and none of these have to do with size exaggeration.

HCF's second argument against human adaptations for speech production is the discovery that not only humans, but also some birds and primates produce formants (time-varying acoustic energy bands) in their vocalizations by manipulating the supralaryngeal vocal tract, a talent formerly thought to be uniquely human. Still, by all accounts such manipulations represent only a fraction of the intricate gestures of lips, velum, larynx, and tip, body, and root of the tongue executed by speakers of all human languages (Browman & Goldstein, 1992; Hauser, 1996). Other evidence also suggests a human adaptation for vocal production. In comparison with extant apes and pre-*sapiens* hominids, modern humans have an enlarged region of the spinal cord responsible for the voluntary control over breathing required for speech production (MacLarnon & Hewitt, 1999).[5] Humans also display greater cortical control over articulation and breathing, compared with the largely subcortical control found in other primates (Deacon, 1997). And as Darwin noted, the innate vocal babbling of human infants is one of the clearest signs that "man has an instinctive tendency to speak."

Nonhuman primates are also notoriously resistant to training of their vocalizations (Hauser, 1996), and as HCF themselves note, they show no ability to learn vocalizations through imitation. HCF try to downplay the difference between humans and primates by pointing out that vocal imitation is not uniquely human. But this is irrelevant to the question of whether vocal imitation evolved for language in the human lineage. The other species that evolved comparable talents, namely certain birds and porpoises, are not ancestral to humans, and must have evolved their talents independently of the course of human evolution.

Moreover, the human capacity for vocal imitation is rather eccentric. Humans can more or less imitate animal noises and car horns and buzz saws, but not as well as some birds; and people can imitate melodies, with a great deal of interindividual variation. Even the ability to convincingly imitate a foreign or regional accent is the exception rather than the rule among human adults, and adults are notoriously poor at imitating the phonetics of a second language. On the other hand, all normal children can imitate the speech pattern of the adults around them in extremely fine and accurate detail. At a crude level this is all "vocal imitation," but there is something particularly fine grained, adept, and species ubiquitous about the child's imitation of the sound pattern of a language, arguing for an imitative specialization for speech, another aspect of the narrow language faculty.

7.5. Phonology

Having the potential to articulate speech sounds—that is, having a vocal tract of the right shape, and controllable in the right ways—is not the same as being able to produce the sounds of a language. The articulatory commands sent to the vocal tract to produce speech are organized in terms of a concatenation of discrete speech segments. Speech segments are drawn from a finite structured repertoire of phonemes, each defined by a set of discrete articulatory or acoustic feature values such as voicing, place of articulation, and mode of onset and release. The concatenation of speech segments is structured into patterned rhythmic constituents, such as syllables, feet, and prosodic phrases, upon which are superimposed systematic patterns of stress and pitch. The composition of the segments can be modified in rule-governed ways according to their contexts (as in the three pronunciations of the past tense suffix in *walked, jogged,* and *patted*). Languages differ in their repertoire of speech segments, their repertoire of syllable and intonation patterns, and in constraints, local and nonlocal, on how one sound can affect the pronunciation of others. This system of patterns and constraints is couched in terms of *phonological structure.*

The set of phonological structures of a language forms a "discrete infinity" (to use Chomsky's term), in that any language has an unlimited number of phonological structures, built from a finite number of discrete units. One can always concatenate segments into longer and longer well-formed phonological sequences (whether meaningful or not). Although the segmental/syllabic aspect of phonological structure is discretely infinite and hierarchically structured, it is not technically recursive: for instance, a syllable cannot be embedded in another syllable. Full syllables can only be concatenated, an operation that does not require true recursion.[6]

Is phonological structure specific to language, or does it serve other more general purposes? Hierarchically and featurally organized gestures characterize other domains of motor control, such as manual manipulation. However, the kinds of constituents, the principles of combination, and the nature of the adjustment processes in phonology appear to be specific to language. And unlike motor programs, phonological structure is a level of representation that is crucially used both in perception and production.[7] Moreover, every language contains phonological rules, a set of partly arbitrary, learned conventions for assigning stress and prosody and for adjusting the form of various segments to their context. These are not just general-purpose real-time adjustments to ease articulation or clarity.

Rhythmic organization similar to that of phonology appears in music, but with somewhat different implementation. The two rhythmic components might be homologous the way fingers and toes are; hybrids of the two appear in poetry, song, and chant (Jackendoff, 1989; Jackendoff & Lerdahl, 2006; Lerdahl & Jackendoff, 1983). We do not know of other human capacities that have been shown to reflect this formal organization, though it is an interesting open question.

Is phonological structure uniquely human? It appears that some combinatorial properties of phonology have analogues in some species of birdsong, and perhaps in some cetacean song, but not in any primates, suggesting that these properties evolved separately in humans. The rhythmic properties of language and music may well be unique to humans: informal observations suggest that no other primate can easily be trained to move to an auditory beat, as in marching, dancing, tapping the feet, or clapping the hands (Brown, Merker, & Wallin, 2000, p. 12). This is surely one of the most elementary characteristics of the human rhythmic response, displayed spontaneously by young children. And the rule-governed recombination of a reper- toire of tones, which appears in different guises in music, tone languages, and more subtly in intonation contours of language, is as far as we know unparalleled else- where. So overall, major characteristics of phonology are specific to language (or to language and music), uniquely human, discretely infinite, and not recursive. Thus phonology represents a major counterexample to both parts of the recursion-only hypothesis.

There are good adaptive reasons for a distinct level of combinatorial phonolog- ical structure to have evolved as part of the language faculty. As noted as early as Hockett (1960), "duality of patterning"—the existence of two levels of rule-governed combinatorial structure, one combining meaningless sounds into morphemes, the other combining meaningful morphemes into words and phrases—is a universal design feature of human language. A combinatorial sound system is a solution to the problem of encoding a large number of concepts (tens of thousands) into a far smaller number of discriminable speech sounds (dozens). A fixed inventory of sounds, when combined into strings, can encode a large number of words without requiring lis- teners to make finer and finer analogue discriminations among physically similar sounds. This observation has been borne out in computer simulations of language evolution (Nowak & Krakauer, 1999).

Phonological adjustment rules also have an intelligible rationale. Phonologists have long noted that many of them act to smooth out articulation or enhance dis- criminability. Because these two requirements are often at cross-purposes (slurred speech is easy to produce but hard to discriminate; exaggerated enunciation vice- versa), a fixed set of rules delineating which adjustments are mandated within a speech community may act in service of the "parity" requirement of language (Liberman & Mattingly, 1989; Slobin, 1977), namely, that the code be usable both by speakers and hearers.

Whether or not these hypotheses about the adaptive function of phonology are correct, it is undeniable that phonology constitutes a distinct level of organization of all human languages, in many respects special to language, and with only very partial analogues at best in other species.

7.6. Words

We now come to an aspect of language that is utterly essential to it: the word. In the minimal case, a word is an arbitrary association of a chunk of phonology and a chunk of conceptual structure, stored in speakers' long-term memory (the lexicon). Some words, such as *hello*, *ouch*, *yes*, and *allakazam*, do not combine with other words (other than trivially, as in direct quotes). But most words (as well as smaller morphemes such as affixes) can combine into syntactic phrases, as well as into complex words such as compounds (e.g., *armchair*) and other derived forms (e.g., *squeezability*) according to principles of morphology. Morphology and syntax constitute the classical domain of recursion.

Words have several properties that appear to be uniquely human. The first is that there are so many of them—50,000 in a garden-variety speaker's lexicon, more than 100 times the most extravagant claims for vocabulary in language-trained apes or in natural primate call systems (Wallman, 1992). The second is the range and precision of concepts that words express, from concrete to abstract (*lily*, *joist*, *telephone*, *bargain*, *glacial*, *abstract*, *from*, *any*). Third, they all have to be learned. This certainly requires proficiency at vocal imitation (see section 7.4.). But it also requires a prodigious ability to construct the proper meaning on the basis of linguistic and nonlinguistic contexts. Children come into their second year of life expecting the noises other people make to be used symbolically; much of the job of learning language is figuring out what concepts (or sets of things in the world, depending on your view of semantics) these noises are symbols for.

HCF observe that "the rate at which children build the lexicon is so massively different from nonhuman primates that one must entertain the possibility of an independently evolved mechanism." They also note that "unlike the best animal examples of putatively referential signals, most of the words of human language are not associated with specific functions" (1576) and may be "detached from the here and now," another feature of words that may be "uniquely human." These observations threaten their claim that recursion is the only uniquely human component of the faculty of language. They attempt to deal with this apparent problem by suggesting that word learning is not specific to language, citing a hypothesis, which they attribute to Bloom (1999) and Markson and Bloom (1997) that "human children may use domain-general mechanisms to acquire and recall words." Actually, although Bloom and Markson did argue against a dedicated system for learning words, they did not conclude that words are acquired by a *domain-general* mechanism. Rather, they argued that word learning is accomplished by the child's Theory of Mind, a mechanism specific to the domain of intuitive psychology, possibly unique to humans.

In any case, the conclusion that there are no mechanisms of learning or representation specific to words may be premature. The experiment by Bloom and Markson cited by HCF showed that children display similar levels of recognition memory after a single exposure to either a new word or a new fact (e.g., "My uncle gave it to me"). But on any reasonable account, words and facts are stored using the same kinds of neural mechanisms responsible for storage, retention, and forgetting. A demonstration that word learning and fact learning have this property in common does not prove they have all their properties in common.

Markson and Bloom's case that word learning can be reduced to a Theory of Mind mechanism is most tenable for the basic act of learning that a noun is the label for a perceptible object. But words are not just names for things (see Bloom, 1999). They also are marked for a syntactic category (verb, preposition, and so on), for obligatory grammatically encoded arguments (agent, theme, path, and so on), and for restrictions on the syntactic properties of their complements (e.g., whether each one is headed by a preposition, a finite verb, or a nonfinite verb) (Gentner, 1981; Jackendoff, 2002; Pinker, 1989). This information is partly idiosyncratic to each word and therefore must be stored in the lexicon. It cannot be identified with the conceptual database that makes up general world knowledge. It has close linguistic, psychological, and neurological ties to syntax (Caramazza & Shapiro, 2004; Gentner, 1981; Pinker, 1989; Shapiro, Pascual-Leone, Mottaghy, Gangitano, & Caramazza, 2001), and requires, at least in part, syntactic analysis in order to be acquired (Gleitman, 1990; Pinker, 1994a).

Moreover, functional morphemes such as articles, auxiliaries, and affixes are also part of the lexicon (as each involves a pairing between a sound and some other information, both specific to the particular language), yet the information they encode (case, agreement, finiteness, voice, and so on) is continuous with the information encoded by syntax. Such words are not used, and presumably could not be acquired, in isolation from syntactic context. So, although Theory of Mind is undoubtedly involved in word learning, it is hard to see how words can be carved away from the narrow language faculty altogether.

Even in the case of learning nouns, there is some reason to believe that children treat facts and words in different ways, reflecting the hallmarks of words that distinguish them from other kinds of factual knowledge. One is that words are bidirectional and arbitrary ("Saussurean") signs: a child, upon hearing a word used by a speaker, can conclude that other speakers in the community, and the child himself or herself, may use the word with the same meaning and expect to be understood (Hurford, 1989). This is one of the assumptions that allows babies to use words upon exposure to them, as opposed to having to have their vocal output shaped or reinforced by parental feedback. Diesendruck and Markson (2001) (see also Au & Glusman, 1990) show that young children tacitly assume that speakers share a code. If one speaker labels a novel object as a *mep* out of earshot of a second speaker, and the second speaker then asks about a *jop*, the children interpret the second speaker as referring to a different object. Presumably this is because they attribute common knowledge of a name (*mep*) to that speaker, even though they had never witnessed that speaker learning the name. In contrast, if one speaker mentions a *fact* about an object (e.g., "my sister gave it to me") out of earshot of a second speaker, and the second speaker then asks about an object characterized by another fact (e.g., "dogs like to play with it"), they do not interpret the second speaker as referring to a different object. Presumably this is because they do not attribute common knowledge of facts to the members of a speech community in the way they do with words. Somewhat to their surprise, Diesendruck and Markson conclude, "Interestingly, the present findings lend indirect support to the idea that in some respects, word learning *is* special" (p. 639).

Another hallmark of words is that their meanings are defined not just by the relation of the word to a concept but by the relation of the word to other words, forming organized sets such as superordinates, antonyms, meronyms (parts), and avoiding true synonyms (Clark, 1993; Deacon, 1997; Miller, 1991; Miller & Fellbaum, 1991). Behrend and collaborators (Behrend, Scofield, & Kleinknecht, 2001; Scofield & Behrend, 2003), refining a phenomenon discovered by Markman (1989), showed that 2-year-old children assign a novel word to an object they are unfamiliar with rather than to one they are familiar with (presumably a consequence of an avoidance of synonymy), but they show no such effect for novel facts.

Another distinctive feature about words is that (with the exception of proper names, which in many regards are more like phrases than words; see Bloom, 1994b) they are generic, referring to kinds of objects and events rather than specific objects and events (di Sciullo & Williams, 1987). Waxman and Booth (2001) and Behrend, Scofield, and Kleinknecht (2001) showed that children generalize a newly learned *noun* to other objects of the same kind, but do not generalize a newly learned *fact* (e.g., "my uncle gave it to me") to other objects of the same kind. Similarly, Gelman and Heyman (1999) showed that children assume that a person labeled with the word *carrot-eater* has a taste for carrots, whereas one described as eating carrots (a fact about the person) merely ate them at least once.

Our assessment of the situation is therefore that words, as shared, organized linkages of phonological, conceptual, and (morpho-)syntactic structures, are a distinctive language-specific part of human knowledge. The child appears to come to social situations anticipating that the noises made by other humans are made up of words, and this makes the learning of words different in several regards from the learning of facts. Moreover, a good portion of people's knowledge of words (especially verbs and functional morphemes) consists of exactly the kind of information that is manipulated by recursive syntax, the component held to make up the narrow language faculty, and therefore cannot be segregated from it and the process of the evolution of language in general.

7.7. Syntax

We finally turn to syntactic structure, the principles by which words and morphemes are concatenated into sentences. In our view, the function of syntax is to help determine how the meanings of words are combined into the meanings of phrases and sentences. Every linguist recognizes that (on the surface, at least) syntax employs at least four combinatorial devices. The first is collecting words hierarchically into syntactic phrases, where syntactic phrases correspond (in prototypical cases) to constituents of meaning. (For example, word strings such as *Dr. Ruth discussed sex with Dick Cavett* are ambiguous because their words can be grouped into phrases in two different ways.) This is the recursive component emphasized by HCF. The second is the ordering of words or phrases within a phrase, for example, requiring that the verb of a sentence fall in a certain position, such as second, or that the phrase serving as topic come first. Many languages of the world are not as strict about word order as English, and often the operative principles of phrase order concern topic and focus, a fairly marginal issue in English grammar. A third major syntactic device is agreement, whereby verbs or adjectives are marked with inflections that correspond to the number, person, grammatical gender, or other classificatory features of syntactically related nouns. The fourth is case-marking, whereby noun phrases are marked with inflections (nominative, accusative, etc.) depending on the grammatical and/or semantic role of the phrase with respect to a verb, preposition, or another noun.

Different languages rely on these mechanisms to different extents to convey who did what to whom, what is where, and other semantic relations. English relies heavily on order and constituency, but has vestigial agreement and no case, except on pronouns. The Australian language Warlpiri has virtually free word order and an exuberant system of case and agreement; Russian and Classical Latin are not far behind. Many languages use the systems redundantly, for instance German, with its rich gender and case systems, moderate use of agreement, and fairly strong constraints on phrase order.

And this barely scratches the surface. Languages are full of devices like pronouns and articles, which help signal information the speaker expects to be old or new to the hearer; quantifiers, tense and aspect markers, complementizers, and auxiliaries, which express temporal and logical relations, and restrictive or appositive modification (as in relative clauses); and grammatical distinctions among questions, imperatives, statements, and other kinds of illocutionary force, signaled by phrase order, morphology, or intonation. A final important device is long-distance dependency, which can relate a question word or relative pronoun to a distant verb, as in *Which theory did you expect Fred to think Melvin had disproven last week?*, where *which theory* is understood as the object of *disprove*.

Is all this specific to language? It seems likely, given that it is special-purpose machinery for regulating the relation of sound and meaning. What other human or nonhuman ability could it serve? Yet, aside from phrase structure (in which a noun phrase, e.g., can contain a noun phrase, or a sentence can contain a sentence) and perhaps long-distance dependencies,[8] none of it involves recursion per se. A case marker may not contain another instance of a case marker; an article may not contain an article; a pronoun may not contain a pronoun, and so on for auxiliaries, tense features, and so on. Although these devices often depend on phrase structure for their implementation, their existence is not predictable from the existence of recursion, so they weaken the hypothesis that the narrow language faculty consists *only* of recursion.

7.8. The Status of Recursion

Let us turn more directly to HCF's hypothesis that recursion is uniquely human and specific to the language faculty. They speculate that recursion may have "evolved for reasons other than language," for instance, "to solve other computational problems such as navigation, number quantification, or social relations," in a module that was "impenetrable with respect to other systems. During evolution, the modular and highly domain-specific system of recursion may have become penetrable and domain-general. This opened the way for humans, perhaps uniquely, to apply the power of recursion to other problems" (Hauser et al., 2002, p. 1578).[9]

We agree with HCF that recursion is not unique to language (although language is the only recursive natural communication system). Indeed, the only reason language *needs* to be recursive is because its function is to express recursive *thoughts*. If there were no recursive thoughts, the means of expression would not need recursion either. Along with HCF, we invite detailed formal study of animal cognition and other human capacities, to ascertain which abilities require recursive mental representations and which do not. Plausible candidates include music (Lerdahl & Jackendoff, 1983), social cognition (Jackendoff, 2007), and the formulation of complex action sequences (Badler et al., 2000; Jackendoff, 2007; Miller, Galanter, & Pribram, 1960; Schank & Abelson, 1975).

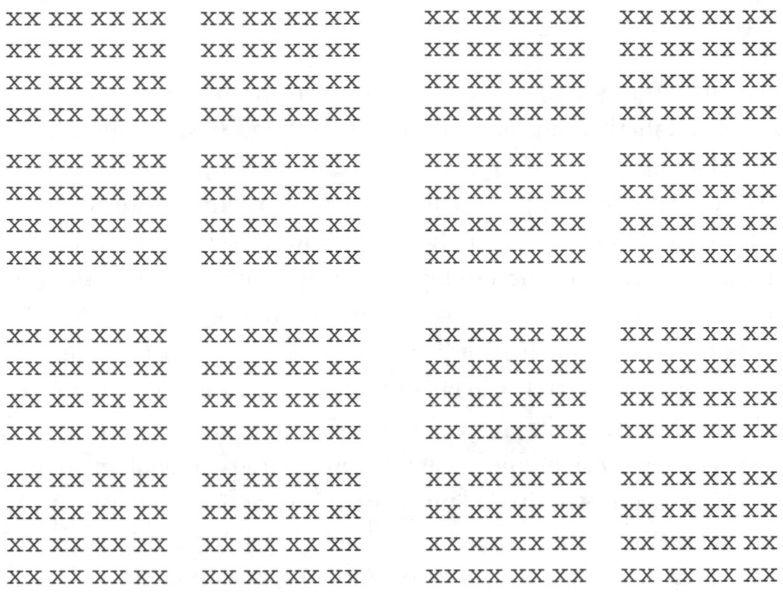

```
XX XX XX XX    XX XX XX XX    XX XX XX XX    XX XX XX XX
XX XX XX XX    XX XX XX XX    XX XX XX XX    XX XX XX XX
XX XX XX XX    XX XX XX XX    XX XX XX XX    XX XX XX XX
XX XX XX XX    XX XX XX XX    XX XX XX XX    XX XX XX XX

XX XX XX XX    XX XX XX XX    XX XX XX XX    XX XX XX XX
XX XX XX XX    XX XX XX XX    XX XX XX XX    XX XX XX XX
XX XX XX XX    XX XX XX XX    XX XX XX XX    XX XX XX XX
XX XX XX XX    XX XX XX XX    XX XX XX XX    XX XX XX XX


XX XX XX XX    XX XX XX XX    XX XX XX XX    XX XX XX XX
XX XX XX XX    XX XX XX XX    XX XX XX XX    XX XX XX XX
XX XX XX XX    XX XX XX XX    XX XX XX XX    XX XX XX XX
XX XX XX XX    XX XX XX XX    XX XX XX XX    XX XX XX XX

XX XX XX XX    XX XX XX XX    XX XX XX XX    XX XX XX XX
XX XX XX XX    XX XX XX XX    XX XX XX XX    XX XX XX XX
XX XX XX XX    XX XX XX XX    XX XX XX XX    XX XX XX XX
XX XX XX XX    XX XX XX XX    XX XX XX XX    XX XX XX XX
```

Figure 7.1. Recursion in visual grouping.

A very clear example comes from visual cognition. Consider Figure 7.1. This display is perceived as being built recursively out of discrete elements that combine to form larger discrete constituents: pairs of x's, rows of four pairs, rectangles of four rows, arrays of four rectangles, and so on. One could further combine Figure 7.1 with three more copies to form a still larger array, and continue the process indefinitely. So we have here a domain of "discrete infinity" with hierarchical structure of unlimited depth, its organization in this case governed by gestalt principles. Presumably, the principles that organize Figure 7.1 play a role in perceiving objects in terms of larger groupings, and in segregating objects into parts. Similar principles of grouping apply in music (Lerdahl & Jackendoff, 1983). This shows that recursion per se is not part of the narrow faculty of language.

What is distinctive about recursion in syntax is that (a) each constituent belongs to a specifically syntactic category such as N or VP, and (b) one member of each constituent has a distinguished status as head. Headed hierarchies are found elsewhere in cognition, for instance, in syllabic structure (which is not recursive), in conceptual structure, and in certain aspects of musical structures (Jackendoff, 1987, pp. 249–251). Thus, like many other aspects of language, syntactic recursion may be a novel combination of newly retuned capacities found elsewhere in cognition, with the addition of certain *sui generis* elements such as the repertoire of syntactic categories.

7.9. Some Genetic Evidence

Recent findings from genetics also cast doubt on the recursion-only hypothesis. There is a rare inherited impairment of language and speech caused by a dominant allele of a single gene, *FOXP2* (Lai, Fisher, Hurst, Vargha-Khadem, & Monaco, 2001). The gene has been sequenced and subjected to comparative analyses, which show that the normal version of the gene is universal in the human population, that it diverged from the primate homologue subsequent to the evolutionary split between humans and chimpanzees, and that it was a target of natural selection rather than a product of genetic drift or other stochastic evolutionary processes (Enard et al., 2002). The phenotype is complex and not completely characterized, but it is generally agreed that sufferers have deficits in articulation, production, comprehension, and judgments in a variety of domains of grammar, together with difficulties in producing sequences of orofacial movements (Bishop, 2002; Gopnik & Crago, 1991; Ullman & Gopnik, 1999; Vargha-Khadem, Watkins, Alcock, Fletcher, & Passingham, 1995). The possibility that the affected people are impaired only in recursion is a nonstarter. These findings refute the hypothesis that the only evolutionary change for language in the human lineage was one that grafted syntactic recursion onto unchanged primate input–output abilities and enhanced learning of facts. Instead, they support the notion that language evolved piecemeal in the human lineage under the influence of natural selection, with the selected genes having pleiotropic effects that incrementally improved multiple components.

Moreover, *FOXP2* is just the most clearly identified one of a number of genetic loci that cause impairments of language or related impairments, such as stuttering and dyslexia (Dale et al., 1998; Stromswold, 2001; The SLI Consortium, 2002; van der Lely, Rosen, & McClelland, 1998). None of these impairments eliminate or compromise recursion alone. Even in the realm of speech perception, genetic evidence may point to adaptation for language. A recent comparison of the genomes of mice, chimpanzees, and humans turned up a number of genes that are expressed in the development of the auditory system and that have undergone positive selection in the human lineage (Clark et al., 2003). As speech is the main feature that differentiates the auditory environments of humans and of chimpanzees in nature, the authors speculate that these evolutionary changes were in the service of enhanced perception of speech.

As more genes with effects on speech and language are identified, sequenced, and compared across individuals and species, additional tests contrasting the language-as-adaptation hypothesis with the recursion-only hypothesis will be available. The latter predicts heritable impairments that completely or partially knock out recursion but leave the people with abilities in speech perception and speech production comparable to those of chimpanzees. Our reading of the literature on language impairment is that this prediction is unlikely to be true.

7.10. Summary of Evidence

Let us summarize the state of the evidence for the content and provenance of the language capacity, as revealed by the larger design of language.

- A typical word is an association of a piece of phonological structure, a piece of syntactic structure, and a piece of conceptual structure. Words appear to be tailored to language; besides including grammatical information, they are bidirectional, shared, organized, and generic in reference. The existence of words is a language universal in the traditional sense.
- Conceptual structure, which captures the algebraic aspects of meaning relevant to linguistic expression (e.g., excluding sensory and motor imagery), is a combinatorial and potentially recursive mental representation that supports formal inference and is present in simpler form in nonlinguistic organisms such as apes and babies (Jackendoff, 1983, 2002; Pinker, 1989, 1994b). Most of the semantic information associated with utterances comes from the conceptual structures of the words themselves. All languages are built to express conceptual structure.
- What distinguishes true language from just collections of uttered words is that the semantic relations *among* the words are conveyed by recursive syntactic and morphological structures, which are largely unique to humans and to language (though recursion per se is considerably more general). In particular, the division of words into syntactic categories, and the role of syntactic and morphological structures in case, agreement, pronouns, argument structure, topic, focus, auxiliaries, question markers, and the like is specifically linguistic, though many of the categories in question are not present in all languages.
- At the other end of the architecture of language, despite early setbacks, the current evidence is strong that there is a human specialization for speech perception, going beyond the general auditory capacities of other primates.
- In speech production, control of the supralaryngeal vocal tract is incomparably more complex in human language than in other primate vocalizations. Vocal imitation and vocal learning are uniquely human among primates (talents that are consistently manifested only in speech). And syllabic babbling emerges spontaneously in human infants.
- Speech perception and production are in the service of phonology, which encodes sound patterns in terms of a discretized and patterned sequence of phonological segments, chosen from a discretized and structured repertoire

of speech sounds. The patterns in the sequence of sounds involve rhythmic and prosodic structure, as well as interactions among the featural contents of segments. The patterns form a discrete infinity and a headed hierarchy, but are not recursive. To the extent that patterned sound exists in other species, it arguably has an independent evolutionary source, as there is nothing comparable in other primates. Certain aspects of phonology, in particular rhythmic organization and certain tendencies of pitch contour, are shared with music, but much appears unique to human language, though again the exact realization of phonological structure shows considerable crosslinguistic variation.

We conclude that the narrow language faculty contains several components other than recursion. Indeed, recursion itself does not belong to the narrow language faculty, as it is actually not unique to language. We have also seen that much of the narrow faculty is overlaid on previously existing capacities such as the capacity for combinatoriality, which in some cases but not others gives rise to recursion. This makes it difficult to peel off just those aspects of language that are unique to human and unique to language. But this is what we should expect of a capacity arising through natural selection.

Key Further Readings

This chapter is based on Pinker and Jackendoff (2005) and Jackendoff and Pinker (2005), which are commentaries on Hauser et al. (2002) and Fitch, Hauser, and Chomsky (2005). Additional issues in the debate over whether language is a product of natural selection may be found in the target article, commentaries, and reply in Pinker and Bloom (1990). Good overviews of natural selection and adaptation include Dawkins (1986, 1996), Maynard Smith (1986, 1989), Ridley (1986), Weiner (1994), and Williams (1966). Specific language impairment is explained in Leonard (1998) and van der Lely, Rosen, and McClelland, (1998). An overview of the genetics of language can be found in Stromswold (2001). Methods for detecting natural selection in molecular genetic data are reviewed in Aquadro (1999), Kreitman (2000), and Przeworski, Hudson, and Di Rienzo (2000). For a broader perspective of our vision of the language capacity, see Jackendoff (2002).

Notes

1 This article is adapted from Pinker and Jackendoff (2005) and Jackendoff and Pinker (2005), and appears here with the permission of the publisher of *Cognition*. Supported by NIH grants HD-18381 (Pinker) and DC 03660 (Jackendoff). We thank Stephen Anderson,

Paul Bloom, Susan Carey, Andrew Carstairs-McCarthy, Matt Cartmill, Noam Chomsky, Barbara Citko, Peter Culicover, Dan Dennett, Tecumseh Fitch, Randy Gallistel, David Geary, Tim German, Henry Gleitman, Lila Gleitman, Adele Goldberg, Marc Hauser, Greg Hickok, David Kemmerer, Patricia Kuhl, Shalom Lappin, Philip Lieberman, Alec Marantz, Martin Nowak, Paul Postal, Robert Provine, Robert Remez, Ben Shenoy, Elizabeth Spelke, Lynn Stein, J. D. Trout, Athena Vouloumanos, and *Cognition* referees for helpful comments and discussion.

2 One finds a rough parallel in animals' territoriality, but the human notion of ownership, involving rights and obligations and the possibility of trade (Jackendoff, 2007) appears unique.

3 We leave open whether such concepts are simply impossible without language or whether they are within the expressive power of the conceptual system but require language as a crutch to attain them. They certainly cannot be shared via ostension, so language is in any event necessary for their cultural transmission.

4 R. Remez, commenting in this reference on the work of (Kluender, 1994), notes that Kluender's trained quail failed to distinguish labial and palatal phonemes. He also suggests that the quail's ability to distinguish other place-of-articulation distinctions may hinge on their detecting the salient apical bursts that initiate stop consonants rather than the formant transitions that suffice for such discriminations in humans.

5 The fact that *Homo erectus* had a spinal cord like that of other primates rules out an alternative hypothesis in which the change was an adaptation to bipedal locomotion.

6 Syllables can sometimes be expanded by limited addition of nonsyllabic material; the word *lengths*, for example, may have a syllabic structure along the line of [$_{Syl}$ [$_{Syl}$ length] s]. But there are no syllables built out of the combination of two or more full syllables, which is the crucial case for true unlimited recursion.

7 The existence in monkeys of mirror-neurons (Rizzolatti, Fadiga, Gallese, & Fogassi, 1996), which are active both in the execution and the sight of particular actions, suggests that some kind of representation shared by perception and production antedates the evolution of language in humans. However, the information coded by such neurons appears to be different from phonological representations in two ways. First, they are specific to the semantic goal of an action (e.g., reaching), rather than its physical topography, whereas phonology is concerned with details of articulation. Second, as noted by HCF, they do not support transfer from perception to production, since the ability to imitate is rudimentary or absent in monkeys, whereas humans learn to articulate speech sounds based on what they hear.

8 Long-distance dependency can involve dependencies extending into recursively embedded structures, and on some accounts involves recursive movement of the fronted phrase up through the phrase structure tree.

9 HCF argue that the ability to learn linearly ordered recursive phrase structure is uniquely human. In a clever experiment, Fitch and Hauser (2004) showed that humans but not tamarins can learn the simple recursive language $A^n B^n$ (all sequences consisting of n instances of the symbol A followed by n instances of the symbol B; such a language can be generated by the recursive rule S $\rightarrow$ A(S)B). But the relevance of this result is unclear. Although human languages are recursive, and $A^n B^n$ is recursive, $A^n B^n$ is not a possible human language. No natural language construction has such phrases, which violate the

principles of syntactic headedness (X-bar theory) that are central to syntactic structure. Also unclear is whether the human subjects who learned these artificial languages did so in terms of an A^nB^n grammar. Each stimulus consisted of a sequence of nonsense syllables spoken by a female voice followed by an equal number of syllables spoken by a male voice. Phonological content was irrelevant, and the learning could have been accomplished by counting from the first syllable of each subsequence (*high:1-2-3; low:1-2-3*). This differs from the kind of analysis mandated by a grammar of recursively embedded phrases, namely (*high-[high- [high-low]-low]-low*). Similar questions can be asked about claims by Gentner, Fenn, Margoliash, and Nusbaum (2006) regarding the learning by starlings of allegedly recursive A^nB^n patterns. If HCF's conclusion is that human syntactic competence consists only of an ability to learn recursive languages (which embrace all kinds of formal systems, including computer programming languages, mathematical notation, the set of all palindromes, and an infinity of others), the fact that actual human languages are a minuscule and well-defined subset of recursive languages is unexplained.

References

Anderson, S. R. (2004). *Dr. Dolittle's delusion: Animal communication, linguistics, and the uniqueness of human language*. New Haven: Yale University Press.

Aquadro, C. (1999). The problem of inferring selection and evolutionary history from molecular data. In M. T. Clegg, M. K. Hecht, & J. MacIntyre (Eds.), *Limits to knowledge in evolutionary biology* (pp. 135–149). New York: Plenum.

Au, T. K., & Glusman, M. (1990). The principle of mutual exclusivity in word learning: To honor or not to honor. *Child Development, 61,* 1474–1490.

Badler, N. I., Bindiganavale, R., Allbeck, J., Schuler, W., Zhao, L., & Palmer, M. (2000). A parameterized action representation for virtual human agents. In J. Cassell, J. Sullivan, S. Prevost, & E. Churchill (Eds.), *Embodied conversational agents* (pp. 256–284). Cambridge, MA: MIT Press.

Behrend, D. A., Scofield, J., & Kleinknecht, E. E. (2001). Beyond fast mapping: Young children's extensions of novel words and novel facts. *Developmental Psychology, 37*(5), 698–705.

Bishop, D. V. M. (2002). Putting language genes in perspective. *Trends in Genetics, 18*(2), 57–59.

Bloom, P. (1994a). Generativity within language and other cognitive domains. *Cognition, 51,* 177–189.

Bloom, P. (1994b). Possible names: The role of syntax-semantics mappings in the acquisition of nominals. *Lingua, 92,* 297–329.

Bloom, P. (1999). *How children learn the meanings of words*. Cambridge, MA: MIT Press.

Bregman, A. S., & Pinker, S. (1978). Auditory streaming and the building of timbre. *Canadian Journal of Psychology, 32,* 19–31.

Browman, C. P., & Goldstein, L. F. (1992). Articulatory phonology: An overview. *Phonetica, 49,* 155–180.

Brown, S., Merker, B., & Wallin, N. (2000). An introduction to evolutionary musicology. In N. Wallin, B. Merker, & S. Brown (Eds.), *The origins of music* (pp. 3–24). Cambridge, MA: MIT Press.

Caramazza, A., & Shapiro, K. A. (2004). The representation of grammatical knowledge in the brain. In L. Jenkins (Ed.), *Variation and universals in biolinguistics*. Amsterdam: Elsevier.

Cheney, D., & Seyfarth, R. (1990). *How monkeys see the world*. Chicago: University of Chicago Press.

Cheney, D., & Seyfarth, R. (2006). *Baboon metaphysics*. Chicago: University of Chicago Press.

Clark, A. G., Glanowski, S., Nielsen, R., Thomas, P. D., Kejariwal, A., Todd, M. A., et al. (2003). Inferring nonneutral evolution from human-chimp-mouse orthologous gene trios. *Science, 302*(5652), 1960–1963.

Clark, E. V. (1993). *The lexicon in acquisition*. New York: Cambridge University Press.

Dale, P. S., Simonoff, E., Bishop, D. V. M., Eley, T. C., Oliver, B., Price, T. S., et al. (1998). Genetic influence on language delay in two-year-old children. *Nature Neuroscience, 1*, 324–328.

Dawkins, R. (1986). *The blind watchmaker: Why the evidence of evolution reveals a universe without design*. New York: Norton.

Dawkins, R. (1996). *Climbing mount improbable*. New York: Norton.

Deacon, T. (1997). *The symbolic species: The coevolution of language and the brain*. New York: Norton.

di Sciullo, A. M., & Williams, E. (1987). *On the definition of word*. Cambridge, MA: MIT Press.

Diesendruck, G., & Markson, L. (2001). Children's avoidance of lexical overlap: A pragmatic account. *Developmental Psychology, 37*, 630–644.

Dooling, R. J., & Brown, S. D. (1990). Speech perception by budgerigars (*Melopsittacus undulatus*): Spoken vowels. *Perception and Psychophysics, 47*, 568–574.

Eimas, P. D., & Miller, J. L. (1992). Organization in the perception of speech by young infants. *Psychological Science, 3*(6), 340–345.

Enard, W., Przeworski, M., Fisher, S. E., Lai, C. S. L., Wiebe, V., Kitano, T., et al. (2002). Molecular evolution of *FOXP2*, a gene involved in speech and language. *Nature, 418*, 869–872.

Fitch, W. T., & Hauser, M. D. (2004). Computational constraints on syntactic processing in nonhuman primates. *Science, 303*, 377–380.

Fitch, W. T., Hauser, M. D., & Chomsky, N. (2005). The evolution of the language faculty: Clarifications and implications (Reply to Pinker and Jackendoff). *Cognition, 97*, 179–210.

Gelman, S. A., & Heyman, G. D. (1999). Carrot-eaters and creature-believers: The effects of lexicalization on children's inferences about social categories. *Psychological Science, 10*(6), 489–493.

Gentner, D. (1981). Some interesting differences between verbs and nouns. *Cognition and Brain Theory, 4*, 161–178.

Gentner, T. Q., Fenn, K. M., Margoliash, D., & Nusbaum, H. C. (2006). Recursive syntactic pattern learning by songbirds. *Nature, 440*, 1204–1207

Gleitman, L. R. (1990). The structural sources of verb meaning. *Language Acquisition, 1*, 3–55.

Gopnik, M., & Crago, M. (1991). Familial aggregation of a developmental language disorder. *Cognition, 39*, 1–50.

Hauser, M. D. (1996). *The evolution of communication*. Cambridge, MA: MIT Press.

Hauser, M. D., Chomsky, N., & Fitch, W. T. (2002). The faculty of language: What is it, who has it, and how did it evolve? *Science, 298*, 1569–1579.

Hickok, G., & Poeppel, D. (2000). Towards a functional neuroanatomy of speech perception. *Trends in Cognitive Sciences, 4*(4), 131–138.

Hockett, C. F. (1960). The origin of speech. *Scientific American, 203*, 88–111.

Hurford, J. R. (1989). Biological evolution of the Saussurean sign as a component of the language acquisition device. *Lingua, 77*, 187–222.

Jackendoff, R. (1983). *Semantics and cognition*. Cambridge, MA: MIT Press.

Jackendoff, R. (1987). *Consciousness and the computational mind*. Cambridge, MA: MIT Press.

Jackendoff, R. (1989). A comparison of rhythmic structures in music and language. In P. Kiparsky & G. Youmans (Eds.), *Phonetics and phonology*, (Vol. 1, pp. 15–44), New York: Academic Press.

Jackendoff, R. (1992). *Languages of the mind*. Cambridge, MA: MIT Press.

Jackendoff, R. (1994). *Patterns in the mind: Language and human nature*. New York: Basic Books.

Jackendoff, R. (1996). How language helps us think. *Pragmatics and Cognition, 4*, 1–34.

Jackendoff, R. (2002). *Foundations of language: Brain, meaning, grammar, evolution*. New York: Oxford University Press.

Jackendoff, R. (2007). *Language, consciousness, culture: Essays on mental structure*. Cambridge, MA: MIT Press.

Jackendoff, R., & Lerdahl, F. (2006). The capacity for music: What's special about it? *Cognition, 100*, 33–72.

Jackendoff, R., & Pinker, S. (2005). The nature of the language faculty and its implications for the evolution of language (Reply to Fitch, Hauser, and Chomsky). *Cognition, 97*, 211–225.

Kluender, K. (1994). Speech perception as a tractable problem in cognitive science. In M. Gernsbacher (Ed.), *Handbook of psycholinguistics* (pp. 173–217). San Diego: Academic Press.

Kojima, S., & Kiritani, S. (1989). Vocal-auditory functions in the chimpanzee: Vowel perception. *International Journal of Primatology, 10*, 199–213.

Kreitman, M. (2000). Methods to detect selection in populations with applications to the human, *Annual Review of Genomics and Human Genetics, 1*, 539–559.

Kuhl, P. K. (1991). Human adults and human infants show a "perceptual magnet effect" for the prototypes of speech categories, monkeys do not. *Perception and Psychophysics, 50*(2), 93–107.

Kuhl, P. K., & Miller, J. D. (1975). Speech perception by the chinchilla: Voiced-voiceless distinction in alveolar plosive consonants. *Science, 190*, 69–72.

Lai, C. S. L., Fisher, S. E., Hurst, J. A., Vargha-Khadem, F., & Monaco, A. P. (2001). A novel forkhead-domain gene is mutated in a severe speech and language disorder. *Nature, 413*, 519–523.

Leonard, L. B. (1998). *Children with specific language impairment*. Cambridge, MA: MIT Press.

Lerdahl, F., & Jackendoff, R. (1983). *A generative theory of tonal music*. Cambridge, MA: MIT Press.

Liberman, A. M. (1985). The motor theory of speech perception revised. *Cognition*, *21*, 1–36.

Liberman, A. M. (1991). Afterthoughts on modularity and the motor theory. In I. G. Mattingly & M. Studdert-Kennedy (Eds.), *Modularity and the motor theory of speech perception*. Mahwah, NJ: Erlbaum.

Liberman, A. M., Cooper, F. S., Shankweiler, D. P., & Studdert-Kennedy, M. (1967). Perception of the speech code. *Psychological Review*, *74*, 431–461.

Liberman, A. M., & Mattingly, I. G. (1989). A specialization for speech perception. *Science*, *243*, 489–494.

Lieberman, P. (1984). *The biology and evolution of language*. Cambridge, MA: Harvard University Press.

Lieberman, P. (2003). Motor control, speech, and the evolution of language. In M. Christiansen & S. Kirby (Eds.), *Language evolution: States of the art*. New York: Oxford University Press.

MacLarnon, A., & Hewitt, G. (1999). The evolution of human speech: The role of enhanced breathing control. *American Journal of Physical Anthropology*, *109*, 341–363.

Markman, E. (1989). *Categorization and naming in children: Problems of induction*. Cambridge, MA: MIT Press.

Markson, L., & Bloom, P. (1997). Evidence against a dedicated system for word learning in children. *Nature*, *385*, 813–815.

Maynard Smith, J. (1986). *The problems of biology*. Oxford: Oxford University Press.

Maynard Smith, J. (1989). *Evolutionary genetics*. New York: Oxford University Press.

Miller, G. A. (1991). *The science of words*. New York: W. H. Freeman.

Miller, G. A., & Fellbaum, C. (1991). Semantic networks of English. *Cognition*, *41*(1–3), 197–229.

Miller, G. A., Galanter, E., & Pribram, K. (1960). *Plans and the structure of behavior*. New York: Holt, Rinehart and Winston.

Miller, J. L., & Eimas, P. D. (1983). Studies on the categorization of speech by infants. *Cognition*, *13*(2), 135–165.

Nowak, M. A., & Krakauer, D. C. (1999). The evolution of language. *Proceedings of the National Academy of Science USA*, *96*, 8028–8033.

Peretz, I., Gagnon, L., & Bouchard, B. (1998). Music and emotion: Perceptual determinants, immediacy, and isolation after brain damage. *Cognition*, *68*, 111–141.

Pinker, S. (1989). *Learnability and cognition: The acquisition of argument structure*. Cambridge, MA: MIT Press.

Pinker, S. (1994a). How could a child use verb syntax to learn verb semantics? *Lingua*, *92*, 377–410.

Pinker, S. (1994b). *The language instinct*. New York: HarperCollins.

Pinker, S. (2003). Language as an adaptation to the cognitive niche. In M. Christiansen & S. Kirby (Eds.), *Language evolution: States of the art*. New York: Oxford University Press.

Pinker, S., & Bloom, P. (1990). Natural language and natural selection. *Behavioral and Brain Sciences, 13*, 707–784.

Pinker, S., & Jackendoff, R. (2005). The faculty of language: What's special about it? *Cognition, 95*, 201–236.

Poeppel, D. (2001). Pure word deafness and the bilateral processing of the speech code. *Cognitive Science, 21*(5), 679–693.

Povinelli, D. J. (2000). *Folk physics for apes.* Oxford: Oxford University Press.

Przeworski, M., Hudson, R. R., & Di Rienzo, A. (2000). Adjusting the focus on human variation. *Trends in Genetics, 16*, 296–302.

Remez, R. E. (1989). When the objects of perception are spoken. *Ecological Psychology, 1*(2), 161–180.

Remez, R. E. (1994). A guide to research on the perception of speech. In *Handbook of psycholinguistics* (pp. 145–172). New York: Academic Press.

Remez, R. E., Pardo, J. S., Piorkowski, R. L., & Rubin, P. E. (2001). On the bistability of sine wave analogues of speech. *Psychological Science, 12*(1), 24–29.

Ridley, M. (1986). *The problems of evolution.* New York: Oxford University Press.

Rizzolatti, G., Fadiga, L., Gallese, V., & Fogassi, L. (1996). Premotor cortex and the recognition of motor actions. *Cognitive Brain Research, 3*, 131–141.

Schank, R., & Abelson, R. (1975). *Scripts, plans, goals, and knowledge.* Hillsdale, NJ: Erlbaum.

Scofield, J., & Behrend, D. A. (2003). Two-year-olds differentially disambiguate novel words and facts. *Journal of Child Language, 34*, 875–889.

Shapiro, K. A., Pascual-Leone, A., Mottaghy, F. M., Gangitano, M., & Caramazza, A. (2001). Grammatical distinctions in the left frontal cortex. *Journal of Cognitive Neuroscience, 13*(6), 713–720.

Sinnott, J. M. (1998). Comparative phoneme boundaries. *Current Topics in Acoustical Research, 2*, 135–138.

Sinnott, J. M., & Brown, C. H. (1997). Perception of the American English liquid /ra-la/ contrast by humans and monkeys. *Journal of the Acoustical Society of America, 102*(1), 588–602.

Sinnott, J. M., Brown, C. H., & Borneman, M. A. (1998). Effects of syllable duration on stop-glide identification in syllable-initial and syllable-final position by humans and monkeys. *Perception and Psychophysics, 60*(6), 1032–1043.

Sinnott, J. M., Brown, C. H., Malik, W. T., & Kressley, R. A. (1997). A multidimensional scaling analysis of vowel discrimination in humans and monkeys. *Perception and Psychophysics, 59*(8), 1214–1224.

Sinnott, J. M., & Saporita, T. A. (2000). Differences in American English, Spanish, and monkey perception of the *say-stay* trading relation. *Perception and Psychophysics, 62*(6), 1312–1319.

Sinnott, J. M., & Williamson, T. L. (1999). Can macaques perceive place of articulation from formant transition information? *Journal of the Acoustical Society of America, 106*(2), 929–937.

Slobin, D. I. (1977). Language change in childhood and in history. In J. Macnamara (Ed.), *Language learning and thought*. New York: Academic Press.

Stromswold, K. (2001). The heritability of language: A review and meta-analysis of twin and adoption studies. *Language, 77*, 647–723.

The SLI Consortium. (2002). A genomewide scan identifies two novel loci involved in Specific Language Impairment. *American Journal of Human Genetics, 70*, 384–398.

Tomasello, M., Carpenter, M., Call, J., Behne, T., & Moll, H. (2005). Understanding and sharing intentions: The origins of cultural cognition. *Behavioral and Brain Sciences, 28*, 675–691.

Trout, J. D. (2001). The biological basis of speech: What to infer from talking to the animals. *Psychological Review, 108*(3), 523–549.

Trout, J. D. (2003a, March 27). The biological basis of speech: Talking to the animals and listening to the evidence. *Joint Meeting of the University Seminars on Cognitive and Behavioral Neuroscience & Language and Cognition*, from http://www.columbia.edu/~remez/27apr03.pdf

Trout, J. D. (2003b). Biological specializations for speech: What can the animals tell us? *Current Directions in Psychological Science, 12*(5), 155–159.

Ullman, M. T., & Gopnik, M. (1999). Inflectional morphology in a family with inherited specific language impairment. *Applied Psycholinguistics, 20*, 51–117.

van der Lely, H. K. J., Rosen, S., & McClelland, A. (1998). Evidence for a grammar-specific deficit in children. *Current Biology, 8*, 1253–1258.

Vargha-Khadem, F., Watkins, K., Alcock, K., Fletcher, P., & Passingham, R. (1995). Praxic and nonverbal cognitive deficits in a large family with a genetically transmitted speech and language disorder. *Proceedings of the National Academy of Sciences USA, 92*, 930–933.

Vouloumanos, A., Kiehl, K. A., Werker, J. F., & Liddle, P. F. (2001). Detection of sounds in the auditory stream: Event-related fMRI evidence for differential activation to speech and nonspeech. *Journal of Cognitive Neuroscience, 13*(7), 994–1005.

Vouloumanos, A., & Werker, J. F. (2004a). *A neonatal bias for speech that is independent of experience*. Paper presented at the Fourteenth Biennial International Conference on Infant Studies, Chicago.

Vouloumanos, A., & Werker, J. F. (2004b). Tuned to the signal: The privileged status of speech for young infants. *Developmental Science, 7*, 270–276.

Wallman, J. (1992). *Aping language*. New York: Cambridge University Press.

Waxman, S., & Booth, A. (2001). On the insufficiency of domain-general accounts of word learning: A reply to Bloom and Markson. *Cognition, 78*, 277–279.

Weiner, J. (1994). *The beak of the finch*. New York: Vintage.

Wiese, H. (2004). *Numbers, language, and the human mind*. New York: Cambridge University Press.

Williams, G. C. (1966). *Adaptation and natural selection: A critique of some current evolutionary thought*. Princeton, NJ: Princeton University Press.

8

ON SEMANTIC UNIVERSALS AND TYPOLOGY

Emmon Bach and Wynn Chao

8.1. Language Universals and Typology

At the time of the Dobbs Ferry conference on Language Universals (1961), which culminated in the publication of *Universals of Language* (Greenberg, 1963/1966), American linguistics was in the midst of a transition from a strongly empiricist stance to the more rationalist approach characteristic of generative grammar and various subsequent developments. Perhaps the most influential statement of the empiricist view of the preceding decades is embodied in Bloomfield's (1933) *Language*. The structuralist approach to linguistic research, with its emphasis on rigorous observation and description, is eloquently expressed in Bloomfield's famous dictum, referred to in many of the papers in the *Universals* volume:

> The only useful generalizations about language are inductive generalizations.
>
> (Bloomfield, 1933, p. 20, in Greenberg, 1963/1966,
> pp. 1, 67, 218, 281, 303)[1]

For Bloomfield, "those areas of language study unamenable to such rigorous discipline were simply abandoned or relegated to the periphery: psycholinguistics, philosophy of language, and much of semantics" (Robins, 1988, p. 481).

This prevailing view received a strong challenge with the publication of Chomsky's (1957) *Syntactic Structures*, with its rationalist view that fundamental aspects of language knowledge were to be explained in terms of a universal grammar in the speakers' minds.

This difference was only the most recent manifestation of a longstanding conflict between the rationalist and empiricist approaches to linguistics, which first appears in the arguments between the "rationalist" Stoic (300 BC–529 AD) and the Alexandrian grammarians views on language. With some exceptions, the didactic, descriptive *grammatica civilis* approach predominated until the eleventh century, when the revival of Greek scholarship and the influence of Islamic thought led to the development of the approach described by Campanella as *grammatica philosophica*, which was primarily concerned with "relating a descriptive framework to a theory of language" (Robins, 1988, pp. 463–470).

The seventeenth century Port Royal grammarians, among the main exponents of the philosophical school, explicitly set out to explain universal aspects of language in terms of logical and semantic factors in the speakers' minds (*op. cit.* p. 477). Their rationalist approach is criticized centuries later in Bloomfield (1933, pp. 6–7), who urges us "to return to the problem of general grammar"[2] (*op. cit.* p. 20) only after enough data from enough languages is collected to allow for "not speculative, but inductive" explanations.

In retrospect, the 1961 conference on language universals and its resulting volume marked one of the pivotal events in the twentieth-century engagement between the dominant empiricist and the emerging rationalist-theoretical paradigm. Its legacy endures to this day. Among other influential contributions, Greenberg's paper on universals and the basic word order typology (Greenberg, 1963a) practically spawned (or reinvigorated) a whole subfield of research on language universals and variation. Typological studies initiated by his work have provided a rich mine for linguistic theories, forming the empirical basis for much subsequent research on linguistic universals and universal grammar.[3]

In the Greenberg volume, Charles Hockett discussed the question of the validity of crosslinguistic identification of lexical categories:

> It was at one time assumed that all languages distinguish between nouns and verbs—by some suitable and sufficiently formal definition of those terms. One form of this assumption is that all languages have two distinct types of stems (in addition, possibly, to various other types), which by virtue of their behaviour in inflection (if any) and in syntax can appropriately be labeled nouns and verbs.
>
> (Hockett, 1963/1966, p. 4)

He went on to say that this claim had been invalidated by Nootka [=Nuu-chah-nulth] at the level of stems, but upheld in the higher categories of the syntax.[4]

Hockett acknowledged that "(1.1) The assertion of a language universal must be founded on extrapolation as well as empirical evidence" (p. 2), and "(1.10) The problem of language universals is not independent of our choice of assumptions and methodology in analyzing single languages" (p. 7). Hockett's assessment of the Port Royal grammar is significantly more positive than Bloomfield's (Hockett, 1963/1966, pp. 4–5)[5]:

> The Port Royal Grammar constituted both a putative description of language universals and the basis of a taxonomy. The underlying assumption was that every language must provide, by one means or another, for all points in the grammatico-logical scheme described in the Grammar. Latin, of course, stood at the origin in this particular

coordinate system. Any other language could be characterized typologically by listing the ways in which its machinery for satisfying the universal scheme deviated from that of Latin. This classical view in general grammar and its taxonomy has been set aside not because it is false in some logical sense but because it has proved clumsy for many languages: it tends to conceal differences that we have come to believe are important, and to reveal some that we now think are trivial.

Hockett's disagreement was thus on empirical, not theoretical grounds. Interestingly, the Port Royal Grammar used the exact form of argument that we see in much contemporary work. For example, it appealed to universal categories like Participle, Verb, and Adjective and their typical configurational properties to explain the distribution of agreement facts in the syntax of French. In fact, as pointed out in Bach (1965, 1971), Greenberg's and subsequent proposals about syntactic typology and universals could not be stated without the crucial assumption that syntactic categories across languages can be identified or compared, and the proposals formed a basis for testing linguistic theories.

In this chapter, we take Greenberg's paper as our inspiration. Starting from the assumption that syntactic categories can be universally identified or correlated (whether or not they are instantiated in every languages), we wish to investigate the relation between them and their semantic interpretations, focussing on the nominal domain.[6] Note that there are two possibilities here: first, there might be a universal stock of categories from which individual languages might draw; second, there may be hypotheses that all languages must instantiate particular categories. The situation in phonological systems is illuminating: the stock of possible sounds is given by a general theory of phonetics-phonology, but not all of the categories need be utilized in every language. (Formore on universals see Bach & Chao, in Press)

8.2. Semantic Universals

In another paper in the volume entitled *On the semantic structure of language*, Uriel Weinreich (1963/1966) began by citing two assumptions that would be agreed on by most linguists. One of them sounds like an endorsement of some version of the so-called Sapir-Whorf hypothesis:

> The semantic mapping of the universe by a language is, in general, arbitrary, and the semantic "map" of each language is different from those of all other languages.
>
> (in Greenberg, 1963/1966, pp. 142–216)

Interestingly, Weinreich goes on in the same article to give a quite detailed account of what might fairly be called universals of semantics. So it would seem that rather than denying that that there is any uniform "map of the universe" across languages, he is actually looking for the proper apportionment of parts of the map to the universal and the particular.

One enduring distinction brought out in Weinreich's paper, as well as in the papers by Ullmann and Jakobson in the Greenberg volume, is the distinction between grammatical/structural and lexical meanings. We take this up below and suggest that the distinction may play a crucial role in helping us to reconcile a supposed contradiction between model-theoretic and conceptual approaches to semantics.

One real advance since Dobbs Ferry comes from the logical and philosophical ideas that have become part of the semanticist's toolbox. At the time of Dobbs Ferry, the main logical tools that linguists were aware of were those of first-order logic, and this generally went together with a syntactic view of interpretation. In the following decade and a half, a much richer set of possibilities was opened up. The work of Richard Montague was central, and we will make use of his work and the tradition that followed from it here. Somewhat surprisingly, the model-theoretic approach[7] of Montague and his followers made possible a much closer fit between language and interpretation than in much previous and subsequent work in other traditions.[8]

Example: In the logical tradition going back to Bertrand Russell, it was customary to explicate the meaning of a definite description in a sentence like *the king of France is bald* with a logical form that split the meaning of the subject into three pieces that do not correspond to any constituent of this English sentence:

$$\exists x[\textbf{KingFrance}(x) \text{ \& } \forall y[\textbf{KingFrance}(y) \iff y = x]]$$

where we have an existential quantifier with a variable, an association of the variable with the predicate *King of France*, and a uniqueness clause (if anything is a King of France, it is identical with the entity picked out by the variable). In Montague's most widely read and cited work on English (1973: PTQ), all term phrases are assigned to a single syntactic category with a uniform semantic interpretation as *generalized quantifiers* (more on this below).

In the main, we follow the model-theoretic program in this chapter.

8.2.1. Syntax-Semantics Mapping

Is there a uniform way of mapping linguistic expressions of various sorts to interpretations? We assume that the best answer to this would be *Yes*. If we are asking this question across languages, again the best answer would be *Yes*. Notice that the second question doesn't make much sense unless we can identify or relate syntactic categories across languages.

This answer relies on a methodological strategy we may call "Shoot for the Universal," implicit in a lot of linguistic theorizing (explicitly invoked in Bach, 1968; Hankamer, 1971). The reasoning behind these strategies is that the best way to find out about a domain is to make strong claims and retreat from them only in the face of contradictory evidence. Stronger claims make for more detailed predictions.

In order to talk about these mappings, we need to say something about the structure of the models we are considering.

There are three kinds of questions we can ask about semantic universals and typology from the point of view of model-theoretic semantics:

(a) Are the basic elements of the model structure universal?
(b) Are the relations between the syntactic categories and semantic interpretations universal?
(c) Are there typological patternings related to either of (a) or (b)?

The issues discussed in the foregoing parts of our chapter reflect an ongoing tension in linguistics between description and theory (Bach, 2004). In our view, there should be a fruitful complementarity between theoretically informed description and empirically informed theorizing. Typological study is the natural meeting ground between these two activities.

8.3. Syntax and Semantics

Here's how we proceed. A language is a pairing of expressions and meanings, among other things perhaps.[9] We describe the language by means of an explicit or generative grammar with a lexicon. The grammar tells us about the form of these complex expressions, as well as about the meanings. The form and the meaning of the complex expressions are dependent on the form and meaning of the expressions that are combined. The step by step or locally confined process of assigning form and meaning to a resultant expression as a function of the form and meaning of the input expressions conforms to the requirement of *compositionality* (see below).

What do we mean by a meaning? In the model-theoretic view, a meaning is something that is not language, something that linguistic expressions refer to, or *denotation*. The grammar assigns denotations to linguistic expressions. The whole system of possible denotations makes up a *model structure*.

We hypothesize that the general model structure is the same for all natural languages. It is very simple.

First of all, because some linguistic expressions like names can refer to individuals, we assume that there is a set of entities to which such names can apply and which is available for making general statements by quantification or other means.

Semantic theory places no restrictions on what can be an entity as long as we don't get into any logical problems. In Montague's most often quoted paper on natural language (Montague, 1973), the entities of the grammar are the individuals which correspond to the names *John*, *Mary*, *Bill*, and *ninety* (as well as potential values for an infinite set of variables). We think it is safe to assume that every language provides for proper names. (How they might be constructed is another matter.) Second, we want to say that sentences can be true or false, so we include two truth values.[10]

Third, as a value for predicates like *laughs*, we want to have something like a set of entities—the entities that laugh, in this case. A way to model this is to think that a predicate like the denotation of *laughs* is a function from entities to truth values:

(1) **Guinevere laughs**.

This functional way of looking at semantic expressions that are more complex than simple names is generalized to model all sorts of denotations as functions. Moreover, they can all be modeled as unary functions: taking one thing to give a value, since the value itself can be a function. So, for example, to model simple denotations of transitive verbs, we take them to denote functions from arguments to intransitive verb denotations—that is, to predicates. Here's an example:

(2) **Guinevere ignores Lancelot**.

The phrase *ignores Lancelot* denotes a function from entities to truth values, whereas *ignores* itself denotes a function from entities to predicates or intransitive verb phrase denotations. This choice generalizes to give two-part constructions (binarism) as the general pattern.

A primary benefit of adopting a functional view (in the mathematical sense of *function*) is that we can have all the properties of functions without special stipulation. Here, for example, we can model two place relations or functions like those associated with transitive verbs by a stepwise analysis into unary functions (to functions, etc.). This process is known as *currying*. In this case, the step is well motivated linguistically. A second free benefit is the possibility of combining functions by composition.

One further step is required before we can go on. The names in the examples given so far can be replaced (in English) by a wider set of expressions like *every knight*, *some queen*, or *the giant in the castle*. Montague introduced the idea that such expressions could be interpreted as *generalized quantifiers*, that is, sets of sets, or sets of properties. He assimilated proper names to the same type. So in sentences like the ones used so far, the expression *Guinevere* is taken to denote the set of all Guinevere's properties, including the properties of laughing, ignoring Lancelot, and so on. This move had far-reaching consequences, some of which we mention below.

So far we have a model structure that is appropriate for interpreting sentences that deal with the real world. But natural languages allow us to talk not only about the way things are, but about the way things might be:

(3) **Guinevere might love Arthur**.

We understand this sentence to mean that it is not excluded that Guinevere loves Lancelot, either as things are, or if circumstances were different. The way in which this will be modeled is to introduce the notion of ways that things are or may be. In Montague and related approaches, this leads to the assumption that there is a set of possible worlds to help interpret sentences like (3) as well as other expressions, sometimes instead of or in addition to a set of situations, world-like ways that things might be, but of a "smaller" kind (Bach, 1981, 1986b, Kratzer, 1989, 1995).

Including possible worlds or situations brings with it the possibility of modeling other special kinds of meanings. For example, a function from possible worlds to individuals gives us what Montague called an *individual concept*. A function from possible worlds to sets or predicates gives us one way of thinking about *properties*, ways of finding the sets of entities that are instances of the predicate in any world. We say more about these *intensional* objects below.

In order to talk about this, we need to say something about the structure of the model beyond what we have done so far.

We associate each of the ingredients of the interpretation with a type.

t is the type for truth values;
s is the type of situations or worlds;
e is the type for entities.

So we can model the structure of denotations using these ingredients and notating functional type like this: if **a** and **b** are types, then there is a type of functions from **a**-type things to **b**-type things, which we represent like this: <**a**, **b**>. This way of looking at the structure of denotations forces complex meanings to be built up pairwise. So, the type for transitive verbs (with extensional interpretation) is <**e**, <**e**, **t**>>, as illustrated in Example (2).[11]

8.3.1. Compositionality

The principle of *compositionality* requires that the meaning of a complex expression must be a function of the meaning of the parts and the way in which they are combined.

This requirement is generally appealed to in some form or other, but needs explication (Partee, 2004). In a recent, paper David Dowty (2007) argues that one can't talk about the problem of semantic compositionality without thinking of syntactic options: tighter versus greater degrees of freedom in syntax, strict versus extended categorical grammar; in Montague's general theory these would be the allowed syntactic operations.

So much for a barest sketch of the general denotational space of our semantics. We now turn to some examples and implications for semantic universals and typology.

8.4. Elaborating the Domain of Entities

The general model structure outlined above is not enough to model the distinctions necessary for a good account of natural language semantics. We will look at a number of elaborations of the model structures that have been proposed, but first let us show the limitations of trying to build meanings just out of the ingredients of the model structure as given so far.

Early and late, people have used this basic model structure to construct various kinds of higher-order denotations. A prominent move has been the introduction of various kinds of intensional entities, a move which began (in modern times) with Frege and continued with Montague's own ventures into natural language semantics. Thus, to solve various kinds of puzzles and problems, Montague used individual concepts, properties, and propositions, all of these being functions from worlds (or world-time pairs in PTQ) to various entities and sets. The distinction between *intensions* and *extensions* is one way of reconstructing Frege's distinction between *sense* and *reference* (Sinn and Bedeutung; Frege, 1892).

> *Example:* It may be that the set of two-legged rational animals and the set of humans are the same set in this world. But there are surely worlds where they are not, so we can say that the property of being a two-legged rational animal and the property of being human are not the same. Similarly for individual concepts like those named by *the Morning Star* and *the Evening Star*, both of which refer to the planet Venus.

Often these constructs have not been as fine grained as needed, and various of them have been introduced into the model structures as independent and primitive elements: propositions and properties, for example (Chierchia, 1984; Thomason, 1980).

The principal elaboration that we will follow here goes by way of dividing up the set of entities **A** into *Sorts*. A sort is a distinguished subset of the domain which allows us to make finer discriminations than is offered by the basic model structure. We mention a few sorts that will be used below in our discussion of semantic typologies.

Greg Carlson (1977) introduced *Kinds*, (ordinary) *Individuals*, and *Stages* into the model, all as Sorts of elements in the domain of individuals, but linked by relations such as that between a Kind and instances of the Kind, and between Individuals and Stages, Stages being something like temporal slices of the manifestation of an individual in a history or world or situation.

Chierchia (1984) added *Properties* as independent primitive elements. Chierchia made use of operators that make predicates from properties and properties from predicates, in effect. He also marshalled a considerable amount of evidence for the independence and necessity of treating properties as basic elements.

Plural and *Mass* entities were introduced in Link (1983). Plural objects can be freely formed from the set of singular entities and used to model the denotations of words like "dogs": the denotation of singular "dog" is the set of individual or atomic dogs; "dogs" denotes, among other things, the whole set of dogs as a plural entity as well as all pairs, triples, and so on, such as the three dogs in my house—Fido, Caesar, and Pompey, for example—but minus the atoms. This algebra for modeling the meanings of count nouns was matched by a nonatomic algebra for mass terms and the "stuff" of all entities.

We assume Linkian kinds of structures for the denotations of nouns (Link, 1983; see also Landman, 2000; Scha, 1981), as mentioned. For simplicity, we use singleton sets in place of atoms, but we will still refer to "singulary" elements in the structures as "atoms" (following Rullmann & You, 2006).

Example: Suppose there are three dogs, a, b, and c, in a situation or world. The whole structure looks like this:

{a, b, c}

{a, b} {a, c} {b, c}

{a} {b} {c}

Let's refer to the interpretations for these various elements as *singularities* (or *atoms*) below the line here, *pluralities* above the line, and *transpluralities* for the whole domain. We don't take any position on whether the atoms are to be treated as singleton sets, as suggested by the picture, or as atoms *simpliciter*. The null set is excluded so that predications about dogs, for example, would not be trivially satisfied in dogless worlds.

For English, we can adopt a straightforward association of the various domains of plurality with the different syntactic expressions. As in Link (1983), singular common nouns are taken to denote sets of singular individuals, and plurals to denote sets of pluralities. The union of the two sets of denotations is an appropriate place for expressions of "general number" (Corbett, 2000; and see the discussion in section 8.5).

Taking these suggestions together, we suppose that the domain **A** of entities has at least these Sorts: (ordinary) Individuals, Kinds, and various sorts of individuals that can be modeled in the domains for Plurals, Masses, etc. Kinds can be related by a taxonomic relation ("subspecies of," see Krifka, 1995), and can be instantiated in Individuals by a realization relation (Carlson, 1977; Krifka, 1995).

8.5. Some Semantic Typologies

Logically speaking, typologies require variety. If some property of languages is truly universal, then all languages will be of the same type as far as that property is concerned. So, typological investigations begin by noting or proposing some characteristic that is not universal. Interesting results come when it is possible to see clusterings of properties.

One such area of investigation came directly out of the modeling of the interpretations for term phrases (**DP**'s) as generalized quantifiers, mentioned above. In the course of their detailed study of generalized quantifiers in natural languages, Barwise and Cooper (1981) enunciated the following hypothesis:

> **NP-Quantifier universal**: Every natural language has syntactic constituents (called noun phrases), whose semantic function is to express generalized quantifiers over the domain of discourse.
>
> [Note that NP here corresponds to what is now usually called DP following Abney, 1987]

Research on a number of languages as well as a closer investigation of the possibility of other ways of expressing quantification led to a classification of quantification strategies into so-called *D-Quantification* and *A-Quantification*—see below (Bach, Jelinek, Kratzer, & Partee, 1995; Introduction, and Partee's contribution to that volume; Partee, 1995). This classification has immediate typological consequences, of which we mention one cluster that was made prominent in the work of Eloise Jelinek (1984, 1995):

8.5.1. *Quantification: A and D Quantification*

D-Quantification is the strategy whereby generalized quantifiers are available as the denotations of term phrases (**DP**'s: 4a), and is opposed to **A**-quantification by means of **A**dverbs (and other means, which coincidentally are associated with categories beginning with "**A**": **A**uxiliaries and **A**ffixes), as in examples made prominent by David Lewis (1975, 4b), and brought into linguistics especially in the theories of Irene Heim (1983) and Hans Kamp (1981):

(4)   a.   ***Every commuter* will read a newspaper**.
(4)   b.   ***Usually*, a commuter will read a newspaper**.

Lewis showed that examples like (4b) could not be resolved into the usual sort of quantification on individual variables, but had to be thought of as quantification of instances or cases involving several variables. Adverbs like *usually* in (4b) were treated as *unselective quantifiers*.

Suppose now that there are languages without **A**-quantification, or without **D**-quantification, then we might have a basis for a semantic typology: languages with only one or the other or both. These differences might reflect independent parameters or be consequences of some other property (see discussion of pronominal arguments below).

It has been claimed that there are languages that have no quantification at all, a claim that has led to a widely publicized controversy. See Everett (2005) on Pirahã, critique in Nevins, Pesetsky, and Rodrigues (2007), and reply by Everett (2007).

Investigations and discussions like those just mentioned involve in an essential way both theory and description. The putative universal proposed by Barwise and Cooper (1981; see above) requires specific claims about syntactic structures, semantic interpretations, and the relations between them.

8.5.2. *Pronominal Argument Languages and Generalized Quantifiers*

Jelinek (1984) proposed the *pronominal argument hypothesis* originally to account for differences of configurationality. According to this hypothesis, some languages require that verbs have affixed or cliticized pronouns as their arguments, and not full DP's. Semantically, this would mean that the verbs are in effect to be interpreted as something like open sentences, with unbound variables in the argument slots. Jelinek's hypothesis predicted several characteristics of such languages: free nominal expressions in sentences, as something like adjuncts, relatively free word order, and (Jelinek, 1995) the lack of quantificational DP's. In this second paper, Jelinek drew a further typological consequence. Languages without a noun–verb dichotomy would lack DP's as such, and hence would have no generalized quantifier constituents.

Here is a schematic comparison of a sentence like *John walks* as it might be rendered in a language like English and one like *Straits Salish* (see Bach, 1994, p. 274):

(5)   a.   **"English": "Straits Salish":**
               J' (walk'): walk'(x) & john'(x)

Here, **J'** stands for the generalized quantifier: the set of all John's properties, and the formula is interpreted as saying that this set includes the property of walking. In the pseudo-Straits Salish example, the best paraphrase is something like *he walks and he is John*. No such paraphrase is possible with a formula that would correspond to *every man walks* in a language with no D-quantification. (5b) shows the difference in expressing the generalization in the two strategies. The first expression shows that *every man* can be interpreted in a way exactly parallel to *John*, but in the second instance, with A-quantification there is no unitary generalized quantifier interpretation:

(5)   b.   **[EVERY(man')](walk') ALWAYS[walk'(x), man'(x)]**
               (**ALWAYS**: unselective binder)

8.5.3. Nouns and Verbs

The pronominal argument hypothesis is related to the question about the universality of nouns and verbs as lexical or syntactic categories. Swadesh (1939, pp. 78–79) argues that in Nootka [=Nuu-chah-nulth] all stems can potentially be inflected as predicates; the distinction between **N** and **V** interpretations may not be present in the lexical domain but resurfaces at the level of syntax, where the expression associated with verbal morphology and interpreted as the main predicate is always clause initial:

(6)   **mamo·k-ma   qo·ʔas-ʔi**
        work-3SG IND man-DET
        "The man is working."

(7)   **qo·ʔas-ma   mamo·k-ʔi**
        man-3SG IND work-DET
        The working one is a man.

    This pattern is characteristic of Northwest Coast languages in the Wakashan and Salishan families, as these examples show:

Straits Salish (Jelinek, 1995, p. 490)

(8)   **swiʾqoʾəł +0 ce t'iləm +lə'**
        young man +3ABS DET sing +PAST
        He is a young man, the one who sang.
        The one who sang is a young man.

(9)   **t'iləm +lə'+0 ce swiʾqoʾəł**
        sing + PAST +3ABS DET young man
        He sang, the one who is a young man.
        The young man sang.

Kwakw'ala (retranscribed, Boas, 1947, p. 280; Boas cites other languages here as well):

(10)   **N'ikida bəgwanəm.** "That one said, it was the man."
        n'ik- -ida bəgwanəm
        say- -infl person

(11)   **Bəgwanəmida n'ika.** "It was the man he [i.e. who] said."
        bəgwanəm- -ida n'ik- -a
        person- infl say- -completive

Haisla (EB fieldnotes)

(12)   **guxw** "house"/"(to be a) house"
(13)   **Guxw gada**. house this
        This is a house.

(14)   **Duqwelan qix guxwgaxhga**.
        duqwela-n qix guxw-gaxhga.
        see-I this house-here.
        I see this house.

The noun–verb question continues to cause discussion (see, for example, Demirdache & Matthewson [1995];, Evans & Osada [2005]).

8.5.4. *Kinds and Plurality*

In the last few years, there has been quite a lot of research into variation across languages with respect to nominal structures and their interpretations. Considerable attention has been paid to Mandarin Chinese (Cheng & Sybesma, 1999; Chierchia, 1998a, 1998b; Krifka, 1995; Rullmann & You, 2006, among others).

There are three striking differences between English and Mandarin in the realm of nominal expressions:

   i. All nouns in Mandarin can occur bare.
   ii. There is no expression of a singular–plural distinction in the morphology of the noun.[12]
   iii. Nouns cannot be construed with numerals in Mandarin without the help of a classifier or measure expression.

Because these three properties are matched exactly in English by mass nouns like *blood, mud,* or *furniture,* Mandarin nouns are often claimed to be mass nouns in general. Note that English also has uncountable plurals such as *cattle, police, poultry, three head of cattle, *three cattle* (see Huddleston & Pullum, 2002, p. 345).

A variant of this idea is Chierchia's view that mass nouns are basically plurals, which then leads to the claim that Mandarin nouns are also all basically plural (Chierchia, 1998a).

Mandarin nouns can be interpreted in various ways, depending on the syntax: definite, indefinite, or as names for Kinds (see Chao & Bach, 2004; Cheng & Sybesma, 1999; Rullmann & You, 2006, for details):

(15)   **gǒu**
       "dog, dogs, a dog, the dog, Dogs [generic]"
(16)   **gǒu yǎo guò mǎlù**
       dog want cross road
       "The [*a] dog wants to cross the road." (Cheng & Sybesma, 1999)
(17)   **gǒu ài chī ròu**
       dog like eat meat
       "Dogs love to eat meat." (ibid.)
(18)   **wǒ kànjiàn xióng le**.
       I see bear aspect
       "I saw (some) bears." (Krifka, 1995)

Chierchia (1998a) proposed a set of choices for NP interpretations, which led him to a typology of languages in their nominal systems. These choices were based on two features: **arg** and **pred**, each with *plus* [+] and *minus* [–] values. If the value for **arg** is *plus* for a language, then NP's can occur as arguments (of verbs), if *minus* then not. If the value for **pred** is *plus*, then NP's can act as predicates (restrictors on quantificational DP's); if *minus*, not. Having *minus* for both properties is excluded in principle. This setup leads to predictions for three kinds of languages, as exemplified thus:

> NP[+arg,-pred] nouns refer to kinds, every NP is of type **e**
> Mandarin, Japanese

> NP[-arg, +pred] every noun is of type <**e,t**>: no bare nominals at all
> French
> Italian null D's only if licensed by lexical head

> NP[+arg, +pred] NP's can be freely argumental or predicative
> English and Germanic languages

There have been critical reviews of this typology; see especially Cheng and Sybesma (1999); Krifka (2004); Borer (2005); Schmitt and Munn (1999); Rullmann and You (2006). Some of these discussions have brought in new data from languages that go against Chierchia's typological predictions. For example, Brazilian Portuguese (Schmitt & Munn, 1999) allows bare singulars; a number of languages with optional plurals go against Chierchia's claims that classifiers and plural marking cannot go together. Some of the critiques have claimed that the relevant parameters should be sought in grammar rather than semantics (Schmitt & Munn, 1999).

Rullmann and You (2006) can be cited as a promising typological study on a different semantic base. In their theory, "The crucial parameter [in this domain] does not involve kind reference, but number: in some languages the extension of morphologically unmarked count nouns includes only atoms, whereas in other languages it includes both atoms and pluralities," that is, in our terminology, "transpluralities."

Rullman and You's theory leads to the prediction that in languages with "general number" (with the whole set of transpluralities as domain), a situation involving one or more entities might in principle be described using either a plain or a plural form of a noun. In other words, plural marking will be optional or "facultative" (Corbett, 2000).

There are many open questions at present in this area of research. For our purposes here, we simply want to stress that the explicit model-theoretic semantics has made it possible to propose quite precise hypotheses about the syntax–semantic mapping, and typological consequences, both for syntax and semantics.

8.6. Concepts and Properties

We mentioned above the distinction between grammatical or structural aspects of language and lexical aspects reflected, for example, in the distinction between functional categories and open class lexical categories. We also noted that it may be reasonable to relate this distinction to that between model-theoretic and conceptual approaches to semantics.

We noted also that nominals of various kinds lead a double role, as shown in the last section and as discussed by various writers. On the one hand they are closely related to Kinds and on the other to predicates. Krifka (2004) argues that nouns are to be interpreted in the first place as Properties, and that their double role can be derived from this common base.

This idea fits well with conclusions reached by Bach in a series of papers on word-internal semantics, especially concerned with polysynthetic languages. After trying to come up with a reasonable choice for the basic denotations of elements involved in derivations of words—both stems or roots and affixes—he concludes that the only thing left might be Properties or perhaps nothing model-theoretic at all, perhaps Concepts in the psychological sense (see Bach, 2005, and papers referred to there).

A prime instance is the textbook example of Semitic consonantal roots like **k-t-b**, which underlie a large number of derived lexical items and inflected forms. All the words are vaguely connected with the notion of writing, but it is difficult to see how they can be compositionally built up in a model-theoretic fashion. The same point can be made with English words derived from what is ultimately the Latin root **scrib**-: *describe, inscription, conscription, scripture,* and so on.

It is noteworthy that much of the rich literature on the analysis of word meanings by such writers as Jackendoff, Pustejovsky, and Talmy is frankly based on conceptual foundations (see references under these names).

So, it may be that Model-Theoretic and Conceptual Semantics are complementary rather than competitors for the True Theory, the former suited to grammatical or syntactic structures, the latter to word-building and sublexical meanings. But there is no time or space to pursue this possibility here. In any case, it is worth pointing out again that Model-Theoretic semantics itself is compatible with a view that the denotations are to be sought in psychological models (Zwarts & Verkuyl, 1994).

8.7. Some Other Syntactic-Semantic Investigations

We have touched here on only one area of the syntax-semantics complex. Similar investigations have been carried out in a number of other areas, and some have been related to each other. We simply mention them here, with little by way of elucidation.

Clause structures: Cinque's "cartographic approach" maps out a large number of clausal domains, each with its functional projection and associated Specifiers and/or Modifiers (1999), and makes universal claims about the layering and ordering.

Nominal structures: We mentioned above only the inner and outer parts of the DP systems in several languages. The topic of adjectives, and other nominal modifiers and intermediate parts of the DP has been the topic of crosslinguistic investigation, in part following the ideas of Cinque just mentioned, and as part of the investigation of wide-spread parallels in clausal and nominal structures (Chao, Mui, & Scott[2001]; Chao & Bach [2004]; Scott [2002, 2003]).

Verbal aspect: The syntax and semantics of aspect and aspectual verb classification (Aktionsarten) has been the subject of vigorous study since Verkuyl's and Dowty's pioneering work in the seventies (Bach, 1986a; Dowty, 1972, 1979; Verkuyl, 1972). Distinctions such as those between events (in the narrow sense) and processes, states, achievements, accomplishments, and the like, deriving ultimately from Aristotle, have been modeled in a wide variety of ways, and parallels to the nominal distinctions between count and mass terms have been the locus of much discussion from both a formal and semantic point of view (Verkuyl, de Swart, & van Hout, 2005).

If we add *eventualities* of various types as sorts, we can accommodate special denotations for other categories. For example, it has been suggested that verbal constructions (or some verbal constructions) have an event argument (Kratzer, 1995). The importance of events in the logic of natural language was insisted on by Donald Davidson (1967) long ago.

8.8. Outlook and Conclusions

We began this chapter with the delineation of two views of language universals as reflecting a tension between empiricist and rationalist views of the nature of scientific investigation. There will probably always be a tension between these two impulses, and not only in linguistics. We also suggested that typological studies are the natural meeting ground—or should we say "battle-ground"?—for these two impulses or stances.

We have probably shown our bias in this dichotomy by our choice of examples. Most of the studies cited work squarely within frameworks that treat universals as terms in hypothetico-deductive theories. But far from having no empirical import, most of the claims we have cited have led to fruitful new work on a wide variety of languages. In the last analysis, just as there can be no such thing as pure theory-free description, there cannot be interesting theories without confrontation with crucial empirical consequences.

We hope to have shown that a semantic perspective can lead to far reaching and interesting typological results and questions. The fact that this chapter has been richer in questions than in firm results is a reflection of the vitality of the field.

Key Further Readings

Here are some suggestions for further reading and background material:

A classic defense of model-theoretic semantic is Lewis (1972). Partee (1996) gives a comprehensive survey. For a general introduction to conceptual semantics, see Jackendoff (1996). Semantic typology is the focus of two papers by Chierchia (1998a, b), with special reference to the semantics of nominal expressions. For crosslinguistic studies on quantification, see Bach et al. (1995). Barwise and Cooper (1981) presented the important NP-universal hypothesis and provided a detailed study of the logic of generalized quantifiers.

Cinque (1999) is the basic reference to the cartographic view of clausal structures.

Dowty (1979), and Levin and Rappaport Hovav (1996) are two basic works on lexical semantics. Two recent works on compositionality are Partee (2004) and Dowty (2007). Link (1983) and Landman (2000) are basic for mass terms, events, and plurality.

For additional special topics, check the references in the body of the chapter and footnotes.

Notes

1 An indication of the transitional position of the volume: there are 16 references to Bloomfield in the index to Greenberg, (1963/1966); 5 to Chomsky.

2 The term "general grammar" is used here in the sense of Arnauld and Launcelot's *Grammaire générale et raisonnée* (Anonymous, 1676/1966).

3 The picture we give here needs considerable shading to be accurate: (1) structuralism cannot be equated with American structuralism, and (2) even in America, the influence of Bloomfield and his particular brand of empiricist behaviorism must not be exaggerated.

4 The debate about this claim for universality of the noun–verb distinction continues, compare section 8.4 below and Evans and Osada (2005).

5 Compare Bloomfield, 1933, p. 6.

6 On lexical categories, see also Baker (2003), who makes a particularly strong argument for universal syntactic categories.

7 See below for an exposition of the basic assumptions of model-theoretic semantics. It is to be distinguished from conceptual semantics, which seeks meaning in mental or psychological entitities, and proof-theoretic semantics, which models meanings in symbolic languages. A classic statement of the program of model-theoretic semantics is David Lewis's 1972 paper, "General Semantics."

8 Montague's advice: "Pay attention to natural languages, they may be trying to tell you something." Not his words, but often implicit in a lot of work in this tradition. Compare Montague's famous remark at the beginning of his paper, "English as a formal language" (1970): "I reject the contention that an important theoretical difference exists between formal and natural languages." Like PTQ, this paper is about English and not some other language such as Logical Form that English can be mapped into.

9 The "other things" include aspects of meaning in the broad sense that are better handled in integrated but separate components dealing with presuppositions, pragmatics, implicatures, and the like.

10 Other choices are possible, for example, a three-valued logic, with a third value being "undefined." This elaboration is no doubt necessary if we adopt a model with Sorts as outlined below. For purposes of exposition, we stick to the classical system with two truth values.

11 Note that "function," "functional" occur in at least two uses in linguistics: as a strictly mathematical term as in this paper, and in various syntactic frameworks as referring to "functional" categories as opposed to lexical or open-class categories. (The difference and relation between them is to be taken up in work in progress).

12 We reject the claim that the Chinese suffix—*men*, which attaches to pronouns and some nouns, is an ordinary plural marker (see Li, 1998). We hold that, like the similar Japanese suffix *-tati*, *-men* is a group-forming suffix, most closely corresponding to the English expression "__ *and them*" as in *Joel and them* meaning Joel and some group related to him by some contextually salient or conventional relation.

References

Abney, S. (1987). The English noun phrase in its sentential aspect. Ph.D. dissertation, MIT.

[Arnauld, Antoine, and Claude Lancelot]. Anonymous (1676/1966). *Grammaire générale et raisonnée ou La Grammaire de Port-Royal. Edition critique présenté par Herbert E. Brekle.* Facsimile of the third revised and expanded edition. Stuttgart-Bad Canstatt: Friedrich Frommann Verlag (Guenther Holzboog). First edition: 1660.

Bach, E. (1965). On some recurrent types of transformations. *Georgetown University Monograph Series on Languages and Linguistics, 18,* 3–18.

Bach, E. (1968). Nouns and noun phrases. In E. Bach & R. T. Harms (Eds.), *Universals in linguistic theory* (pp. 90–122). New York: Holt, Rinehart and Winston.

Bach, E. (1971). Questions. *Linguistic Inquiry, 2,* 153–166.

Bach, E. (1981). On time, tense, and aspect: An essay in English metaphysics. In P. Cole (Ed.), *Radical pragmatics* (pp. 63–81). New York: Academic Press.

Bach, E. (1986a). The algebra of events. *Linguistics and Philosophy, 9,* 5–16.

Bach, E. (1986b). Natural language metaphysics. In R. Barcan Marcus, G. J. W. Dorn, & P. Weingartner (Eds.), *Logic, methodology, and philosophy of science VII* (pp. 573–595). Amsterdam: North Holland.

Bach, E. (1994). The semantics of syntactic categories: A crosslinguistic perspective. In J. MacNamara & G. E. Reyes (Eds.), *The logical foundations of linguistic theory* (pp. 264–281). New York and Oxford: Oxford University Press.

Bach, E. (2004). Linguistic universals and particulars. In P. van Sterkenburg (Ed.), *Linguistics today—facing a greater challenge.* Amsterdam/Philadelphia: Benjamins. pp. 47–60. [Invited address presented at the XVII International Congress of Linguists. Prague.]

Bach, E. (2005). Is word-formation compositional? In G. N. Carlson & F. J. Pelletier (Eds.), *Reference and quantification: The partee effect* (pp. 107–112). Stanford: CSLI Publications.

Bach, E., & Chao, W. (2005). Semantics in the Nominal Domain, invited talk, University of Oxford.

Bach, E., & Chao, W. (in press). Language universals from a semantic perspective. To appear in C. Maienborn, K. von Heusinger, & P. Portner (Eds.), *Semantics: An international handbook of natural language meaning.* Berlin: Mouton de Gruyter.

Bach, E., Jelinek, E., Kratzer, A., & Partee, B. H. (Eds.). (1995). *Quantification in natural languages.* Dordrecht: Kluwer.

Baker, M. (2003). *Lexical categories.* Cambridge: Cambridge University Press.

Barwise, J., & Cooper, R. (1981). Generalized quantifiers and natural language. *Linguistics and philosophy, 4,* 159–219.

Bloomfield, L. (1933). *Language.* New York: Henry Holt.

Boas, F. (1947). Kwakiutl grammar with a glossary of the suffixes. In H. B. Yampolsky with the Collaboration of Z. S. Harris (Eds.), *Transactions of the American Philosophical Society.* N.S. Vol. 37, Part 3, pp. 202[?]–377. Reprinted by AMS Press, New York.

Borer, H. (2005). *Structuring sense, volume I: In name only.* Oxford: Oxford University Press.

Carlson, G. N. (1977). *Reference to kinds in English.* Ph.D. dissertation, University of Massachusetts, Amherst. Published 1988. New York, Garland.

Chao, W., & Emmon Bach. ([2004] and [To appear]). Mandarin nominals and modifiers: Types and categories. In Huba Bartos, ed., *Syntactic Categories and their Interpretation in Chinese.* Budapest: Hungarian Academy of Sciences.

Chao, W., Scott, G.-J., & Mui, E. (2001). *The interpretation of adjectives in Chinese.* Paper presented at the North American Association of Chinese Linguistics 13 (NAACL-13), Irvine, California.

Cheng, L. L-S., & Sybesma, R. (1999). Bare and not-so-bare nouns and the structure of NP. *Linguistic Inquiry, 30,* 509–542.

Chierchia, G. (1984). Topics in the syntax and semantics of infinitives and gerunds. Ph.D. dissertation: The University of Massachusetts, Amherst (G.L.S.A.).

Chierchia, G. (1998a). Plurality of mass nouns and the notion of "semantic parameter." In S. Rothstein (Ed.), *Events and grammar* (pp. 53–103). Dordrecht: Kluwer.

Chierchia, G. (1998b). Reference to kinds across languages. *Natural Language Semantics, 6,* 339–405.

Chomsky, N. (1957). *Syntactic structures.* The Hague: Mouton.

Cinque, G. (1999). *Adverbs and functional heads: A crosslinguistic perspective.* New York/Oxford: Oxford University Press.

Corbett, G. G. (2000). *Number.* Cambridge: Cambridge University Press.

Davidson, D. (1967). The logical form of action sentences. In N. Rescher (Ed.), *The logic of decision and action* (pp. 81–120). Pittsburgh: University of Pittsburgh Press. (Reprinted in Davidson 1980.)

Davidson, D. (1980). *Essays on actions and events.* Oxford: Clarendon Press.

Dowty, D. R. (1972). *Studies in the logic of verb aspect and time reference in English.* PhD Dissertation, The University of Texas, Austin.

Davis, S., & Mithun, M. (Eds.). (1979). *Linguistics, philosophy, and Montague grammar.* Austin and London: The University of Texas Press.

Demirdache, H., & Matthewson, L . (1995). On the universality of the Noun Verb distinction. *NELS, 25,* 79–93.

Dowty, D. (2007). Compositionality as an empirical problem. In C. Barker & P. Jacobson (Eds.), *Direct compositionality* (pp. 23–101). Oxford: Oxford University Press.

Dowty, D. R. (1979). *Word meaning and Montague grammar.* Dordrecht: Reidel.

Evans, N., & Osada, T. (2005). The myth of a language without word classes. *Linguistic Typology, 9,* 351–390

Everett, D. L. (2005, August–September). Cultural constraints on grammar and cognition in Pirahã. *Current Anthropology, 46(4),* 621–646.

Everett, D. (2007). Cultural constraints on grammar in PIRAHÃ: A reply to Nevins, Pesetsky, and Rodrigues, from http://ling.auf.net/lingbuzz/000427

Frege, G. (1892). Ueber sinn und bedeutung. *Zeitschrift fuer philosophie und philosophische kritik.N .S. 100,* 25–50.

Greenberg, J. H. (1963a). Some universals of language with particular reference to the order of meaningful elements. In Greenberg (Ed.), pp. 73–111.

Greenberg, J. H., (Ed.). (1963b/1966). *Universals of language.* Cambridge, MA: MIT Press.

Hankamer, J. (1971). Constraints on deletion in syntax. Yale University Ph.D. dissertation, Garland: 1979.

Heim, I. (1983). File change semantics and the familiarity theory of definiteness. In R. Bäuerle, C. Schwarze, & A. von Stechow (Eds.), *Meaning, use, and the interpretation of language*, (Walter de Gruyter) (pp. 164–190). [Reprinted in Portner and Partee 2002: pp. 223–248.]

Hockett, C. F. (1963/1966). The problem of universals in language. In J. H. Greenberg, (Ed.), *Universals of language*. 2nd ed. (pp. 1–29). Cambridge, MA: MIT Press.

Huddleston, R., & Pullum, G. K. (2002). *The Cambridge grammar of the English language*. Cambridge: Cambridge University Press.

Jackendoff, R. (1996). Semantics and cognition. In S. Lappin, (Ed.), *The handbook of contemporary semantic theory* (pp. 539–559). Oxford: Blackwell.

Jelinek, E. (1984). Empty categories, case, and configurationality. *NLLT*, *2*, 39–76.

Jelinek, E. (1995). Quantification in straits salish. In Bach et al., 1995, pp. 487–540.

Kamp, H. (1981). A theory of truth and semantic representation. In J. Groenendijk, T. Janssen, & M. Stokhof (Eds.), *Formal methods in the study of language* (Part 1, pp. 277–322). Amsterdam: Mathematical Centre Tracts 135. [Reprinted in Portner and Partee 2002: pp. 189–222.]

Kratzer, A. (1989). An investigation of the lumps of thought. *Linguistics and Philosophy*, *12*, 607–653.

Kratzer, A. (1995). Stage-level and individual-level predicates. In G. N. Carlson & F. J. Pelletier (Eds.), *The generic book* (pp. 125–175). Chicago and London: University of Chicago Press.

Krifka, M. (1995). Common nouns: A contrastive analysis of Chinese and English. In G. N. Carlson & F. J. Pelletier (Eds.), *The generic book* (pp. 398–411). Chicago and London: University of Chicago Press.

Krifka, M. (2004). Bare NPs: Kind-referring, indefinites, both, or neither? In O. Bonami & P. C. Hofherr (Eds.), *Empirical issues in formal syntax and semantics*, 5, 111–132.

Landman, F. (2000). *Events and plurality*. Dordrecht/Boston/London: Kluwer.

Levin, B., & Rappaport Hovav, M. (1996). Lexical semantics and syntactic structure. In S. Lappin (Ed.), *The handbook of contemporary semantic theory* (pp. 487—507). Oxford: Blackwell.

Lewis, D. (1972). General semantics. In D. Davidson & G. Harman (Eds.), *Semantics of natural language* (pp. 169–218). Dordrecht: Reidel.

Lewis, D. (1975). Adverbs of quantification. In E. L. Keenan (Ed.), *Formal semantics of natural language* (pp. 3–15). Cambridge: Cambridge University Press.

Li, Y.-H. Audrey. (1998). Argument determiner phrases and number phrases. *Linguistic Inquiry*, *29*, 693–702.

Link, G. (1983). The logical analysis of plurals and mass terms. In R. Bäuerle, Ch. Schwarze & A. von Stechow (Eds.), *Meaning, use, and interpretation of language* (pp. 302–323). Berlin: de Gruyter.

Montague, R. (1970). English as a formal language. [Paper 6 in Montague, 1974.]

Montague, R. (1973). The proper treatment of quantification in ordinary English. [Paper 8 in Montague, 1974, originally published in Hintikka, Moravcsik, and Suppes, 1973, pp. 221–242.]

Nevins, A. I., Pesetsky, D., & Rodrigues, C. (2007). Pirahã Exceptionality: A Reassessment, from http://ling.auf.net/lingBuzz/000411

Partee, B. H. (1995). Quantificational structures and compositionality. In E. Bach, E. Jelinek, A. Kratzer, & B. H. Partee (Eds.), *Quantification in natural languages* (pp. 541–601). Dordrecht: Kluwer.

Partee, B. H. (1996). The development of formal semantics in linguistic theory. In S. Lappin (Ed.), *The handbook of contemporary semantic theory* (pp. 11–38). Oxford: Blackwell.

Partee, B. H. (2004). *Compositionality in formal semantics*. Oxford: Blackwell Publishing.

Robins, R. H. (1988). Appendix: History of linguistics. In F. J. Newmeyer (Ed.), *Linguistics: The Cambridge survey* (Vol. I, pp. 462–480). Cambridge: Cambridge University Press.

Rullmann, H., & You, A. (2006). General number and the semantics and pragmatics of indefinite bare nouns in mandarin Chinese. In K. von Heusinger & K. P. Turner (Eds.), *Where semantics meets pragmatics* (pp. 175–196). Amsterdam: Elsevier.

Scha, R. (1981). Distributive, collective and cumulative quantification. In J. Groenendijk, T. Janssen, & M. Stokhof (Eds.), *Formal methods in the study of language*. Amsterdam: Mathematical Center Tracts, Amsterdam. Reprinted in J. Groenendijk, T. Janssen & M. Stokhof (Eds.), *Truth, interpretation, information* (1984, Dordrecht: Foris). [Ref from Landman, 2000.]

Scott, G. (2002). Stacked adjectival modification and the structure of nominal phrases. In G. Cinque et al. (Eds.), *Functional structure in the DP and the IP: The cartography of syntactic structures* (Vol. I, pp. 91–120). New York: Oxford University Press.

Scott, G.-J. (2003). The syntax and semantics of adjectives: A cross-linguistic study. Ph.D. dissertation, SOAS, The University of London.

Schmitt, C., & Munn, A. (1999). Against the nominal mapping parameter: Bare nouns in Brazilian Portuguese. *NELS, 29,* 339–353.

Swadesh, M. (1939). Nootka internal syntax. *IJAL, 9,* 77–102.

Thomason, R. (1980). A model theory for propositional attitudes. *Linguistics and philosophy, 4,* 47–70.

Verkuyl, H. J. (1972). *On the compositional nature of the aspects*. Dordrecht: Reidel.

Verkuyl, H. J., de Swart, H., & van Hout, A. (Eds.). (2005). *Perspectives on aspect*. Dordrecht: Springer.

Weinreich, U. (1963/1966). On the semantic structure of language. In J. H. Greenberg (Ed.), *Universals of language* (pp. 142–216). Cambridge, MA: MIT Press.

Zwarts, J., & Verkuyl, H. (1994). An algebra of conceptual structure: An investigation into Jackendoff's conceptual semantics. *Linguistics and Philosophy, 17,* 1–28.

9

FOUNDATIONS OF UNIVERSAL GRAMMAR IN PLANNED ACTION

Mark Steedman

A close relation has often been remarked between language (and other serial cognitive behavior) and an underlying sensory-motor planning mechanism (Caramazza & Hillis, 1991; Lashley, 1951; Miller, Galanter, & Pribram, 1960; Piaget, 1936; Rizzolatti & Arbib, 1998). The evidence adduced is evolutionary, neuropsychological, and developmental.

This chapter attempts to link the specific form taken by the universal grammatical mechanism that projects the finite lexicon of any given language onto the infinite set of strings of words paired with meanings that constitute that language to a more primitive capacity for *planning*, or constructing sequences of actions that culminate in an intended goal. A central question in defining this system is that of how action representations can be learned from interaction with the physical world.

The formation of novel plans from such elementary actions requires two fundamental operations of *composition*, or sequencing, and *type-raising*, or mapping objects in a situation into their affordances, or contextually supported actions. The paper argues that operations related to composition and type-raising also entirely determine the universal grammatical mechanism that projects language-specific lexicons onto the sentences of the language. This observation suggests that the language faculty is in evolutionary and developmental terms attached to a more primitive planning mechanism to which it is formally entirely transparent.

9.1. Universal Grammar

Two rather different kinds of phenomena trade under the name of *linguistic universals*. The first is, often expressed as implicational rules of the form, "if a language has property P, it has property Q." An example is Greenberg's (1963) Universal 3, "Languages with dominant VSO order are always prepositional." Although

174

sometimes stated as deterministic laws, such rules almost always admit exceptions (as Greenberg 3 does—Dryer, 1992, p. 83), and should be regarded as probabilistic, arising either from the origins of most prepositions as verbs rather than adnominals, or from a requirement for efficient encoding to ensure easy learnability of the grammar as a whole, rather than as rules of universal grammar as such. Languages are free to violate such constraints, just so long as they do not violate so many of them as to make life unreasonably difficult for the child language learner.

The second kind often takes the form of claims such as, "No natural language does X" or "every natural language does Y," and seem more like strict constraints on human language, such as that every language has nouns, or transitive verbs, or relative clauses. This second class of universal is further divided into three types: "substantive" universals, "functional" universals, and "formal" universals, although there is some confusion in the literature concerning the definition of these types.[1]

Substantive universals, such as the ubiquity of nouns and transitive verbs, are to do with content, and are determined by ontology, or the way our interactions with the physical and mental world structure mental representations, and hence semantics, into categories like mothers, dogs, and grasping. Functional universals, such as the ubiquity of complementizers, case, tense, definiteness, and the like, are determined by relations among substantive entities. Both substantive and functional categories are represented lexically by morphemes, although at least some functional categories are almost always morphologically implicit or "unmarked" in any given language. This distinction, therefore, corresponds quite closely to traditional notions of "open class" versus "closed class" items, or "stems" versus "inflections" and "function words."

The third class, the formal universals, are rather different. These relate to the inventory of syntactic operations that combine substantive and functional categories, and project their characteristics and meanings onto sentences and logical forms. Such universals concern the mathematical or automata-theoretic class of operations that are countenanced in the theory of grammar, and take the form of statements such as, "Natural languages fall outside the class of context-free languages" (Chomsky, 1957). Such universals are not statistical in nature: one example of a natural language (or in this case, natural language constructions, as in Huybregts [1984] and Shieber [1985]) that is, provably non-context-free proves the claim, even if natural language constructions in general are, in fact "with overwhelmingly greater than chance frequency," context free.

It is often quite hard to decide to what type a given universal claim should be assigned. Greenberg's Universal 20 claims that only 6 of the 24 possible linear orderings of the categories Dem(onstrative), Num(ber), A(djective), and N(oun) exhibited in English NPs like *These five young lads* are universally attested. Although Greenberg sampled only 30 languages, and 8 further orders have since been attested (Cinque, 2005; Hawkins, 1983), they modify the statement of the universal itself, not its statistical strength.

Similarly, Ross (1970) described a universal relating "gapping" or deletion of the verb under coordination with base constituent order. The pattern can be summarized as follows for the three dominant sentential constituent orders (asterisks indicate the excluded cases):

(1)   SVO: *SO and SVO   SVO and SO
      VSO: *SO and VSO   VSO and SO
      SOV: SO and SOV *SOV and SO

This observation can be generalized to individual constructions within a language: just about any construction in which an element apparently goes missing preserves canonical word order in an analogous fashion. For example, English ditransitive verbs subcategorize for two complements on their right, like VSO verbs. In the following "argument cluster" coordination, it is indeed in the right conjunct that the verb goes missing:

(2)   Give Thelma a book, and Louise a record.

At first glance, this observation looks like an implicational universal, and indeed there were early claims for exceptions from languages like Dutch (SOV) and Zapotec (VSO, Rosenbaum, 1977), which allow both patterns. However, both those languages can be claimed to have mixed base order, and if the claim is relativized to constructions, it can be seen as making a claim about the universal apparatus for projecting lexically specified constructions onto sentences, and hence as a claim about a formal universal.

9.2. Universal Semantics

The most plausible source for substantive, functional, and formal universals of language is a universal semantics, determined in turn by the specific nature of our interactions with the world, and the concepts that those interactions engender (Chomsky, 1965, pp. 27–30; Newmeyer, 2005; Pinker, 1979). The reasoning behind this assumption is as follows. The only reason for natural language grammar to exist at all is to support semantic interpretation as a basis for reasoning about joint action in the world with other members of a language community. Furthermore, we know that syntactic grammars for even the simplest language classes cannot be exactly induced on the basis of exposure to strings from the language alone (Gold, 1967). (Although Horning [1969] showed that grammars of any such class can technically be approximated to any desired degree of probable error by automatically induced statistical models, and such approximations are in fact quite practically applicable to problems such as word disambiguation for automatic speech recognition, such statistical approximation carries exponentially growing computational costs. It is also quite unclear how such approximations can support semantic interpretation.) We also know that exact induction of even quite high classes of (monotonic) grammar from strings paired with labeled trees corresponding to the yield of the grammar for that string is essentially trivial (apart from the problem of noise in the input and consequent error) (Buszkowski & Penn, 1990; Siskind, 1996; Villavicencio, 2002; Zettlemoyer & Collins, 2005). It follows that the simplest hypothesis concerning the way children acquire their native language is that they induce its syntactic grammar from pairings of strings and logical forms representing meaning. On this assumption, language universals must reflect the properties of a universal grammar of logical form, in which the structure of predicates and arguments carves nature (including our own being) at the joints in just one way, ideally suited to reasoning about it.

Of course, to say this much is not terribly helpful. The putative grammar of logical form itself has a syntax, which can in turn only be explained as arising from a semantics that must be specified in a much stronger sense, using a model theory whose details will ultimately be determined by the nature of our own and our remote nonhuman ancestor's interactions with the world. Worse still, our grasp on this kind of semantics is (as Chomsky never tires of pointing out) even shakier than our grasp on linguistic syntax, mainly because our formal and intuitive grasp of such dynamic systems is much weaker than that of static declaritive systems. Nevertheless, this must be where linguistic universals originate.

This is easiest to see in terms of substantive and functional universals—that is, those that relate to content and category of morphemes, words, and constituents. For example, if it is the case that all natural languages have transitive verbs, or that no language has a verb allowing more than four arguments (Newmeyer, 2005, p. 5; Steedman, 1993, 2000b; citing Pesetsky, 1995), then the universal logical form must include all and only such relations.[2] If languages are nevertheless free to specify the position of the verb with respect to its arguments as initial, second position, or final, then we may suspect that the Universal Grammar of logical form specifies only dominance relations, not linear order.[3]

But it is also true of the formal universals—that is, those that govern the types of rules that combine constituents or categories, projecting their properties onto larger structures. For example, the main reason for believing in a formal universal to the effect that natural language grammar formalisms must be of at least the expressive power of context-free grammars is not that intrinsically non-finite-state fragments of languages like English can be identified. All attested and in fact humanly possible instances of such strings can be recognized by covering finite-state machines, and human beings must in some sense actually *be* finite-state machines. The real reason is that no one can see any way to parsimoniously capture the one part of the semantics that we do have a reasonably good understanding of, namely, compositional projection of function-argument relations under constructions like complementization and relative clause formation, governed by the particular type of transitive verbs that take sentences as complement, other than by simulating an infinite-state, push-down automaton.[4]

Unfortunately, that is about as far as our intuitions take us. The way in which individual languages reflect the putative underlying universal is not very transparent to us as linguists (although it must be transparent to the child). For example, some languages like English lexicalize complex causatives like "he was running across the street" with special transitive versions of verbs like *run* taking PP complements. Other languages, like French, appear to lexicalize the elements of the underlying causative logical form more literally, in expressions like "Il était en train de traverser la rue à la course."[5] Moreover, even such apparently painstakingly elaborated expressions do not seem to be anywhere near complete in explicitly identifying sufficient truth conditions for such utterances about a specific situation (such as one in which the subject of the remark never reached the destination), and in fact it is very difficult to specify such truth conditions for any language. The reason is that such conditions seem to include the intentions that motivated the subject's plan of action, together with the "normal" consequences that could be anticipated, as well as the physical action itself. This fact engenders the "imperfective paradox" that it is possible to truthfully say, "He was running across the street" (but not "He ran across the street"), even if the person in question never reached the other side, just in case what he did would normally have resulted in his doing so (see Dowty [1979] and much subsequent work).

This chapter argues that, if one wants to truly understand this semantics, and the form of the linguistic universals that it determines, it is necessary to simultaneously investigate the nature of action representations capable of supporting notions of teleology and change of state together with the ways such representations can be learned in interaction with experience of the world, and the ways in which the specific form that human knowledge representations takes follows from that experience, and determines observed and predicted grammatical universals. The fact that we find it difficult to specify such knowledge representations using the logics that have been developed for other more mathematical inquiries should make us expect to find the form of such grounded and experientially induced knowledge representations quite surprising and rather unlike the hand-built representations for commonsense knowledge or "naive physics" that have been proposed in the Artificial Intelligence (AI) literature (Hayes, 1979, *passim*).

9.3. Representing Change and Reasoning About Action

We know from Köhler (1925) and much subsequent work that some animals can make quite sophisticated plans involving tools. Apes really can solve the monkeys and bananas problem, using tools like old crates to gain altitude in order to reach objects out of reach. Such planning involves retrieving known actions from memory (such as piling boxes on top of one another, and climbing on them) and sequencing them in a way that will bring about a desired state or goal (such as having the bananas).

Köhler showed that, in apes at least, such search seems to be *reactive* to the presence of the tool and (breadth first) *forward chaining*, working forward from the tool to the goal, rather than backward chaining (working from goal to tool). That is, the animal can make a plan in the presence of the tool, but has difficulty with plans that require subgoals of finding tools.[6]

This observation implies that actions are accessed via perception of the objects that mediate them—in other words, that actions are represented in memory *associatively* as properties of objects—in Gibson's (1966) terms, as *affordances* of objects.

Animal planning, therefore, involves *searching* through possible causally related futures generated by the affordances of the available objects in the situation that obtains.

The problem of planning can therefore be viewed as the problem of finding a sequence of actions α, β, etc., through a state space of a kind called a Kripke model, represented in Figure 9.1. This structure, in which blobs represent *states* (which we can think of as vectors of values of facts or propositions) and directed arcs represent *actions* that transform one state into another (which we can think of as finite-state transducers from one state vector to another), is known as a S4 Kripke model. We can define a planning calculus over such models as follows.

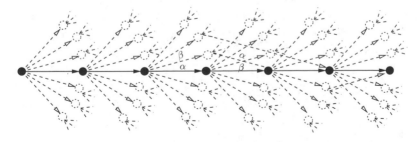

Figure 9.1. S4 Kripke model of causal accessibility relation.

9.3.1. The Linear Dynamic Event Calculus

The way animals and human beings structure their knowledge of change in the world is in terms of event types that can (mostly) be characterized as affecting just a few fluents among a very large collection representing the state of the world. (Fluents are facts or propositions that are subject to change.) Naive event representations that map entire situations to entire other situations are therefore representationally redundant and inferentially inefficient. A good representation of affordances must get around this "frame problem" (McCarthy & Hayes, 1969; Shanahan, 1997; Steedman, 2002).

The Linear Dynamic Event Calculus (LDEC) combines the insights of the Event Calculus of Kowalski and Sergot (1986), itself a descendant of the Situation Calculus of McCarthy and Hayes and the STRIPS planner of Fikes and Nilsson (1971), with the Dynamic and Linear Logics that were developed by Harel (1984), Girard (1987), and others.

STRIPS represented actions as sets of *preconditions* and localized *updates* to a model or database representing the changing state of the world, as in the following (simplified) definition of the operator *push* (as applied to doors), in which the variables x,y are implicitly universally quantified over:

(3)   OPERATOR: *push* (x, y)
      PRECONDITIONS: *door* (x)
                               closed (x)
      DELETIONS: *closed* (x)
      ADDITIONS: *open* (y)

The fact that STRIPS represents change in terms of database update means that it solves both the representational and computational forms of the frame problem of McCarthy and Hayes (1969), eliminating large numbers of "frame axioms" explicitly stating such banalities as that the color of the walls is the same before and after pushing a door, and the expensive inference that might otherwise be a need to identify the color of the walls after numerous such events.

Dynamic logics are a form of modal logic in which the $\square$ and $\lozenge$ modalities are relativized to particular events. For example, if a (possibly nondeterministic) program or command α computes a function F over the integers, then we may write the following:

(4) $n \geq 0 \Rightarrow [\alpha]\,(y = F(n))$

This can be read as, "if n is positive and you take action α, y always becomes set to $F(n)$."[7]

We can think of the dynamic modalities [α] as defining a logic whose models are Kripke diagrams in which accessibility between possible worlds corresponds to state-changing events, as in Figure 9.1.

The events α can accordingly be defined as mappings between situations or partially specified possible worlds, defined in terms of conditions on the antecedent, which must hold for them to apply (such as that $n \geq 0$ in (4)), and consequences (such as that $y = F(n)$) that hold in the consequent.

The particular dynamic logic that we will be interested in here is one that includes the following dynamic axiom, which says that the operator ; is *sequence*, an operation related to *functional composition* over events, viewed as functions from situations to situations:

(5) $[\alpha][\beta]P \Rightarrow [\alpha; \beta]P$

Using this notation, we can conveniently represent, say, a plan for an agent y *getting outside* as the composition of y *pushing* a door x and then *going through* it, written as follows:

(6)   *push'(x,y);go-through'(x,y).*

Composition is one of the most primitive *combinators*, or operations, combining functions, which Curry and Feys (1958) call **B**, writing the above sequence $\alpha; \beta$ as **B**$\beta\alpha$, where

(7)   **B**$\beta\alpha \equiv \lambda s.\beta(\alpha(s))$

Plans like *push';go-through'* could be written in Curry's notation as **B***go-through' push'*

B is the first of two fundamental planning operators that will later turn up as a cornerstone of the syntactic projection mechanism of Universal Grammar. However, for planners, it is more readable to write it as ";".

9.3.2. Situation/Event Calculi and the Frame Problem

To avoid the frame problem in both its representational and computational aspects, we need a new form of logical implication, distinct from the standard or intuitionistic $\Rightarrow$ we have used up till now. We will follow Bibel del Cerro, Fronhfer, and Herzig (1989) and others in using *linear* logical implication $\multimap$ rather than intuitionistic implication $\Rightarrow$ in those rules that change the value of fluents.

For example, we can represent the knowledge needed to come up with plan (6)—that is, events involving doors in a world (greatly simplified for purposes of exposition) in which there are two places, *out* and *in*, separated by a door that may be *open* or *shut*—as follows[8]:

(8) $affords(push(y,x)) \wedge shut(x) \multimap [push(y,x)]open(x)$
(9) $affords(go\text{-}through(y,x)) \wedge in(y) \multimap [go\text{-}through(y,x)]out(y)$

These rules say that if the situation affords you pushing something and the something is shut, then it stops being shut and starts being open, and that if the situation affords you going through something, and you are in, then you stop being in and start being out.

Linear implication has the effect of building into the representation the update effects of actions—that once you apply the rule, the proposition in question is "used up" and cannot take part in any further proofs, while a new fact is added. The formulae therefore say that if something is shut and you push it, it becomes open (and vice versa), and that if you are in and you go through something, then you become out (and vice versa). This linear deletion effect is only defined for facts—that is, ground literals. $affords(go\text{-}through(y,x))$ is a derived proposition, so it will hold or not in the consequent state according to whether it can be proved or not in that state.

In order to know when we can apply such rules, we also need to define the conditions that *afford* actions of pushing and going through. Here ordinary nonlinear intuitionistic implication is appropriate:

(10)   a. $door(x) \wedge open(x) \Rightarrow affords(go\text{-}through(y,x))$
        b. $door(x) \wedge shut(x) \Rightarrow affords(push(y,x))$

These rules say (oversimplifying wildly) that if a thing is a door and is open, then it's possible to go through it, and that if a thing is a door and it's shut, then it's possible to push it.

We also need to define the transitive property of the possibility relation, as follows, using the definition (5) of event sequence composition:

(11) $affords(\alpha) \wedge [\alpha]affords(\beta) \Rightarrow affords(\alpha; \beta)$

This says that any situation that affords an action α, in which actually doing α gets you to a situation that affords an action β, is a situation that affords α, *then* β.

To interpret linear implication as it is used here in terms of proof theory and proof search, we need to think of possible worlds in the Kripke diagram in Figure 9.1 as states of a single updatable STRIPS database of facts. Rules like (8) and (9) can then be interpreted as (partial) functions over the states in the model that map states to other states by removing facts and adding other facts. Linear implication and the dynamic box operator are here essentially used as a single state-changing operator: you can't have one without the other.

The effect of such rules can be exemplified as follows. If the initial situation is that you are in and the door is shut:

(12) $in(you) \wedge door(d) \wedge shut(d)$

then intuitionistic rule (10b) and the linear rule (8) mean that attempts to prove the following propositions concerning the state of the door in the situation that results from pushing the door will all succeed, because they are all facts in the database that results from the action $push(you,d)$ in the initial situation (12):

(13)   a. $[push(you,d)]open(d)$
        b. $[push(you,d)]door(d)$
        c. $[push(you,d)]in(you)$

On the other hand, an attempt to prove the proposition (14) will fail because rule (8a) removes the fact in question from the database that results from the action $push(you,d)$[9]:

(14) $[push(you,d)]shut(d)$

The advantage of interpreting linear implication in this way is that it builds the STRIPS treatment of the frame problem into the proof theory and entirely avoids the need for inferentially cumbersome reified frame axioms of the kind proposed by Kowalski (1979) and others (see Shanahan, 1997).

This fragment gives us a simple planner in which starting from the world (15) where you are *in* and the door is *shut*, and stating the goal (16) meaning "find a series of actions that the situation affords that will get you *out*," can, given a suitable search control, be made to automatically deliver a constructive proof that one such plan is (17), the composition of *pushing* and *going through* the door:

(15) $in(you) \wedge door(d) \wedge shut(d)$
(16) $affords(\alpha) \wedge [\alpha]out(you)$
(17) $\alpha = push(you,d);go\text{-}through(you,d).$

The situation that results from executing this plan in the start situation (12) is one in which the following conjunction of facts is directly represented by the database:

(18) $out(you) \wedge door(d) \wedge open(d)$

Because we can regard actions as functions from situations to situations, rule (11) defines *function composition* B as the basic plan-building operator of the system. Composition is one of the simplest of a small collection of combinators, which Curry and Feys (1958) used to define the foundations of the λ-calculus and other applicative systems in which new concepts can be defined in terms of old. As the knowledge representation that underlies human cognition and human language could hardly be anything *other* than an applicative system of some kind, we should not be surprised to see it turn up as one of the basic operations of planning systems.[10]

By making the calculus affordance based, we provide the basis for a simple forward-chaining reactive style of planning that seems to be characteristic of non-linguistic animal planning. This kind of planning is not purely reactive in the sense of Brooks (1986) and Agre and Chapman (1987): the notion of state representation plays a central role, as Bryson has proposed within the Behavior-Based AI approach (Bryson & Stein, 2001).

There are two ways of thinking about computing plans with the LDEC. One is as a logic programming language with sideeffects, much like Prolog. Poole (1993) shows how the Horn clauses of such a representation can be associated with a Bayesian Network probability model. However, there are problems in scaling such logicist representations to realistically sized cases. We noted earlier that STRIPS/LDEC operators can be thought of as finite-state transducers (FSTs) over state space vectors. We can think of these operators, more specifically, as FSTs over *sparse* vectors, because they treat most values as irrelevant, STRIPS style. Crucially, FSTs are closed under composition (Kaplan & Karttunen, 1994). It follows that it is also possible to think of LDEC operators in terms of neural network representations of associative memory (McClelland, McNaughton, & O'Reilly, 1995), and in particular, in terms of a very simple device called the Associative Network, or Willshaw Net (Willshaw, 1981), which is specialized for representing associations between sparse vectors.

In either case, Steedman (2004, p. 61) and Botvinick and Plaut (2004) suggest that Simply Recurrent Networks (SRN: Elman, 1990) can be used to learn such sequences in order to automate or memo-ize them in the style of explanation-based learning (EBL; van Harmelen & Bundy, 1988), so that they can be used as elements of higher-level or hierarchical plans. However, such a process should not be confused with planning itself, or the with learning basic actions.

9.4. Formalizing Affordance in LDEC

We can define the affordances of objects directly in terms of LDEC preconditions (and deletions). Thus, the affordances of boxes are things like *falling, climbing on, putting-on* things, and *putting-things-on*:

$$(19) \quad affordances(box) = \left\{ \begin{array}{l} \lambda x_{box}.fall(x) \\ \lambda x_{box} \lambda y.climb\text{-}on(y, x) \\ \lambda x_{box} \lambda y \lambda z.put\text{-}on(x, y, z) \lambda x \lambda y_{box} \lambda z.put\text{-}on(x, y, z) \end{array} \right\}$$

This provides the basis for reactive, affordance-based, forward-chaining plan construction that is characteristic of primates.

Note that these affordances are heterogeneous in type, involving the box, respectively, in roles of *agent*, *patient*, and *thing affected*.

The Gibsonian affordance-based box schema in (19) can in turn be defined as a function mapping boxes into (second-order, polyadic) functions from their affordances like falling, climbing on, and putting on something, into the results of those actions:

(20) $box = \lambda x_{box}.\lambda p_{affordances(box)}.p(x)$

where p ranges over the function types in (19)

The operation of turning an object of a given type into a function over those functions that apply to objects of that type is the second primitive combinator central to the planning capability. It is called T, or *type-raising*, so (20) can be rewritten as $box' = \lambda x_{box}.Tx$, where

(21) $Ta \equiv \lambda p.p(a)$

9.5. Linguistic Reflexes of Affordance

The fact that object concepts like (19) are affordance based and type-raised to support planning shows up in natural language lexicons in two main ways:

- Some languages, like Navajo, seem to lexicalize default affordance directly, and to also reflect types of verbal arguments like *animate object* in a system of *nominal classifiers*.
- other languages, such as Latin, reflect roles like *agent*, *patient*, and *thing affected* in (19) a system of (*nominative/ergative*, *accusative/absolutive*, *dative*, etc.) *case*.

Of course, some languages mix these markers, whereas while others, like English, encode case in word order, rather than morphology.

9.5.1. Navajo

Many North American Indian languages, such as the Athabascan group that includes Navajo, are comparatively poorly off for nouns. Many nouns for artifacts are morphological derivatives of verbs. For example, "door" is *ch'é'étiin*, meaning "something has a path horizontally out," a gloss which has an uncanny resemblance to (9). This process is completely productive: "towel" is *bee 'ádít'oodí*, glossed as "one wipes oneself with it," or perhaps "wherewith you wipe yourself," and "towelrack"

is *bee 'ádít'oodí bąąh dah náhidiiltsos*—roughly, "one wipes oneself with it is repeatedly hung on it" or "whereon you hang wherewith you wipe yourself" (Young &
Morgan, 1987).

Such languages thus appear to lexicalize nouns as a *default affordance* (T) and
to *compose* such affordances (B). Of course, we should avoid naive Whorfean inferences about Navajo speakers' reasoning about objects. Though productive, these
lexicalizations are as conventional as our own.[11]

Navajo nouns are also implicitly classified by animacy, shape, and consistency.
However, rather than being realized via a rich gender system, as in some other
Athabaskan languages such as Koyukon, this classification is in Navajo reflected in
verbal morphology. For example, the classifier *-iltsos* on the verb *náhidiiltsos*, "hung,"
marks it as predicated of flat, flexible things like towels, so that a more faithful gloss of
the Navajo for "towel rack" might be "whereon you hang flat flexible objects wherewith you wipe yourself." A belt rack or a gun rack would have a different classifier.

Wikipedia gives the following table of Navajo classifiers (the orthographic conventions are slightly different from those used in the examples from Young &
Morgan, 1987).

(22)   *Navajo Classifiers*:

Classifier + Stem	Label Explanation	Examples
-'ą	SRO Solid Roundish Object	bottle, ball, boot, box, etc.
-yí	LPB Load, Pack, Burden	backpack, bundle, sack, saddle, etc.
-ł-jool	NCM Non-Compact Matter	bunch of hair or grass, cloud, fog, etc.
-lá	SFO Slender Flexible Object	rope, mittens, socks, pile of fried onions, etc.
-tą	SSO Slender Stiff Object	arrow, bracelet, skillet, saw, etc.
-ł-tsooz	FFO Flat Flexible Object	blanket, coat, sack of groceries, etc.
-tłéé'	MM Mushy Matter	ice cream, mud, slumped-over drunken person, etc.
-nil	PLO1 Plural Objects 1	eggs, balls, animals, coins, etc.
-jaa'	PLO2 Plural Objects 2	marbles, seeds, sugar, bugs, etc.
-ką	OC Open Container	glass of milk, spoonful of food, handful of flour, etc.
-ł-tí	ANO Animate Object	microbe, person, corpse, doll, etc.

As a consequence, the English verb "give" is expressed by 11 different forms in
Navajo, depending on the charateristics of the object given, including *níłjool* (give-
NCM), used in "give me some hay" and *nítjjh* (give-SSO), used in "give me a
cigarette."[12]

The appearance of such pronominal classifiers on the verb appears to be an example of a "head marking" system of *case*, inasfar as the final position of such classifiers "structurally" mark the fact that they are patients of the action (cf. Blake, 2001, p. 13). The interest of such classifiers and their reflex in Navajo nominalizations as a form of case marking agreement is twofold. First, if these classifiers appear explicitly in Navajo, one might expect that they reflect a universal ontology of entities. The advantage of such ontologies is that they allow an agent to generalize the notion of affordances of doors to other actions applying to objects of that class. The extension to a system of case allows even further generalization to the full range of transitive actions.

9.5.2. Latin

The type-raising combinator T is even more directly related to more familiar and morphologically transparent case systems, as in the following fragment of Latin:

(23)   a. Balb*us* ambulat.
              "Balbus walks."
          b. Livia Balb*um* amat.
              "Livia loves Balbus."
          c. Livia Balb*o* murum dabit.
              "Livia gave Balbus a wall."

This involves the following fragment of Latin lexicon:

(24)
$$
\left\{
\begin{array}{lll}
\text{Balb} + us & : & \lambda p_{(e,t)} \cdot p \; balb' \\
\text{Balb} + um & : & \lambda p_{(e,(e,t))} \lambda y \cdot p \; balb' y \\
\text{Balb} + o & : & \lambda p_{(e,(e,(e,t)))} \lambda y \lambda z \cdot p \; balb' yz
\end{array}
\right\}
$$

"Balbus" is the word. Its semantic correlate is *balb'*. The logical form is homomorphic to the object concept but has a distinct (left-associative) notation. Case affixes are type-raisers.

We shall see in the next section that even English posesses a case system in this sense.

9.6. **B, T,** and the Combinatory Projection Principle

Besides supporting the basic operations of seriation and object orientation that planning depends upon, syntactic versions of combinators B and T support a rebracketing and reordering calculus of exactly the kind that is needed to capture natural language syntax and provide the basis of Combinatory Categorial Grammar (CCG; Ades & Steedman, 1982; see Steedman [2000b] for references).

CCG eschews language-specific syntactic rules like (25) for English. Instead, all language-specific syntactic information is *lexicalized* via lexical entries, like (26) for the English transitive verb:

(25) S → NP VP
        VP → TV NP
        TV → $\{proved, finds, \ldots\}$

(26)   proved: $= (S\backslash NP)/NP$

This syntactic "category" identifies the transitive verb as a function, and specifies the type and directionality of its arguments and the type of its result, /NP indicating an NP argument to the right, $\backslash NP$ indicating an NP argument to the left, and the brackets indicating that the rightward argument is the first argument to combine.

Category (26) also reflects its semantic type ($e \rightarrow (e \rightarrow t)$), expressed in (27a) below as a lambda term paired with it via a colon operator, in which primes mark constants, nonprimes are variables, and concatenation denotes function application under a "left associative" convention, so that the expression *prove′xy* is equivalent to (*prove′x*)*y*.

We follow Baldridge (2002) in generalizing this notation to freer word order languages, as follows, where brackets {} enclose one or more sets of arguments that can combine in any order, and the preceding slash /, \, or | indicates that all members of the set must be found to the right, left, or either direction, respectively. We also generalize the semantic notation using a parallel argument set notation for lambda terms and a convention that pairs the unordered syntactic arguments with the unordered semantic arguments in the left-to-right order in which they appear on the page. Typical transitive verb categories then appear as follows[13]:

(27)   a. English: $(S\backslash NP)/NP : \lambda x \lambda y.prove′xy$
        b. Latin: $S|\{NP_{nom}, NP_{acc}\} : \lambda\{y, x\}.prove′xy$
        c. Tagalog: $S/\{NP_{nom}, NP_{acc}\} : \lambda\{y, x\}.prove′xy$
        d. Japanese: $S\backslash\{NP_{nom}, NP_{acc}\} : \lambda\{y, x\}.prove′xy$

Such categories should be thought of as schemata covering a finite number of deterministic categories like (27a).

Some very general syntactic rules, corresponding to function application, and the combinators B and T, together with a third combinator S, which we will pass over here, but which is parallel in every respect to B, then constitute the universal mechanism of syntactic derivation or projection onto the set of all and only the sentences of the language specified by its CCG lexicon. This universal set of rules is the following:

(28)   *The functional application rules*

a. $X/_* Y : f \quad Y : a \Rightarrow X : fa$ (>)

b. $Y : a \quad X\backslash_* Y : f \Rightarrow X : fa$ (<)

(29)   *The functional composition rules*:

a. $X/_\diamond Y : f \quad Y/_\diamond Z : g \Rightarrow_B \quad X/_\diamond Z : \lambda x.f(gx)$ (>B)

b. $Y\backslash_\diamond Z : g \quad X\backslash_\diamond Y : f \Rightarrow_B \quad X\backslash_\diamond Z : \lambda x.f(gx)$ (<B)

c. $X/_x Y : f \quad Y\backslash_x Z : g \Rightarrow_B \quad X\backslash_x Z : \lambda x.f(gx)$ (>B$_x$)

d. $Y/_x Z : g \quad X/_x Y : f \Rightarrow_B \quad X/_x Z : \lambda x.f(gx)$ (<B$_x$)

(30)   *The order-preserving type-raising rules*:

a. $X : a \Rightarrow_T \quad T/_i(T\backslash_i X) : \lambda f.fa$ (>T)

b. $X : a \Rightarrow_T \quad T\backslash_i(T/_i X) : \lambda f.fa$ (<T)

The types $*$, $\diamond$, and $\times$ on the slashes in rules (28) restrict the categories that may combine by them. Although all categories seen so far have the unadorned slash types /, \, or |, which can combine by any rule, the language-specific lexicon can restrict the combinatory potential of lexical function categories using these slash types. Thus, coordinators like *and* are restricted via the $*$ type to *only* combine by the application rules:

(31)   and: $= (X\backslash_* X)/_* X$

The $\diamond$ slash type on a function category means that it can combine *either* by the application rules (28) *or* by the rules >B and <B bearing that slash type in (29), but *not* by the rules >B$_x$ or <B$_x$. In English (as opposed to, say, Latin), adjectives are retricted using this slash type, because they are entirely fixed in terms of linear order with respext to the head, unlike adverbs, and it is the latter rules that allow reordering:

(32)   young: $= N/_\diamond N$

The variable i type on the type-raising rules (30) means that the raised category inherits the slash type of its argument.

The composition rules are all generalized to cover cases where the "lower" function $Y|Z$ and the result $X|Z$ are of higher valency $(Y|Z)|W$ and $(X|Z)|W$, etc., up to some low value, such as 4 $(((Y|Z)|W)|V)|U$ and $(((X|Z)|W)|V)|U$, which appears to be the highest valency in the universal inventory of lexical types (Newmeyer, 2005, citing Pesetsky, 1995). It is the combination of crossed composition, as in >B$_x$ and <B$_x$, and this generalization that increases the expressive power of the formalism to the lowest known trans-context-free level of the "mildly context-sensitive" class identified by Joshi, Vijay-Shanker, and Weir (1991) and discussed by Stabler in Chapter 10, weakly equivalent to basic Lexicalized Tree-Adjoining Grammars (LTAG and its Tree-Local Multicomponent variant) and Linear

Indexed Grammars (LIGs). The theory thus embodies a very strong claim about a formal universal, namely, that all natural languages fall into this low-power class.

A number of principles that amount to the following statement mean that these are the *only* combinatory rules that are available to Universal Grammar:

(33)   *The Strict Lexicalization Principle*
         The universal combinatory rules must project, and may not override, the direction-
         ality and slash type specified in the language-specific lexicon.

This theory has been applied to the linguistic analysis of coordination, relativiza-tion, and intonational structure in English and many other languages (Baldridge, 1998, 2002; Bozsahin, 1998; Hoffman, 1995; Komagata, 1999; Steedman, 1996, 2000a). For example, we can define relativization without syntactic movement or empty categories, as in (35), via the following category for the relative pro-noun:

(34) $that := (N\backslash_\diamond N)/(S/NP)$

This category yields the following derivation:

(35)   (The woman)   that   Thelma   met
         $\overline{(N\backslash_\diamond N)/(S/NP)}$ $\overline{S/(S\backslash NP_{3SG})}^{>T}$ $\overline{(S\backslash NP_{3SG})/NP}$
                                               $\underline{\hspace{6cm}}^{>B}$
                                                        S/NP
         $\underline{\hspace{10cm}}^{>}$
                                  $N\backslash_\diamond N$

Such "extractions" are correctly predicted to be unbounded, because composition can operate across clause boundaries:

(36)   (The woman)   that   Thelma   says   she   met
       $\overline{(N\backslash_\diamond N)/(S/NP)}$ $\overline{S/(S\backslash NP_{3SG})}^{>T}$ $\overline{(S\backslash NP_{3SG})/S}$ $\overline{S/(S\backslash NP_{3SG})}^{>T}$ $\overline{(S\backslash NP_{3SG})/NP}$
                                    $\underline{\hspace{5cm}}^{>B}$ $\underline{\hspace{5cm}}^{>B}$
                                          S/S
                                    $\underline{\hspace{8cm}}^{>B}$
                                                    S/NP
       $\underline{\hspace{11cm}}^{>}$
                             $N\backslash_\diamond N$

It is the lexical category (34) of the relative pronoun that establishes the long-range dependency between noun and verb (through the semantics defined in the lexi-con via the logical form (not shown here): syntactic derivation merely projects it onto the phrasal logical form via strictly type-dependent combinatory operations of composition and type-raising, together with application, applying only to adjacent derivational constituents.

In the terms of the Minimalist Program, CCG therefore has the effect of reducing MOVE to MERGE.[14]

The conjunction category (31) allows a related movement- and deletion-free account of right node raising, as in (37):

(37)

$$
\begin{array}{cccc}
\underbrace{\text{[Thelma met]}}_{\displaystyle S/NP}\!\!>\!B & \underbrace{\text{and}}_{\displaystyle (X\backslash_\star X)/_\star X} & \underbrace{\text{[Fred says he likes]}}_{\displaystyle S/NP}\!\!>\!B & \underbrace{\text{Louise}}_{\displaystyle S\backslash(S/NP)}\!\!<\!T
\end{array}
$$

$$
\cfrac{\cfrac{}{(S/NP)\backslash_\star(S/NP)}>}{\cfrac{\cfrac{}{(S/NP)}<}{S}<}
$$

The $\star$ modality on the conjunction category (31) means that it can *only* combine like types by the application rules (28). Hence, the across-the-board condition (ATB) on extractions from coordinate structures (including the "same case" condition) is captured:

(38)   a. A woman [that$_{(N\backslash_\circ N)/(S/NP)}$ [[Thelma met]$_{S/NP}$ and [Louise likes]$_{S/NP}$]$_{S/NP}$]$_{N\backslash_\circ N}$
        b. A woman [that$_{(N\backslash_\circ N)/(S/NP)}$ *[[Thelma met]$_{S/NP}$ and [likes Louise]$_{S\backslash NP}$]$_{S/NP}$]$_{N\backslash_\circ N}$
        c. A woman that$_{(N\backslash_\circ N)/(S/NP)}$ *[[Thelma met]$_{S/NP}$ and [Louise likes her]$_{S}$]]
        d. A woman that$_{(N\backslash_\circ N)/(S/NP)}$ *[[Thelma met her]$_{S}$ and [Louise likes]$_{S/NP}$]

CCG offers startlingly simple analyses of a wide variety of further coordination phenomena, including English "argument-cluster coordination," "backward gapping" and "verb-raising" constructions in Germanic languages, and English gapping. The first of these is illustrated by the following analysis, from Dowty (1988 — cf. Steedman, 1985), in which the ditransitive verb category $(VP/NP)/NP$ is abbreviated as DTV, and the transitive verb category VP/NP is abbreviated as TV[15]:

(39)

$$
\begin{array}{ccccccc}
\underbrace{\text{give}}_{\displaystyle DTV} & \underbrace{\text{Thelma}}_{\displaystyle TV\backslash DTV}\!\!<\!T & \underbrace{\text{a book}}_{\displaystyle VP\backslash TV}\!\!<\!T & \underbrace{\text{and}}_{\displaystyle (X\backslash_\star X)/_\star X} & \underbrace{\text{Louise}}_{\displaystyle TV\backslash DTV}\!\!<\!T & \underbrace{\text{a record}}_{\displaystyle VP\backslash TV}\!\!<\!T
\end{array}
$$

$$
\cfrac{\cfrac{\cfrac{\cfrac{}{VP\backslash DTV}\!<\!B \qquad\qquad \cfrac{}{VP\backslash DTV}\!<\!B}{(VP\backslash DTV)\backslash_\star(VP\backslash DTV)}>}{VP\backslash DTV\backslash}<}{VP}<
$$

The universal set of combinatory rules does not allow any derivation for word orders like the following, given the lexicon of English:

(40)   *Thelma a book and give Louise a record.

Thus, the universal noted by Ross (1970) concerning the direction of gapping and the base order of constituents in constructions is a theorem of the theory of extraction without movement based on combinatory projection with rules based on B and T. In the terms of the minimalist program, CCG therefore also reduces COPY and/or DELETE to MERGE.

It should be evident from the fact that the type-raising operation in (35) turns the NP *Thelma* into a function over predicates $S\backslash NP$, and in (39) it turns the same word into a function over ditransitive verbs $(VP/NP)\backslash((VP/NP)/NP)$ and the NP *a book* into a function over transitive verbs $VP\backslash(VP/NP)$ that type-raising, even in English, is simply (respectively: nominative, dative, and accusative) grammatical *case*, albeit marked "structurally" by position with repect to the verb, rather than morphologically, an in Latin *Thelma, Thelmæ, Thelmam*. We have seen that notions of case and affordance are highly related. Thus sentence (39) can be seen as composing pairs of functions over affordances and conjoining the result.

It is likely that a number of other universals concerning possible word orders can be base generated on similar assumptions of a universal projection principle based on the combinators **B** and **T**. Universal 20 of Greenberg (1963) concerning the possible base orders of Dem, Num, A, and N, as expanded by Hawkins (1983) and Cinque (2005), is particularly promising in this respect, as Hawkins (1983, pp. 121–122) points out.

The close relation between the combinatory syntactic primitives and those involved in planned action should not come as a surprise. If we turn to those aspects of language that presumably reflect its origin most directly, namely, its use to manipulate the actions of others to our own advantage, then it is clear that this is, quintessentially, a planning problem, rather than a distinctively linguistic one. For example, the fact that the utterance most likely to effect the manipulation of getting the window shut is often not the imperative "Shut the window" but the declarative "It's cold in here" can be captured in essentially the same terms of affordance and change in knowledge state that are used to plan with doors and locations, the main difference lying in the fact that representation of the state of other minds is required, as discussed in Steedman (2002, 2007b).

9.7. Conclusion

This chapter has sketched a theory of the way in which experience shapes object and action concepts, how they are used to plan purposive actions in dynamic worlds, and how this system forms a basis for language, to which the latter is almost entirely transparent. The linguistic theory that exhibits this transparent mapping is "nearly context free"—that is, at the lowest trans-context-free level of the "mildly context-sensitive" systems, discussed in Chapter 10 of this volume by Stabler. The involvement of syntactic combinatory rules corresponding to composition and type-raising allows such powerful operations as MOVE, COPY, and DELETE, as proposed in other linguistic frameworks, to be reduced to MERGE, defined as type-dependent combination of string-adjacent constituents.

Such grammars are "monostratal," in the sense of having only one level of representation, namely, logical form. They are also monotonic, in that the rules that relate such meanings to surface strings are purely type driven, and never alter representational form. It follows that the first stages of language acquisition reduce to the problem of identifying which words correspond with which elements of logical form from repeated exposure to (possibly noisy, possibly contextually ambiguous) pairings of strings and contextually supported meanings. Villavicencio (2002) and Zettlemoyer and Collins (2005) offer computational models of this process. In such models, much of the baggage of traditional accounts of language acquisition, including notions like "parameter setting," "core and periphery," "trigger," and "subset principle" (Fodor & Sakas, 2005), can be eliminated or seen as emergent from simple statistical parsing models.

The present chapter has remained conspicuously silent on the question of how STRIPS-like rules can be induced from sensory-motor data arising from interaction with the world. Nevertheless, it seems likely that a proper theory of action representation will have to embody the ideas of object orientation and dynamism that are assumed here, embodied in associative memory mechanisms of a kind that have long been associated with the hippocampus. The fact that the language faculty, whose syntactic aspects have long been thought to be quite mysterious and unique, appears to reflect these same properties so simply and directly may strengthen this expectation.

Acknowledgments

Thanks to Chris Geib, Kira Mourão, Ron Petrick, and Matthew Stone, and to the editors and the anonymous reviewers for this volume. The work was supported in part by the SE Edinburgh-Stanford Link grant Sounds of Discourse and EU IST grant FP6-2004-IST-4-27657 PACO-PLUS.

Key Further Readings

Probably the best (and certainly the most readable) introduction to the physiological and behavioral basis for the relation between planning and serial cognitive behavior is Miller et al. (1960), which builds on inspiring work by Lashley (1951). A more recent survey and theoretical proposal, drawing on modern brain-imaging techniques and neural-computational models, is Pulvermüller (2002). Developmental aspects of sensory-motor serial behavior related to planning in children in the period preceding the onset of language are discussed in Piaget (1936), which is particularly valuable for a large number of anecdotal examples and observations. Evolutionary aspects of the relation are discussed in Chapter 17 of Maynard-Smith and Szathmáry (1995) and in a more linguistic vein by my Edinburgh colleague Jim Hurford (2007).

AI planning, include reactive planning and the event calculus, is helpfully reviewed in Russell and Norvig (2003). The project of inducing grounded cognition in a robot via machine learning from interaction with the world is being pursued in a number of laboratories in Europe and North America, but the problem remains extremely hard, and the theoretical results so far remain little more than promissory notes and metaphorical speculations. However, once such a conceptual representation and the corresponding logical forms are established, the problem of attaching a specific language to it is comparitively simple—see Zettlemoyer and Collins (2005), for example.

Notes

1   The following distinctions follow Chomsky (1995). Chomsky (1965, pp. 27–30) distinguishes only between substantive and formal universals. However, the specific instances of formal universal cited there include some that under the definition of Chomsky (1995, pp. 54–55) would be classified as substantive or functional. To the extent that formal universals are discussed at all in Chomsky (1995, pp. 16, 222), it is clear that the definition is the restricted one stated below, in contrast to that in Lasnik and Uriagereka (2005, p. 12), where functional universals are referred to in passing as "formal," threatening to lose an important distinction.

2   I shall use the term "transitive" indiscriminately to cover all verbs taking a second argument such as NP, PP, VP, or S in addition to the subject.

3   The fact that UG "cannot count beyond two"—that is, that no language requires its verb to be in third position, next-to-last position, etc. (Newmeyer, 2005, 4)—must also be semantic, say, because of an association between first position and notions such as "topic."

4   In this sense, the emphasis in Hauser, Chomsky, and Fitch (2002) on the evolution of recursion itself as the crucial element distinguishing human cognition and language from animal cognition may be misplaced. It must be the evolution of *concepts that intrinsically require recursive definitions* that separates us from other animals. Recursive concepts of mutual belief seem to be plausible candidates, as Tomasello (1999) has suggested.

5   Many of these explicit elements like "à la course" are of course often elided in actual French utterance in context, making the problem of automatic translation much harder.

6   This seems a sensible way for an animal to plan. If there *is* a short plan using available resources, breadth-first forward chaining will find it. Even when evolution has provided tools with very general affordances, such as credit cards, cell phones, and fast-food delivery, backward breadth-first chaining is expensive and risky.

7   Dynamic logic also includes "diamond" operators $\langle\alpha\rangle$ which, if used in place of the "box" operator $[\alpha]$ in (4), has the effect of replacing "always" by "sometimes" in this gloss. The present dynamic logic is "box only"—that is, it represents action as deterministic in spite of the fact that the word does not always behave that way.

8   We follow a logic-programming convention that all variables appearing in the consequent are implicitly universally quantified and all *other* variables are implicitly existentialy

quantified. Because in the real world doors don't always open when you push them, box must be read as *default* necessity, meaning "usually."

9 We follow a further logic-programming convention of "negation as failure," according to which a proposition is treated as false if it cannot be positively proved to be true.

10 This calculus is developed further in Steedman (1997, 2002) in application to more ambitious plans, and a number of generalizations of the frame problem, using a novel analysis of *durative* events extending over intervals of time, in which such events are represented by instantaneous inceptive and culminative events, which repectively add and remove facts about the event being in progress and the consequences, if any, of its culmination. This representation has a number of advantages over more standard interval-based representations such as those of Allen (1984) and; Allen and Hayes (1989), including a solution to the imperfective paradox. These ramifications are passed over here.

11 Navajo speakers find equally exotic the propensity of English to generate denominal verbs, like "table" and "pocket," with equal productivity, and find compounds like "workshop" astonishingly unspecific about who or what is doing the working.

12 I once read a transcript of a Navajo radio broadcast in which the participants were discussing how to translate the name of the band called Hootie and the Blowfish. They had no trouble with "Hootie" and "fish," but thought "blow" deplorably vague, needing to know exactly *who* was blowing exactly *what* and with *what result* in order to come up with the correct translation—roughly, "fish that inflates itself."

13 These categories are deliberately simplified for expository purposes, and certainly overstate the degree to which alternative constitutent orders are semantically equivalent in these languages.

14 Steedman (2000b, 2007a) shows that this claim also extends to the "covert" variety of movement that has been invoked to explain ambiguities of quantifier scope in sentences like the following:

(i) Some man loves every woman.

15 In more recent work, Dowty has disowned this analysis because of the implicit "intrinsic" use of logical form that it entails.

References

Ades, A., & Steedman, M. (1982). On the order of words. *Linguistics and Philosophy, 4,* 517–558.

Agre, P., & Chapman, D. (1987). Pengi: An implementation of a theory of activity. In *Proceedings of the sixth national conference on artificial intelligence (AAAI-87)*. Los Altos, CA: Morgan Kaufmann.

Allen, J. (1984). Towards a general theory of action and time. *Artificial intelligence, 23,* 123–154.

Allen, J., & Hayes, P. (1989). Moments and points in an interval-based temporal logic. *Computational intelligence, 5,* 225–238.

Baldridge, J. (1998). *Local scrambling and syntactic asymmetries in Tagalog*. Master's thesis, University of Pennsylvania.

Baldridge, J. (2002). *Lexically specified derivational control in combinatory categorial grammar*. Ph.D. thesis, University of Edinburgh.

Bibel, W, Farinas del Cerro, L., Fronhfer, B., & Herzig, A. (1989). Plan generation by linear proofs: On semantics. In *German workshop on artificial intelligence—GWAI'89*, vol. 216 of *Informatik-Fachberichte*. Berlin: Springer Verlag.

Blake, B. (2001). *Case* (2nd ed.). Cambridge: Cambridge University Press.

Botvinick, M., & Plaut, D. (2004). Doing without schema hierarchies: A recurrent connectionist approach to normal and impaired routine sequential action. *Psychological Review, 111*, 395–429.

Bozsahin, C. (1998). Deriving predicate-argument structure for a freeword order language. In *Proceedings of COLING-ACL'98, Montreal* (pp. 167–173). Cambridge, MA: MIT Press.

Brooks, R. A. (1986). A robust layered control system for a mobile robot. *IEEE Journal of Robotics and Automation, 2*, 14–23.

Bryson, J. (2001). Intelligent control requires more structure than the theory of event coding provides. *Behavioral and Brain Sciences, 24*, 878–879. Open peer commentary on Hommel et al. (2001).

Bryson, J., & Stein, L. A. (2001). Modularity and design in reactive intelligence. In *Proceedings of the 17th international joint conference on artificial intelligence*. Menlo Park, CA: AAAI.

Buszkowski, W., & Penn, G. (1990). Categorial grammars determined from linguistic data by unification. *Studia Logica, 49*, 431–454.

Caramazza, A., & Hillis, A. E. (1991). Lexical organization of nouns and verbs in the brain. *Nature, 349*, 788–790.

Chomsky, N. (1957). *Syntactic structures*. The hague: Mouton.

Chomsky, N. (1965). *Aspects of the theory of syntax*. Cambridge, MA: MIT Press.

Chomsky, N. (1995). *The minimalist program*. Cambridge, MA: MIT Press.

Cinque, G. (2005). Deriving greenberg's universal 20 and its exceptions. *Linguistic Inquiry, 36*, 315–332.

Curry, H. B., & Feys, R. (1958). *Combinatory Logic* (Vol. I). Amsterdam: North Holland.

Dowty, D. (1979). *Word meaning in Montague grammar*. Dordrecht: Reidel. 2nd edition with additions, (1991).

Dowty, D. (1988). Type-raising, functional composition, and nonconstituent coordination. In T. Richard, O. Emmon Bach, & D. Wheeler (Eds.), *Categorial grammars and natural language structures* (pp. 153–198). Dordrecht: Reidel.

Dryer, M. (1992). The greenbergian word order correlations. *Language, 68*, 81–138.

Elman, J. (1990). Finding structure in time. *Cognitive Science, 14*, 179–211.

Fikes, R., & Nilsson, N. (1971). STRIPS: A new approach to the application of theorem proving to problem solving. *AI Journal, 2*, 189–208.

Fodor, J. D., & Sakas, W. (2005). The subset principle in syntax: Costs of compliance. *Journal of Linguistics, 41*, 513–569.

Gibson, J. (1966). *The senses considered as perceptual systems*. Boston, MA: Houghton-Mifflin Co.

Girard, J.-Y. (1987). Linear logic. *Theoretical Computer Science, 50*, 1–102.

Gold, E. M. (1967). Language identification in the limit. *Information and Control, 16*, 447–474.

Greenberg, J. (1963). Some universals of grammar with particular reference to the order of meaningful elements. In J. Greenberg (Ed.), *Universals of language*, 73–113. Cambridge MA: MIT Press.

Harel, D. (1984). Dynamic logic. In D. Gabbay & F. Guenthner (Eds.), *Handbook of philosophical logic* (Vol. 2, pp. 497–604). Dordrecht: Reidel.

van Harmelen, F., & Bundy, A. (1988). Explanation-based generalisation = partial evaluation. *Artificial Intelligence, 36*(3), 401–412.

Hauser, M., Noam, C., & Fitch, W. T. (2002). The faculty of language: What is it, who has it, and how did it evolve? *Science, 298*, 1569–1579.

Hawkins, J. (1983). *Word order universals*. New York: Academic.

Hayes, P. (1979). The naive physics manifesto. In D. Michie (Ed.), *Expert systems in the microeletronics age* (pp. 242–270). Edinburgh: Edinburgh University Press.

Hoffman, B. (1995). *Computational analysis of the syntax and interpretation of "free" word-order in turkish*. Ph.D. thesis, University of Pennsylvania. IRCS Report 95–17.

Horning, J. (1969). *A study of grammatical inference*. Ph.D. thesis, Stanford.

Hurford, J. (2007). *Origins of meaning*. Oxford: Oxford University Press.

Huybregts, R. (1984). The weak inadequacy of context-free phrase-structure grammars. In G. de Haan, M. Trommelen, & W. Zonneveld (Eds.), *Van Periferie naar Kern*. Dordrecht: Foris.

Joshi, A., Vijay-Shanker, K., & Weir, D. (1991). The convergence of mildly context-sensitive formalisms. In P. Sells, S. Shieber, & T. Wasow (Eds.), *Processing of linguistic structure* (pp. 31–81). Cambridge, MA: MIT Press.

Kaplan, R., & Karttunen, L. (1994). Regular models of phonological rule systems. *Computational linguistics, 20*, 331–378.

Köhler, W. (1925). *The mentality of apes*. New York: Harcourt Brace and World.

Komagata, N. (1999). *Information structure in texts: A computational analysis of contextual appropriateness in english and japanese*. Ph.D. thesis, University of Pennsylvania.

Kowalski, R. (1979). *Logic for problem solving*. Amsterdam: North Holland.

Kowalski, R., & Sergot, M. (1986). A logic-based calculus of events. *New generation computing, 4*, 67–95.

Lashley, K. (1951). The problem of serial order in behavior. In L. A. Jeffress (Ed.), *Cerebral mechanisms in behavior* (pp. 112–136). New York: Wiley. Reprinted in Saporta (1961).

Lasnik, H., & Uriagereka, J. (2005). *A course in minimalist syntax*. Oxford: Blackwell.

Maynard-Smith, J., & Szathmáry, E. (1995). *The major transitions in evolution*. Oxford: W. H. Freeman/Spektrum.

McCarthy, J., & Hayes, P. (1969). Some philosophical problems from the standpoint of artificial intelligence. In B. Meltzer & D. Michie (Eds.), *Machine intelligence* (Vol. 4, pp. 473–502). Edinburgh: Edinburgh University Press.

McClelland, J., McNaughton, B., & O'Reilly, R. (1995). Why there are complementary learning systems in the hippocampus and cortex. *Psychological review, 102*, 419–457.

Miller, G., Galanter, E., & Pribram, K. (1960). *Plans and the structure of behavior*. New York, NY: Henry Holt.

Newmeyer, F. (2005). *Possible and probable languages*. Oxford: Oxford University Press.

Pesetsky, D. (1995). *Zero syntax*. Cambridge, MA: MIT Press.

Piaget, J. (1936). *La naissance de l'intelligence chez l'enfant*. Paris: Delachaux et Niestle; Translated (1953) as *The origin of intelligence in the child*, London: Routledge and Kegan Paul.

Pinker, S. (1979). Formal models of language learning. *Cognition, 7*, 217–283.

Poole, D. (1993). Probabilistic horn abduction and bayesian networks. *Artificial Intelligence, 64*, 81–129.

Pulvermüller, F. (2002). *The neuroscience of language*. Cambridge University Press.

Rizzolatti, G., & Arbib, M. (1998). Language within our grasp. *Trends in Neuroscience, 21*, 188–194.

Rosenbaum, H. (1977). Zapotec gapping as counterevidence to some universal proposals. *Linguistic Inquiry, 8*, 379–395.

Ross, J. R. (1970). Gapping and the order of constituents. In M. Bierwisch & K. Heidolph (Eds.), *Progress in linguistics* (pp. 249–259). The Hague: Mouton.

Russell, S., & Norvig. P. (2003). *Artificial intelligence: A modern approach* (2nd ed.). Upper Saddle River, NJ: Prentice Hall.

Saporta, S. (Ed.). (1961). *Psycholinguistics: A book of readings*. New York: Holt Rinehart Winston.

Shanahan, M. (1997). *Solving the frame problem*. Cambridge, MA: MIT Press.

Shieber, S. (1985). Evidence against the context-freeness of natural language. *Linguistics and Philosophy, 8*, 333–343.

Siskind, J. (1996). A computational study of cross-situational techniques for learning word-to-meaning mappings. *Cognition, 61*, 39–91.

Steedman, M. (1985). Dependency and coordination in the grammar of Dutch and English. *Language, 61*, 523–568.

Steedman, M. (1993). Categorial grammar. *Lingua, 90*, 221–258.

Steedman, M. (1996). *Surface structure and interpretation*. Cambridge, MA: MIT Press. No. 30 in Linguistic Inquiry Monographs.

Steedman, M. (1997). Temporality. In J. van Benthem & A. ter Meulen (Eds.), *Handbook of logic and language* (pp. 895–938). Amsterdam: North Holland/Elsevier.

Steedman, M. (2000a). Information structure and the syntax-phonology interface. *Linguistic Inquiry, 34*, 649–689.

Steedman, M. (2000b). *The syntactic process*. Cambridge, MA: MIT Press.

Steedman, M. (2002). Plans, affordances, and combinatory grammar. *Linguistics and Philosophy, 25*, 723–753.

Steedman, M. (2004). Where does compositionality come from? In S. Levy & R. Gaylor (Eds.), *Proceedings of the AAAI Fall Symposium on Compositional Connectionism in Cognitive Science* (pp. 59–62). Menlo Park: AAAI. Technical Report FS-04-03.

Steedman, M. (2007a). On "The Computation". In G. Ramchand & C. Reiss (Eds.), *The Oxford handbook of linguistic interfaces* (pp. 575–611). Oxford: Oxford University Press.

Steedman, M. (2007b). *Compositional semantics of intonation*. Edinburgh: University of Edinburgh.

Tomasello, M. (1999). *The cultural origins of human cognition*. Cambridge, MA: Harvard University Press.

Villavicencio, A. (2002). *The acquisition of a unification-based generalised categorial grammar*. Ph.D. thesis, University of Cambridge.

Willshaw, D. (1981). Holography, association and induction. In G. Hinton & J. Anderson (Eds.), *Parallel models of associative memory* (pp. 83–104). Hillsdale, NJ: Erlbaum.

Young, R., & Morgan, W. (1987). *The Navaho language*. Albuquerque, NM: University of New Mexico Press.

Zettlemoyer, L., & Collins, M. (2005). Learning to map sentences to logical form: Structured classification with probabilistic categorial grammars. In *Proceedings of the 21st Conference on Uncertainty in AI (UAI)* (pp. 658–666). ACL. Menlo Park, CA: AAAI.

10

COMPUTATIONAL MODELS OF LANGUAGE UNIVERSALS: EXPRESSIVENESS, LEARNABILITY, AND CONSEQUENCES

Edward P. Stabler

E very linguist is struck by similarities among even the most different and most culturally isolated human languages. It is natural to assume that some of these common properties, these language universals, might reflect something about the way people can learn and use languages. In some relevant sense, some of these properties may arise and be maintained even in culturally isolated languages because of special restrictions on the range of structural options available for human language learners. A bolder idea is that some of these language universals may guarantee that the whole class of languages with such properties is "learnable," in a relevant sense. Although considerable progress has been made on finding ways to clearly articulate and assess possibilities of these sorts in precise computational models, there has also been a shift to more sophisticated versions of a long-standing traditional perspective: it may not be so much the formal structure of human languages, but the special kinds of fit between form and meaning that give human languages their most distinctive properties, in which case some early work on language acquisition may have characterized inappropriately difficult learning problems. A more reasonable perspective on the learners' predicament may recognize a certain *nonarbitrariness* in the relation between structures and their semantic values, so that only certain kinds of structures are expected to carry certain sorts of semantic values. This can allow semantic properties of expressions to provide clues about syntactic structure, and vice versa, enriching the evidence available to the learner. This chapter will review some fundamental results in this line of inquiry, from universals formulated in terms of the expressive power of grammars, to results on learnable subsets of the languages defined by those grammars, leading finally to recent views on semantically characterized grammatical universals. Even restricting attention to hypotheses that are most empirically secure and independent of any particular choice among the major traditions in grammatical theory, the modern perspective is surprising in many respects and quite different from anything that could have been conceived at the 1961 Conference on Language Universals (Greenberg, 1963).

10.1. Universals of Language Complexity

Chomsky and others in the 1950s noticed that languages can be classified by the kinds of grammars that generate them, and that a straightforward classification in terms of grammar also corresponds to a classification of the kinds of resources needed to recognize those languages (Chomsky, 1956). This "Chomsky hierarchy" has been considerably elaborated and integrated into the theory of automata and complexity (Hopcroft & Ullman, 1979). Finding the place of human languages in this hierarchy is of interest because it provides an indication of what resources (memory, time) are required to recognize and produce them. This may sound straightforward, but it actually requires some sophistication to understand the project. In the first place, human linguistic behavior is influenced by many things; we would like to abstract away from coughs, interruptions, and memory limitations of various sorts. We adopt similar abstractions when we say that a calculator computes the sum or product function on integers. Such a claim is not refuted by the behavior of the device when its power fails or when the inputs exceed the memory limitations of the device.[1] The motivation for these abstractions is not merely simplicity. Rather, as in any science, we hope to be factoring the explanation along lines that correspond to the real causal sources of the behavior. The mechanisms involved in coughing or in responding to interruptions are relevantly different from those involved in producing or perceiving a fluent utterance. Consequently, to place human languages in the Chomsky hierarchy is to adopt a certain kind of explanation of human linguistic behavior, and so controversy is expected even among the best-informed researchers.

There is another reason for interest in properties of human languages, regarded as sets of sequences. These sequences, as produced in context and subject to various kinds of "noise," certainly comprise one of the most important sources of evidence available to language learners. We would like to understand how perceptible properties of these unanalyzed sequences shape early language acquisition. Grammatically sophisticated notions like "subject," "modifier," or "verb phrase" are used in framing most familiar universals, but to understand the earliest stages of language acquisition it is useful to identify universals that can apply before such sophisticated analyses are available.[2]

A third reason for being interested in claims about language complexity is that it provides a common basis for comparing grammars of very different kinds. Linguists are often very concerned with the exact nature of the description they provide of linguistic structures, and this concern is completely reasonable. For one thing, given the complexity of the domain being described, the simplicity of our description is a practical concern. But this also leads to a proliferation of descriptive formalisms—several major, distinct traditions and many very significant variants in each tradition—which can be an obstacle to effective communication and critical assessment. In the great diversity of formal proposals, though, an astounding convergence among a great range of independently proposed formalisms has been discovered.

In the work of Joshi, Vijay-Shanker, and Weir (1991), Seki, Matsumura, Fujii, and Kasami (1991), and Vijay-Shanker and Weir (1994), four independently proposed grammar formalisms are shown to define exactly the same languages: a kind of head grammars (HGs), combinatory categorial grammars (CCGs), tree-adjoining grammar (TAGs), and linear indexed grammars (LIGs). Furthermore, this class of languages is included in an infinite hierarchy of languages that are defined by multiple context-free grammars (MCFGs), multiple component tree-adjoining grammars (MCTAGs), linear context-free rewrite systems (LCFRSs), and other systems. Later, it was shown a certain kind of "minimalist grammar" (MG), a formulation of the core mechanisms of Chomskian syntax—using the operations merge, move, and a certain strict "shortest move condition"— define exactly the same class of languages (Harkema, 2001; Michaelis, 1998, 2001; Stabler, 1997). These classes of languages are positioned between the languages defined by context-free grammars (CFGs) and those defined by context-sensitive grammars (CSGs) like this:

(1) $\text{CFG} \subset \boxed{\text{TAG} \equiv \text{CCG} \ldots} \subset \boxed{\text{MCTAG} \equiv \text{MCFG} \equiv \text{MG} \ldots} \subset \text{CSG}$

where $\subset$ indicates proper subset relations between the definable languages and $\equiv$ relates formalisms that define exactly the same languages. The equivalence $\equiv$ is often called "weak" because it considers only the definable sequences and not the structures of derivations, but an inspection of the proofs of these weak equivalence results reveals that they are not very difficult. The proofs provide recipes for taking a grammar from one formalism and converting it into an exactly equivalent grammar in another formalism. The recipes are not difficult because, in an intuitive sense that has not yet been formally captured, the recursive mechanisms of each of these formalisms are rather similar. Furthermore, unlike earlier very expressive grammar formalisms (Berwick, 1981; Johnson, 1988; Peters & Ritchie, 1973; Torenvliet & Trautwein, 1995; Trautwein, 1995), it is known that the two classes boxed in (1) can both be recognized feasibly by "polynomial time" computations.

It may be a universal structural fact about human languages that they are always included in one of the classes boxed in (1). Joshi (1985) proposes a slightly weaker hypothesis, namely, that human languages are "mildly context sensitive" (MCS) in the sense that they have (i) limited crossing dependencies, (ii) constant growth, and (iii) polynomial parsing complexity. A language is said to have "constant growth" if there is a bound k such that whenever two sentences have lengths that differ by more than k, there is a sentence of intermediate length. The intuition here is that sentences are built up by simple combinations of smaller constituents (and so, for example, they do not allow an operation of unbounded copying). The notion of polynomial recognizability is discussed in any standard introduction to formal languages and computing (Hopcroft, Motwani, & Ullman, 2000; Lewis & Papadimitriou, 1981, for example). Both TAG languages and MCFG languages are MCS in this sense, but other classes are too.

The claims that human languages are definable by TAGs or MCFGs, or that they are MCS, are very strong claims with significant computational consequences. Mainstream work in linguistic theory can be seen as aiming to sharpen these results with more precise characterizations of the recursive mechanisms of grammar. But the basic claims mentioned here are also being challenged on empirical grounds. For example, there are proposals to the effect that the grammars need certain kinds of copying mechanisms (Kobele, 2006; Michaelis & Kracht, 1997; Stabler, 2004), and this may require placing human languages in a slightly larger class. The parallel multiple context-free grammars (PMCFGs) defined by Seki et al. (1991) allow this kind of copying, and remain efficiently recognizable, but they lack the constant growth property. Many linguists like Joshi remain unpersuaded that anything like reduplication is needed anywhere in the syntax (cf. Pullum, 2006). Other possible but less plausible threats to the MCS claims are more drastic; many seemingly minor variations on MCS grammars yield systems that can define any "recursively enumerable" language (Gärtner & Michaelis, 2005; Kobele, 2005; Kobele & Michaelis, 2005, for example), in which case the mechanisms of grammar would tell us essentially nothing about human languages beyond the fact that they are finitely representable. But many linguists feel that even the strong claim that human languages are universally in the classes boxed in (1) is actually rather weak. They think this because, in terms of the sorts of things linguists describe in human languages, these computational claims tell us little about what human languages are like.

10.2. Learnable Syntactic Patterns: Gold

Perhaps stronger universal claims about language structure will come from computational models of learning. Some basic syntactic universals may reflect properties of the language learning mechanism, and it might even be the case that some of these properties guarantee the "learnability" of human languages, in some relevant sense.

One framework for addressing these issues is provided by Gold and others (Gold, 1967; Jain, Osherson, Royer, & Sharma 1999). Noting that human learners seem to succeed without explicit instruction or feedback (Bowerman, 1988; Braine, 1971), one model of the evidence available to a learner is a "(positive) text." Given any language L, a text for that language is an infinite sequence containing all and only strings of the language. A learner can then be regarded as a function from longer and longer finite initial sequences of such a text to grammars. We say the learner "converges," if on some initial sequence of the text the learner makes a guess that does not change with any longer initial sequence. We say the learner successfully learns the text if the learner converges on a grammar that generates the language of the text. The learner is said to be able to learn the language L if the learner learns every text for that language. And finally a learner can learn a class of languages $\mathcal{L}$ if and only if it learns every language in the class.

Obviously, this is not meant to provide a realistic picture of human learning, but the framework is of interest for the insight it provides into the conditions in which a generalizing learner can be guaranteed to succeed in this simple sense of correctly identifying a text. A precise characterization of the classes of languages that can be learned from positive text, in the sense just defined, was provided by Angluin's (1980) subset theorem, which can be formulated this way (see Figure 10.1):

> A collection $\mathcal{L}$ of (recursively enumerable) languages is learnable just in case for every language L in the collection you can find a finite subset D_L such that no language L' in the collection includes D_L and is properly included in L.

> In other words, roughly, a class of languages is learnable only if each language L has a finite subset, a "cue," indicating either that the target language is either L or a language that can provide positive evidence to disconfirm the hypothesis that it is L.

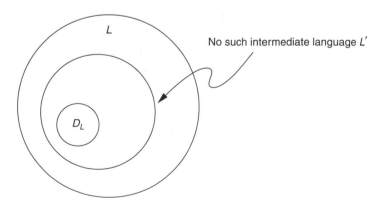

Figure 10.1.

Using this theorem, it is easy to show that no learner can learn any class $\mathcal{L}$ that contains all the finite languages and also one or more infinite languages. The intuition behind this demonstration is clear: roughly, to conclude that a finite sample of data indicates an infinite pattern is to conclude that the data is not simply a finite stipulation that does not generalize. As the class of all finite languages is one where every finite set of data might be a stipulation in this sense, it is not learnable. It also follows that none of the classes indicated in (1) are learnable because they contain all the finite languages together with some infinite ones. We can also use Angluin's subset theorem to show that any finite class of languages $\mathcal{L}$ is learnable from positive examples.

It is worth briefly sketching a more interesting example to illustrate the kind of result we would like to obtain for human languages, a class that is learnable because of some interesting universal structural property. A finite state language can be defined by a machine like the one in Figure 10.2.

The states of the machine are circled; 0 is the initial state; the final states are doubly circled; and a string is in the language defined by the machine just in case that it labels a path along the arcs from the initial state to a final state. So the machine in Figure 10.2 defines a language containing just two strings, namely,

(2)   dp vp
       dp vp pp

This finite state machine is deterministic in the sense that (i) it has at most one initial state, and (ii) no two arcs leaving any state have the same label. It is not hard to show that no deterministic machine with fewer states can define this same language.

We can reverse a machine like the one shown in Figure 10.2 by (i) changing start states to final states, (ii) changing final states to start states, and (iii) reversing every arc. It is clear that the reverse of the machine shown is not deterministic, because the reverse has two initial states. Now following Angluin (1982), we define a finite state language L as reversible just in case the result of reversing the smallest deterministic finite state machine for L yields another deterministic machine. Clearly then, every language consisting of a single string is reversible, and so the class of reversible languages is infinite. But example (2) shows that the class of reversible

Figure 10.2.

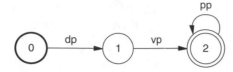

Figure 10.3.

languages does not include every finite language. And it is easy to see that the class includes infinitely many infinite languages, like the one defined by this machine (Figure 10.3).

Because of the loop on the final state, this machine defines the language containing sentences with dp vp followed by 0 or more pp's. In fact, Angluin proves that this infinite language is the smallest reversible language that contains the two sentences in (2). In other words, if a learner knows that the target language is reversible and sees the two strings in (2), then the most conservative guess the learner can make is that the target language is the infinite language defined by Figure 10.3. It turns out that given any sample of input strings, the smallest reversible language containing that sample can be efficiently computed, and a learner that always guesses this language will successfully learn any reversible language.

Do human languages have a universal structural property that similarly guarantees the learnability of human languages? There are two important points to make here. The first is that the grammars (or machines) in the examples above generate the data available to the learner. But in traditional approaches to human language we factor the grammar into parts. The syntax may determine the order of morphemes, but morphological and phonological processes also have an influence on what is available to the learner. In particular, notice that the definition of *reversible* explicitly depends on the identities of the elements labeling each arc, requiring a kind of forward and backward nonambiguity. All interesting positive learning results are like this: the learner must be able to figure out the language structure from the identities and positions of the elements in the data (Kanazawa, 1996; Yokomori, 2003). So, obviously, in human languages, we can expect structural universals to emerge from learning only when the data available to the learner is reflecting structural properties. Most structural properties would be hidden if every morpheme were silent or if every morpheme sounded exactly like every other. So already we have a preliminary problem. Human languages allow homophony of various kinds, and there is no apparent fixed, finite bound to the extent of homophony. There are patterns of systematic homophony (syncretism) found in human languages, and there is also some "random" accidental homophony (Bobaljik, 2002; Pertsova, 2006; Williams, 1994), and we would like to specify these things in such a way that we could determine the sorts of structural properties that should be visible nevertheless.

For the moment, the standard move is to adopt a linguistically nonstandard understanding of the grammar and of what we mean by "structural property," extending these notions down to the identities of perceived forms (e.g., morpheme sequences). And we adopt a psychologically nonstandard view of the data available to the learner: morpheme sequences. We would like to remove these simplifications eventually, but they provide a preliminary way to return to our question: Do human languages have a universal structural property that guarantees the learnability of human languages? Recent work suggests that some phonotactic domains may have a basic property that guarantees learnability (Heinz, 2006), but for syntax (extended in the way just suggested to define languages of morpheme sequences), no such property is known.[3] For example, in reversible languages, if a word can be added to the end of a sentence, that word can be iterated any number of times, but this does not hold in human languages. For example, in English, although sentence-final modifiers might be iterable, optional final words cannot always be iterated:

> I see
> I see it
> * I see it it

To determine how humans will generalize, what constructions can iterated or extracted from, it seems we need to be able to identify things like modifiers, arguments, and predicates. The way the learner generalizes must, it seems, be based on an analysis of the input in terms of this kind. How can such analyses be learned? The standard response is that we require semantic information to obtain such analyses, and the evidence for this suggestion is that terms like *modifier, argument*, and *predicate* are semantically loaded. But it is quite possible for items with distinctive semantic properties to also have distinctive syntactic ones. We return to this matter in section 10.4. below.

10.3. Learnable Syntactic Patterns: Probably Approximately Correct

A different idea about a shortcoming of the Gold framework for learning sketched above is that it does not accommodate "noise" of any kind (coughs, slips, false starts, intrusions of other languages) and the exact identification criterion of success is too strict. We might get a rather different picture of what is required for learning by adopting a probabilistic criterion of success. One proposal of this kind is presented by Valiant (1984). Suppose that a learner is presented with expressions according to some probability distribution μ, where each expression is categorized as either being in the target language L or not. In this setting, we can quantify the degree

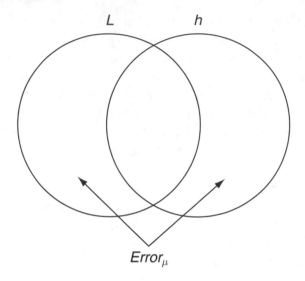

Figure 10.4.

to which the learner's hypothesis h misses the target by letting it be the probability of expressions in $L - h$ and $h - L$ (Figure 10.4).

As before, the learner is a function from samples to hypotheses h, but now the samples are drawn according to some arbitrary probability μ and classified according to whether they are in the target language or not. We say a class of languages (or "concepts") is learnable if the learner will always be "probably approximately correct" (PAC) after some number m of examples, where m can depend on how probably δ we want to be approximately ϵ correct. A class $\mathcal{L}$ is "PAC learnable" if and only if there is a learner and a function m such that for all probability distributions μ, for every language L in $\mathcal{L}$, for every level of confidence $0 < \delta < 1$, and for every margin of error $0 < \epsilon < 1$, the learner's guess after $m(\epsilon, \delta)$ samples will be a hypothesis h, where the probability that the hypothesis is within ϵ of the target is at least $1 - \delta$:

$$\mu(error_\mu \leq \epsilon) \geq (1 - \delta).$$

Mastering this success criterion takes some study, but it has the very nice property that a learner can be counted as successful even when some extremely rare expressions would be misclassified. And some classes of languages can be PAC learned by learners that only revise their hypotheses in response to "positive data," data that is classified as being in the target language. Furthermore, the PAC criterion has been shown to be the discrete analog of a standard criterion for the consistent statistical approximation of real-valued functions by "empirical risk minimization" and related methods (Alon, Ben-David, Cesa-Bianchi, & Haussler, 1997; Mendelson, 2004; Mukherjee, Niyogi, Poggio, & Rifkin, 2004; Poggio, Rifkin, Niyogi, & Mukherjee, 2004). The classes $\mathcal{L}$ that are learnable in this sense turn out to have a certain combinatorial simplicity: a class $\mathcal{L}$ is PAC learnable if and only if it has a finite "VC dimension."[4] This convergence of results, the coincidence of independently proposed criteria of success on such a simple combinatorial bound, suggests that this work has in fact identified a robust and natural notion. So it is perhaps no surprise that some researchers have proposed, "Applying this approach to natural language . . . one concludes that the family of learnable grammars must have a finite Vapnik Chervonenkis (VC) dimension" (Niyogi, 2004, p. 941; cf. also Poggio et al., 2004). This would be a very significant restriction on the class of available languages. But the proposal requires an important qualification.

Many classes with infinite VC dimension are efficiently learnable in other looser but still reasonable senses. For example, consider the problem of learning conjunctions of positive or negated atomic propositions (these conjunctions are often called *monomials*) from a sample of the situations of models that makes them true in a propositional calculus with infinitely many propositional symbols. This space has infinite VC dimension, but if we "parameterize" the space by the number n of proposition symbols used, then the complexity of the learning problem grows only polynomially with respect to n, $1/\epsilon$, and $1/\delta$ (Kearns & Vazirani, 1994, Thm.1.2). When we consider language-oriented problems like learning reversible languages, we find that the space of reversible languages has infinite VC dimension.[5] But in this case, it has been difficult to find a way to parameterize the problem to appropriately reveal its efficiency (Pitt, 1989; Freund et al., 1997; Yokomori, 2003).

In sum, to expect finite VC dimension for the available human languages when we do not find it for the monomials or the reversible languages seems unreasonable. A possible response is to say that, in a clear sense, the *whole class* of monomials and the *whole class* of reversible languages is not efficiently learnable. That's true, but in the first place, on reasonably sized reversible language learning problems, Angluin's learner is efficient. And in the second place, there seems to be no principled (linguistic or cognitive) dividing line between the "reasonably sized" problems that we are likely to encounter and the rest.

A more important point about this direction of research is this: the adoption of the PAC success criterion or something similar obviously does not address the main concern mentioned at the end of the previous section. That is, we have not discovered how to define the kinds of generalizations made by human learners, and our universals of language complexity in section 10.1. were rather weak, so these models do not yet explain the sorts of similarities across languages noticed by linguists.

10.4. Syntactic/Semantic Relations: Languages as Logics

The common descriptions of language are all semantically laden.[6] Subjects, objects, predicates, modifiers, names, anaphors, etc.—these are all traditionally identified with criteria that are at least in part semantic. The typological universals identified by Greenberg and others in the 1960s are all expressed in such terms, as are more recent proposals in that tradition (Hawkins, 2005, for example). Much of recent syntactic theory is so semantically laden that the distinctions between semantic and syntactic arguments can be difficult to discern. Furthermore, psychological studies of acquisition confirm the commonsense idea that children and other language learners use multiple cues to figure out what is meant by utterances. For example, in one recent paper we find this suggestion:

> . . . the learning procedure in some way makes joint use of the structures and situations that cooccur with verbs so as to converge on their meanings. Neither source of evidence is strong or stable enough by itself, but taken together they significantly narrow the search space.
>
> (Lidz, Gleitman, & Gleitman, 2004)

Can we provide computational models of how this works? There has been much activity in this area—much of it focused on making sense of the Augustine (398) idea that the meaning of a word like *cat* might be determined in part by noticing a common element in many of the situations where that word is used. But here we will very briefly discuss two fundamental questions about the potential and limits of such learning strategies: What is the nature of the fit between syntax and semantics such that a learner could expect to find semantic evidence of syntactic structure, and vice versa? And what kind of compositional structure do we find in human languages?

10.4.1. The Syntactic/Semantic Fit and "Bootstrapping"

The fundamental approaches to learning discussed in sections 10.2. and 10.3. extend immediately to language learning situations where the target is a grammar that defines form-meaning associations, and where the samples available to the learner are (at least sometimes) of this form too. It is completely clear that the availability of both forms and meanings in the data completely changes the situation! For example, in the Gold paradigm, it is obvious that some (sentence, meaning) texts are learnable where the text of sentences alone is not. We can prove this with a simple example. Consider any class of languages containing all the finite languages and an infinite language—known to be unlearnable in the Gold sense, as discussed in section 10.2. Now pair each sentence with a meaning in the following way: let the expressions in the finite languages all have distinct meanings (e.g., let them each denote distinct numbers), but let all the expressions in the infinite language all denote the same thing (e.g., the number 1). Then, after seeing any two different (sentence, meaning) pairs, the learner is in a position to know whether the target language is infinite or not, and in either case, the learner has a strategy for successful identification. It is also easy to define unlearnable classes of (sentence, meaning) languages where the corresponding sentence-only languages are easily identifiable. So we immediately conclude that when paired semantic and syntactic information is available, the nature of the learning problem varies fundamentally with the nature of the syntax-semantics relation.

Simple, artificial logics provide some useful examples of languages where the meanings of expressions is not arbitrary. A logic is typically given by a syntax that defines a set of expressions, a semantics that associates these sequences with semantic values, and an inference relation that is defined on expressions but which also preserves some semantic property. In systems like this, there is a fit between syntactic and semantic properties; for example, expressions that semantically denote binary functions on truth values are syntactically elements that combine with two sentential expressions. More interestingly, when there is a syntactic restriction on the number of elements that play a certain syntactic role, the elements with that syntactic role typically denote in semantic domains that are similarly restricted.

This perspective is extended to human languages by Keenan and Stabler (2003) with particular attention to the extreme case of the "syntactic constants," elements that play unique roles in the grammar. Although one proper name can typically be replaced by any another without changing structure in any human language, the syntactic constants are those words with unique roles, elements that cannot be replaced by any other, in the expressions of the language. In every sentence of standard English, for example, we can replace the name *Bill* by *Sam* without affecting structural properties, but there is no other element that can replace every occurrence of the infinitival *to*, no other element can replace the auxiliary *be*, and so on, for many other elements. These syntactic constants, "grammatical words," have a semantic distinction too: on any reasonable approach, they do not denote the same kinds of things that things like names or transitive verbs denote. Rather, they tend to denote "semantic constants," that is, semantic values that are constant in the sense (roughly) that they do not depend on which individuals have which properties.[7] Names like *Tarski* and predicates like *loves* are obviously interpreted in a way that depends on particular individuals, but a grammatical passive marker, interpreted as a function from transitive predicates to intransitive ones, is not dependent on individuals. It is a semantic constant.

This is of particular interest in the present context for two reasons. In the first place, it defines a setting in which various kinds of syntactic evidence could bear on semantic properties, and vice versa. Clearly, in this kind of setting, it is possible to get evidence about the semantic values of elements that could not be learned with the Augustinian method of correlating utterances with the situations of utterance. If the learner has access to both syntax and to syntactically characterizable relations of plausible inference, then obviously the bearing on semantic hypotheses can be even more direct.

A second reason to take note of this kind of fit between syntax, semantics, and inference is that very prominent directions in current syntactic research suggest that human languages may tie semantic value and syntactic properties together very tightly across languages. For example, Szabolcsi has proposed in a series of papers that quantifiers of various kinds occupy distinct syntactic positions across languages (Szabolcsi, 1996a; Szabolcsi & Brody, 2003). And Cinque has proposed in a series of works that, across languages, adverbial elements appear in a fixed order (Cinque, 1999, 2001). These are but two examples from an enormous range of proposals that share the idea that the ties between syntactic role and semantic values may be very rich indeed (Grimshaw, 1981; Levin & Rappaport Hovav, 1995; Pinker, 1984).

10.4.2. Compositional Structure

Although it is now a commonplace that complex expressions take their semantic values as a function of the semantic values of their parts, it is still difficult to formulate this idea in a fully general, precise, and substantial way, so that it can underpin substantial linguistic universals, and so that we can properly understand its relation to language acquisition and use.

Suppose we think of a human language as the set of expressions generated from a lexicon by some structure-building rules (again setting aside the worry that we want to factor the grammar into a syntax and some kind of morphology, or other parts). To allow for structural ambiguity, let's regard the semantics as assigning semantic values to derivations. Then, a simple idea about compositional structure is this: the lexical elements have meanings, and with each way of composing the parts is associated a function from the meanings of the parts to the meanings of the resulting complex. The language learner can master the whole language by identifying the meanings of the parts and the semantic significance of the ways of combining expressions. This simple picture cannot be right. It raises a puzzle about how the language learner could proceed: What evidence from situations could lead the language learner to the meanings of each component of that phrase? And we would like a solution to this puzzle that is compatible with the fact that human languages have so many idioms, so many complex expressions with meanings that seem idiosyncratic— not just phrasal idioms (*kick the bucket, pop the question, chew the fat, . . .*) but also idiomatic compounds and fixed phrases (*by and large, in short, every which way, do away with, spick and span, break a leg, monkey wrench, sunflower, traffic light, deadline,...*) and special verb-particle constructions (*take up/down/in/out/back/over, turn up/down/over/in/out/around/off, hold up/down/off/out/over,...*).

It is reasonable to suppose that, at least to a good first approximation, the learner's first evidence about what the morphemes of a language are is not semantic but combinatorial (Brent, 1999; Goldsmith, 2006; Harris, 1957). In that case, language learners may sometimes realize that an expression is complex and sometimes even have a good idea from situational cues what it means, but not know the meanings of the parts. Under what circumstances can such a learner proceed from information about the meanings of sentences to an idea about the meanings of the parts of those sentences? One approach to this idea has been inspired by a simple proposal from (Frege, 1884, section 60): "It is enough if the sentence as a whole has meaning; it is this that confers on its parts also their content."

Following Hodges (2001) and Westerståhl (2004), suppose a language is given by a lexicon $\{a, b, c, \ldots, a_1, b_1, \ldots\}$ together with some rules $\{f_1, f_2, \ldots f_n\}$ for building complexes. A derivation can be given as a function expression like $f_1(a, b)$, and the semantics μ can be a partial function from these derivations into some semantic domain. Let's say that two derivations, d_1 and d_2, are synonymous with this semantics, $d_1 \equiv_\mu d_2$, just in case they have the same meaning $\mu(d_1) = \mu(d_2)$. Then, the language is compositional if for every rule f, $f(a_1, \ldots, a_n) \equiv_\mu f(b_1, \ldots, b_n)$, whenever for each i between 1 and n, $\mu(a_i) = \mu(b_i)$. In other words, the semantics is compositional if substituting one synonymous element for another in a derivation leaves the meaning of the complex unchanged. In this setting, suppose that a language learner has acquired a fragment of English with a total compositional semantics, and then the speaker hears an idiom like *let the cat out of the bag* for the first time, with some evidence that it means something like *reveal the secret*. Now it is clear that there are several ways to provide a compositional extension of the language that accommodates this. One can maintain compositionality by assuming the rules assembling the idiom are different from the usual ones, leaving us free to set the interpretation of the idiom even when the parts have exactly their usual meanings. But a more appealing extension introduces new senses for some of the words—for example, *cat* could be interpreted as the *secret* and *bag* might even be interpreted as "concealment," in which case the complex could be interpreted compositionally. But for idioms lacking compositionally interpretable parts (like perhaps *kick the bucket*), new senses could be introduced with no meanings specified for them.

In sum, a simple version of compositionality appears to be compatible with a reasonable range of proposals about how a language learner might handle idioms and collocations of various kinds. Something like this seems to represent a consensus now in the field,[8] and although much remains mysterious in our models of language recognition and production, this picture seems compatible with results of acquisition research. In particular, some studies indicate that children do, in fact, look for compositional analyses of new phrases (Gibbs, 1991,1994). One hopes that this recent work may lead to models of language acquisition and use that will properly predict the range of idiomatic constructions found across languages and be part of a picture in which we can make sense of the way language learners identify semantic properties of linguistic elements. These preliminaries appear to be essential first steps toward a realistic conception of how semantically characterized elements appear in the configurations we find across languages.

10.5. Conclusions

The fact that humans notice certain kinds of patterns in small samples of sentences, patterns that extend well beyond the sample, has the consequence that many languages cannot be learned (as we see, in different ways, in the formal results of Gold, Angluin, Valiant). It is natural to assume that the human way of doing this will determine some structural universals of human languages. Our understanding of this matter has been shaped by two rather recent developments. First, there has been an astounding convergence among grammar formalisms on a certain "mildly context sensitive" (MCS) level of combinatorial complexity. There are still many controversies in this area, but it appears that Joshi's hypothesis that human languages are MCS may be right or very close to right. Second, there has been a remarkable convergence among independent characterizations of the learnable patterns. Again, there are controversies, but it is clear that the VC dimension provides a relevant measure of learning complexity. With these two major convergences, our understanding of language structure and learning complexity has advanced considerably.

We began by asking, Do nontrivial universal properties of language structure reflect important properties of human language learning? And do some of these structural properties guarantee that the class of all languages with those properties is a "learnable" class in some relevant sense? This last question certainly must be answered negatively if by "structural" we refer to purely syntactic structure. Because purely structural properties typically determine neither the sequences of perceptible forms nor their semantic properties, structure alone is not enough to determine the learning problem. Human language learning depends, for example, on the fact that the pronunciation *dog* does not change arbitrarily in every utterance, and on the fact that many utterances of *dog* are perceptibly different from at least many other morphemes, but these are not matters of syntactic structure. So, to set the stage for learning structural properties of expressions, we need to worry about the bounds or pressures limiting syncretism and accidental homophony. Standardly, one proceeds by adopting simplifying assumptions, assuming that such bounds will be forthcoming. Still, our initial questions remain largely open.

The standard idea about why these questions remain open is that we must first bridge the gulf between the perceptible properties of unanalyzed linguistic input and the terms of linguistic analysis (cf. note 2). In computational models, we can stipulate that one or another expression is a subject or a modifier or whatever, but this does not take us toward an explanation until the stipulations are understood and hence removable. To get to such terms without stipulation, it is typically assumed that semantic cues may be essential, as discussed at the end of section 10.2. and in section 10.4., but even this is not established. In particular, the role of grammatical constants as indicators of structure has not been fully explored. When the computational bases of traditional analyses are better understood, then can hope for explanations of how traditional universals emerge.

Obtaining clear open questions is an achievement, and the terms for addressing them must derive from secure foundations in learning and complexity theory. The computational foundations reviewed here are almost entirely new since the 1961 meeting on universals. It is certain that the next 40 years will yield a much deeper and more comprehensive understanding of language universals and how they emerge.

Key Further Readings

For basic background on language complexity, there are good introductory texts written mainly for computer scientists, like Hopcroft et al. (2000), and Lewis Papadimitriou (1981). There is also a three-volume handbook that surveys many topics at a fairly advanced level: Rozenberg and Salomaa (1997). The particular results mentioned in the present chapter are mainly recent and available only in the cited original sources.

The basic mathematical notion of invariance, mentioned by Jakobson in the 1961 Conference (Jakobson, 1963, pp. 263–264), is fundamentally algebraic (see note 7). This notion is explicitly treated at length and applied to the study of language universals in Keenan and Stabler (2003), with references there to relevant antecedents. See also Hodges (2001) and Westerståhl (2004).

There are many good texts on computational models of language learning. On the Gold paradigm: Kanazawa (1998) and Jain et al. (1999). On the PAC paradigm and variants: Alpaydin (2004), Kearns and Vazirani (1994), and Anthony and Biggs (1992). Related work on learning real-valued functions, with some attention to linguistic domains: Duda, Hart, and Stork (2001) and Hastie, Tibshirani, and Friedman (2001). A tutorial but mathematically sophisticated treatment of language learning and language change is provided by Niyogi (2006).

There are also many relevant formal and empirical studies of syntactic-semantic relations. Form-meaning relations, especially those that could underpin "bootstrapping" or "linking" or "coalition" theories of acquisition, are very widely discussed in the psychological literature (Grimshaw, 1981; Hirsh-Pasek & Golinkoff, 1996; Pinker, 1984; Snedeker & Gleitman, 2004). I think it is also useful to look at some of the earlier papers like Fodor (1966): although much has changed in the field, the basic structure of the learning situation is still described clearly and succinctly here. Fundamental relations between syntax, semantics, and pragmatics have gotten clearer since then, in the work of philosophers (Dummett, 1981, 1991; Hodges, 2001; Westerståhl, 2004), logicians (Prawitz, 1971, 1998, 2005; Pagin, 1998), and linguists (Bernardi, 2002; Cinque, 1999; Szabolcsi, 1996b, 2004). For a historical perspective on these fundamentals, there are the brief remarks in Augustine (398, I.8) that inspired the famous response in Wittgenstein (1958). This short list of papers certainly omits very many important lines of inquiry.

Notes

1   This is standardly recognized in the literature. For example, in Chomsky's 1956 paper we find,

> We might avoid this consequence by an arbitrary decree that there is a finite upper limit to sentence length in English. This would serve no useful purpose, however . . . (Chomsky, 1956, p. 115)

And in recent introductions to formal languages and computation, we find remarks like this:

> Viewing the computer as a finite state system . . . is not satisfying mathematically or realistically. It places an artificial limit on memory capacity, thereby failing to capture the real essence of computation. (Hopcroft & Ullman, 1979, p. 14)

The suggestion is not that the limitations are unimportant or uninteresting, but just that we may get a more revealing and accurate understanding from an account that factors the definition of grammatical patterns away from the interfering factors.

2   This point has been noted often before in both linguistic work and studies of language acquisition. For example,

> In short, a problem that is central to understanding the learning of syntax is that of arriving at a theory of how the child determines appropriate base structures for the types of sentences that appear in the corpus. However, the peculiarly abstract relation between base structures and sentences unfits any of the usual learning mechanisms for explaining their assimilation. (Fodor, 1966, p. 113)

... in the case of Universal Grammar ... we want the primitives to be concepts that can plausibly be assumed to provide a preliminary, prelinguistic analysis of a reasonable selection of presented data. It would be unreasonable to incorporate, for example, such notions as subject of a sentence or other grammatical notions, since it is unreasonable to suppose that these notions can be directly applied to linguistically unanalyzed data. (Chomsky, 1981, p. 10)

The problem with almost every nonsemantic property that I have heard proposed as inductive biases is that the property is itself defined over abstract symbols that are part of the child's input, that themselves have to be learned. For example, some informal proposals I have heard start from the assumption that the child knows the geometry of the phrase structure tree of a sentence, or, even worse, the syntactic categories and grammatical relations of phrases. (Pinker, 1984, p.51)

3 The seminal work of Wexler and Culicover (1980) defines a learnable class and proposes a number of interesting structural properties for human syntax, but it is based on an early grammatical framework; a penetrating analysis of this work is provided by Osherson, Weinstein, and Stob (1986), showing that it allows only a finite range of grammars. There are many other less interesting ways to restrict the range of human grammars to a finite set (Chomsky, 1981; Osherson, Weinstein, & Stob, 1984; Pinker, 1982): one can simply stipulate that only a finite set of (unspecified) properties are really relevant "core" properties, and of course many nonlinguistic factors (lifespan, attention span) conspire to make our concerns finite. After one such proposal, it is appropriately remarked, "As with many learnability presentations, the account just given has an air of science fiction about it" (Pinker, 1982, p. 675). Compare also the remarks in note 1. The interesting question is whether there really are principled, empirically motivated, syntactic properties of language that guarantee learnability, properties which would explain the sorts of properties traditionally noticed by linguists (Greenberg, 1966, for example). As suggested at the outset, what we really want to know is how human learners generalize from the finite data they are given, such that we end up with languages like the ones we have.

4 The precise definition of "VC dimension" is very simple. Given an arbitrary subset S of the domain, if $\{L \cap S| L \in \mathcal{L}\}$ is the set of all subsets of S, then we say S is "shattered" by the class $\mathcal{L}$. The VC dimension of $\mathcal{L}$ is the size of the largest set Y that is shattered by $\mathcal{L}$. The relation between PAC learnability and VC dimension is from Blumer, Ehrenfeucht, Haussler and Warmuth (1989), building on Vapnik and Chervonenkis (1971). VC dimension is introduced and carefully discussed in standard texts (Alpaydin, 2004; Anthony & Biggs, 1992; Kearns & Vazirani, 1994).

5 It is obvious that the space $\mathcal{L}_{rev}$ of reversible languages has infinite VC dimension, but I have not seen this in the literature before, so I sketch a proof. We need to show that there is no finite bound on the size of the sets that are shattered by $\mathcal{L}_{rev}$. For any finite $k \geq 0$, let the language $L_k = \{b_i ab_i| 0 \leq i \leq k\}$. It is clear that every such L_k is reversible (see Figure 10.5).

Furthermore, it's clear that every subset of this language is reversible as it will be defined by the result of deleting any number of the a-arcs (and then removing any states and arcs that

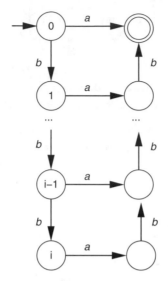

Figure 10.5.

are not on a path from the start state to the final state). Clearly, the size of L_k grows with k, and every such set can be shattered by $\mathcal{L}_{\text{rev}}$ because, every subset of L_k is also reversible.

6 Jakobson dismisses attempts to separate syntactic and semantic components of language at the 1961 Conference on Universals with the amusing remark, "Fortunately, in his quest for universals of grammar Greenberg does not share the whimsical prejudice against 'semantics oriented definitions,' which, strange as it seems, may have filtered even into our Conference on Language Universals" (Jakobson, 1963, p. 271).

7 These notions are defined precisely in Keenan and Stabler (2003). What we here call "*semantic constancy*" is sometimes called *isomorphism invariance* or *permutation invariance*. This is a familiar notion in semantics (e.g., van Benthem, 1986, section 1.7), closely following the classical notions of invariance from Klein (1893) and Tarski (1986).

8 Cf., for example, Westerståhl (2004), Hodges (2001), McGinnis (2002), Nunberg, Wasow, and Sag (1994), Keenan and Stabler (2003), Kracht (1998). Contrasting views can be found in earlier work like Jackendoff (1997) and Di Sciullo and Williams (1987).

References

Alon, N., Ben-David, S., Cesa-Bianchi, N., & Haussler, D. (1997). Scale-sensitive dimensions, uniform convergence, and learnability. *Journal of the Association for Computing Machinery*, 44(4), 615–631.

Alpaydin, E. (2004). *Introduction to machine learning*. Cambridge, MA: MIT Press.

Angluin, D. (1980). Inductive inference of formal languages from positive data. *Information and Control*, 45, 117–135.

Angluin, D. (1982). Inference of reversible languages. *Journal of the Association for Computing Machinery*, 29, 741–765.

Anthony, M., & Biggs, N. (1992). *Computational learning theory*. New York: Cambridge University Press.

Augustine. 398. *Confessions*. Reprinted with commentary by J. J. O'Donnell. New York: Oxford University Press, (1992).

Bernardi, R. (2002). *Reasoning with polarity in categorial type logic*. Utrecht: Ph.D. thesis, University of Utrecht.

Berwick, R. C. (1981). Computational complexity of lexical functional grammar. *Proceedings of the 19th Annual Meeting of the Association for Computational Linguistics, ACL'81*, 7–12.

Blumer, A., Ehrenfeucht, A., Haussler, D., & Warmuth, M. K. (1989). Learnability and the Vapnik-Chervonenkis dimension. *Journal of the Association for Computing Machinery, 36*, 929–965.

Bobaljik, J. D. (2002). Syncretism without paradigms: Remarks on Williams 1981, 1994. In G. Booij & J. van Marle (Eds.), *Yearbook of morphology 2001* (pp. 53–85). Dordrecht: Kluwer.

Bowerman, M. (1988). The "no negative evidence" problem: How do children avoid constructing an overly general grammar? In J. A. Hawkins (Ed.), *Explaining language universals*. Oxford: Blackwell.

Braine, M. (1971). On two types of models of the internalization of grammars. In D. I. Slobin (Ed.), *The ontogenesis of grammar: A theoretical symposium*. New York: Academic Press.

Brent, M. R. (1999). An efficient, probabilistically sound algorithm for segmentation and word discovery. *Machine Learning, 34*, 71–105.

Chomsky, N. (1956). Three models for the description of language. *IRE Transactions on Information Theory, IT-2*, 113–124.

Chomsky, N. (1981). *Lectures on government and binding*. Dordrecht: Foris.

Cinque, G. (1999). *Adverbs and functional heads: A cross-linguistic perspective*. Oxford: Oxford University Press.

Cinque, G. (2001). The status of "mobile" suffixes. In W. Bisang, (Ed.), *Aspects of typology and universals* (pp. 13–19). Berlin: Akademie Verlag.

Di Sciullo, A. M., & Williams, E. (1987). *On the definition of word*. Cambridge, MA: MIT Press.

Duda, R. O., Hart, P. E., & Stork, D. G. (2001). *Pattern classification*. New York: Wiley.

Dummett, M. (1981). *Frege: Philosophy of language* (2nd ed.). London: Duckworth.

Dummett, M. (1991). *The logical basis of metaphysics* (p. 23). London: Duckworth.

Fodor, J. A. (1966). How to learn to talk: Some simple ways. In F. Smith & G. A. Miller (Ed.), *The genesis of language: A psycholinguistic approach* (pp. 105–122). Cambridge, MA: MIT Press.

Frege, G. (1884). *Die grundlagen der arithmetik*. Koebner, Breslau. J. L. Austin's translation available as *The foundations of arithmetic*. Evanston, IL: Northwestern University Press, (1980).

Freund, Y., Kearns, M., Ron, D., Rubinfeld, R., Schapire, R. E., & Sellie, L. (1997). Efficient learning of typical finite automata from random walks. *Information and Computation, 138*, 23–48.

Gärtner, H-M., & Michaelis, J. (2005). A note on the complexity of constraint interaction. In *Logical Aspects of Computational Linguistics, LACL'05, Lecture Notes in Artificial Intelligence LNCS-3492* (pp. 114–130). New York: Springer.

Gibbs, R. W. (1991). Semantic analyzability in children's understanding of idioms. *Journal of Speech and Hearing Research, 35*, 613–620.

Gibbs, R. W. (1994). *The poetics of mind.* New York: Cambridge University Press.

Gold, E. M. (1967). Language identification in the limit. *Information and Control, 10,* 447–474.

Goldsmith, J. (2006). An algorithm for the unsupervised learning of morphology. *Natural Language Engineering, 12*(4), 353–371.

Greenberg, J. (1963). *Universals of language: Report of a conference held at Dobbs Ferry,* New York, April 13–15, 1961. Cambridge, MA: MIT Press.

Greenberg, J. (1966). Some universals of language with particular attention to the order of meaningful elements. In J. Greenberg (Ed.), *Universals of human language.* Cambridge, MA: MIT Press.

Grimshaw, J. (1981). Form, function and the language-acquisition device. In C. L. Baker & J. J. McCarthy (Eds.), *The logical problem of language acquisition.* Cambridge, MA: MIT Press.

Harkema, H. (2001). A characterization of minimalist languages. In P. de Groote, G. Morrill, & C. Retor'e (Eds.), *Logical aspects of computational linguistics,* Lecture Notes in Artificial Intelligence, No. 2099 (pp. 193–211). New York: Springer.

Harris, Z. S. (1957). Cooccurrence and transformations in linguistic structure. *Language, 33,* 283–340. Reprinted in H. Hiz (Ed.), *Papers on syntax.* Reidel: Boston, 1981.

Hastie, T., Tibshirani, R., & Friedman, J. H. (2001). The elements of statistical learning: Data mining, inference, and prediction. Springer Series in Statistics. New York: Springer.

Hawkins, J. A. (2005). *Efficiency and complexity in grammars.* New York: Oxford University Press.

Heinz, J. (2006). Learning quantity insensitive stress systems via local inference. In *Proceedings of the Eighth Meeting of the ACL Special Interest Group in Computational Phonology at HLT-NAACL* (pp. 21–30). New York: The Association for Computational Linguistics.

Hirsh-Pasek, K., & Golinkoff, R. M. (1996). *The origins of grammar: Evidence from early language comprehension.* Cambridge, MA: MIT Press.

Hodges, W. (2001). Formal features of compositionality. *Journal of Logic, Language and Information, 10,* 7–28.

Hopcroft, J. E., Motwani, R., & Ullman, J. D. (2000). *Introduction to automata theory, languages and computation* (2nd ed.). Addison-Wesley, Reading, Massachusetts.

Hopcroft, J. E., & Ullman, J. D. (1979). Introduction to automata theory, languages and computation. Addison-Wesley, Reading, Massachusetts.

Jackendoff, R. S. (1997). *The architecture of the language faculty.* Cambridge, MA: MIT Press.

Jain, S., Osherson, D., Royer, J. S., & Sharma, A. (1999). Systems that learn: An introduction to learning theory (2nd ed.). Cambridge, MA: MIT Press.

Jakobson, R. (1963). Implications of language universals for linguistics. In J. Greenberg (Ed.), *Universals of language: Report of a conference held at Dobbs Ferry,* New York, April 13–15 (1961). Cambridge, MA: MIT Press.

Johnson, M. (1988). *Attribute Value Logic and The Theory of Grammar.* Number 16 in CSLI Lecture Notes Series. Chicago: CSLI Publications.

Joshi, A. (1985). How much context-sensitivity is necessary for characterizing structural descriptions. In D. Dowty, L. Karttunen, & A. Zwicky (Eds.), *Natural language processing: Theoretical, computational and psychological perspectives* (pp. 206–250). New York: Cambridge University Press.

Joshi, A. K., Vijay-Shanker, K., & Weir, D. (1991). The convergence of mildly context sensitive grammar formalisms. In P. Sells, S. Shieber, & T. Wasow (Eds.), *Foundational issues in natural language processing* (pp. 31–81). Cambridge, MA: MIT Press.

Kanazawa, M. (1996). Identification in the limit of categorical grammars. *Journal of Logic, Language, and Information, 5*, 115–155.

Kanazawa, M. (1998). *Learnable classes of categorial grammars.* Stanford, CA: CSLI Publications.

Kearns, M. J., & Vazirani, U. V. (1994). *An introduction to computational learning theory.* Cambridge, MA: MIT Press.

Keenan, E. L., & Stabler, E. P. (2003). *Bare grammar.* Stanford, CA: CSLI Publications.

Klein, F. (1893). A comparative review of recent researches in geometry: Programme on entering the philosophical faculty and the senate of the university of Erlangen in 1872. *Bulletin of the New York Mathematical Society, 2*, 215–249. Translation by M. W. Haskell of the original October 1872 publication, with a prefatory note by the author.

Kobele, G. M. (2005). Features moving madly: A note on the complexity of an extension to MGs. *Research on Language and Computation, 3*(4), 391–410.

Kobele, G. M. (2006). *Generating copies: An investigation into structural identity in language and grammar.* Ph.D. thesis, University of California, Los Angeles.

Kobele, G. M., & Michaelis, J. (2005). Two type 0 variants of minimalist grammars. In J. Rogers (Ed.), *Proceedings of the 10th Conference on Formal Grammar and the 9th Meeting on Mathematics of Language, FGMOL05.* The European Summer School in Logic, Language and Information.

Kracht, M. (1998). Strict compositionality and literal movement grammars. In *Proceedings, Logical Aspects of Computational Linguistics, LACL'98* (pp. 126–142). New York: Springer.

Levin, B., & Hovav, M. R. (1995). *Unaccusativity: At the syntax-lexical semantics interface.* Cambridge, MA: MIT Press.

Lewis, H. R., & Papadimitriou, C. H. (1981). *Elements of the theory of computation.* Englewood Cliffs, NJ: Prentice-Hall.

Lidz, J., Gleitman, H., & Gleitman, L. R. (2004). Kidz in the 'hood: Syntactic bootstrapping and the mental lexicon. In D. G. Hall & S. R. Waxman (Eds.), *Weaving a lexicon* (pp. 603–636). Cambridge, MA: MIT Press.

McGinnis, M. (2002). On the systematic aspect of idioms. *Linguistic Inquiry, 33*(4), 665–672.

Mendelson, S. (2004). Geometric parameters in learning theory. In V. D. Milman & G. Schechtman (Eds.), *Geometric aspects of functional analysis*, Lecture notes in mathematics. Berlin: Springer.

Michaelis, J. (1998). Derivational minimalism is mildly context-sensitive. In *Proceedings, Logical Aspects of Computational Linguistics, LACL'98*, New York: Springer.

Michaelis, J. (2001). Transforming linear context free rewriting systems into minimalist grammars. In P. de Groote, G. Morrill, & C. Retor'e (Eds.), *Logical aspects of computational linguistics, lecture notes in Artificial Intelligence* (Vol. 2099, pp. 228–244), New York: Springer.

Michaelis, J., & Kracht, M. (1997). Semilinearity as a syntactic invariant. In C. Retoré (Ed.), *Logical aspects of computational linguistics* (pp. 37–40). New York: Springer-Verlag. (Lecture Notes in Computer Science [1328].)

Mukherjee, S., Niyogi, P., Poggio, T., & Rifkin, R. (2004). Learning theory: Stability is sufficient for generalization and necessary and sufficient for consistency of empirical risk minimization. *Advances in Computational Mathematics, 25*(1–3), 161–193.

Niyogi, P. (2006). *The computational nature of language learning and evolution.* Cambridge, MA: MIT Press.

Nunberg, G., Wasow, T., & Sag, I. A. (1994). Idioms. *Language, 70*(3), 491–538.

Osherson, D., Weinstein, S., & Stob, M. (1984). Learning theory and natural language. *Cognition, 17,* 1–28.

Osherson, D., Weinstein, S., & Stob, M. (1986). An analysis of a learning paradigm. In W. Demopoulos & A., Marras (Eds.), *Language learning and concept acquisition* (pp. 103–116.). Norwood, NJ: Ablex.

Pagin, P. (1998). Bivalence: Meaning theory vs. metaphysics. *Theoria; a Swedish Journal of Philosophy and Psychology, 64,* 157–186.

Pertsova, K. (2006). Lexical meanings of morphemes. 80th Annual Meeting of the LSA, Albuquerque, New Mexico.

Peters, P. S., & Ritchie, R. W. (1973). On the generative power of transformational grammar. *Information Sciences, 6,* 49–83.

Pinker, S. (1982). A theory of the acquisition of lexical interpretive grammars. In J. Bresnan, (Ed.), *The mental representation of grammatical relations.* Cambridge, MA: MIT Press.

Pinker, S. (1984). *Language learnability and language development.* Cambridge, MA: Harvard University Press.

Pitt, L. (1989). Inductive inference, DFAs, and computational complexity. In K. P. Jantke (Ed.), *Workshop on analogical and inductive inference,* Volume 397 of *Lecture Notes in Artificial Intelligence* (pp. 18–44). Berlin: Springer Verlag.

Poggio, T., Rifkin, R., Niyogi, P., & Mukherjee, S. (2004). General conditions for predictivity in learning theory. *Nature, 428,* 419–422.

Prawitz, D. (1971). Ideas and results in proof theory. In Fenstad, J. E. (Ed.), *Proceedings of the Second Scandinavian Logic Symposium.* North-Holland, Amsterdam, pages 235–307. Partially reprinted as "Gentzen's analysis of first order proofs," In R. I. G. Hughes, *A philosophical companion to first order logic.* Hackett: Indianapolis, (1993).

Prawitz, D. (1998). Comment on Peter Pagin's paper. *Theoria; a Swedish Journal of Philosophy and Psychology, 64,* 304–318.

Prawitz, D. (2005). Meaning approached via proofs. *Synthese, 148*(3), 507–524.

Pullum, G. K. (2006). *On syntactically mandated phrase reduplication.* Cambridge, MA: Unpublished handout, Linguistics Colloquium, Massachusetts Institute of Technology.

Rozenberg, G., & Salomaa, A. (Ed.). (1997). *Handbook of formal languages, volume 2: Linear modeling: Background and application*. New York: Springer.

Seki, H., Matsumura, T., Fujii, M., & Kasami, T. (1991). On multiple context-free grammars. *Theoretical Computer Science, 88*, 191–229.

Snedeker, J., & Gleitman, L. R. (2004). Why it is hard to label our concepts. In D. G. Hall & S. R. Waxman (Eds.), *Weaving a lexicon* (pp. 257–293). Cambridge, MA: MIT Press.

Stabler, E. P. (1997). Derivational minimalism. In C. Retoré (Ed.), *Logical aspects of computational linguistics* (pp. 68–95). New York: Springer-Verlag. (Lecture Notes in Computer Science [1328].)

Stabler, E. P. (2004). Varieties of crossing dependencies: Structure dependence and mild context sensitivity. *Cognitive Science, 93*(5), 699–720.

Szabolcsi, A. (1996a). Strategies for scope-taking. In A. Szabolcsi (Ed.), *Ways of scope taking*. Boston: Kluwer.

Szabolcsi, A. (Ed.). (1996b). *Ways of scope taking*. Kluwer, Boston.

Szabolcsi, A. (2004). Positive polarity—negative polarity. *Natural Language and Linguistic Theory, 22*(2), 409–452.

Szabolcsi, A., & Brody, M. (2003). Overt scope in Hungarian. *Syntax, 6*, 19–51.

Tarski, A. (1986). What are logical notions? *History and Philosophy of Logic, 7*, 143–154.

Torenvliet, L., & Trautwein, M. (1995). A note on the complexity of restricted attribute-value grammars. In M. Moll & A. Nijholt (Ed.), *Proceedings of Computational Linguistics in the Netherlands, CLIN5* (ISBN 90-75296-03-7 pp. 145–164). Twente, The Netherlands: Department of Computer Science, University of Twente.

Trautwein, M. (1995). The complexity of structure-sharing in unification-based grammars. In *Proceedings of Computational Linguistics in the Netherlands, CLIN5* (pp. 165–180).

Valiant, L. (1984). A theory of the learnable. *Communications of the Association for Computing Machinery, 27*(11), 1134–1142.

van Benthem, J. (1986). *Essays in logical semantics*. Dordrecht: Reidel.

Vapnik, V. N., & Chervonenkis, A. Y. (1971). On the uniform convergence of relative frequencies of events to their probabilities. *Theory of Probability and its Applications, 16*, 264–280.

Vijay-Shanker, K., & Weir, D. (1994). The equivalence of four extensions of context free grammar formalisms. *Mathematical Systems Theory, 27*, 511–545.

Westerståhl, D. (2004). On the compositional extension problem. *Journal of Philosophical Logic, 33*(6), 549–582.

Wexler, K., & Culicover, P. W. (1980). *Formal principles of language acquisition*. Cambridge, MA: MIT Press.

Williams, E. (1994). Remarks on lexical knowledge. *Lingua, 92*, 7–34. Reprinted in L. Gleitman & B. Landau (Eds.), *The acquisition of the lexicon*, MIT Press, (1994).

Wittgenstein, L. (1958). *Philosophical investigations*. New York: MacMillan. This edition published in 1970.

Yokomori, T. (2003). Polynomial-time identification of very simple grammars from positive data. *Theoretical Computer Science, 298*, 179–206.

11

LANGUAGE UNIVERSALS IN THE BRAIN: HOW LINGUISTIC ARE THEY?

RALPH-AXEL MÜLLER

11.1. Do Language Universals Need a Brain?

Anybody's search for language universals will depend on certain assumptions that are not themselves scientific in the strict sense of the empirical sciences, because they cannot be subjected to experimental testing. These basic assumptions are onto-logical, as they imply convictions of how those universals might *exist*, and they are epistemological because their mode of existence will determine how one can *find out* about them. Although I do not intend to digress into philosophical questions, it is nonetheless necessary at the outset to clarify certain preconceptions that will char-acterize this chapter. These are physicalist in nature and therefore the information I will provide in the discussions below will resonate most with those who believe that minds are organized in certain ways because brains are.

There are alternative positions one could take regarding universals. For exam-ple, to Saussure (1915/1972) universal principles of "langue" were communica-tive in nature (i.e., derived from social interaction), rather than individual minds or brains.[1] In more recent cognitive science, minds have sometimes been likened to software that can be implemented on just about any computational hardware (cf. Fodor, 1976; Gardner, 1987, p. 78f). The implication of this position would be that some universals of mind may exist without corresponding universals of brain. Conversely, Chomsky—arguably the most prominent thinker in modern linguistics—has insisted that "linguistic universals [are] principles that hold of lan-guage quite generally as a matter of biological (not logical) necessity," which is ultimately based on a "genetically determined initial state" (Chomsky, 1980, p. 232).

The physicalist approach taken in this chapter does not deny the possibility of universal principles of language that are not based on a unique neural architec-ture. In other words, different speakers (including speakers of different languages) may abide by abstract universal principles, but these principles—though universal descriptively—may be subserved by diverse types of neural processes. This universality could be called *shallow* because it is not found in neurocognitive architecture, but only in the description of linguistic behavior. *Deep universality*, on the contrary, would involve neurofunctional principles shared by all typically developing brains. I will argue below that from a developmental neuroscience point of view, it is not very likely that any deeply universal principles are specifically linguistic. Functional domains that begin to develop before the onset of language acquisition (such as visuomotor coordination, polymodal integration, joint attention, and working memory) present us with much more probable roots for linguistic universals.

11.2. What Is Universal in Human Brains?

When examining human brains, either on a macroscopic level of large anatomical landmarks (e.g., the inferior frontal gyrus; the Sylvian fissure; Figure 11.1) or on a more microscopic level (e.g., the layered architecture of cortex), seeing universality or variability depends on viewpoint in similar ways as seeing a glass half full or half empty. With a human gene "code" that contains probably no more than 35,000 genes (Ewing & Green, 2000), a full a priori specification of the brain's entire architecture (let alone that of other bodily organs) is unlikely. Because development is

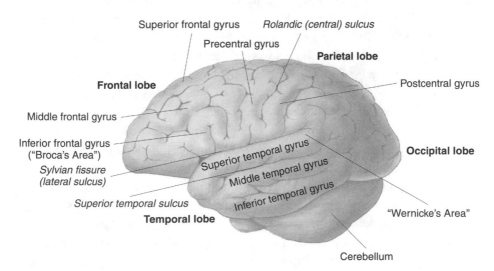

Figure 11.1. The location of some basic anatomical loci referred to in this chapter is indicated on the left hemisphere. The four lobes of the brain are labeled in bold; sulci are labeled in italics.

therefore largely epigenetic in nature, the high degree of phenotypic universality, at least within the spectrum of what we call "typical development," is surprising.

As a macroscopic example, every typically developing brain has two almost (but not quite) symmetric hemispheres, and each hemisphere in every such brain has a central sulcus (Figure 11.1), just posterior of which we find cells that increase their firing rates during tactile or somatosensory stimulation. Even more, in every such brain different body parts are organized on this postcentral gyrus in a roughly topographic manner, the face being represented at the bottom, and legs and feet at the top, with hands and trunk in between. However, the basic universal blueprint of neuroanatomy is also subject to great individual variability. For example, the precise shape of the central sulcus or the postcentral gyrus will never be the same across individuals. Indeed, this variability of individual brain morphology is one of the insistent problems in functional neuroimaging studies, which rely on our ability to pool brains of individual subjects for statistical group analyses. The process of "spatial normalization" reflects the duality of discernible universality (the brain in "standard space") and observed individual variability (the brain in "native space"; Brett, Johnsrude, & Owen, 2002).

For an example of microscopic universality, neocortex in every typically developed human brain examined with suitable methods, such as Golgi or Nissl stains, has been found to consist of six layers, with different cell types and specific connectivity patterns for each layer (Amaral, 2000). Although the textbook assumption of six distinct "laminae" defies the true complexity of neocortex (Braitenberg & Schüz, 1991), the principle of layered architecture is universal within the species, and it is also universal across different neocortical regions within each individual (Creutzfeldt, 1977). However, with respect to this intraindividual universality, there are interesting variations that correspond to function. Layer IV containing cells that receive axons with sensory inputs from the thalamus is well developed in sensory cortex (e.g., postcentral somatosensory cortex), but virtually nonexistent in primary motor cortex located just anteriorly, in the precentral gyrus.

This difference between primary sensory and motor cortices has obvious functional relevance. It invites the question whether similar functionally relevant differences may exist with regard to more complex cognitive domains, such as language. Although language use involves sensory and motor functions (auditory processing of speech; planning and execution of complex movements of the vocal tract, etc.), such functions are usually not considered relevant to core language universals because they appear peripheral and shared with other domains (e.g., auditory perception of music; motor execution in playing an instrument). Of greater interest would be species-universal architectural specificity in cortex suspected to play crucial roles in core language components, such as morphosyntax. I will return to this question in detail later in section 11.6. Suffice it to emphasize here that in Broca's area in the left inferior frontal gyrus—probably the most obvious candidate for such a "language area"—there is indeed some species-universal specificity that distinguishes this cortex from primary sensory or motor areas, but this universal blueprint is again accompanied by substantial individual variability (Amunts et al., 1999).

Universality can be found, not only in the vertical organization of cortex (in the layered architecture described above), but also in its horizontal architecture. This *columnar* organization was first described by Hubel and Wiesel (1968) in their electrophysiological studies of visual cortex in the monkey. Since then, columnar organization has been documented across cerebral cortical regions, not only for unimodal sensorimotor cortices, but also for multimodal association cortices (Mountcastle, 1997). Columns are characterized by intrinsic features (i.e., tight vertical interconnectivity with limited local horizontal connections) and by extrinsic organization (e.g., specific afferents from thalamus; specific efferents to other brain regions). Although this organizational principle appears largely universal across cerebral cortex, there is variability with regard to cell types and connectivity between regions. Whereas the basic blueprint of columnar organization can be considered as ultimately driven by genetic information (but note the caveats in the following section), relatively little is known about individual variability of cytoarchitecture and columnar organization in the human brain that may be based on experiential factors.[2]

11.3. What Can Genes Do for Universality in the Brain?

As alluded to above, brain organization is unlikely to be fully specified by genes. Nonetheless, it is almost certain that genes play a crucial role in brain anatomical and architectural universality, while being instrumental for neural variability at the same time. In rodents, regulatory genes such as *Emx2* and *Pax6* have been identified that are expressed in graded fashion along the anterior–posterior axis of the developing brain. Mutations of these genes result in distorted proportions of posterior visual cortex versus more anterior somatosensory and auditory cortices (O'Leary & Nakagawa, 2002; Pallas, 2001). Genetic effects on brain morphology have also been demonstrated in humans. Thompson and colleagues (2001) found that monozygotic twins were less different in local gray matter volume compared to dizygotic twins, who in turn showed fewer regional differences than unrelated subjects. Interestingly, the putatively gene-driven similarity between monozygotic twins differed from region to region, with some regions of the brain showing variability similar to what was seen in unrelated subjects. This latter finding suggests the importance of experiential and other nongenetic effects (see below and section 11.6).

When considering what in the gross morphology of the brain or the microarchitecture of cortex might be genetically determined, it is important to appreciate that if a feature is "innate" (i.e., present at birth) it is not necessarily driven by genes, for at least two reasons. First, the brain developing in utero is by no means isolated from the external world. Although low-pass filtered and muffled, the fetus can perceive sounds including language stimuli in utero, and some evidence suggests transnatal auditory learning, that is, postnatal retention of stimuli received in utero (Moon & Fifer, 2000). In one study by Moon, Cooper, and Fifer (1993), infants who were only about 2 days old showed a preference for native language versus foreign language stimuli, which may be attributed to prenatal experience.

Second, the prenatal brain is highly active and some of the ultimate functional organization of the brain appears to be driven by this activity, rather than by intrinsic information that might directly reflect gene expression. As reviewed by Rakic, Ang, and Breunig (2004), the differentiation of cerebral cortex into functionally specific areas is driven partly by intrinsic, partly by extrinsic factors, among which afferent activity plays a predominant role. For example, Schlaggar and O'Leary (1991) showed that when cortex from the occipital lobe (typically visual cortex) is transplanted into the postcentral region (typically somatosensory cortex) in rat embryos, these rats will develop almost normal somatosensory barrel fields from the transplanted cortex, that is, receptive fields for individual sensory hairs (whiskers). This cortical differentiation into barrel fields is presumably determined by afferent activity from somatosensory regions of the thalamus, as opposed to intrinsic information in the transplanted cortex itself, which would have resulted in development of visual specialization.

11.4. What Can Genes Do for Language?

With regard to the question of "genes for language," the predominant empirical approach has been similar to the traditional lesion approach in neuropsychology that investigates brain organization based on specific deficits resulting from localized damage (see section 11.5). Analogously, the focus has been on genetic defects associated with developmental language impairments (Bishop, 2002; Tomblin & Buckwalter, 1994). A series of studies that received much attention was dedicated to familial aggregation of specific language impairment (SLI) in family KE (Gopnik, 1990; Gopnik & Crago, 1991). Speech disorder in this family was later found to be an autosomal-dominant trait involving a single gene on chromosome 7 (Fisher, Vargha-Khadem, Watkins, Monaco, & Pembrey, 1998; Lai, Fisher, Hurst, Vargha-Khadem, & Monaco, 2001). The studies by Gopnik and colleagues (1990, 1991) initially suggested a selective linguistic deficit specifically related to aspects of morphosyntax (such as past tense formation). Subsequent testing by Vargha-Khadem and colleagues on a broader battery of tests revealed, however, that deficits in affected family members were by no means exclusively morphosyntactic. For instance, affected family members had significantly lower *nonverbal* IQ scores than unaffected members. They were also affected by orofacial dyspraxia, and their phonological working memory was impaired (Vargha-Khadem, Watkins, Alcock, Fletcher, & Passingham, 1995; Watkins, Dronkers, & Vargha-Khadem, 2002). Magnetic resonance imaging (MRI) findings in family KE (Watkins et al., 2002) demonstrating gray matter reduction mostly in motor areas of the brain support the conclusion that basic impairments are non-linguistic and that apparently specific morphosyntactic deficits are secondary to orofacial motor, phonemic, and other impairments.

The findings of impairments beyond the language domain in affected members of family KE serve as a caution to developmental linguists such as Pinker (2001), who has speculated that the genes involved "may have a causal role in the development of the normal brain circuitry that underlies language and speech." As mentioned, in family KE (as well as one unrelated case; Lai et al., 2001) the relevant mutation associated with speech disorder has been located to a region on chromosome 7 (7q31), and specifically to a gene named *FOXP2* (forkhead box P2). This gene belongs to a group of so-called forkhead transcription factors, which are involved in the synthesis of ribonucleic acid (RNA) from deoxyribonucleic acid (DNA). Forkhead proteins play a role in various rather general functions related to cellular proliferation and differentiation, as well as signal transduction (Marcus & Fisher, 2003). Since *FOXP2* is expressed not only in the brain but also in other body organs, such as the lungs and the heart, it appears unlikely that it could play a specialized role in neurocognitive development, let alone a specific function in morphosyntax. Nonetheless, recent work including larger samples of patients with verbal dyspraxia suggests that a specific coding change within the *FOXP2* gene may more specifically affect the developing central nervous system and make it vulnerable to defects in complex and fast orofacial muscular sequencing (MacDermot et al., 2005). This specific genetic abnormality was found in about 6% of patients with verbal dyspraxia. While it is thus unlikely to account for a majority of cases with developmental language impairment, *FOXP2* appears to be one gene that may be importantly involved in the development of orofacial neuromuscular abilities, which may in turn be one of the prerequisite for typical language development (cf. Fisher & Marcus, 2006). From this perspective, *FOXP2* may contribute—in rather indirect ways—to linguistic universality within the spectrum of typically developing children. It is notable, however, that this gene plays a role in precursor functions (orofacial muscular control) that are not per se linguistic. Indeed, the link between orofacial dyspraxia and grammatical impairments may appear mysterious, unless one considers that motor functions may serve as precursors to some aspects of language acquisition. I will return to this issue in section 11.6.

11.5. Where in the Brain Does Language Happen?

The previous section highlights how little is known about the genetic bases for language acquisition in typically developing children. The language impairment associated with a single-gene defect in family KE provides probably no more than a tiny fraction of a large set of genes that may be prerequisites for language acquisition through their involvement in brain maturation and developing sensorimotor systems. A comprehensive model of the genes involved in language acquisition that may be responsible for its universality is thus unavailable and will probably remain so for a long time. An alternative and more promising approach to the biological bases of language universality will therefore seek to identify brain areas known to participate in language processing. In this regard, a striking universality can indeed be found among an overwhelming majority of human individuals.

To begin with, the percentage of people who process language predominantly in their left hemispheres is very high, probably around 95% for right-handed adults. Interestingly, this rule does not apply to some individuals (relatively many left-handers, in fact), whose language nonetheless falls within the normal spectrum (Tzourio, Crivello, Mellet, Nkanga-Ngila, & Mazoyer, 1998). Hemispheric asymmetry on its own can therefore not account for universal principles of language. However, there is more to neuroanatomical universality. Even though either hemisphere may in principle be able to support language (see section 11.6.2), the particular regions within a hemisphere that activate during language processing appear to be very consistent across members of the species.

Historically, most of our knowledge of the brain organization for language originates from studies of lesion patients. Leborgne, Broca's (1861) legendary case, as well as aphasic lesion patients later studied by Wernicke (1874), provided the basis for our current understanding of language areas in perisylvian cortex (cortex surrounding the lateral sulcus) of the left hemisphere. In section 11.6, I will return to the question of what exactly it means when we talk about a "language area." Although the role of Broca's area in inferior frontal cortex and Wernicke's area in the posterior superior temporal region as "language areas" was originally established based on lesion patients, their important participation in language processing has been more recently confirmed in numerous neuroimaging studies (Cabeza & Nyberg, 2000), including studies using languages other than English, such as Chinese (Mandarin; Chee et al., 2000), Japanese (Homae, Hashimoto, Nakajima, Miyashita, & Sakai, 2002), Italian (Moro et al., 2001), French (Crozier et al., 1999), German (Friederici, Ruschemeyer, Hahne, & Fiebach, 2003), Finnish (Laine, Rinne, Krause, Tereas, & Sipilea, 1999), and Dutch (Indefrey, Hagoort, Herzog, Seitz, & Brown, 2001).Functional imaging has also identified additional regions frequently activated bylanguage tasks, such as parts of the cerebellum (Fiez & Raichle, 1997), and the middle and inferior temporal gyri (Martin & Chao, 2001; Martin, Haxby, Lalonde, Wiggs, & Ungerleider, 1995).

This apparent universality of neuroanatomic substrates yields a promising approach to linguistic universality. Maybe these regions contain some special cellular architecture, or maybe they are interconnected in ways that are universal within the human species and permit specifically linguistic processing. I will examine this possibility in the following section. However, first it needs to be acknowledged that apparent universality of "language regions" within our species could be an illusory result of conventional statistical procedures in functional neuroimaging.

With very few exceptions, imaging studies of language are based on groupwise analyses of typical adults. As mentioned above, this requires spatial normalization that at least partially removes the pronounced anatomical variability of individual brains. Groupwise analyses that typically employ t-statistics, however, also remove functional variability. Indeed, this variability is considered noise, or "error" (Smith, 2001). In view of the thousands of functional neuroimaging papers published every year, surprisingly few have examined individual functional variability for language. In a positron emission tomography (PET) study, Herholz et al. (1996) found consistent activation in left inferior frontal area 45 associated with verb generation in all of their seven right-handed participants. However, there was variability of activation within the inferior frontal lobe, which was only partly accounted for by anatomical variation. Functional variability appeared even more pronounced in other frontal and in temporo-parietal regions. Xiong and colleagues (2000) quantified functional variability in a second PET study of 20 young adults, also using a verb generation paradigm. Interestingly, the highest consistency of activation was seen not in left perisylvian cortex, but in the mediofrontal supplementary motor area. This latter activation was probably related to the presence of a motor response in the experimental, but not the control condition. The finding suggests that motor processing is associated with less functional variability than language processing. When examining larger regions, consistency of activation $\geq 80\%$ was, however, seen in inferior frontal and superior temporal areas. Nonetheless, it is remarkable that a few participants did *not* show significant activation in one of these regions, given that they are considered core language areas. Even in participants with activation in these regions, activation peaks occurred at a mean Euclidian distance of more than 10 mm from the peak loci identified in groupwise analyses. This extent of variability in inferior frontal and lateral temporal cortex has more recently been replicated in a functional magnetic resonance imaging (fMRI) study by Seghier and coworkers (2004), who used a phonological rhyme detection and a semantic categorization task in 30 right-handed young adults (see also Burton, Noll, & Small, 2001).

In conclusion, neuroimaging studies suggest—in accordance with the lesion literature—that there are a few perisylvian regions in the inferior frontal lobe and in lateral temporal cortex of the left hemisphere that participate relatively consistently in language tasks such as word retrieval. These areas may be called "language areas," although this denomination requires several important qualifications. First, there is individual variability and some people do not seem to rely on these brain regions in typical ways during language processing. Correspondingly, some patients with damage to these regions do not become aphasic (Alexander & Annett, 1996; Hund-Georgiadis, Zysset, Weih, Guthke, & von Cramon, 2001). Second, the precise loci of activity within these large language areas vary substantially between individuals. Third, individual subjects will typically show activation in many sites outside these regions and these sites will be characterized by great variability. Fourth, the finding of activity related to a language task will depend very much on the precise nature of the chosen task. Studies of individual variability have focused mostly on simple lexical retrieval tasks, whereas little is known about variability for morphosyntactic and other language functions. All this, however, leaves open the theoretical possibility of some special processing architecture within language areas that is universal across the species, although it may be anatomically organized in slightly varying loci. In the following section, I will examine more closely what it might mean for a brain region to qualify as a language area and what a developmental account of a language area implies with regard to universality.

11.6. What's in a "Language Area"?

The exemplary part of the brain selected for this discussion will be Broca's area. The term originated as a misnomer related to Paul Broca's (1861, 1866) reports on patient Leborgne, who suffered from severe expressive (or nonfluent) aphasia— uttering nothing but his legendary "tan-tan" and a curse word ("qué [=sacré] nom de dieu"). Postmortem examination showed a large lesion that Broca himself identified as primarily left inferior frontal. Later study of the preserved brain, ironically, showed that the damage went far beyond "Broca's area" (i.e., inferior frontal cortex; Signoret, Castaigne, Lhermitte, Abelanet, & Lavorel, 1984). Nonetheless, the term is still widely used almost a century and a half later, although there is no complete consensus on its precise anatomical meaning. While it certainly includes the pars opercularis of the inferior frontal gyrus (roughly corresponding to Brodmann area 44), many will also consider the pars triangularis (area 45; e.g., Amunts et al., 1999; Caplan, Alpert, Waters, & Olivieri, 2000; Dronkers, Pinker, & Damasio, 2000; Friederici, 2002) and possibly the more inferior area 47 as part of Broca's area (e.g., Cooke et al., 2002; Keller, Carpenter, & Just, 2001).

Since there is no consensus as to its precise anatomical substrate, it is not surprising that there is also considerable debate about the functional role of the region. Among the strongest recent proposals is Grodzinsky's (2000), according to which area 44 exclusively specializes in syntactic transformations. This hypothesis is related to earlier work in linguistics and neurolinguistics, particularly in the study of agrammatism, which was originally considered a selective loss of grammatical functors and morphemes, with retained lexicosemantic knowledge (Friedmann & Grodzinksy, 1997; Kean, 1985). In some functional neuroimaging studies pursuing this hypothesis (e.g., Caplan et al., 2000; Indefrey, Hellwig, Herzog, Seitz, & Hagoort, 2004; Stromswold, Caplan, Alpert, & Rauch, 1996), apparently, "modular" activation foci in the left inferior frontal gyrus have indeed been found to be associated with syntactic complexity.

11.6.1. Cellular Architecture

As mentioned earlier, apparent functional specificity could reflect a distinct type of cortical architecture specifically tuned to morphosyntactic processing. Such architecture in left inferior frontal cortex could be universal within the species (i.e., identical in every individual), possibly based on intrinsic genetic information. Unfortunately, the literature on cytoarchitecture in Broca's area is small. Simonds and Scheibel (1989) studied 17 brains of deceased infants and young children (3–72 months of age), examining dendritic complexity. They found that the homologue to Broca's area in the right hemisphere had an early advantage in dendritic development, with pronounced left inferior frontal development kicking in at the beginning of the second year. In brains of 4- to 6-year olds, Broca's area in the left hemisphere showed greater dendritic length compared to its homologue and adjacent premotor cortex in both hemispheres. These findings could reflect intrinsically driven cytoarchitectonic developments specifically enabling left inferior frontal cortex to assume morphosyntactic functions. Amunts and colleagues showed that there is substantial individual variability in the cytoarchitecture and boundaries of cytoarchitectonic fields within the inferior frontal cortex (Amunts et al., 1999). Area 44, often considered the "core" or exclusive site of Broca area (see above), is "dysgranular," containing only a very thin layer of granular cells in layer IV. Interestingly, this feature is shared with motor cortex and makes area 44 an unlikely candidate for a substrate specifically involved in morphosyntactic or any other kind of nonmotor linguistic processing. This finding is consistent with dendritic complexity in area 44, which on most parameters (such as dendritic spine density) resembles premotor cortex more than it resembles prefrontal association cortex (Jacobs et al., 2001).

Amunts, Schleicher, Ditterich, and Zilles (2003) also examined developmental changes in the cytoarchitecture of inferior frontal fields, focusing on the gray level index (GLI; i.e., the fraction of cortical volume taken up by neuronal cell bodies). One finding was that GLI asymmetries in area 44 (but not 45) were leftward in the first decade of life—roughly corresponding with the "critical period" for language acquisition—but reversed in early adulthood, turning robustly rightward in people aged 50 years and older. However, the GLI may not be a precise enough measure to illuminate developmental changes in specific processing capacities possibly related to language acquisition. Indeed, it remains unclear whether the results from these developmental studies, including those from Scheibel's group mentioned above, reflect intrinsic cytoarchitectonic changes that are causative of Broca's area's capacity to play an important role in language acquisition—as opposed to changes that are secondary *results* of this area's language involvement. This causality conundrum is quite common in developmental cognitive neuroscience because it is known that, while brain structure affords function, function in turn affects structure. In other words, there is reciprocal or circular causality in the interaction between neuroanatomy and functional physiology that makes it almost impossible to determine the "root cause" of a developmental outcome.

11.6.2. Plasticity

Studies on the cellular architecture of Broca's area are thus inconclusive with regard to the question of universal processing specificity. However, the question can be addressed in a more indirect way using a more traditional neuropsychological approach (i.e., the study of lesion patients). It is known that in adults, left inferior frontal lesion usually results in nonfluent aphasia (Caplan, Hildebrandt, & Makris, 1996; Pedersen, Jørgensen, Nakayama, Raaschou, & Olsen, 1995), which may be consistent with universal specificity (aside from the caveat raised earlier in this section). The same is not true for lesion effects in children. As a most striking example, left hemispherectomy (i.e., resection or complete disconnection of the entire left hemisphere) following early-onset lesion is often associated with good long-term language outcome if the right hemisphere remains intact (Mariotti, Iuvone, Torrioli, & Silveri, 1998; Vanlancker-Sidtis, 2004; Vargha-Khadem & Mishkin, 1997; Vargha-Khadem et al., 1997), although underlying etiology affects the specifics of language outcome (Curtiss, de Bode, & Mathern, 2001).

The above clinical behavioral studies have been more recently complemented by neuroimaging work demonstrating the readiness of the right hemisphere to assume language functions following early left hemisphere injury. Some studies in typically developing children shed light indirectly on the relevant developmental plasticity, suggesting that the participation of Broca's area of the left hemisphere in word generation gradually increases between the ages of 7 and 18 years (Holland et al., 2001), which may be incompatible with the idea of an innately predetermined specifically linguistic and species-universal architecture in left inferior frontal cortex. However, the findings reported by Holland and colleagues were based on only 17 subjects, and apparent age-related effects may have been confounded by differences in behavior, which was unmonitored in a covert word generation paradigm. A more recent study including 95 right-handed children and adults between the ages of 7 and 32 years (Brown et al., 2005) in several overt word generation tasks found that activation for several lexical tasks in Broca's area was age independent, whereas activity in more superior portions of premotor cortex increased with age. The location of these effects suggests that they may be related to speech articulatory development rather than core language components, such as morphosyntax.

Functional neuroimaging of clinical patients yields evidence that is even more telling with regard to the search for a potential innately prespecified and species-universal language-related functional architecture in Broca's area. Consistent with the behavioral studies described above, imaging studies in children with early-onset damage to the left hemisphere demonstrate a significantly greater potential for reorganization of language functions into homotopic right hemisphere areas, such as right inferior frontal cortex, in comparison to adults with late onset lesions (Müller, Behen et al., 1999; Müller, Rothermel et al., 1999). More recent fMRI studies in children with early-onset left hemisphere lesions (Liegeois et al., 2004) and in adult patients with a history of pre- or perinatal left hemisphere lesions (Staudt et al., 2002) confirm the readiness of right-hemisphere cortex homotopic to typical left-hemisphere perisylvian language cortex to assume language functions early in development. Indeed, this potential for reorganization appears to be greater in the language domain than it is for motor control. This effect could be shown statistically in a study of a group of nine pediatric patients with early-onset unilateral left hemisphere damage (Müller, Rothermel et al., 1998), but can be illustrated more easily in single case examples (Figure 11.2). Bearing in mind that group statistical approaches to the study of brain-damaged patients are always limited by variance related to numerous clinical and demographic parameters, these results suggest that the cortical architecture subserving language functions in Broca's area is less "hard-wired" than the architecture in precentral cortex subserving motor control.

11.6.3. Connectivity

As discussed earlier, neuroimaging studies of morphosyntactic processing have quite consistently reported activation in left inferior frontal gyrus. However, when considering the entire neuroimaging literature relevant to Broca's area, any exclusive syntactic specialization of area 44 begins to appear rather improbable (Duncan & Owen, 2000). In particular, left inferior frontal activation has been reported for nonsyntactic language processing as, for example, in lexicosemantic and phonological tasks (see review in Heim, 2005). More intriguingly, such activity is also found associated with tasks that are traditionally considered as nonlinguistic, such as

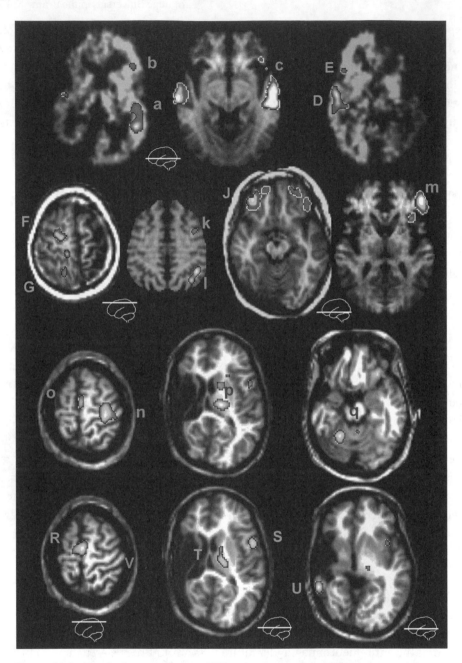

Figure 11.2. Results from single-case PET activation studies. All images are axial
(horizontal) slices at locations indicated by the lines across the small brain icons
underneath the corresponding images. In each image, task-related activations (blood
flow increases) are superimposed onto grayscale brain anatomy except for two
images on the left and on the right of the top row where the grayscale images
represent resting blood flow. Lowercase caption letters (blue in color plate) stand

imitation (Buccino et al., 2004; Iacoboni et al., 1999), motor imagery (Binkofski et al., 2000; Gerardin et al., 2000), object manipulation (Binkofski et al., 1999), motor preparation and complex motor planning (Fincham, Carter, van Veen, Stenger, & Anderson, 2002; Krams, Rushworth, Deiber, Frackowiak, & Passingham, 1998), digit sequence learning (Haslinger et al., 2002; Toni, Schluter, Josephs, Friston, & Passingham, 1999), working memory (Chen & Desmond, 2005;

←——

Figure 11.2. *(continued)* for typical activation foci, uppercase letters (green in color plate) for foci suggesting reorganization, and V for absence of typical activation. Images are shown in radiological convention (i.e., the left side of each image represents the right hemisphere). Top row: A patient with congenital Sturge Weber syndrome, which leads to progressive calcification and shrinkage in only one hemisphere (here: the right), shows a pattern of left-hemisphere activation in temporal (a) and inferior frontal regions (b) during listening to sentences, resembling the pattern seen in healthy adults (c). In a second patient with the same disorder, in this case affecting the left hemisphere, right hemisphere activation in temporal (D) and inferior frontal regions (E) is almost a mirror image of the typical pattern. This can be interpreted as homotopic interhemispheric reorganization. Second row: Activation patterns for an expressive language paradigm, in which subjects generate sentences based on an input sentence and a prompt word ("He listened to the radio . . . – *Television*," with the usual response, "He watched television"). Blood flow increases are shown for the comparison with sentence repetition. Another patient with unilateral calcification (of the left hemisphere) caused by Sturge Weber syndrome shows right-hemispheric activations in prefrontal (F), inferior parietal (G), and inferior frontal regions (J), which are homotopic to corresponding activations seen in healthy control subjects (k-m). Two bottom rows: Activations associated with finger tapping (compared to rest) in a young adult with a history of perinatal right middle cerebral artery stroke. Activations during finger movement in the unaffected right hand show a normal pattern, with foci in primary motor cortex (n), supplementary motor area (o), thalamus and basal ganglia (p) of the left hemisphere, as well as in the ipsilateral cerebellum (q). For the weak left hand, activity patterns are very different, with focus on the supplementary motor area (R), inferior premotor cortex (S), and thalamus (T) ipsilateral to the movement, as well as an activation in what appears to be temporal cortex in the vicinity of the damaged area (U). Remarkably, there is no activation in ipsilateral primary motor cortex (V), suggesting that interhemispheric reorganization in the motor domain is primarily nonhomotopic (see Müller, Rothermel et al., 1998; Müller, Watson et al., 1998). (See Plate 1)

Goldberg, Berman, Randolph, Gold, & Weinberger, 1996), rule shifting (Konishi et al., 1998), response selection (Thompson-Schill, D'Esposito, Aguirre, & Farah, 1997), and response inhibition (Kemmotsu, Villalobos, Gaffrey, Courchesne, & Müller, 2005; Rubia et al., 2001).

Some of these findings are probably related to results from monkey studies demonstrating the existence of neurons in area F5—arguably homologous to area 44 in humans (see below)—that display increased firing rates, not only when a monkey performs a specific action, but also when the monkey *observes* another monkey perform the same action, or even when the monkey looks at an object (such as a tool) that is typically associated with this action (Fadiga, Fogassi, Gallese, & Rizzolatti, 2000; Ferrari, Rozzi, & Fogassi, 2005). These functional characteristics of inferior frontal neurons have been attributed to a "mirror neuron system" (Rizzolatti, Fogassi, & Gallese, 2002). Because mirror neurons show increased spiking rates during observation of actions, they have been hypothesized to be crucial for the meaningful interpretation of actions performed by others and the ability in monkeys (and presumably in humans) to relate an observed action to similar action performed by themselves. Mirror neurons may thus be instrumental for action understanding (Rizzolatti & Craighero, 2004), and possibly for "mind reading" or "theory of mind" (Gallese, 2003).

However, it appears misleading to attribute such functional roles to a set of neurons in a small anatomical location (such as F5 in the monkey or Broca's area in the human). Instead, it is certain that inferior frontal mirror neurons can display the described firing patterns only based on their connectivity with distributed brain regions of a mirror-neuron circuit. Aside from inferior frontal cortex, crucial regions within this circuit are the superior temporal sulcus, whose role in the perception of biological motion is known (Puce & Perrett, 2003), and a rostral portion of the inferior parietal lobe (area PF in the monkey brain; Rizzolatti & Craighero, 2004). The mirror neuron system can be considered part of what has been traditionally called the dorsal stream of visual perception (Rizzolatti & Matelli, 2003). Originally described as a visuospatial pathway, the dorsal system has been more recently characterized as a system of "vision for action," additionally incorporating portions of prefrontal cortex (Goodale & Westwood, 2004). Although primary functions of the mirror neuron system relate to visuomotor and audiomotor (Kohler et al., 2002) coordination, it has been argued that this system plays a pivotal role in language development, both phylogenetically and in child language acquisition (Rizzolatti & Arbib, 1998).

A number of functional neuroimaging studies have examined the suggestion of Broca's area being a homologue of area F5 in the monkey and thus the site of mirror neurons (Grèzes & Decety, 2001; Nishitani, Schurmann, Amunts, & Hari, 2005; Rizzolatti & Arbib, 1998). These studies have confirmed the participation of left inferior frontal cortex in functions attributed to the mirror neuron system, such as action imitation (Iacoboni et al., 1999), motor imagery (Binkofski et al., 2000), action observation and recognition (Buccino et al., 2001, 2004), and observation and imitation of lip movements (Nishitani & Hari, 2002).

A few functional imaging studies have attempted to relate mirror neuron functions directly to linguistic processing. Tettamanti and colleagues (2005) found a significant effect in the pars opercularis of left inferior frontal gyrus when comparing comprehension of action-related sentences to comprehension of abstract sentences (not referring to any body movement), which were matched for syntactic complexity. The results suggest that mirror neuron activity can be prompted, not only by observation and imagery of actions as previously shown, but also by listening to corresponding linguistic stimuli. Based on the design in this study, it cannot be ruled out that these stimuli simply evoked action imagery, which, in turn, activated inferior frontal cortex. However, given the intimate proximity of activity identified in the study by Tettamanti and colleagues, and inferior frontal activity observed for syntactic decoding of sentences in many other studies (e.g., Friederici et al., 2003; Indefrey et al., 2004), it would appear that cortical resources may be shared between functions attributed to the mirror neuron system and linguistic functions.

One fMRI study by Hamzei and coworkers (2003) directly compared linguistic and mirror-neuron-related effects in a small sample of healthy adults. In a conjunction analysis, the investigators found three sites of convergent activity for action recognition, action imitation, and covert verb generation. These were in parietal cortex (possibly homologous with area PF in the monkey brain, as described above), on the border of inferior frontal and premotor cortex, and in pars opercularis of inferior frontal cortex (Broca's area), all in the left hemisphere. When inspecting statistical maps in individual subjects, Hamzei and colleagues found that activity for action recognition was always immediately adjacent to, and often overlapping with, activity for verb generation, but no consistent spatial relation between the two could be identified. Although it is beyond the spatial resolution of fMRI to isolate the function of individual "mirror neurons" or even small sets of these, the spatial proximity of effects suggests that mirror neuron and language-related functions share cortical resources in inferior frontal cortex.

The evidence of developmental neurofunctional plasticity and of inferior frontal participation in the mirror neuron circuit laid out above underscores the need for cautious interpretation of clinical and imaging results. It is true that most adult patients with left inferior frontal damage will experience speech impairment and grammatical deficits; and it is true that most functional imaging studies manipulating morphosyntactic complexity (or a variety of other language-related variables) will identify left inferior frontal activation; and indeed it is true that whenever researchers have bothered to examine activation maps intraindividually, they have found that most right-handed adults show such language-related activation in left inferior frontal cortex, albeit in slightly varying loci. But does this imply that Broca's area is a piece of human cortical tissue uniquely and universally prespecified to process language functions, be they morphosyntactic or other? A view from an adult perspective that ignores development may suggest affirmation. However, the discussion and evidence presented above should have elucidated why such an "adults-only" approach to explaining the functional organization of the brain is gravely misleading. A truly explanatory model of a brain region's function requires an account of the interaction of intrinsic information (based on genes and gene expression) with extrinsic information. The latter has many meanings and implications. For instance, as discussed in section 11.3, the functional differentiation of developing neocortex is largely determined by input activity. If thalamic input activity is driven by visual stimuli, the receiving cortex will assume visual functions, regardless of its location and intrinsic information.

This approach to understanding a cortical region's functional role, however, yields more intricate answers when it comes to complex functional domains such as language that are not driven by a single sensory modality and are governed by principles that appear modality independent. Nonetheless, a developmental approach strongly constrains the set of potential models that are reasonable from a neuroscientific perspective. The functional specificity of Broca's area is unlikely to be fully determined by thalamic or other subcortico-cortical afferents. The evidence on the mirror neuron circuit discussed above suggests that the functional role of Broca's area is in part determined by cortico-cortical connectivity. In view of this evidence, the linguistic role of Broca's area can be understood in two ways: either as coincidental vis-à-vis its involvement in the mirror neuron circuit, or as meaningful from the developmental perspective. In-depth discussion is beyond the scope of this chapter, but developmental neuroscience shows that nothing is coincidental in functional brain organization (because, for example, organization reflects activity, which in turn is a prerequisite for trophic supply and thus survival of neurons; Jessell & Sanes, 2000). Before completing the picture of developmental specification in Broca's area, it is important to note that this region is likely to participate in many circuits besides the mirror neuron circuit. The role of the arcuate fasciculus in connecting posterior and anterior perisylvian regions has been established for a long time (for recent evidence from diffusion-tensor MRI, see Catani, Jones, and ffytche, (2005)). More important is the connectivity with brain regions that provide access to meaningful object representation.[3]

It was mentioned above that evidence for a mirror neuron circuit is in part related to what has been more traditionally known as the dorsal stream of visual processing (Rizzolatti & Matelli, 2003). The dorsal stream plays a crucial role in both visuospatial processing ("where") and in visuomotor coordination ("how"), whereas ventral stream is instrumental for the perception and meaningful interpretation of visual objects ("what"; Goodale, 2004; Ungerleider & Mishkin, 1982). An analogous organization of the auditory system into "where" and "what" pathways has been recently documented based on monkey and human neuroimaging data (Arnott, Binns, Grady, & Alain, 2004; Rauschecker & Tian, 2000). Indeed, a study by Kohler and colleagues (2002) demonstrated the existence of audiovisual mirror neurons with increased firing rates for specific actions, regardless of whether they are heard, seen, or performed by a monkey.

Interestingly, tracer studies in the monkey show that visual association cortex in anterior temporal cortex, involved in complex object recognition along the visual ventral stream, and auditory association cortex in the superior temporal gyrus involved in complex auditory processing along the auditory ventral stream, both connect to inferior frontal cortex (areas 47 and 45; Romanski, Bates, & Goldman-Rakic, 1999). This suggests that Broca's area is a site of converging connectivity from dorsal stream, including the mirror neuron circuit, and ventral stream. This convergence would gather within a small cortical territory afferent information that can be considered crucial to a child's capacity for language acquisition.

Returning to the findings of apparently nonlinguistic activation in Broca's area listed above, what initially appeared puzzling can be demystified from a developmental neuroscience point of view that takes adequate account of the mechanisms involved in the functional differentiation of cortex and the importance of interregional connectivity. The participation of Broca's area in a wide variety of functions (from imitation, to action understanding, to working memory, and response inhibition), rather than being coincidental or mysterious, is *explanatory*; that is, it accounts for this area's capacity to assume language-related functions in the young child's brain. This, of course, cannot imply that all of the mentioned nonlinguistic functions are fully developed precursors by the time language acquisition begins (say, around 1 year of age). Rather, some basic domain-specific functions (of imitation, working memory, inhibition, etc.) precede language acquisition, but development in these domains continues alongside language acquisition, throughout childhood. These nonlinguistic domains, therefore, provide "ingredients" of language acquisition, rather than, strictly speaking, precursors.[4] From this perspective, ingredient domains—although traditionally considered nonlinguistic—are in fact intimately linked to language acquisition.

11.7. Conclusion

The search for potential linguistic universals first leads to genes. A simple biological account of universality would be based on species-universal genes, defects of which result in specific language impairment. Despite some intriguing findings, as those related to coding changes in the *FOXP2* gene, it is certain that such an account is not just too simple, but in fact misleading. Neural specificity for complex cognitive domains such as language can only be understood from a developmental perspective that takes into account the interplay between intrinsic and extrinsic information and between structure and function. Rather than being intrinsically (genetically) predetermined, local architecture (e.g., in Broca's area) is largely an *outcome* of function and activity. Specificity is shaped by afferent and efferent connectivity. It is therefore not surprising that studies of the cellular architecture in Broca's area have not identified any signs of a special processor that might be uniquely endowed to perform morphosyntactic or other specifically linguistic operations. A much more likely account of the unique and grossly universal functional characteristics of Broca's area relates to its pivotal position in functional networks, in particular the dorsal pathways of visual and auditory perception, which are instrumental for sensorimotor integration, and include mirror neuron circuits crucial for action understanding, and the ventral visual stream, which provides access to meaningful object interpretation and thus to semantic representations.

The most promising neurobiological approach to language universals is thus *nonlinguistic*, referring to processing domains that begin to develop even before the child starts learning words and grammar. Some of these "language ingredient functions" are related to the participation of Broca's area in the sensorimotor circuits mentioned above. Other functional characteristics, such as working memory and response inhibition, rely on additional network participation that could not be discussed in this chapter (cf. Kemmotsu et al., 2005; Lenartowicz & McIntosh, 2005). Convergence of these networks in inferior frontal cortex provides Broca's area with an array of inputs (information) that is crucial for language acquisition. Since input-output connectivity in Broca's area is unique within the brain, it assumes linguistic functions universally, that is, in every typically developing brain. Even in many atypically developing brains with early-onset damage to Broca's area in the left hemisphere, functional reallocation will favor the homologue in inferior frontal cortex of the right hemisphere.

Although much of the above discussion focused on the role of Broca's area as a generally agreed upon neural substrate for language processing, the conclusions that can be drawn from the investigation of developing functional specificity and universality in Broca's area will probably apply to any other brain region participating in language processes, such as superior and middle temporal gyri, inferior parietal lobes, or cerebellar cortex. This general conclusion implies that universal principles of language cannot be intrinsically specified (by genetically encoded specific architecture), but emerge from developmental embedding in and interaction

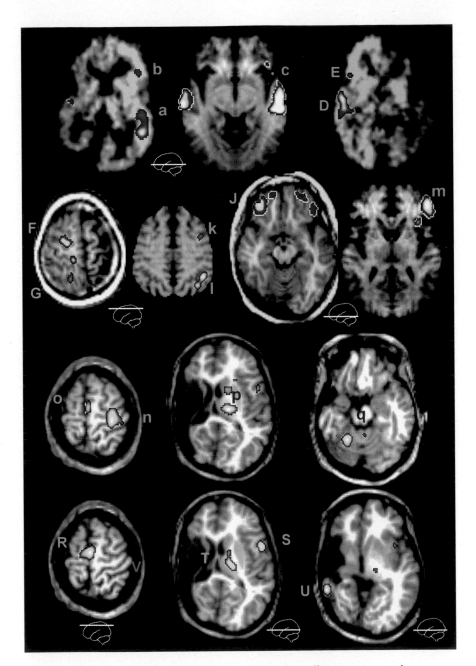

Plate 1. Results from single-case PET activation studies. All images are axial (horizontal) slices at locations indicated by the lines across the small brain icons underneath the corresponding images. In each image, task-related activations (blood flow increases) are superimposed onto grayscale brain anatomy except for two images on the left and on the right of the top row where the grayscale images

(continued)

Plate 1. *(continued from previous page)* represent resting blood flow. Lowercase caption letters (blue in color plate) stand for typical activation foci, uppercase letters (green in color plate) for foci suggesting reorganization, and V for absence of typical activation. Images are shown in radiological convention (i.e., the left side of each image represents the right hemisphere). Top row: A patient with congenital Sturge Weber syndrome, which leads to progressive calcification and shrinkage in only one hemisphere (here: the right), shows a pattern of left-hemisphere activation in temporal (a) and inferior frontal regions (b) during listening to sentences, resembling the pattern seen in healthy adults (c). In a second patient with the same disorder, in this case affecting the left hemisphere, right hemisphere activation in temporal (D) and inferior frontal regions (E) is almost a mirror image of the typical pattern. This can be interpreted as homotopic interhemispheric reorganization. Second row: Activation patterns for an expressive language paradigm, in which subjects generate sentences based on an input sentence and a prompt word ("He listened to the radio . . . – *Television*," with the usual response, "He watched television"). Blood flow increases are shown for the comparison with sentence repetition. Another patient with unilateral calcification (of the left hemisphere) caused by Sturge Weber syndrome shows right-hemispheric activations in prefrontal (F), inferior parietal (G), and inferior frontal regions (J), which are homotopic to corresponding activations seen in healthy control subjects (k-m). Two bottom rows: Activations associated with finger tapping (compared to rest) in a young adult with a history of perinatal right middle cerebral artery stroke. Activations during finger movement in the unaffected right hand show a normal pattern, with foci in primary motor cortex (n), supplementary motor area (o), thalamus and basal ganglia (p) of the left hemisphere, as well as in the ipsilateral cerebellum (q). For the weak left hand, activity patterns are very different, with focus on the supplementary motor area (R), inferior premotor cortex (S), and thalamus (T) ipsilateral to the movement, as well as an activation in what appears to be temporal cortex in the vicinity of the damaged area (U). Remarkably, there is no activation in ipsilateral primary motor cortex (V), suggesting that interhemispheric reorganization in the motor domain is primarily nonhomotopic (see Müller, Rothermel et al., 1998; Müller, Watson et al., 1998). (See Figure 11.2)

with multiple nonlinguistic functional networks that provide crucial ingredient functions to language acquisition.

The linguistic reader, who is used to very specific claims regarding innate principles of universal grammar, will surely be disappointed by the lack of such specific proposals in this chapter. This reader may accept some of the claims regarding developmental embedding in ingredient function, but will wonder what those universal principles are that would result from such embedding. For example, recursive properties and hierarchical organization are considered key characteristics of human language. Although there have been computational proposals, such as "neurally inspired" connectionist approaches to recursion in language (e.g., Voegtlin & Dominey, 2005), neuroscience itself does not currently offer conclusive models. Indeed, it appears too early to even pinpoint what level of neuroscientific research one would have to target. Could it be cellular architecture or specific connectivity patterns (as discussed above in section 11.6), or the organizational properties typically found in the left hemisphere (cf. Semenza et al., 2006)? As an alternative, the developmental cognitive neuroscientist may trust the linguistic community to identify such principles. Once such "shallow universals" (as defined in section 11.1) are identified based on satisfactory consensus in the linguistic community, a neurodevelopmental account needs to be sought that can establish "deep" (i.e., biologically meaningful) universals. As concluded from the review above, such a neurodevelopmental account is most likely to be founded on the organization and interplay of nonlinguistic "ingredient processes."

Key Further Readings

A useful, though slightly technical review of the interplay between intrinsic (genetically driven) and extrinsic factors in brain development and the emergence of regional functional specialization is provided by O'Leary and Nakagawa (2002). Recommended readings more specifically related to the genetic underpinnings of language and to language universals are Marcus and Fisher (2003), and a more recent update by Fisher and Marcus (2006). These reviews focus on *FOXP2* and its potential role in typical language acquisition and specific language impairment.

The work by Amunts and colleagues (1999, 2003) provides insight into the complex regional differences and developmental changes in cellular architecture, with specific focus on Broca's area. It is thought-provoking with regard to the question of what it might mean, on the microscopic level of cell types and connectivity patterns, for a brain region to be considered as a potentially specialized linguistic processor. Brown et al. (2005) add important information on developmental changes in this regard from a much more macroscopic perspective, using functional MRI and a set of standard language paradigms in large samples of children and adults. This study is currently the most thorough examination of changes in language organization in typically developing children.

Rizzolatti and Craighero (2004) provide a recommended background reading for a better understanding of language networks emerging from "nonverbal" functional networks, such as the mirror neuron system. Nishitani, Schurmann, Amunts, and Hari (2005) add important aspects specifically related to Broca's area to this approach. This paper reviews the cellular architecture of inferior frontal cortex and the functional implications of its connectivity patterns, with emphasis on action understanding. The reviews by Rizzolatti and Craighero (2004) and Nishitani et al. (2005) are important as they discuss the organization of functional networks that may provide a developmental basis for the emergence of language universals.

Acknowledgments

Preparation of this chapter was supported by NIH R01-NS43999 and R01-DC006155

Notes

1 "...la langue... [est] à la fois un produit social de la faculté du langage et un ensemble de conventions necessaires..." [Language is a social product of the language faculty and at the same time a set of necessary conventions; ibid.: p. 25.]

2 For a review of animal studies suggesting substantial experiential impact, see Buonomano and Merzenich (1998). A single case human postmortem study by Amunts, Schleicher, and Zilles (2004) found unusual cytoarchitecture in inferior frontal areas 44 and 45 in an individual with exceptional language abilities, who was fluent in 60 languages; a group study by Jacobs, Schall, and Scheibel (1993) suggests experiential effects on dendritic complexity in Wernicke's area.

3 The argument here is related to a critique of the assumption of "residual normality" in the study of developmental disorders by Thomas and Karmiloff-Smith (2002).

4 Note that this use of the term ingredient does not relate to subcomponents of language (such as phonology, morphology, syntax, etc.), but to functional domains not conventionally considered to belong to language.

References

Alexander, M. P., & Annett, M. (1996). Crossed aphasia and related anomalies of cerebral organization: Case reports and a genetic hypothesis. *Brain and Language*, 55(2), 213–239.

Amaral, D. G. (2000). The anatomical organization of the central nervous system. In E. R. Kandell, J. H. Schwartz, & T. M. Jessell (Eds.), *Principles of neural science* (4th ed., pp. 317–336). New York: McGraw-Hill.

Amunts, K., Schleicher, A., Burgel, U., Mohlberg, H., Uylings, H. B., & Zilles, K. (1999). Broca's region revisited: Cytoarchitecture and intersubject variability. *The Journal of Comparative Neurology*, *412*(2), 319–341.

Amunts, K., Schleicher, A., Ditterich, A., & Zilles, K. (2003). Broca's region: Cytoarchitectonic asymmetry and developmental changes. *The Journal of Comparative Neurology*, *465*(1), 72–89.

Amunts, K., Schleicher, A., & Zilles, K. (2004). Outstanding language competence and cytoarchitecture in Broca's speech region. *Brain and Language*, *89*(2), 346–353.

Arnott, S. R., Binns, M. A., Grady, C. L., & Alain, C. (2004). Assessing the auditory dual-pathway model in humans. *Neuroimage*, *22*(1), 401–408.

Binkofski, F., Amunts, K., Stephan, K. M., Posse, S., Schormann, T., Freund, H. J., et al. (2000). Broca's region subserves imagery of motion: A combined cytoarchitectonic and fMRI study. *Human Brain Mapping*, *11*(4), 273–285.

Binkofski, F., Buccino, G., Stephan, K. M., Rizzolatti, G., Seitz, R. J., & Freund, H. J. (1999). A parieto-premotor network for object manipulation: Evidence from neuroimaging. *Experimental Brain Research*, *128*(1–2), 210–213.

Bishop, D. V. (2002). The role of genes in the etiology of specific language impairment. *Journal of Communication Disorders*, *35*(4), 311–328.

Braitenberg, V., & Schüz, A. (1991). *Anatomy of cortex. Statistics and geometry*. Berlin: Springer.

Brett, M., Johnsrude, I. S., & Owen, A. M. (2002). The problem of functional localization in the human brain. *Nature Reviews Neuroscience*, *3*(3), 243–249.

Broca, P. (1861). Remarques sur le siège de la faculté du langage articulé, suivies d'une observation d'aphémie (perte de la parole). *Bulletins et Mémoires de la Société Anatomique de Paris*, *36*, 330–357.

Broca, P. (1866). Discussion sur la faculté du langage und aphasie traumatique. *Bulletins de la Société d'Anthropologie de Paris*, *1*, 377–385 & 396–379.

Brown, T. T., Lugar, H. M., Coalson, R. S., Miezin, F. M., Petersen, S. E., & Schlaggar, B. L. (2005). Developmental changes in human cerebral functional organization for word generation. *Cerebral Cortex*, *15*(3), 275–290.

Buccino, G., Binkofski, F., Fink, G. R., Fadiga, L., Fogassi, L., Gallese, V., et al. (2001). Action observation activates premotor and parietal areas in a somatotopic manner: An fMRI study. *The European Journal of Neuroscience*, *13*(2), 400–404.

Buccino, G., Vogt, S., Ritzl, A., Fink, G. R., Zilles, K., Freund, H. J., et al. (2004). Neural circuits underlying imitation learning of hand actions: An event-related fMRI study. *Neuron*, *42*(2), 323–334.

Buonomano, D. V., & Merzenich, M. M. (1998). Cortical plasticity: From synapses to maps. *Annual Review of Neuroscience*, *21*, 149–186.

Burton, M. W., Noll, D. C., & Small, S. L. (2001). The anatomy of auditory word processing: Individual variability. *Brain and Language*, *77*(1), 119–131.

Cabeza, R., & Nyberg, L. (2000). Imaging cognition ii: An empirical review of 275 PET and fMRI studies. *Journal of Cognitive Neuroscience*, *12*, 1–47.

Caplan, D., Alpert, N., Waters, G., & Olivieri, A. (2000). Activation of Broca's area by syntactic processing under conditions of concurrent articulation. *Human Brain Mapping*, *9*, 65–71.

Caplan, D., Hildebrandt, N., & Makris, N. (1996). Location of lesions in stroke patients with deficits in syntactic processing in sentence comprehension. *Brain, 119*, 933–949.

Catani, M., Jones, D. K., & ffytche, D. H. (2005). Perisylvian language networks of the human brain. *Annals of Neurology, 57*(1), 8–16.

Chee, M. W. L., Weekes, B., Lee, K. M., Soon, C. S., Schreiber, A., Hoon, J. J., et al. (2000). Overlap and dissociation of semantic processing of Chinese characters, English words, and pictures: Evidence from fMRI. *Neuroimage, 12*(4), 392–403.

Chen, S. H., & Desmond, J. E. (2005). Cerebrocerebellar networks during articulatory rehearsal and verbal working memory tasks. *Neuroimage, 24*(2), 332–338.

Chomsky, N. (1980). *Rules and representations.* New York: Columbia UP.

Cooke, A., Zurif, E. B., DeVita, C., Alsop, D., Koenig, P., Detre, J., et al. (2002). Neural basis for sentence comprehension: Grammatical and short-term memory components. *Human Brain Mapping, 15*(2), 80–94.

Creutzfeldt, O. D. (1977). Generality of the functional structure of the neocortex. *Naturwissenschaften, 64*(10), 507–517.

Crozier, S., Sirigu, A., Lehaericy, S., van de Moortele, P. F., Pillon, B., Grafman, J., et al. (1999). Distinct prefrontal activations in processing sequence at the sentence and script level: An fMRI study. *Neuropsychologia, 37*(13), 1469–1476.

Curtiss, S., de Bode, S., & Mathern, G. W. (2001). Spoken language outcomes after hemispherectomy: Factoring in etiology. *Brain and Language, 79*(3), 379–396.

Dronkers, N. F., Pinker, S., & Damasio, A. R. (2000). Language and the aphasias. In E. R. Kandell, J. H. Schwartz, & T. M. Jessell (Eds.), *Principles of neural science* (4th ed., pp. 1169–1187). New York: McGraw-Hill.

Duncan, J., & Owen, A. M. (2000). Common regions of the human frontal lobe recruited by diverse cognitive demands. *Trends in Neurosciences, 23*(10), 475–483.

Ewing, B., & Green, P. (2000). Analysis of expressed sequence tags indicates 35,000 human genes. *Nature Genetics, 25*(2), 232–234.

Fadiga, L., Fogassi, L., Gallese, V., & Rizzolatti, G. (2000). Visuomotor neurons: Ambiguity of the discharge or "motor" perception? *International Journal of Psychophysiology, 35*(2–3), 165–177.

Ferrari, P. F., Rozzi, S., & Fogassi, L. (2005). Mirror neurons responding to observation of actions made with tools in monkey ventral premotor cortex. *Journal of Cognitive Neuroscience, 17*(2), 212–226.

Fiez, J. A., & Raichle, M. E. (1997). Linguistic processing. In J. D. Schmahmann (Ed.), *The cerebellum and cognition* (pp. 233–254). San Diego: Academic Press.

Fincham, J. M., Carter, C. S., van Veen, V., Stenger, V. A., & Anderson, J. R. (2002). Neural mechanisms of planning: A computational analysis using event-related fMRI. *Proceedings of the National Academy of Sciences of the United States of America, 99*(5), 3346–3351.

Fisher, S. E., & Marcus, G. F. (2006). The eloquent ape: Genes, brains and the evolution of language. *Nature Reviews Genetics, 7*(1), 9–20.

Fisher, S. E., Vargha-Khadem, F., Watkins, K. E., Monaco, A. P., & Pembrey, M. E. (1998). Localisation of a gene implicated in a severe speech and language disorder. *Nature Genetics, 18*(2), 168–170.

Fodor, J. A. (1976). *The language of thought*. Hassocks (Sussex): Harvester Press.

Friederici, A. D. (2002). Towards a neural basis of auditory sentence processing. *Trends in Cognitive Sciences*, 6(2), 78–84.

Friederici, A. D., Ruschemeyer, S. A., Hahne, A., & Fiebach, C. J. (2003). The role of left inferior frontal and superior temporal cortex in sentence comprehension: Localizing syntactic and semantic processes. *Cerebral Cortex*, 13(2), 170–177.

Friedmann, N., & Grodzinksy, Y. (1997). Tense and agreement in agrammatic production: Pruning the syntactic tree. *Brain and Language*, 56, 397–425.

Gallese, V. (2003). The roots of empathy: The shared manifold hypothesis and the neural basis of intersubjectivity. *Psychopathology*, 36(4), 171–180.

Gardner, H. (1987). *The mind's new science* (2nd ed.). New York: Basic Books.

Gerardin, E., Sirigu, A., Lehericy, S., Poline, J.-B., Gaymard, B., Marsault, C., et al. (2000). Partially overlapping neural networks for real and imagined hand movements. *Cerebral Cortex*, 10(11), 1093–1104.

Goldberg, T. E., Berman, K. F., Randolph, C., Gold, J. M., & Weinberger, D. R. (1996). Isolating the mnemonic component in spatial delayed response: A controlled PET 15O-labeled water regional cerebral blood flow study in normal humans. *Neuroimage*, 3(1), 69–78.

Goodale, M. A. (2004). Perceiving the world and grasping it: Dissociations between conscious and unconscious visual processing. In M. S. Gazzaniga (Ed.), *The cognitive neurosciences* (3rd ed., pp. 1159–1172). Cambridge, MA: The MIT Press.

Goodale, M. A., & Westwood, D. A. (2004). An evolving view of duplex vision: Separate but interacting cortical pathways for perception and action. *Current Opinion in Neurobiology*, 14(2), 203–211.

Gopnik, M. (1990). Feature blindness: A case study. *Language Acquisition: A Journal of Developmental Linguistics*, 1(2), 139–164.

Gopnik, M., & Crago, M. B. (1991). Familial aggregation of a developmental language disorder. *Cognition*, 39(1), 1–50.

Grodzinsky, Y. (2000). The neurology of syntax: Language use without Broca's area. *Behavioral and Brain Sciences*, 23(1), 1–71.

Grèzes, J., & Decety, J. (2001). Functional anatomy of execution, mental simulation, observation, and verb generation of actions: A meta-analysis. *Human Brain Mapping*, 12(1), 1–19.

Hamzei, F., Rijntjes, M., Dettmers, C., Glauche, V., Weiller, C., & Büchel, C. (2003). The human action recognition system and its relationship to Broca's area: An fMRI study. *Neuroimage*, 19(3), 637–644.

Haslinger, B., Erhard, P., Weilke, F., Ceballos-Baumann, A. O., Bartenstein, P., Grafin von Einsiedel, H., et al. (2002). The role of lateral premotor-cerebellar-parietal circuits in motor sequence control: A parametric fMRI study. *Cognitive Brain Research*, 13(2), 159–168.

Heim, S. (2005). The structure and dynamics of normal language processing: Insights from neuroimaging. *Acta Neurobiologiae Experimentalis*, 65(1), 95–116.

Herholz, K., Thiel, A., Wienhard, K., Pietrzyk, U., von Stockhausen, H.-M., Karbe, H., et al. (1996). Individual functional anatomy of verb generation. *Neuroimage*, 3, 185–194.

Holland, S. K., Plante, E., Weber Byars, A., Strawsburg, R. H., Schmithorst, V. J., & Ball, W. S., Jr. (2001). Normal fMRI brain activation patterns in children performing a verb generation task. *Neuroimage, 14*(4), 837–843.

Homae, F., Hashimoto, R., Nakajima, K., Miyashita, Y., & Sakai, K. L. (2002). From perception to sentence comprehension: The convergence of auditory and visual information of language in the left inferior frontal cortex. *Neuroimage, 16*(4), 883–900.

Hubel, D. H., & Wiesel, T. N. (1968). Receptive fields and functional architecture of monkey striate cortex. *The Journal of Physiology, 195*(1), 215–243.

Hund-Georgiadis, M., Zysset, S., Weih, K., Guthke, T., & von Cramon, D. Y. (2001). Crossed nonaphasia in a dextral with left hemispheric lesions: A functional magnetic resonance imaging study of mirrored brain organization. *Stroke, 32*(11), 2703–2707.

Iacoboni, M., Woods, R. P., Brass, M., Bekkering, H., Mazziotta, J. C., & Rizzolatti, G. (1999). Cortical mechanisms of human imitation. *Science, 286*(5449), 2526–2528.

Indefrey, P., Hagoort, P., Herzog, H., Seitz, R. J., & Brown, C. M. (2001). Syntactic processing in left prefrontal cortex is independent of lexical meaning. *Neuroimage, 14*(3), 546–555.

Indefrey, P., Hellwig, F., Herzog, H., Seitz, R. J., & Hagoort, P. (2004). Neural responses to the production and comprehension of syntax in identical utterances. *Brain and Language, 89*(2), 312–319.

Jacobs, B., Schall, M., Prather, M., Kapler, E., Driscoll, L., Baca, S., et al. (2001). Regional dendritic and spine variation in human cerebral cortex: A quantitative golgi study. *Cerebral Cortex, 11*(6), 558–571.

Jacobs, B., Schall, M., & Scheibel, A. B. (1993). A quantitative dendritic analysis of Wernicke's area in humans. II. Gender, hemispheric, and environmental factors. *Journal of Comparative Neurology, 327,* 97–111.

Jessell, T. M., & Sanes, J. N. (2000). The generation and survival of nerve cells. In E. R. Kandel, J. H. Schwartz, & T. M. Jessell (Eds.), *Principles of neural science* (4th ed., pp. 1042–1062). New York: Elsevier.

Kean, M.-L. (Ed.). (1985). *Agrammatism.* Orlando: Academic Press.

Keller, T. A., Carpenter, P. A., & Just, M. A. (2001). The neural bases of sentence comprehension: A fMRI examination of syntactic and lexical processing. *Cerebral Cortex, 11*(3), 223–237.

Kemmotsu, N., Villalobos, M. E., Gaffrey, M. S., Courchesne, E., & Müller, R.-A. (2005). Activity and functional connectivity of inferior frontal cortex associated with response conflict. *Cognitive Brain Research, 24,* 335–342.

Kohler, E., Keysers, C., Umilta, M. A., Fogassi, L., Gallese, V., & Rizzolatti, G. (2002). Hearing sounds, understanding actions: Action representation in mirror neurons. *Science, 297*(5582), 846–848.

Konishi, S., Nakajima, K., Uchida, I., Kameyama, M., Nakahara, K., Sekihara, K., et al. (1998). Transient activation of inferior prefrontal cortex during cognitive set shifting. *Nature Neuroscience, 1*(1), 80–84.

Krams, M., Rushworth, M. F., Deiber, M. P., Frackowiak, R. S., & Passingham, R. E. (1998). The preparation, execution and suppression of copied movements in the human brain. *Experimental Brain Research, 120*(3), 386–398.

Lai, C. S., Fisher, S. E., Hurst, J. A., Vargha-Khadem, F., & Monaco, A. P. (2001). A forkhead-domain gene is mutated in a severe speech and language disorder. *Nature*, *413*(6855), 519–523.

Laine, M., Rinne, J. O., Krause, B. J., Tereas, M., & Sipilea, H. (1999). Left hemisphere activation during processing of morphologically complex word forms in adults. *Neuroscience Letters*, *271*(2), 85–88.

Lenartowicz, A., & McIntosh, A. R. (2005). The role of anterior cingulate cortex in working memory is shaped by functional connectivity. *Journal of Cognitive Neuroscience*, *17*(7), 1026–1042.

Liegeois, F., Connelly, A., Cross, J. H., Boyd, S. G., Gadian, D. G., Vargha-Khadem, F., et al. (2004). Language reorganization in children with early-onset lesions of the left hemisphere: An fMRI study. *Brain*, *127*(Pt. 6), 1229–1236.

MacDermot, K. D., Bonora, E., Sykes, N., Coupe, A. M., Lai, C. S., Vernes, S. C., et al. (2005). Identification of foxp2 truncation as a novel cause of developmental speech and language deficits. *American Journal of Human Genetics*, *76*(6), 1074–1080.

Marcus, G. F., & Fisher, S. E. (2003). Foxp2 in focus: What can genes tell us about speech and language? *Trends in Cognitive Sciences*, *7*(6), 257–262.

Mariotti, P., Iuvone, L., Torrioli, M. G., & Silveri, M. C. (1998). Linguistic and nonlinguistic abilities in a patient with early left hemispherectomy. *Neuropsychologia*, *36*(12), 1303–1312.

Martin, A., & Chao, L. L. (2001). Semantic memory and the brain: Structure and processes. *Current Opinion in Neurobiology*, *11*, 194–201.

Martin, A., Haxby, J. V., Lalonde, F. M., Wiggs, C. L., & Ungerleider, L. G. (1995). Discrete cortical regions associated with knowledge of color and knowledge of action. *Science*, *270*, 102–105.

Moon, C. M., Cooper, R. P., & Fifer, W. P. (1993). Two-day-olds prefer their native language. *Infant Behavior and Development*, *16*(4), 495–500.

Moon, C. M., & Fifer, W. P. (2000). Evidence of transnatal auditory learning. *Journal of Perinatology*, *20*(8, Pt. 2), S37–S44.

Moro, A., Tettamanti, M., Perani, D., Donati, C., Cappa, S. F., & Fazio, F. (2001). Syntax and the brain: Disentangling grammar by selective anomalies. *Neuroimage*, *13*, 110–118.

Mountcastle, V. B. (1997). The columnar organization of the neocortex. *Brain*, *120*(Pt. 4), 701–722.

Müller, R.-A., Behen, M. E., Rothermel, R. D., Muzik, O., Chakraborty, P. K., & Chugani, H. T. (1999). Brain organization for language in children, adolescents, and adults with left hemisphere lesion: A PET study. *Progress in Neuropsychopharmacology and Biological Psychiatry*, *23*, 657–668.

Müller, R.-A., Rothermel, R. D., Behen, M. E., Muzik, O., Chakraborty, P. K., & Chugani, H. T. (1999). Language organization in patients with early and late left hemisphere lesion: A PET study. *Neuropsychologia*, *37*, 545–557.

Müller, R.-A., Rothermel, R. D., Behen, M. E., Muzik, O., Mangner, T. J., & Chugani, H. T. (1998). Differential patterns of language and motor reorganization following early left hemisphere lesion: A PET study. *Archives of Neurology*, *55*, 1113–1119.

Müller, R.-A., Watson, C. E., Muzik, O., Chakraborty, P. K., & Chugani, H. T. (1998). Motor organization following intrauterine middle cerebral artery stroke: A PET study. *Pediatric Neurology, 19,* 294–298.

Nishitani, N., & Hari, R. (2002). Viewing lip forms: Cortical dynamics. *Neuron, 36*(6), 1211–1220.

Nishitani, N., Schurmann, M., Amunts, K., & Hari, R. (2005). Broca's region: From action to language. *Physiology (Bethesda), 20,* 60–69.

O'Leary, D. D., & Nakagawa, Y. (2002). Patterning centers, regulatory genes and extrinsic mechanisms controlling arealization of the neocortex. *Current Opinion in Neurobiology, 12*(1), 14–25.

Pallas, S. L. (2001). Intrinsic and extrinsic factors that shape neocortical specification. *Trends in Neurosciences, 24*(7), 417–423.

Pedersen, P. M., Jørgensen, H. S., Nakayama, H., Raaschou, H. O., & Olsen, T. S. (1995). Aphasia in acute stroke: Incidence, determinants, and recovery. *Annals of Neurology, 38,* 659–666.

Pinker, S. (2001). Talk of genetics and vice versa. *Nature, 413*(6855), 465–466.

Puce, A., & Perrett, D. (2003). Electrophysiology and brain imaging of biological motion. *Philosophical Transactions of the Royal Society of London. Series B, Biological Sciences, 358*(1431), 435–445.

Rakic, P., Ang, E. S. B. C., & Breunig, J. (2004). Setting the stage for cognition: Genesis of the primate cerebral cortex. In M. S. Gazzaniga (Ed.), *The cognitive neurosciences* (3rd ed., pp. 33–49). Cambridge, MA: MIT Press.

Rauschecker, J. P., & Tian, B. (2000). Mechanisms and streams for processing of "what" and "where" in auditory cortex. *Proceedings of the National Academy of Sciences of the United States of America, 97*(22), 11800–11806.

Rizzolatti, G., & Arbib, M. A. (1998). Language within our grasp [see comments]. *Trends in Neurosciences, 21*(5), 188–194.

Rizzolatti, G., & Craighero, L. (2004). The mirror-neuron system. *Annual Review of Neuroscience, 27,* 169–192.

Rizzolatti, G., Fogassi, L., & Gallese, V. (2002). Motor and cognitive functions of the ventral premotor cortex. *Current Opinion in Neurobiology, 12*(2), 149–154.

Rizzolatti, G., & Matelli, M. (2003). Two different streams form the dorsal visual system: Anatomy and functions. *Experimental Brain Research, 153*(2), 146–157.

Romanski, L. M., Bates, J. F., & Goldman-Rakic, P. S. (1999). Auditory belt and parabelt projections to the prefrontal cortex in the rhesus monkey. *Journal of Comparative Neurology, 403*(2), 141–157.

Rubia, K., Russell, T., Overmeyer, S., Brammer, M. J., Bullmore, E. T., Sharma, T., et al. (2001). Mapping motor inhibition: Conjunctive brain activations across different versions of go/no-go and stop tasks. *Neuroimage, 13*(2), 250–261.

Saussure, F. (1915/1972). *Cours de linguistique générale.* Paris: Payot.

Schlaggar, B., & O'Leary, D. (1991). Potential of visual cortex to develop an array of functional units unique to somatosensory cortex. *Science, 252,* 1556–1560.

Seghier, M. L., Lazeyras, F., Pegna, A. J., Annoni, J. M., Zimine, I., Mayer, E., et al. (2004). Variability of fMRI activation during a phonological and semantic language task in healthy subjects. *Human Brain Mapping*, *23*(3), 140–155.

Semenza, C., Delazer, M., Bertella, L., Grana, A., Mori, I., Conti, F. M., et al. (2006). Is math lateralized on the same side as language? Right hemisphere aphasia and mathematical abilities. *Neuroscience Letters*, *406*(3), 285–288.

Signoret, J. L., Castaigne, P., Lhermitte, F., Abelanet, R., & Lavorel, P. (1984). Rediscovery of Leborgne's brain: Anatomical description with ct scan. *Brain and Language*, *22*(2), 303–319.

Simonds, R. J., & Scheibel, A. B. (1989). The postnatal development of the motor speech area: A preliminary study. *Brain and Language*, *37*, 42–58.

Smith, S. (2001). Overview of fMRI analysis. In P. Jezzard, P. Mathews, & S. Smith (Eds.), *Functional MRI: An introduction to methods* (pp. 215–227). Oxford: Oxford University Press.

Staudt, M., Lidzba, K., Grodd, W., Wildgruber, D., Erb, M., & Krageloh-Mann, I. (2002). Right-hemispheric organization of language following early left-sided brain lesions: Functional MRI topography. *Neuroimage*, *16*(4), 954–967.

Stromswold, K., Caplan, D., Alpert, N., & Rauch, S. (1996). Localization of syntactic comprehension by positron emission tomography. *Brain and Language*, *52*, 452–473.

Tettamanti, M., Buccino, G., Saccuman, M. C., Gallese, V., Danna, M., Scifo, P., et al. (2005). Listening to action-related sentences activates fronto-parietal motor circuits. *Journal of Cognitive Neuroscience*, *17*(2), 273–281.

Thomas, M., & Karmiloff-Smith, A. (2002). Are developmental disorders like cases of adult brain damage? Implications from connectionist modeling. *Behavioral and Brain Sciences*, *25*(6), 727–750.

Thompson, P. M., Cannon, T. D., Narr, K. L., van Erp, T., Poutanen, V. P., Huttunen, M., et al. (2001). Genetic influences on brain structure. *Nature Neuroscience*, *4*(12), 1253–1258.

Thompson-Schill, S. L., D'Esposito, M., Aguirre, G. K., & Farah, M. J. (1997). Role of left inferior prefrontal cortex in retrieval of semantic knowledge: A reevaluation. *Proceedings of the National Academy of Sciences of the United States of America*, *94*(26), 14792–14797.

Tomblin, J. B., & Buckwalter, P. R. (1994). Studies of genetics of specific language impairment. In R. V. Watkins & M. L. Rice (Eds.), *Specific language impairments in children* (pp. 17–34). Baltimore: Paul H. Brookes.

Toni, I., Schluter, N. D., Josephs, O., Friston, K., & Passingham, R. E. (1999). Signal-, set- and movement-related activity in the human brain: An event-related fMRI study [published erratum appears in cereb cortex 1999 mar;9(2):196]. *Cerebral Cortex*, *9*(1), 35–49.

Tzourio, N., Crivello, F., Mellet, E., Nkanga-Ngila, B., & Mazoyer, B. (1998). Functional anatomy of dominance for speech comprehension in left-handers vs right-handers. *Neuroimage*, *8*(1), 1–16.

Ungerleider, L. G., & Mishkin, M. (1982). Two cortical visual systems. In D. J. Ingle, M. A. Goodale, & R. J. W. Mansfeld (Eds.), *Analysis of visual behavior* (pp. 549–586). Cambridge, MA: MIT Press.

Vanlancker-Sidtis, D. (2004). When only the right hemisphere is left: Studies in language and communication. *Brain and Language*, *91*(2), 199–211.

Vargha-Khadem, F., Carr, L. C., Isaacs, E., Brett, E., Adams, C., & Mishkin, M. (1997). Onset of speech after left hemispherectomy in a nine-year-old boy. *Brain*, *120*, 159–182.

Vargha-Khadem, F., & Mishkin, M. (1997). Speech and language outcome after hemispherectomy in childhood. In I. Tuxhorn, H. Holthausen, & H. E. Boenigk (Eds.), *Paediatric epilepsy syndromes and their surgical treatment* (pp. 774–784). Eastleigh, UK: John Libbey.

Vargha-Khadem, F., Watkins, K. E., Alcock, K., Fletcher, P., & Passingham, R. E. (1995). Praxic and nonverbal cognitive deficits in a large family with a genetically transmitted speech and language disorder. *Procedures of the National Academy of Science USA*, *92*, 930–933.

Voegtlin, T., & Dominey, P. F. (2005). Linear recursive distributed representations. *Neural Networks*, *18*(7), 878–895.

Watkins, K. E., Dronkers, N. F., & Vargha-Khadem, F. (2002). Behavioural analysis of an inherited speech and language disorder: Comparison with acquired aphasia. *Brain*, *125*(Pt. 3), 452–464.

Watkins, K. E., Vargha-Khadem, F., Ashburner, J., Passingham, R. E., Connelly, A., Friston, K. J., et al. (2002). MRI analysis of an inherited speech and language disorder: Structural brain abnormalities. *Brain*, *125*(Pt. 3), 465–478.

Wernicke, C. (1874). *Der aphasische symptomenkomplex* (repr. 1974 ed.). Berlin: Springer.

Xiong, J., Rao, S., Jerabek, P., Zamarripa, F., Woldorff, M., Lancaster, J., et al. (2000). Intersubject variability in cortical activations during a complex language task. *Neuroimage*, *12*(3), 326–339.

12

LANGUAGE, INNATENESS, AND UNIVERSALS

ANDY CLARK AND JENNIFER B. MISYAK

12.1. Universals and the Brain

If one were to look for the neurobiological instantiations of language universals in the human brain, what kinds of candidate possibilities should one consider? In linguistics, theoretical biology, and philosophy of mind, we find proponents of Universal Grammar, genetic determinism, symbolic representationalism, and functionalism. In these cases, traditional approaches would focus upon such matters as the hardwiring of an inborn language apparatus, the maturation of a genetic "blueprint," or a structural isomorphism between symbolic mental atoms and combinatorial form relations. In many philosophical treatments, such views are entwined with an image of innate mental knowledge encoded in a propositional quasi-linguistic format (e.g., the "Language of Thought" hypothesis; Fodor, 1975). Such a plethora of proposals[1] reflects a tendency to regard innate cognitive endowments as implying a preexisting, often high, degree of structural and/or functional specification within the cerebral cortex, typically without much recourse to experience-based learning (i.e., positing little more than normal maturation or minimal "triggering").

Yet, elsewhere in contemporary psychology and allied interdisciplines,[2] neuroconstructivist perspectives (cf. Karmiloff-Smith, 1998; Mareschal et al., 2007) encourage us to temper our empiricist leanings (as classically imputed to Locke, 1690/1964) with an appreciation of the power of simple biases, subsequently influenced by developmental processes, occurring at multiple interacting levels. This stance dovetails, too, with the conceptualization of internal knowledge representation advanced by connectionist theories of the mind. As connectionism blurs the classical distinction between architecture and representation, it eschews the traditional expectation that mental content be *propositionally* specifiable in form and, instead, describes knowledge along *pattern-completing* lines. What one might potentially seek at the biological level need not be either architecturally or representationally innate specification. Instead, one might look to scenarios whereby *small initial biases* might nonetheless make a crucial difference to some complex interplay of processing factors—potentially leading to the emergence of reliable behavior patterns (including complex, species-universal ones), given a range of predictable (external) inputs and some initial (general) state.[3] A possible parallel in developmental psychobiology would be the example model afforded by probabilistic epigenesis (Gottlieb, 1998), in which the development and environment of an organism interacts with responsive genetic factors amid an assumed backdrop of species-typical experiences. On these accounts, germinal parameters (including timing variations) and gently biased architectures could in principle serve as possible sources for the biological bases of linguistic universals.

Accordingly, we shall not explore all the proposed options for neurobiological realizers of presumed language universals. Instead, drawing upon connectionist work in cognitive science and offering philosophical arguments sympathetic to the connectionist framework, we aim to draw attention to this less visited subspace of possibilities. By considering whether universals could be intrinsic in this subtler manner, we also develop some insights that may ultimately point toward another stronger conclusion, namely, that diverse natural languages ubiquitously embody certain regularities because they themselves are possessed by humans with distinctive cognitive developmental profiles. Before arriving there, though, as the center frame for casting these ideas into neuroscientific relief, we begin by closely engaging the assessment laid out by Müller in Chapter 11.

12.2. A Closer Look: The Argument by Müller[4]

Müller develops an argument of the following form:

1. If language universals are to be real, genetically determined features of the mind, and not simply convenient descriptions of certain regularities in human languages, then they had better show up as distinctive, and genetically controlled, features of the brain.
2. If language universals are going to show up in the brain, they are expected to show up as some kind of genetically controlled language-oriented specificity of neural structure or function (linguistic specificity of "architecture or processing mode").
3. But language universals do not show up in this way (as some kind of language-oriented specificity of neural structure or function), not even if we look at the best suspects such as Broca's area (or better, area 44/45).

Instead, we find a convergence of some important processing characteristics and pathways, none of them specifically linguistic in nature.

4. Hence, there are no genetically controlled language-specific elements in the brain, and no "linguistic universals" in the sense described in premise 1.

At first glance, it looks as if all the work in this argument is done by premise 3. And indeed, it is premise 3 that Müller sets out mainly to defend. He convincingly shows, for example, that Broca's area, though often depicted as specialized for syntax, does not meet the innateness criteria (genetically controlled linguistic specificity of architecture or processing mode) set out in premise 2. In the case of Broca's area, the claim of linguistic specificity is undermined by neuroimaging results that show much wider involvement, for example, in translating visual percepts into motor plans, and by the fact that the area exhibits no language-specific cellular organization, or "cytoarchitecture" (other cortical areas can support language if the need arises, the typical choice being the right hemisphere equivalent area). What both those areas have in common, Müller argues, is (not a special cytoarchitecture but) a kind of language-favoring developmental positioning. They are locations at which several of the key nonlinguistic elements implicated in language use converge. These key nonlinguistic elements include circuitry-supporting imitation, working memory, joint attention, object perception, and capacities of multimodal integration. What all this suggests, Müller concludes, is that (in the test case of Broca's area) the area is not innately specialized for language. But despite this, it is no surprise that important language skills typically come, over developmental time, to depend on it.

The reasoning is clear enough. One doesn't have an innately specified beer-glass-lifting muscle group. But it is no surprise, given what it takes to lift a beer glass, that the task recruits the resources it does. Ditto, Müller is suggesting, for language. Perhaps (to generalize the result beyond the specific example of Broca's area) we exhibit no innate specialization for language at all. Language universals, insofar as they exist in the brain at all, may do so only as the emergent upshots of the activity of multiple nonlanguage-specific processing features.

12.3. An Alternative View

We should concede premise 1 but take another look at premise 2. Premise 2 states that if language universals are going to show up in the brain, they must show up as some kind of genetically controlled language-oriented specificity of neural structure or function (linguistic specificity of "architecture or processing mode"). But does looking at specificity of architecture or processing mode really exhaust the options for genetically controlled language-specific adaptation? Why must genetically controlled language-specific adaptation take such a structural form? Why (to take a concrete example) couldn't the emergence of language universals be genetically controlled by, for example, some tweaks of timing that (in the normal linguistic environment) favor the acquisition of languages exhibiting certain structural forms?

Examples of such subtle modes of adaptation are certainly available. Elman et al. (1996) develop several case studies that demonstrate how the provision of a gently biased neural architecture can lead, in rich developmental and ecological context, to the reliable (and reliably neurally located) emergence of specific bodies of knowledge. One such study involves the development of knowledge about human face structure. Here, some high-contrast blob detectors filter visual input so that (in normal ecological context) faces dominate the training of a downstream neural network, and a face area reliably emerges (Elman et al., 1996, pp. 115–118). Similarly, gentle biases of timing (e.g., the staged, wavelike, onset of plasticity in specific neural subsystems) could, in principle, lead to the reliable emergence (in the normal ecological context of exposure to language) of, say, a neural area specializing in some aspect of syntactic processing. Even if that area did many other things as well, it might still be "language specific" in that the selective pressure for that tweak of timing was the need to rapidly and reliably acquire some key linguistic skill.

Our question is, why shouldn't this count as the discovery of a genetically controlled language-specific endowment? This would be a kind of "minimal nativism" (Clark, 1993).

12.4. Objections and Another Direction

Someone might object that, in the kinds of cases described, the genetically controlled element does not do all (or even most of) the language-supporting work. But there is no reason to insist that the genes do all (or even most of) the work. Instead, the genetic tweak may rely on a wide variety of organism-external factors and forces to bring about its effect. Thus, we can follow Wheeler and Clark (1999) in depicting genes as differences selected to make a difference, against the enabling backdrop of a rich developmental and ecological context. To take a technological parallel, for instance, consider a LISP program that one might use for doing tax returns (among other things), where the expressions, commands, and symbols in the script must be evaluated and implemented by a host of external functions, utilities, and structures on one's computer that the script references and depends upon. Such a program only specifies a process that yields the desired result (in this instance, of telling you how much money to part with), given the context of a rich backdrop of assumed background processes that make available various operations of transposition, concatenation, and so on, among script elements. In this sense, then, there are no *self-contained* codes or programs at all, so it's hardly surprising that genes turn out not to be self-contained codes or programs either! As but one biological exemplification, within the prenatal environment, epigenetic factors are understood to provide for differential (and malleable) methylation patterns of otherwise identical genes; and given different ecological contexts as well, the interpretation or expression of those very same genetic complexes may be vastly different (see also Chapter 13). The search for genetically specified language universals needs to be open then to the very wide and subtle range of ways that nature might have found to encourage skills with language, and to effectively gift an organism with unearned knowledge of the linguistic world.

Having said all that, however, we would like to conclude by suggesting that, even when one takes into account the range of possible subtle modes of influence we have been canvassing, there may still be good reason to agree with Müller's conclusion. That is to say, despite the lacuna in the argument itself, it may indeed prove to be the case that there are no language-specific adaptations. For, it may be that the real story proceeds pretty much in the opposite direction to the one stressed by the fans of linguistic nativism.

We have in mind the thought (see Chapter 3) that languages can be adapted to the idiosyncrasies of users as much as users to the idiosyncrasies of language. Thus, insofar as there are subtle features of human development (the timing of certain kinds of plasticity and the onset of certain important nonlinguistic capacities) that favor the rapid and reliable acquisition of linguistic skill, it may, to a large degree, be the languages that have adapted to exploit such (preexisting) biases rather than the biases that have developed to support language. According to this alternative story, the languages that we have may have been tuned and selected so as to be preferentially acquirable by beings whose cognitive and developmental profile is like our own. Successful languages would then be Human Acquisition Devices (HADs).

Such an account need not invoke language universals though it can accommodate their attenuated existence, as biases to which languages adapt (e.g., as suggested by Kirby & Christiansen, 2003). But crucially, such human-specific adaptation would situate these features more squarely within the languages themselves as reflections of human biases realized by biological brains (in interaction with their environments). Deciding whether universals are realized in this manner requires an appraisal of relevant evidence using a more open characterization (e.g., as "statistical tendencies with varying degrees of universality" [Christiansen & Chater, 2008], rather than fundamental properties derived from a system of formal constraints). Within the larger cognitive scientific landscape, the alternative direction, we are only sketching resonates with an externalist and dynamical conception of the mind, one that extends the cognitive reach of brain processes beyond the body and out into the impinging world. Seen from this bird's-eye view, a vision of language commonalities inhering "outside" of the brain, either as imprinted upon socioculturally transmitted products and/or distributed among interacting networks of minds spanning across ambiguous boundaries, appears no less unnatural than (and may even be seen as the logical complement or extension of) the search for realizers of such universals within the individual human brain.

So now, after casting a wide metaphorical net over our topic by venturing from tiny brain parameters to the all-encompassing world in a matter of mere pages (!) we can see that the distinctions made while deciding whether universals could be accorded real existence in human biological wetware—that is, those concerning language specificity of origins, temporal dynamics of onset/development, and direction of adaptation—may prove equally important on this larger stage. Thus, we may ask

Do language [universals] require a linguistically-specific neuroarchitectural genesis—or may they be "specific" in another sense, possibly arising from non-language-specific foundations and biases? How should we best construe the relations between epigenome, phenotype, and environment (and their complex timing interactions) in supporting the manifestation of language [universals]? With regard to language [universal] patterns and language users, in which direction does adaptation primarily flow?

We began by briefly considering whether linguistic universals could result from a minimally native endowment of the human brain, informed by an appreciation of the subtle ways this could unfold over developmental time. In so doing, the larger questions we have stumbled across along the way may shed some light on the evolution of language and the features promoting its persistence and use. The postulated *language/human universals* suggest a quest that looks both inward and outward, to the biological brain and to the larger cultural and developmental wholes, in which it participates.

Key Further Readings

Clark (1993) develops a theoretical treatment of the minimally nativist position, or "minimal rationalism," explored here. This account provides a nuanced reinterpretation of the nature of innate knowledge, set in contrast to classical (and formal linguistic) nativist views in philosophy. The theoretical subspace of minimal nativism is further described as existing along a continuum of varying degrees of connectionist nativisms, in ways made precise by reference to the details of connectionist computational architectures.

For further discussion of how developmental processes working in tandem with small intrinsic biases and low-level perceptual constraints may lead to the emergence of "higher-level" cognitive competencies, Elman et al.'s *Rethinking Innateness: A Connectionist Perspective on Development* (1996) is an invaluable resource. As the title implies, this book also reconsiders the notion of "innateness" from a connectionist stance, fleshed out with arguments, modeling examples, and neurobiological case studies, and including an informative chapter on brain development and sections that address human language (e.g., Chapters 3 and 7).

On the interpretation of genetic influence deployed in this chapter, the paper by Wheeler and Clark (1999) offers three criteria for internal (genic) representation and discusses how genes can have special explanatory relevance in developmental/behavioral accounts despite the complexity of codetermining interactions among coupled organisms and environments. Importantly, genes are not to be construed as self-contained programs, but as additional biases embedded within a normative biochemical and ecological context.

Finally, on the important question of where language universals might fit within the "big picture" of human language evolution, we recommend the review article by Christiansen and Kirby (2003). This paper surveys existing controversies and trends in the field, with special attention to the multiple timescales and complex interactive dynamics (spanning individual learning, cultural transmission, and biological evolution) that underpin the evolution of natural languages.

Notes

1 Other proposals in this area include Calvin and Bickerton (2000), Chomsky (1980), Crain (1991), Lightfoot (1989), and others.

2 Insights from developmental cognitive neuroscience and artificial neural network approaches are usefully combined in Quartz (1999) and Quartz and Sejnowski (1997).

3 These learning (i.e., processing) changes could also involve alteration or reorganization of the architecture and of the representational resources of a system.

4 This short paper is based on an original commentary by Clark, on Ralph-Axel Müller "Language universals in the brain: How linguistic are they?" presented at the Language Universals Symposium, Cornell University, May 2004.

References

Calvin, W. H., & Bickerton, D. (2000). *Lingua ex machina: Reconciling Darwin and Chomsky with the human brain*. Cambridge, MA: MIT Press.

Chomsky, N. (1980). *Rules and representations*. New York: Columbia University Press.

Christiansen, M. H., & Chater, N. (2008). Language as shaped by the brain. *Behavioral and Brain Sciences, 31*(5), 489–509.

Christiansen, M. H., & Kirby, S. (2003). Language evolution: Consensus and controversies. *Trends in Cognitive Sciences, 7*, 300–307.

Clark, A. (1993). Minimal rationalism. *Mind, 102*, 587–610.

Crain, S. (1991). Language acquisition in the absence of experience. *Behavioral and Brain Sciences, 14*, 597–611.

Elman, J. L., Bates, E. A., Johnson, M. H., Karmiloff-Smith, A., Parisi, D., & Plunkett, K. (1996). *Rethinking innateness: A connectionist perspective on development.* Cambridge, MA: MIT Press.

Fodor, J. A. (1975). *The language of thought.* Cambridge, MA: Harvard University Press.

Gottlieb, G. (1998). Normally occurring environmental and behavioral influences on gene activity: From central dogma to probabilistic epigenesis. *Psychological Review, 105,* 792–802.

Karmiloff-Smith, A. (1998). Development itself is the key to understanding developmental disorders. *Trends in Cognitive Sciences, 2,* 389–398.

Kirby, S., & Christiansen, M. H. (2003). From language learning to language evolution. In M. H. Christiansen & S. Kirby (Eds.), *Language evolution* (pp. 272–294). Oxford, UK: Oxford University Press.

Lightfoot, D. (1989). The child's trigger experience: Degree-0 learnability. *Behavioral and Brain Sciences, 12,* 321–334.

Locke, J. (1964). *An essay concerning human understanding.* Cleveland: World. (Original work published 1690).

Mareschal, D., Johnson, M. H., Sirois, S., Spratling, M. W., Thomas, M. S. C., & Westermann, G. (2007). *Neuroconstructivism: How the brain constructs cognition.* Oxford: Oxford University Press.

Quartz, S. (1999). The constructivist brain. *Trends in Cognitive Sciences, 3,* 48–57.

Quartz, S., & Sejnowski, T. (1997). The neural basis of cognitive development: A constructivist manifesto. *Behavioral and Brain Sciences, 20,* 537–596.

Wheeler, M., & Clark, A. (1999). Genic representation: Reconciling content and causal complexity. *British Journal for the Philosophy of Science, 50,* 103–135.

13

EVOLUTION, DEVELOPMENT, AND EMERGING UNIVERSALS

BARBARA L. FINLAY

B emusement is this biologist's response when straying into cognitive territory regarding its denizens prospecting for the universals of language and cognition. What could they be looking for, and what would the demonstration of a universal feature of language learning signify to them? If the language prospectors believe the world to be unstructured, the vehicles of perception and production unlimited, the content of communication, and the evolutionary possibilities of the brain relevant to communication unconstrained, then the appearance of "language universals" in independent language learners would be a remarkable and illuminating finding. Some special hardware in all the language learners or users must have been installed. But if any aspect of the world is structured, if available information has predictable content or history, or if information-processing capacities were limited, universals could arise from any or all of these sources, if we may draw parallels with other biological information-transmission devices. No doubt, though, features of universal structure would be a good point to start from in the quest for sources of organization in language. Some recognized universals in the organization of the genome, body plan, and basic physiology have served this purpose in biology, and they present some interesting parallels with language universals.

Scientific fields are rich sources of metaphor for each other, and rather than indulge in academic handwringing over the imprecision of what is signified by terms like "universal" or "constraint" or "module" or "adaptation" across fields, I would advocate leaping in now and sorting out later. Schrödinger's cat, for example, as a vehicle for the concept of the effects of observation on the observed, has intruded usefully in areas as diverse as the biological nature of consciousness to research in the effectiveness of psychotherapies without the unnecessary intrusion of quantum mechanics. If some developmental, cognitive, or linguistic operation proves

261

to be reminiscent of the action of Hox genes in setting up the body plan, if only in the most metaphorical sense, for example, perhaps we'll save ourselves some work.

Are there any instructive generalities that have emerged in the examination of universals in basic biology? Researchers and theorists in language evolution and in evolutionary biology (Buss & Schmitt, 1993; Chomsky, 1975; Cosmides et al., 1995) have argued explicitly that universals betray a genetic source of constraint. An overview of organismal biology, however, does not confirm that the presence of a universal feature either within or across species betrays a single source or type of source, whether an overwhelming environmental regularity or a genetically selected device (Jablonka & Lamb, 2005). Nevertheless, recent progress in evolutionary biology very much puts universal structure in the organismal organization as the centerpiece of a new discipline, the study of evolution and development together, "evo-devo" (Gerhart & Kirschner, 1997; Kirschner & Gerhart, 2005). The developmental scaffolding of the body plan, the fundamental physiology of cells, and the rules for hooking up neurons are shockingly similar in worms, wasps, whales, and women (and men). The basic core of organizational genes, Hox genes, which produce the fundamental head-to-tail polarization of the embryo contains eight genes unrolled in strict but overlapping sequence, duplicated four times; construction and degradation of lipids alone requires over 300 catalytic enzymes; the "wiring diagram" of the cat cortex, a cortex of moderate size, contains about 60 areas with about 1200 connections between them (Scannell, Blakemore, & Young, 1995). In fact, one of the battlefields of evolutionary biology and creation "science" is whether such universal networks are irreducibly complex and require a singular point of intelligent creation. The arguments for intelligent design from irreducible complexity bear an uncomfortable similarity to that originally posited for the necessity of a genetically specified universal grammar (Chomsky, 1975), and more current proposals for language development and evolution that posit multiple sources for language's complex structure are essentially asserting that any complex structure in biology must be decomposable (Elman et al., 1996; Fisher & Marcus, 2006; Pinker & Jackendoff, Chapter 7).

Such elaborate networks, however, should give any scientist pause. The oft-quoted statement by Darwin on the eye (1882, p. 143), in this case about a structure with an apparent excess of adaptive detail, is the prototypical example:

> To suppose that the eye, with all its inimitable contrivances for adjusting the focus to different distances, for admitting different amounts of light, and for the correction of spherical and chromatic aberration, could have formed by natural selection, seems, I freely confess, absurd in the highest degree possible.

The first response to such overcomplex diagrams is often an intellectual version of terror management, involving either reductive denial of the problem on the one hand or appeal to content-free formalizations on the other. A number of persistent intellects have taken Darwin's specific challenge, and the results are exceptionally encouraging (Fernald, 2004; Land & Nilsson, 2001). We now know with some confidence how many separate times image-forming eyes have appeared, how "intermediate" forms of photoreception are adaptive in their own right, something of how common aspects of the genome are used in diverse species to produce species-typical eyes, and so on, in much detail. Language, given its briefer stay on earth, is probably not more complex than eyes and vision, or oxidative physiology.

Principals have emerged from such studies of evolving networks and body plans that should be of much use in thinking about evolved components of language. The reader is directed to several current books that can lay these ideas out in the space and detail they require, notably Kirschner and Gerhart's *The Plausibility of Life* (2005), which takes on directly the problem of underlying structure in complex evolved circuits, and Jablonka and Lamb's *Evolution in Four Dimensions* (2005), which discusses the propagation of information structures past those directly encoded in the genome, by interaction with epigenetic, environmental and social structure. I will mention a few ideas as potential examples from these rich sources.

First, the genome does not evolve by a process of continuous modification and elaboration of a single substrate away from its original state (Gerhart & Kirschner, 1997). One of the major forms of genetic evolution is duplication, and following that, modification and elaboration of some of the doubled substrate. Duplications range from parts of genes to the entire genome, with vigorous evolutionary radiations often associated with massive duplications. The benefit to evolving systems is that initial function is need not be discarded nor overwritten, but can co-exist in parallel with functional modifications in the existing genome. Systematic examination of possible sources for such exaptations in the realm of language and cognition should be further encouraged. Edelman (1998) has taken essentially such an exaptation position, noting the structural similarities of the problems of visual form recognition and language processing, and proposing language may exploit aspects of the computational problem already solved in vision. The genome represents its instructions in a massively parallel way; finding an organizational similarity in the massively parallel wiring of the cortex allows some freer thinking about the advantages of this kind of organizational plan.

Second, a set of instructions as represented in genes, or expressed in epigenetic processes becomes nonsensical out of the context in which they evolved. Selection and adaptation properly refer to this whole complex of information, not to genes alone (Jablonka & Lamb, 2005). Developing organisms continuously require information and often instruction about the nature of life they are to encounter, from biochemical milieu to the structure of sensory information, to the nature of the social world. Identical genomes in only slightly varying environments can produce completely different morphological and behavioral phenotypes: consider the social insects. In the case of language, studying the properties of the adult speaker independent from the instructional environment makes unusually little sense (Goldstein, King, & West, 2003).

Third, variation in components and scaling of biological systems is expected, and the responses to normal variation and scaling are typically graceful (Finlay, Silveira, & Reichenbach, 2005). Because evolved systems carry the residue of commonly encountered challenges, in both the nature of developmental programs that have survived and in how they are implemented at various scales, individual variation gives more insight into fundamental mechanisms used by the genome than one might guess. The expression of individual variation after millions of years of evolution is not random, but highly structured. Because language is a species singularity, and because of an initial, generally held egalitarian view that every individual mastering a language must command the same complex structure as any other, the language competence of different users of the same language has perhaps been treated as more monolithic than it may be. If biology instructs, there will be useful information in the variations of individual language users that can give evidence about the absent information of cross-species variation. The permutations of language competence in specific disorders, such as autism, or in individuals with specific sensory or neural deficits is already proving a source of insight into the various routes to language competence, but the dissection of "normal" variation should supply still more.

Overall, if language were approached as another example of a complex biological system, more direct progress could be made toward understanding it. Little effort is wasted debating whether there are human-specific adaptations in the eye, or in oxidative physiology: of course there are! But such adaptations must take their place and be understood in a much vaster array of existing mechanisms and evolutionary history serving the normal development of morphology and physiology. Cognition and language seem unlikely to be fundamentally different.

Key Further Readings

A good introduction to the emerging field of evo-devo is Kirschner and Gerhart's *The Plausibility of Life: Resolving Darwin's Dilemma* (2005), which systematically examines the kind of organizational structure found in evolving systems. Jablonka and Lamb in *Evolution in Four Dimensions* (2005) lay out an emerging new view of evolving systems, in which conservation of information is no longer posited to be a function solely of the genes, but a system distributed between cellular, niche, environmental, and behavioral/social sources.

References

Buss, D. M., & Schmitt, D. P. (1993). Sexual strategies theory: An evolutionary perspective on human mating. *Psychological Review, 100*, 204–232.

Chomsky, N. (1975). *Reflections on language*. New York: Pantheon.

Cosmides, L., & Tooby, J. (1995). Beyond intuition and instinct blindness: Toward an evolutionary rigorous cognitive science. In J. Mehler & S. Franck (Eds.), *Cognition on cognition* (pp. 69–108). Bradford Books Cambridge, MA: MIT Press.

Darwin, C. (1882). *The origin of species by means of natural selection* (6th ed., p. 143). London: John Murray.

Edelman, S. (1998). Representation is representation of similarities. *Behavioral and Brain Sciences, 21*, 449–498.

Elman, J.L., Bates, E.A., Johnson, M.H., Karmiloff-Smith, A., Parisi, D., & Plunkett, K. (1996). *Rethinking innateness: A connectionist perspective on development*. Cambridge, MA: MIT Press.

Fernald, R. D. (2004). Eyes: Variety, development and evolution. *Brain, Behavior, and Evolution, 64*, 141–147.

Finlay, B. L., Silveira, L. C. L., & Reichenbach, A. (2005) Comparative aspects of visual system development. In J. Kremers (Ed.), *The structure, function and evolution of the primate visual system* (pp. 37–72). West Sussex, England: John Wiley and Sons.

Fisher, S. E., & Marcus, G.F. (2006). The eloquent ape: Genes, brains, and the evolution of language. *Nature Reviews Genetics, 7*, 10–20.

Gerhart, J., & Kirschner, M. (1997). *Cells, embryos and evolution*. Malden, MA: Blackwell Science.

Goldstein, M. H., King, A. P., & West, M. (2003). Social interaction shapes babbling: Testing parallels between birdsong and speech. *Proceedings of the National Academy of Sciences of the United States of America, 100*, 8030–8035.

Jablonka, E., & Lamb, M. (2005). *Evolution in four dimensions*. Cambridge, MA: MIT Press.

Kirschner, M. W., & Gerhart, J. C. (2005). *The plausibility of life: Resolving Darwin's dilemma*. Yale University Press: New Haven.

Land, M., & Nilsson, D.-E. (2001). *Animal eyes*. Oxford: Oxford University Press.

Scannell, J. W., Blakemore, C., & Young, J. (1995). Analysis of connectivity in the cat cerebral cortex. *Journal of Neuroscience, 15*, 1463–1483.

14

ON THE NECESSITY OF AN INTERDISCIPLINARY APPROACH TO LANGUAGE UNIVERSALS

Florencia Reali and Morten H. Christiansen

14.1. Toward an Interdisciplinary Theory of Language Universals

There is considerable variation across the languages of the world, nonetheless it is possible to discern common patterns in how languages are structured and used. The underlying source of this variation as well as the nature of crosslinguistic universals is the focus of much debate across different areas of linguistics. Some linguists suggest that language universals derive from the inner workings of Universal Grammar (UG)—a set of innate constraints on language acquisition (e.g., see Bever, Chapter 6; Hornstein & Boeckx, Chapter 5; and Pinker & Jackendoff, Chapter 7). Others see universals as emerging from patterns of language use, primarily because of processes taking place over diachronic rather than synchronic timescales (Bybee, Chapter 2; Hawkins, Chapter 4). Yet, other linguists propose that universals may derive from some combination of language acquisition and use (Hurford, Chapter 3). Even within the same theoretical linguistic framework, there is often little agreement about what the exact universals are. For example, when surveying specific universals proposed by different proponents of UG, Tomasello (2004) found little overlap between proposed universals.

We believe that a resolution to this debate is unlikely to be forthcoming from within linguistics itself; instead, it must be sought by adopting an interdisciplinary approach to language universals, integrating linguistic insights with those of other relevant disciplines. Thus, we need to understand the possible biological bases for language universals (see Clark & Misyak, Chapter 12; Finlay, Chapter 13; and Müller, Chapter 11, for discussion), their potential psychological underpinnings (Bever, Chapter 6), and how they may relate to semantics, computation, and learnability

(Bach & Chao, Chapter 8; Stabler, Chapter 10; and Steedman, Chapter 9), just to mention a few key constraining factors on a broad theory of language universals. Importantly, though, such a theory will also have to take seriously the widespread diversity that can be observed across the languages of the world in terms of phonology, morphology and syntax (Evans & Levinson, to appear). In this chapter, we discuss a single case in which a broader interdisciplinary approach may help shed additional light on the UG perspective on language universals. We note, however, that other approaches to universals are likely also to benefit from a broader interdisciplinary perspective.

14.2. Language Universals and Universal Grammar

Boeckx (2006) describe the research agenda of generative linguistics, including the ways in which its specific aims have evolved over the past five decades up to the current Minimalist Program (see also Bever, Chapter 6). Since Chomsky (1965), generative linguistics has been explicitly grounded on the assumption of an innate linguistic endowment, providing the basis for language acquisition, a UG. On this account, language universals derive from the properties of UG. The necessity of UG rests primarily on the Poverty of Stimulus (POS) argument for innateness of linguistic-specific constraints. Originally proposed by Chomsky (1980a, b), POS is based on the assumption that the information in the linguistic environment is too impoverished for language to be learnable. As noted by Boeckx (2006) and others, the logic of the argument is powerful: If the data in the primary linguistic input is insufficient for correct grammatical generalization, then language acquisition requires an endogenous biological explanation. If the premises are valid, the conclusion seems unavoidable. However, a critical appraisal of POS inevitably brings up the crucial question raised by Boeckx (2006): How good are the premises?

Until recently, the POS premises have been taken for granted based on intuitive observations. Here, however, we argue that one of the weaknesses of the argument stems from the difficulty in assessing the informativeness of the input, and from the imprecise and intuitive definition of what counts as "insufficient information" available to the learner. Moreover, we underscore the need for an interdisciplinary approach to POS, where no discipline is primary. Along these lines, we describe recent research in cognitive science that has begun to posit serious theoretical challenges to the fundamental assumptions of POS. In particular, we discuss studies that have contested the traditional views by focusing on the paradigmatic linguistic example used by Boeckx (2006) to illustrate POS: Auxiliary fronting in complex Yes/No interrogatives.

14.3. Learning Structure from Regularities

Recent work in cognitive science has begun to call POS assumptions into question, including its underlying assumptions about the nature of the linguistic input and the learning abilities of young infants. Much of this research has contributed to a substantial reappraisal of the role of statistical learning in language acquisition.

The ability to infer structure from statistical regularities in the input is a ubiquitous strategy throughout cognition (e.g., Goldstone, 2000; Markman & Gentner, 1993). Despite the growing bulk of work underscoring the role of statistical learning in perception and cognition, traditional generative linguistic approaches have argued over the past five decades that probabilistic information—including distributional, phonological, prosodic, and semantic cues—may be insufficient for acquisition of the rules of grammar (e.g., Chomsky, 1957; Crain & Pietroski, 2001; Fodor & Crowther, 2002; Hornstein & Lightfoot, 1981; Laurence & Margolis, 2001; Legate & Yang, 2002). Recent research in psycholinguistics, however, has started to demonstrate that distributional regularities may provide an important source of information for bootstrapping syntax (e.g., Mintz, 2002, 2003; Reali & Christiansen, 2005; Redington, Chater, & Finch, 1998; Solan, Horn, Ruppin, & Edelman, 2005). Moreover, distributional information is especially useful when it is integrated with other probabilistic cues such as prosodic or phonological information (e.g., Monaghan, Christiansen, & Chater, 2007; Morgan, Meier, & Newport, 1987; Reali, Christiansen, & Monaghan, 2003).

Behavioral studies over the last decade have shown that young infants are quite competent statistical learners (for reviews, see Gómez & Gerken, 2000; Saffran, 2003). For example, 8-month-old infants have access to powerful mechanisms to induce statistical regularities between linguistic elements (e.g., Gómez, 2002; Saffran, Aslin, & Newport, 1996; Saffran & Wilson, 2003), and by 1 year, children's perceptual attunement is likely to allow them to use language-internal probabilistic cues (Jusczyk, 1997). A recent line of research in natural language processing and connectionist modeling has revealed many properties of statistical learning of potential relevance for language acquisition (e.g., Christiansen & Chater, 1999; Elman, 1993; Lewis & Elman, 2001; Manning & Schütze, 1999). For instance, even though the primary linguistic input may be primarily characterized by a lack of *explicit* negative evidence, computational work suggest that learners could rely on *implicit* negative evidence, which may result from predictive learning algorithms (e.g., Elman, 1993; Rohde & Plaut, 1999). For example, Spivey-Knowlton and Saffran (1995) proposed a learning method that employs a type of feedback overlooked in most discussions on language learnability. In principle, a child could evaluate a general hypothesis about the target language by observing whether the *predictions* generated by the hypothesis are borne out in the speech she hears. As the child listens to others speak, she predicts that certain elements will follow one another. Thus, the child learns by listening to utterances rather than by producing them, and generates his or her own negative evidence by comparing the predicted input with the actual input (for further discussion, see Rohde & Plaut, 1999). Connectionist models such as Simple Recurrent Networks (SRNs; Elman, 1990) employ learning techniques that are consistent with prediction-feedback learning. When SRNs are trained to predict the next element in a sequential input (Elman, 1990, 1993), they produce implicit predictions regarding upcoming materials. By comparing a given prediction to the actual incoming input, the network produces an immediate error signal that can be functionally interpreted as implicit negative evidence derived from incorrect predictions.

During the 1980s, generative analysis of language learnability emphasized the unavailability of positive examples, shifting away from the focus on negative evidence (for further discussion, see MacWhinney, 2004). Thus, Chomsky's (1980a, b) statement of the poverty of stimulus argument applied to the case of multiclausal Yes/No questions relies on the notion of learning in the absence of positive evidence: "A person might go through much or all of his life without ever having been exposed to the relevant evidence, but he will nevertheless unerringly employ the structure-dependent generalization, on the first relevant occasion" (Chomsky, 1980a, p. 40). However, the notion of absence of positive evidence has been seriously contested by recent studies that indicate that child-directed speech may contain sufficient statistical information to distinguish between grammatical and ungrammatical multiclause Yes/No questions.

14.4. A Case Study: Auxiliary Fronting in Yes/No Questions

Auxiliary fronting in Yes/No questions is one of the most often cited examples used to illustrate the logic of POS argument. The ubiquity of this example is partly motivated by the study of Crain and Nakayama (1987), which provided empirical evidence suggesting that children only entertain structure-dependent hypotheses when they are prompted to produce multiclausal Yes/No questions. Moreover, Legate and Yang (2002) present corpus analyses of child-directed-speech indicating that relevant examples of grammatical Yes/No questions—that is, interrogatives containing an embedded "competing" auxiliary—appear to be extremely infrequent in the primary linguistic input. Specifically, they found that core examples constitute less than 1% of all sentences, and conclude that the information does not suffice for generalization, partly because the numbers suggest that examples may not be available to *every* child. Assuming that every child is capable of correct generalization, the necessity for a more endogenous, biological explanation seems to be needed.

The vast majority of literature discussion on POS has concentrated on whether examples of multiclause interrogatives such as, *Will the man who is tall leave now?*, are available to the child (e.g., Boeckx, 2006; Crain & Nakayama, 1987; Legate & Yang, 2002; cf. Pullum & Scholz, 2002; see Scholz & Pullum, 2002, for discussion). However, it has been recently proposed that such a characterization of what counts as relevant evidence may be too narrow, failing to take into account the possibility of implicit statistical information in the primary linguistic input (e.g., Lewis & Elman, 2001; Reali & Christiansen, 2005). These studies suggest that more *indirect sources* of statistical information may provide additional cues for making the appropriate grammatical generalizations. For example, Lewis and Elman (2001) trained SRNs on data from an artificial grammar that generated questions of the form, "auxiliary noun-phrase adjective?," and sequences of the form, "A_i noun phrase B_i" (where A_i and B_i represent a variety of different material). Crucially, the networks were not trained with core examples of multiclausal Yes/No interrogatives. Lewis and Elman found that the networks were better at making predictions for grammatical multiclause questions compared to ungrammatical ones involving incorrect auxiliary fronting. A possible caveat in this study, however, is that the networks were trained using an artificial grammar lacking the complexity of an actual child-directed speech corpus.

Recently, Reali and Christiansen (2005) conducted a series of corpus analyses of child-directed speech showing that there is indirect statistical information sufficient for distinguishing between grammatical and ungrammatical generalizations in multiclause Yes/No questions. First, they trained simple statistical models based on pairs (bigrams) and triples (trigrams) of words drawn from the Bernstein-Ratner (1984) corpus of child-directed speech. The Bernstein-Ratner corpus contains transcripts of speech from nine mothers to their children. The speech was recorded over a 4–5-month period when children were between 13 and 21 months of age. This corpus is relatively small and very noisy, mostly containing short sentences with simple grammatical structure. Importantly, there are no explicit examples of multiclause interrogatives in the corpus.

Bigram and trigram models (e.g., Jurafsky & Martin, 2000) measure how frequently pairs or triples of adjacent words occur in a linguistic corpus. Based on the probability of its fragments, the probability of a sentence can be calculated (for a more detailed description of the methods, see Reali & Christiansen, 2005). After training the bigram and trigram models, the authors compared the probabilities of a hundred test sentences that consisted of correct multiclause interrogatives (e.g., *Is the bunny that is on the chair sleeping?*) and their ungrammatical counterpart (e.g., **Is the bunny that on the chair is sleeping?*). Reali and Christiansen hypothesized that indirect statistical information in the form of word co-occurrences provided sufficient evidence for distinguishing grammatical from ungrammatical multiclause questions. In line with their prediction, they found a significant difference in the likelihood of these two alternative hypotheses: Grammatical versions were more probable than ungrammatical versions in more than 95% of the cases.

In a second series of analyses, they tested the bigram and trigram models trained on the Bernstein-Ratner corpus on the same sentences used in the Crain and Nakayama original study. In the Crain and Nakayama study, 3- to 5-year old children spontaneously produced sentences like, *Is the boy who is watching Mickey Mouse happy?*, and never produced sentences like, **Is the boy who watching Mickey Mouse is happy?*. Reali and Christiansen found that according to the bigram and trigram models the grammatical versions of the multiclause interrogatives were significantly more probable than their ungrammatical counterparts. In a subsequent series of simulation studies, they showed that simple learning devices, such as SRNs, were capable of exploiting the statistical cues captured by the bigram and trigram models. When trained on the full-blown child-directed speech corpus, the networks produced a bias toward grammatical multiclause questions when compared to their ungrammatical counterparts. The results indicate that a noisy child-directed speech corpus contains enough indirect statistical information to distinguish between grammatical and ungrammatical multiclause Yes/No questions.

Reali and Christiansen (2005) argue for a possible way in which exposure to fine-grain statistical information may translate into production biases. Crucially, the pattern of network predictions they found can be interpreted as providing statistical constraints on real-time production. Following previous connectionist work (Christiansen & Chater, 1999), they propose that the SRN's output predictions could be construed as a set of possible sentence *continuations* during production. For example, semantic factors being equal, after the speaker produces the fragment, *The boy who . . .*, she would be biased to continue the sentence using an auxiliary (e.g., *is*) rather than a verb in progressive form or an adjective (e.g., *watching* or *happy*). This is because chunks of the form "who is" are considerably more frequent than chunks of the form "who watching" or "who happy." They found that the Yes/No questions generated in this fashion are consistent with children production data found in Crain and Nakayama (1987).

Importantly, statistical regularities result from the nonrandomness in the distribution of linguistic elements. Thus, the importance of the underlying syntactic structure should not be underestimated. Linguistic structure is a prerequisite for statistical learning because it is the constituent properties of well-formed sentences that make distributional cues useful in the first place. Therefore, a language without reliable structural regularities would not be learnable from a statistical perspective. Reali and Christiansen concluded that sequential statistics could help explain why children tend not to make many auxiliary-fronting errors. Moreover, the model predicted that children should make fewer errors involving high-frequency word chunks compared to low-frequency ones. Interestingly, this prediction has been confirmed by a recent question elicitation study (Ambridge, Rowland, & Pine, 2008). For example, they found higher rates of auxiliary-doubling error for questions where such errors involved high-frequency word category combinations (e.g., more errors such as *Is the boy who is washing the elephant is tired?* than *Are the boys who are washing the elephant are tired?*).

Although these results only pertain to a single linguistic construction, on the theoretical side they point toward the necessity of a serious reassessment of the type of information that should be considered useful for learning a particular linguistic structure. More generally, the POS assumption may have to be revisited in the light of the statistical richness present in the primary linguistic input.

14.5. A Broader Perspective

A remaining question is where universal patterns of language structure derive from. It seems clear that at least of some aspects of language universals are determined by innate constraints. The key question, however, is whether these constraints are best characterized as being specifically linguistic[1] in nature, or whether they may derive from more general cognitive and perceptual constraints on learning and processing. Interdisciplinary work on the evolution of language supports the latter view (e.g., Batali, 2002; Brighton, 2002; Christiansen & Chater, 2008; Christiansen, Dale, Ellefson, & Conway, 2002; Christiansen, Reali, & Chater, 2006; Deacon, 1997; Kirby & Christiansen, 2003). According to this perspective, most language universals may derive from nonlinguistic constraints on the statistical learning mechanisms themselves and from general functional and pragmatic properties of communicative interactions. Additional common features of language might have emerged through processes of cultural transmission across generations of human learners and through grammaticalization (e.g., Bybee, Chapter 2; Hurford, Chapter 3; Givón, 1998; Heine & Kuteva, 2002). Thus, language could be regarded as "piggy-backing" on more general cognitive mechanisms adapted for other functions. These mechanisms, in turn, determine the cognitive constraints that are brought to bear on language acquisition.

The cognitive mechanisms used to learn language may be not qualitatively different from those used to learn other aspects of cognition and perception. According to this view, complex linguistic tasks would be performed using similar machinery to that used by other cognitive systems, providing a possible framework for a unification of theories of representation. This view is supported by research in neuroanatomy and neurophysiology, suggesting that similar architectures underlie language and other cognitive processes. For example, the study of cortical areas indicates that brain structures are quite homogenous across different functional areas. In fact, the cortex has been compared with a multidimensional plaid (Kingsbury & Finlay, 2001) that is more suitable for the implementation of fine-grained distributed architectures than for the implementation of computer-like modules functioning independently and interchanging discrete packets of information (see also Finlay, Chapter 13; Müller, Chapter 11; and Clark & Misyak, Chapter 12).

In sum, a remaining challenge for the language sciences is the question of whether our innate language-acquisition biases are better characterized as part of domain-specific or domain-general cognitive mechanisms. An effective research program designed to investigate the nature and constraints of cognitive mechanisms should be grounded within an interdisciplinary approach in which no single discipline is primary.

Key Further Readings

For reappraisals of POS arguments and the logical problem of language acquisition, we recommend the articles by Scholz and Pullum (2002) and Pullum and Scholz (2002). These two articles are part of *The Linguistic Review* special issue: A review of "The Poverty of stimulus argument." This special issue consists of a discussion paper by Geoffrey Pullum and Barbara Scholz with responding articles by various contributors. Pullum and Scholz provide an insightful reevaluation of POS argument when applied to various frequently used examples, including the case of plurals in noun–noun compounding, auxiliary sequences, anaphoric one, and Yes/No questions in English. We also recommend the discussion article by Brian MacWhinney (2004), *A multiple process solution to the logical problem of language acquisition* (and associated peer commentaries). In this paper, MacWhinney discusses alternatives to the UG hypothesis in the context of language acquisition, including item-based learning, indirect negative evidence, and multiple-cue integration.

For an empirical reevaluation of children's spontaneous production of multiclause Yes/No questions, we recommend a recent article by Ambridge, Rowland, and Pine (2008). They found that children's errors in auxiliary fronting were consistent with input-based learning predictions.

For an introduction to linguistic alternatives to the generative framework, we recommend the book *Probabilistic Linguistics* edited by Bod, Jay, and Jannedy (2003). This book comprises the contribution of various authors, providing empirical and computational evidence for the probabilistic nature of linguistic behavior at various levels of representation, ranging from phonetics to discourse. The work covered in the book indicates that linguistic competence is far from discrete, challenging core assumptions of generative approaches and providing a new probabilistic framework for the study of language.

Acknowledgments

MHC was supported by a Charles A. Ryskamp Fellowship from the American Council of Learned Societies.

Note

1 The term "specifically linguistic innate knowledge" refers to *representational innateness* as defined in Elman et al. (1996). Representational innateness is the strongest and most specific form of linguistic nativism. It allows for an innately specified encoding of detailed grammatical knowledge (for discussion, see Chapter 7, Elman et al., 1996).

References

Ambridge, B., Rowland, C., & Pine, J. (2008). Is structure dependence an innate constraint? New experimental evidence from children's complex question production. *Cognitive Science, 32,* 222–255.

Batali, J. (2002). The negotiation and acquisition of recursive grammars as a result of competition among examples. In E. Briscoe (Ed.), *Linguistic evolution through language acquisition: Formal and computational models* (pp. 111–172). Cambridge: Cambridge University Press.

Bernstein-Ratner, N. (1984). Patterns of vowel modification in motherese. *Journal of Child Language, 11,* 557–578.

Bod, R., Jay, J. H., & Jannedy, S. (Eds.). (2003). *Probabilistic linguistics.* Cambridge, MA: MIT Press.

Boeckx, C. (2006). *Linguistic minimalism: Origins, concepts, methods, and aims.* New York: Oxford University Press.

Brighton, H. (2002). Compositional syntax from cultural transmission. *Artificial Life, 8,* 25–54.

Chomsky, N. (1957). *Syntactic structures.* The Hague: Mouton & Co.

Chomsky, N. (1965). *Aspects of the theory of syntax.* Cambridge, MA: MIT Press.

Chomsky, N. (1980a). The linguistic approach. In M. Piatelli-Palmarini (Ed.), *Language and learning: The debate between Jean Piaget and Noam Chomsky.* Cambridge, MA: Harvard University Press.

Chomsky, N. (1980b). *Rules and representations.* Cambridge, MA: MIT Press.

Christiansen, M. H., & Chater, N. (1999). Toward a connectionist model of recursion in human linguistic performance. *Cognitive Science, 23,* 157–205.

Christiansen, M. H., & Chater, N. (2008). Language as shaped by the brain. *Behavioral and Brain Sciences, 31,* 489–558.

Christiansen, M. H., Dale, R. A. C., Ellefson, M. R., & Conway, C. M. (2002). The role of sequential learning in language evolution: Computational and experimental studies. In A. Cangelosi & D. Parisi (Eds.), *Simulating the evolution of language* (pp.165–187). London: Springer-Verlag.

Christiansen, M. H., Reali, F., & Chater, N. (2006). The Baldwin effect works for functional, but not arbitrary, features of language. In A. Cangelosi, A. Smith, & K. Smith (Eds.), *Proceedings of the sixth international conference on the evolution of language* (pp. 27–34). London: World Scientific Publishing.

Crain, S., & Nakayama, M. (1987). Structure dependence in grammar formation. *Language*, *63*, 522–543.

Crain, S., & Pietroski, P. (2001). Nature, nurture, and universal grammar. *Linguistics and Philosophy*, *24*, 139–186.

Deacon, T. W. (1997). *The symbolic species: The coevolution of language and the brain*. New York: WW Norton.

Elman, J. L. (1990). Finding structure in time. *Cognitive Science*, *14*, 179–211.

Elman, J. L. (1993). Learning and development in neural networks: The importance of starting small. *Cognition*, *48*, 71–99.

Elman, J. L., Bates, E. A., Johnson, M. H., Karmiloff-Smith, A., Parisi, D., & Plunkett, K. (1996). *Rethinking innateness*. Cambridge, MA: MIT Press.

Evans, N., & Levinson, S. (to appear). The myth of language universals: Language diversity and its importance for cognitive science. *Behavioral and Brain Sciences*.

Fodor, J. D., & Crowther, C. (2002). Understanding stimulus poverty arguments. *The Linguistic Review*, *19*, 105–145.

Givón, T. (1998). On the co-evolution of language, mind, and brain. *Evolution of Communication*, *2*, 45–116.

Goldstone, R. L. (2000). Unitization during category learning. *Journal of Experimental Psychology: Human Perception and Performance*, *26*, 86–112.

Gómez, R. L. (2002). Variability and detection of invariant structure. *Psychological Science*, *13*, 431–436.

Gómez, R. L., & Gerken, L. A. (2000). Infant artificial language learning and language acquisition. *Trends in Cognitive Sciences*, *4*, 178–186.

Heine, B., & Kuteva, T. (2002). On the evolution of grammatical forms. In A. Wray (Ed.), *Transitions to language* (pp. 376–397). Oxford, UK: Oxford University Press.

Hornstein, N., & Lightfoot, D. (Eds.). (1981). *Explanation in linguistics*. London: Longman.

Jurafsky, D., & Martin, J. H. (2000). *Speech and language processing*. Upper Saddle River, NJ: Prentice Hall.

Jusczyk, P. (1997). The discovery of spoken language. Cambridge, MA: MIT Press.

Kingsbury, M. A., & Finlay, B. L. (2001). The cortex in multidimensional space: Where do cortical areas come from? *Developmental Science*, *4*, 125–157.

Kirby, S., & Christiansen, M. H. (2003). From language learning to language evolution. In M. H. Christiansen & S. Kirby (Eds.), *Language evolution* (pp. 272–294). Oxford, UK: Oxford University Press.

Laurence, S., & Margolis, E. (2001). The poverty of the stimulus argument. *British Journal for the Philosophy of Science, 52*, 217–276.

Legate, J. A., & Yang, C. (2002). Empirical re-assessment of stimulus poverty arguments. *Linguistic Review, 19*, 151–162.

Lewis, J. D., & Elman, J. L. (2001). Learnability and the statistical structure of language: Poverty of stimulus arguments revisited. In *Proceedings of the twenty-sixth annual Boston University conference on language development* (pp. 359–370). Somerville, MA: Cascadilla Press.

MacWhinney, B. (2004). A multiple process solution to the logical problem of language acquisition. *Journal of Child Language, 31*, 883–914.

Manning, C. D., & Schütze, H. (1999). *Foundations of statistical natural language processing.* Cambridge, MA: MIT Press.

Markman, A. B., & Gentner, D. (1993). Structural alignment during similarity comparisons. *Cognitive Psychology, 25*, 431–467.

Mintz, T. H. (2002). Category induction from distributional cues in an artificial language. *Memory and Cognition, 30*, 678–686.

Mintz, T. H. (2003). Frequent frames as a cue for grammatical categories in child-directed speech. *Cognition, 90*, 91–117.

Monaghan, P., Christiansen, M. H., & Chater, N. (2007). The phonological-distributional coherence hypothesis: Crosslinguistic evidence in language acquisition. *Cognitive Psychology, 55*, 259–305.

Morgan, J. L., Meier, R. P., & Newport, E. L. (1987). Structural packaging in the input to language learning: Contributions of prosodic and morphological marking of phrases to the acquisition of language. *Cognitive Psychology, 19*, 498–550.

Pullum, G. K., & Scholz, B. (2002). Empirical assessment of stimulus poverty arguments. *Linguistic Review, 19*, 9–50.

Reali, F., & Christiansen, M. H. (2005). Uncovering the richness of the stimulus: Structural dependence and indirect statistical evidence. *Cognitive Science, 29*, 1007–1028.

Reali, F., Christiansen, M. H., & Monaghan, P. (2003). Phonological and distributional cues in syntax acquisition: Scaling up the connectionist approach to multiple-cue integration. In R. Alterman & D. Kirsh (Eds.), *Proceedings of the twenty-fifth annual conference of the Cognitive Science Society* (pp. 970–975). Mahwah, NJ: Lawrence Erlbaum.

Redington, M., Chater, N., & Finch, S. (1998). Distributional information: A powerful cue for acquiring syntactic categories. *Cognitive Science, 22*, 425–469.

Rohde, D. L. T., & Plaut, D. C. (1999). Language acquisition in the absence of explicit negative evidence: How important is starting small? *Cognition, 72*, 67–109.

Saffran, J. R. (2003). Statistical language learning: Mechanisms and constraints. *Current Directions in Psychological Science, 12*, 110–114.

Saffran, J. R., Aslin, R., & Newport, E. L. (1996). Statistical learning by 8-month-old infants. *Science, 274*, 1926–1928.

Saffran, J. R., & Wilson, D. P. (2003). From syllables to syntax: Multi-level statistical learning by 12-month-old infants. *Infancy, 4*, 273–284.

Scholz, B., & Pullum, G. K. (2002). Searching for arguments to support linguistic nativism. *Linguistic Review, 19,* 185–223.

Solan, Z., Horn, D., Ruppin, E., & Edelman, S. (2005). Unsupervised learning of natural languages. *Proceedings of the National Academy of Sciences, 102,* 11629–11634.

Spivey-Knowlton, M., & Saffran, J. R. (1995). Inducing a grammar without an explicit teacher: Incremental distributed prediction feedback. In J. D. Moore & J. F. Lehman (Eds.), *Proceedings of the seventeenth annual conference of the cognitive science society* (pp. 230–235). Hillsdale, NJ: Erlbaum.

Tomasello, M. (2004). What kind of evidence could refute the UG hypothesis? *Studies in Language, 28,* 642–644.

AUTHOR INDEX

The letter 'n' denotes note numbers in the respective pages

SUBJECT INDEX

The letter 'n' denotes note numbers in the respective pages